T0331793

# Innovations in Software-Defined Networking and Network Functions Virtualization

Ankur Dumka
*University of Petroleum and Energy Studies, India*

A volume in the Advances in Systems Analysis, Software Engineering, and High Performance Computing (ASASEHPC) Book Series

Published in the United States of America by
    IGI Global
    Engineering Science Reference (an imprint of IGI Global)
    701 E. Chocolate Avenue
    Hershey PA, USA 17033
    Tel: 717-533-8845
    Fax: 717-533-8661
    E-mail: cust@igi-global.com
    Web site: http://www.igi-global.com

Library of Congress Cataloging-in-Publication Data

Names: Dumka, Ankur, 1984- editor.
Title: Innovations in software-defined networking and network functions
   virtualization / Ankur Dumka, editor.
Description: Hershey, PA : Engineering Science Reference, [2018] | Includes
   bibliographical references.
Identifiers: LCCN 2017020273| ISBN 9781522536406 (hardcover) | ISBN
   9781522536413 (ebook)
Subjects: LCSH: Software-defined networking (Computer network technology)
Classification: LCC TK5105.5833 .I67 2018 | DDC 004.6--dc23 LC record available at https://lccn.
loc.gov/2017020273

This book is published in the IGI Global book series Advances in Systems Analysis, Software Engineering, and High Performance Computing (ASASEHPC) (ISSN: 2327-3453; eISSN: 2327-3461)

British Cataloguing in Publication Data
A Cataloguing in Publication record for this book is available from the British Library.

All work contributed to this book is new, previously-unpublished material.
The views expressed in this book are those of the authors, but not necessarily of the publisher.

For electronic access to this publication, please contact: eresources@igi-global.com.

# Advances in Systems Analysis, Software Engineering, and High Performance Computing (ASASEHPC) Book Series

ISSN:2327-3453
EISSN:2327-3461

Editor-in-Chief: Vijayan Sugumaran, Oakland University, USA

## MISSION

The theory and practice of computing applications and distributed systems has emerged as one of the key areas of research driving innovations in business, engineering, and science. The fields of software engineering, systems analysis, and high performance computing offer a wide range of applications and solutions in solving computational problems for any modern organization.

The **Advances in Systems Analysis, Software Engineering, and High Performance Computing (ASASEHPC) Book Series** brings together research in the areas of distributed computing, systems and software engineering, high performance computing, and service science. This collection of publications is useful for academics, researchers, and practitioners seeking the latest practices and knowledge in this field.

## COVERAGE

- Storage Systems
- Virtual Data Systems
- Parallel Architectures
- Network Management
- Performance Modelling
- Computer Networking
- Software engineering
- Metadata and Semantic Web
- Engineering Environments
- Computer graphics

IGI Global is currently accepting manuscripts for publication within this series. To submit a proposal for a volume in this series, please contact our Acquisition Editors at Acquisitions@igi-global.com or visit: http://www.igi-global.com/publish/.

# Titles in this Series

701 East Chocolate Avenue, Hershey, PA 17033, USA
Tel: 717-533-8845 x100 • Fax: 717-533-8661
E-Mail: cust@igi-global.com • www.igi-global.com

# Table of Contents

# Detailed Table of Contents

**Chapter 1**
*Himanshu Sahu, University of Petroleum and Energy Studies, India*
*Misha Hungyo, R&D Nokia, India*

Software defined network (SDN) and Network function virtualization (NFV) are the two new networking paradigms changing the way traditional networks work. SDN works on the concept of centralization so that all the decisions related to controlling the networks is done in a centralized place in a centralized manner. To provide a centralized control, SDN decouples the control plane and data from the traditional routing devices to take it in the centralized position. The data plane is still intact with the routing devices, but they now become mere forwarding devices and the decisions are made at the centralized place called the controller. The controller is basically the x86 server that is connected to the forwarding devices and communicates with them for all control decisions such as routing. NFV is based on virtualization of network functions in the form of software running over a high end server. This kind of virtualization helps in easy setup of networks as well as easy migration.

**Chapter 2**
*Vishal Kaushik, University of Petroleum and Energy Studies, India*
*Ajay Sharma, SRM University - Haryana, India*
*Ravi Tomar, University of Petroleum and Energy Studies, India*

Software-defined networking (SDN) is an emerging network architecture that facilitates the network administrator to control and manage network behavior dynamically. Different from traditional networks, software-defined networks support dynamic and scalable computing. The dynamic behavior is achieved by decoupling or disassociating the system. The swing of control from tightly bound individual networks to assessable computing devices enables infrastructure abstraction. Due to the abstraction, the network can be considered as a logical or virtual entity. In this chapter, relation between network function virtualization (NFV) and software-defined networking (SDN) has been outlined. This chapter focuses on describing the pros and cons of NFV technologies. network functions virtualization (NFV) was founded under the work of the European Telecommunications Standards Institute (ETSI).

**Chapter 3**

    *Mohit Kumar Jaiswal, University of Petroleum and Energy Studies,*
       *India*

The SDN controller is interfaced with the hardware of the network (i.e., with switches and routers) using OpenFlow. Basically, OpenFlow is an open interface used for configuring the forwarding tables of network switch according to the desired path derived by the SDN controller. OpenFlow enables more innovation in controller platforms and applications, and describes a solution for each frame or packet flow. OpenFlow is based on an ethernet switch with an internal flow-table and a standardized interface to add and remove flow entries of forwarding table of the system. The control mechanism from each one of the switch and router up to SDN controller are encrypted with the transport layer security (TLS) and secure socket layer (SSL) OpenFlow protocols to provide the additional security inside the network.

**Chapter 4**

    *Sujitha S., Thiagarajar College of Engineering, India*
    *Manikandan M. S. K., Thiagarajar College of Engineering, India*
    *Ashwini G., Thiagarajar College of Engineering, India*

Designing and organizing networks has become extra innovative over the past few years with the assistance of SDN (software-defined networking). The software implements network protocols that undergo years of equivalence and interoperability testing. Software-defined networking (SDN) is a move toward computer networking that allows network administrators to programmatically initialize, manage, alter, and direct network behavior dynamically through open interfaces and abstraction of lower-level functionality. SDN controller is an application in software-defined networking (SDN) that manages run control to permit clever networking. SDN controllers are based on protocols, such as OpenFlow, that permit servers to inform switches where to send packets. This chapter explores SDN controllers.

# Chapter 5

The chapter explores the various types and functionalities of controllers present in the field of software-defined networking. It is responsible for providing a bridge between various application interfaces. It enables smart networking and is solely responsible for having an authority over the network. It takes input from one API, processes it, and returns output for the high-level interface or API. They instruct the switch as to what functions to perform and can be of two types: either pure or hybrid. The controller at the central layer performs all the functions of the "evergreen" existing switches. The data plane of the router is solely the foreground for the switch to apply all its powers, while in hybrid switch software-defined networking and existing technologies work hand in hand. An administrator can build up the SDN tools to manage the traffic, whereas the existing network protocols progressively move the various incoming packets onto the network. This engenders hybrid network. Here the existing and SDN technologies or switches, work under the similar conditions.

This chapter is focused on SDN practical approach with Cisco controllers APIC, APIC-EM, and the application programming interfaces with real-world benefits and challenges. The chapter uses Cisco SDN way of managing, administering, maintaining, and implementing platforms using an external tool. This chapter will also discuss the controller API structures, management model of the controller, and using POSTMAN tool to push API requests and talk to the APIC controller. The chapter also discusses some of the important APIC EM applications like PnP, Easy QoS, IWAN, etc.

# Chapter 7

Mininet is a stage for working extensive systems on the assets of a finest single little framework or virtual machine. Mininet is made for initiating research in software-defined networking (SDN) and OpenFlow. Mininet permits executing predefined code intuitively on virtual equipment machine on a basic PC. Mininet gives an accommodation and authenticity at less cost. The auxiliary to Mininet is equipment test beds, which are quick and precise, yet extremely costly and shared. The other alternative is to utilize Mininet test system, which is low cost, yet some of the time moderate and requires code substitution. Mininet gives convenience, execution precision, and versatility.

**Chapter 8**

*Lalit Pandey, Independent Researcher, India*

This chapter is focused on the traditional network architecture limitations with NFV benefits. Discussion of NFV architecture and framework as well as management and orchestration has been discussed in this chapter. Cisco VNF portfolio and virtual network functions implementation is included with software implementation of the architecture of NFV (network function virtualization). Management and orchestration functional layers as per ETSI standard. The challenges in NFV implementation is also a concern today, which is a part of this chapter.

**Chapter 9**

*Ankur Dumka, University of Petroleum and Energy Studies, India*

With the advancement in the requirement of data, the need for stringent quality of service guarantee is a demand of the current world, which brings the network programmers to design the network protocols that certify certain guaranteed performance in terms of service delivery. Here, focus is on the quality of service within the SDN network with its comparison and implementation using simulation. Types of quality of service are also discussed in this chapter with a focus on the ways of implementation of quality of service. The authors define a QoS management and orchestration architecture that allow them to manage the network in a modular manner. Performing the operation and results in such a network is shown as are the outputs for the same.

**Chapter 10**

*Ankur Dumka, University of Petroleum and Energy Studies, India*
*Hardwari Lal Mandoria, G. B. Pant University of Agriculture and*
*    Technology, India*
*Anushree Sah, University of Petroleum and Energy Studies, India*

The chapter surveys the analysis of all the security aspects of software-defined network and determines the areas that are prone to security attacks in the given software-defined network architecture. If the fundamental network topology information is poisoned, all the dependent network services will become immediately affected, causing catastrophic problems like host location hijacking attack, link fabrication attack, denial of service attack, man in the middle attack. These attacks affect the following features of SDN: availability, performance, integrity, and security. The flexibility in the programmability of control plane has both acted as a bane as well as a boon to SDN. Like the ARP poisoning in the legacy networks, there are several other vulnerabilities in the SDN architecture as well.

In this chapter, a general structure for a product-characterized remote sensor is arranged where the controller is actualized at the base station and the SDN-WSN system by talking about and breaking down. The execution and vitality utilization of SDN-WSN system is superior to other vitality-effective conventions.

Software-defined networking (SDN) is an emerging network design and management paradigm that offers a flexible way for reducing the complexity of the network management and configuration. SDN-based wireless sensor networks (SDWSNs) consist of a set of software-defined sensor nodes equipped with different types of sensors. In SDWSN, sensor node is able to conduct different sensing tasks according to the programs injected into it and functionalities of these nodes can also be dynamically configured by injecting different application-specific programs. SDWSNs adopt the characteristics of SDN and can provide energy efficient solutions for various problems such as topology management, sleep scheduling, routing, and localization, etc. This chapter discusses how to apply SDN model in the design of an energy-efficient protocol for wireless sensor networks and also presents an overview of SDN model proposed for wireless sensor networks and SDN-based resource management, routing, sleep scheduling algorithm, localization for SDWSNs. Finally, open research challenges are summarized.

SDS along with SDN and software-defined compute (SDC; where in computing is virtualized and software defined) creates software-defined infrastructure (SDI). SDI is the set of three components—SDN, SDS, and SDC—making a new kind of software-defined IT infrastructure where centralization and virtualization are the main focus. SDI is proposed to have infrastructure developed over commodity hardware and software stack defined over it. SDS is exploiting the same concept of decoupling and centralization in reference to storage solutions as in SDN. The SDN works on decoupling the control plane with the data plane from a layer, three switches, or router, and makes a centralized decision point called the controller. The SDS works in a similar way by moving the decision making from the storage hardware to a centralized server. It helps in developing new and existing storage solutions over the commodity storage devices. The centralization helps to create a better dynamic solution for satisfying the customized user need. The solutions are expected to be cheaper due to the use of commodity hardware.

# Chapter 14

The idea of software-defined networking (SDN) is a paradigm shift in computer networking. There are various advantages of SDN (e.g., network automation, fostering innovation in network using software, minimizing the CAPEX and OPEX cost with minimizing the power consumption in the network). SDN is one of the recently developed network-driven methodologies where the core of all lower-level services is operated by one centralized device. Developers tried to develop such approaches to make it easy for an administrator to control information flow from one node to another node. To obtain these services, lower-level static architecture is decoupled for the higher level. This chapter introduces a new approach that is based on complex network processing and forecasting for an event.

# Preface

Th editor of this book would like to thank IGI Global for agreeing to publish this book and the cooperation extended during the development of this book. The final version of this book contains 14 chapters which are related to emerging technology of software defined network and network function virtualization and areas and problems related to this field. The areas covered in this book relate to software defined network, Network function virtualization, controllers, protocols related to software defined network, software defined storage and wireless sensor network related to software defined network.

This book will provide to be a vulnerable resource for undergraduate, graduate and post graduate doing research in the field of software defined network and network function virtualization. This book will also provide valuable to the researchers, developers of software defined networks and network function virtualization.

Software-Defined Network (SDN) and Network Function Virtualization (NFV) are the latest technologies that fuel latest hype bubble in the networking industry and service provider environment. The book primary covers different features and aspects related to SDN and NFV including the practical knowledge that would paved up the way for the researchers for their work in this field. The book explains SDN with need for SDN with giving the practical knowledge taking implementation using real environment and simulation. The protocol used for SDN, OpenFlow is also discussed and explained with scalability and challenges related to OpenFlow.

Open flow is a new protocol that used to decouple control plane from data plane. This book focusses on basics of OpenFlow protocol, its benefits and drawback. Book also focusses on controllers and their working which are used to control the control plane of all the nodes within the network. Subsequent chapters also discusses on number of controllers available in the market and difference in the manner of working and operations.

Controllers which are heart of SDN technology are discussed in details which include the working of controllers within SDN network. Controllers which are used for solving the networking problems with their own intelligence. The controllers are present on the top-most layer which works as a cloud which has the power to regulate, maintain and making decisions both manually and automatically. The controllers underlies with many application services like message routing, data storage and formatting etc. Discussion over different types of controllers available for SDN networks are discussed with their comparison with each other which will make the choice for controller selection easier.

Security aspects related to SDN networks are discussed which covers many aspects related to SDN security including attacks like DoS, DDoS with different solutions to minimize the effect of these attacks. Quality of Service within SDN network is focused which includes different strategy being used for implementation of quality of service and their performance comparison by using simulation results.

Discussion of SDN technology with respect to associated technologies are also discussed in the chapters following. SDN technology relation with wireless sensor network, in terms of it's working with wireless sensor network and the research area related to the topics has been discussed. The connection of software defined area with software defined area has been discussed with automation of software defined area has been discussed in this book.

A different perspective in terms of software defined area has been discussed in terms of software defined storage has been discussed and explained that how large data can be managed in terms of software defined storage which gives a different perspective for this book. These all topics all together make this book a different approach towards the topic of software defined network and network function virtualization which make this book different and unique from other. Thus focusing from the beginner to the advanced topic has been discussed in this book.

The first chapter defined about software defined network which is not a new technology- we have been using concept of programmable networks for decades, this chapter describe the motivation behind SDN movement, its principles and perfect use cases and numerous technology related with SDN. Software defined network (SDN) and Network function virtualization (NFV) are the two new networking paradigms which are changing the way the traditional networks works. The SDN is the technology that works on the concept of centralization so that all the decision related to controlling the networks should be taken on centralized place in a centralized manner. To provide a centralized control the SDN decouples the control plane and data from the traditional routing devices to take it in the centralized position. The data plane still intact with the routing devices but they now become a mere forwarding devices and the decisions are taken at the centralized place called the controller. Controller is basically the x86 server that are connect to the forwarding devices and communicate with them for all control decisions such as routing. NFV is based on virtualization of network functions in the form of software running over high end server. This kind of virtualization helps in easy setup of networks as well as easy migration.

The second chapter discusses about network function virtualization. This chapter outline the benefits, enablers and challenges for network function virtualization. This chapter emphasizes that how the NFV is highly complementary to SDN. This chapter describe how NFV improve the flexibility of network service provisioning and reduce the time to market of new services. By leveraging virtualization technologies and commercial off-the-shelf programmable hardware, such as general-purpose servers, storage, and switches, NFV decouples the software implementation of network functions from the underlying hardware. As an emerging technology, NFV brings several challenges to network operators, such as the guarantee of network performance for virtual appliances, their dynamic instantiation and migration, and their efficient placement. This chapter presents brief overview of NFV, explain its requirements and architectural framework, present several use cases, and discuss the challenges and future directions in this burgeoning research area.

The third chapter discuss about open flow protocol. The SDN controller is interfaced with the hardware of the network i.e., with switches and routers using OpenFlow. Basically, OpenFlow is an open interface used for configuring the forwarding tables of network switch according to the desired path derived by the SDN controller. OpenFlow enables more innovation in controller platforms, applications and describes a solution for each frame or packet flow. OpenFlow is based on an Ethernet switch, with an internal flow-table, and a standardized interface to add and remove flow entries of forwarding table of the system. The control mechanism from each one of the switch and router up to SDN controller are encrypted with the Transport Layer Security (TLS) and Secure Socket Layer (SSL) OpenFlow protocols are used to provide the additional security inside the Network.

The fourth chapter discusses about controllers of software defined networks. Designing and organizing networks has become extra innovative over the past few years with the assist of SDN (software-defined networking). The software implements network protocols that undergo years of equivalence and interoperability testing. Software-defined networking (SDN) is an move toward to computer networking that allows network administrators to programmatically initialize, manage, alter, and direct network behavior dynamically through open interfaces and abstraction of lower-level functionality. SDN controller is an application in software-defined networking (SDN) so as to manages run control to permit clever networking. SDN controllers are based on protocols, such as OpenFlow, that permit servers to inform switches where to send packets. So controller is the a large amount important thing in Software Defined Networking.

The fifth chapter discusses the working of different types of controllers and their working. The chapter is to gloss over the various types and functionalities of controllers present in the field of Software Defined Networking. It is responsible for providing a bridge between various application interfaces. It enables smart networking and is solely responsible for having an authority over the network. It takes input from one API, process it and return output for the high level interface or API. They instruct the switch as to what functions to perform and can be of two types either pure or hybrid. The controller at the central layer performs all the functions of the "evergreen" existing switches. The data plane of the router is solely the foreground for the switch to apply all its powers. While in hybrid switch Software defined networking and existing technologies work hand in hand. An administrator can build up the SDN tools to manage the traffic whereas the existing network protocols progressively move the various incoming packets onto the network. This engenders hybrid network. Here the existing and SDN technologies or switches, work under the similar conditions.

The sixth chapter presents the practical approach of software defined network with Cisco. This chapter focusses on SDN Practical approach with Cisco Controllers APIC, APIC-EM and the application programming Interfaces with real world benefits and challenges. The chapter is using Cisco SDN way of managing, administering, maintaining & implementing platforms using an external tool. This chapter will also discuss the controller API structures, Management Model of the controller and using POSTMAN tool to push API requests and talk to the APIC Controller. Chapter also discussed some of the important APIC EM applications like Plug and Play (PnP), Easy Quality of Service, IWAN, etc.

The seventh chapter presents the simulation of software defined network with Mininet simulators. Mininet is a stage for working extensive systems on the less assets of a finest single little framework or Virtual Machine. Mininet is made for initiating research in Software Defined Networking (SDN) and OpenFlow. Mininet is permits executing of predefined code intuitively on virtual equipment machine on a basic PC. Mininet gives an accommodation and authenticity at less cost. The auxiliary to Mininet is equipment test beds which are quick, precise yet extremely costly and shared. The other alternative is to utilize Mininet test system which is low cost yet some of the time moderate and require code substitution. Mininet gives convenience, execution precision and versatility.

The eight chapter presents practical application of network function virtualization. This chapter is focused on the traditional Network architecture limitations with Network Function Virtualization (NFV) Benefits. Discussion of NFV Architecture & Framework as well as Management and Orchestration has been discussed in this chapter. Cisco VNF Portfolio and Virtual Network Functions Implementation is included with Software Implementation of the architecture of Network Function Virtualization. Management & Orchestration functional layers as per ETSI Standard. Challenges in NFV implementation is also a concern today which is a part of this chapter.

The ninth chapter discusses about quality of services (QoS) in software defined network and its applications. This chapter focuses on the quality of service within the SDN network with its comparison and implementation using simulation. Types of quality of service is also discussed in this chapter with focusses on types of ways of implementation of quality of service. QoS management and orchestration architecture are also discussed here that allow us to manage the network in a modular manner. Performing our operation and results in such a network and shown the outputs for the same.

The tenth chapter presents the security architecture of software defined network and different aspects related to security of software defined network. In this chapter, author discusses about Distributed denial-of-service (DDoS) which is a rapidly growing problem. The multitude and variety of both the attacks and the defense approaches is overwhelming. This chapter is a survey on the problem of denial-of-service (DoS) and Distributed Denial of Service (DDoS) attacks and proposed ways to deal with it. We describe the nature of the problem and look for its root causes, further presenting brief insights and suggested approaches for defending against DDoS. We point out both the positive and negative sides of each potential solution. Future work identifies and justifies open research issues. In conclusion, we give a brief summary of what has realistically been achieved so far, as well as what are the key missing components. In this paper, we present a classification of available mechanisms that are proposed in literature on preventing Internet services from possible DDoS attacks and discuss the strengths and weaknesses of each mechanism. This provides better understanding of the problem and enables a security administrator to effectively equip his arsenal with proper prevention mechanisms for fighting against DDoS threat.

The eleventh chapter discusses about WSN structure based on SDN. SDN based Wireless Sensor Networks (SDWSNs) consists of a set of software-defined sensor node equipped with different types of sensors. In SDWSN, sensor node is able to conduct different sensing tasks according to the programs injected in it and functionalities of these nodes can also be dynamically configured by injecting different application-specific programs. SDWSNs adopt the characteristics of SDN and can provide energy efficient solutions for various problems such as topology management, sleep scheduling, routing and localization etc. This chapter has discussed how to apply SDN model in the design of an energy efficient protocol for wireless sensor networks and also presents an overview of SDN model proposed for wireless sensor networks and SDN based resource management, routing, sleep scheduling algorithm, localization for SDWSNs. In last, open research challenges are summarized.

The twelfth chapter discusses about SDN paradigm in wireless sensor network. Software Defined Networking (SDN) into wireless sensor networks (WSNs) for sparing vitality/control and proficient administration. The majority of the Generic Architectures executes for the base station in a product characterized remote sensor organize. A general structure for a product characterized remote sensor is arranged where the controller is actualized at the base station and the SDN-WSN system by talking about and breaking down, the execution and vitality utilization of SDN-WSN system is superior to other vitality effective conventions.

The thirteenth chapter presents software defined storage. Due to the emergence of cloud computing and mobile computing as well as exponential growth of internet users the rate of digital data generation has increased many folds. The storage of the data and processing requirement has also increased to store the huge data. So storage technology has geared up to find better storage techniques and develop better solutions. One of the recent technologies is known as "Software Defined Storage (SDS)" inspired by the success of "Software Defined Networks (SDN)". SDS along with SDN and Software Defined Compute (SDC) (where in computing is virtualized and software defined), creates Software Defined Infrastructure (SDI). SDI is the set of 3 components SDN, SDS and SDC making a new kind of software defined IT infrastructure where centralization and virtualization are the main focus. SDI is proposed to have infrastructure developed over commodity hardware and software stack defined over it SDS is exploiting the same concept of decoupling and centralization in reference to storage solutions as in SDN. The SDN works on decoupling the control plane with the data plane from a layer 3 switches and make a centralized decision point called the controller. The SDS works in the similar way by moving the decision making from the storage hardware to a centralized server. It helps in developing new and existing storage solutions over the commodity storage devices. The centralization helps to create a better dynamic solution for satisfying the user need. It also provides cheaper solution due to use of commodity hardware.

The fourteenth chapter discusses about learning of SDN with software defined area. In this chapter, author tried to introduce a new approach which is based on the complex network processing and forecasting for an event. As we know the Internet is one of the finest examples of complex networks, we consider a networking device as a processing node where information comes in the form of packets and processed by the device. This functionality can be organized with a combination of machine learning algorithm and static nature of unprocessed network. Because of periodic request and response based services one network can be easily automated and controlled by a single administrator. Such type of functionalities can be made better if we can design our network having more iterative nature. Iterative nature means where request and responses are similar in nature. A network is very vulnerable to attack so considering time series analysis of past finite time duration dataset, our network can be secured by periodic attack types.

This book covers the emerging definition, protocols, standards for software defined networks and network function virtualization and their surroundings and associated terminologies. The book covers the topics such that it would be beneficial for beginners, research scholars to find area of working, industry for getting practical exposure of implementation of network using software defined networks and network function virtualization. The book also contain data regarding automation in SDN which is hot topics for researchers finding the area of working in this field. The practical and simulation of SDN and NFV paved a way to learn the implementation of SDN and NFV network in real time and simulated environment. The discussion on security and quality of service also enable the reader to find the loopholes and area of research in the subsequent field of SDN. Integration of SDN with wireless sensor network is further enhance the content of book and paved a new research area in the field of SDN. Software defined storage is another area which make this book different from others. Thus, this book is said to provide a complete reference in the field of SDN and NFV which nearly covers all the topics related to SDN and NFV which make this book complete in itself.

# Acknowledgment

First of all, I would like to thank the Almighty.

Acknowledgement when honestly given is a reward without price. I am thankful to the publishing team at IGI Global accepting to publish this edited book. I thank Mariah Gilbert, Marianne Caesar, development editor, for helping me in bringing this project to a successful end. I would also thank Jan Travers, Kayla Wolfe, Meghan Lamb, and Jacqueline Sternberg of IGI Global team for their various supports.

Writing this part is probably the most difficult task. Although the list of people to thank heartily is long, making this list is not the hard part. The difficult part is to search the words that convey the sincerity and magnitude of my gratitude and love.

I express my deep gratitude to my parents for their moral support, blessings and encouragement throughout my life. I am greatly indebted to my wife and best friend for her constant support in every aspect of life and also responsible for encouraging me to finish this book. She has paid the real cost for this work by sacrificing many of her desires and carrying out our combined social responsibilities alone. I want to acknowledge her contributions and convey my sincere thankfulness. I am heartily thankful to Naina, my lovely daughters and inspiration, blessed by God. She always generates enthusiasm and spark in my work by their warm welcome and blossom smile at home.

# Chapter 1
# Introduction to SDN and NFV

**Himanshu Sahu**
*University of Petroleum and Energy Studies, India*

**Misha Hungyo**
*R&D Nokia, India*

## ABSTRACT

*Software defined network (SDN) and Network function virtualization (NFV) are the two new networking paradigms changing the way traditional networks work. SDN works on the concept of centralization so that all the decisions related to controlling the networks is done in a centralized place in a centralized manner. To provide a centralized control, SDN decouples the control plane and data from the traditional routing devices to take it in the centralized position. The data plane is still intact with the routing devices, but they now become mere forwarding devices and the decisions are made at the centralized place called the controller. The controller is basically the x86 server that is connected to the forwarding devices and communicates with them for all control decisions such as routing. NFV is based on virtualization of network functions in the form of software running over a high end server. This kind of virtualization helps in easy setup of networks as well as easy migration.*

## INTRODUCTION

Information and Communication technology (ICT) has seen evolution of new technologies and trends such as mobile and cloud computing, social media and IOT. These new technology requires ubiquitous accessibility, high bandwidth and dynamic management (Xia, Wen, Foh & Niyato, 2015). The current networking technology seems inept to satisfy these dynamic requirements due to ossification inherited in the traditional one by the use of propriety hardware devices. Software defined network (SDN) and Network function virtualization (NFV) are the two

DOI: 10.4018/978-1-5225-3640-6.ch001

new networking paradigms that are changing the way the traditional networks are functioning. These new technologies seem promising in handling the current and future requirements in the ICT. SDN (ONF White Paper 2012) is a technology which works on the concept of centralization to provide centralized decision making for the entire network whereas NFV (NFV-ISG, White paper 2015) is a technology which is based on virtualization to virtualize the network functions (NF). SDN decouples the control plane and the data plane from the traditional networking devices i.e. routers leaving behind data plane intact with the device making them mere forwarding devices following the decision of the centralized controller. The benefit of centralization is to have a centralized information regarding topology which provides easy monitoring and fault tolerance. SDN also provides the network programmability which helps to cope the dynamic nature of today's networks. NFV, on the other hand, is based on virtualization of network functions in the form of software running over high end server. This kind of virtualization helps in easy setup of networks as well as easy migration. The NFV is initiated from the Telecom Service Provider (TSP) so that they can achieve high return of investment i.e. ROI along with a flexible infrastructure where deployment and integration is faster and easier.

This chapter consists of two sections. The first section will cover the SDN definitions, evolution and architecture of SDN along with challenges and future trends. The second section will cover the NFV definitions, evolutions and architecture of NFV along with challenges and future trends.

## INTRODUCTION TO SOFTWARE DEFINED NETWORK (SDN)

(Haleplidis, Pentikousis, Salim, Meyer, koufopavlou(2015)) in RFC 7426 describes Software Defined Networks as:

*Software-Defined Networking (SDN) refers to a new approach for network programmability, that is, the capacity to initialize, control, change, and manage network behavior dynamically via open interfaces. SDN emphasizes the role of software in running networks through the introduction of an abstraction for the data forwarding plane and, by doing so, separates it from the control plane.*

By following the above definition we can deduce the following salient features of a SDN network:

1. Programmable Network
2. Centralized Management
3. Dynamically Configurable Networks

4.    Open Protocols and Interfaces
5.    Easily Monitored and Fault Tolerant Network

## Need of SDN

According to Gens, F. (2012), as we follow recent trends in ICT due to the emergence of Cloud Computing, Mobile Computing and IOT the network traffic has growing exponentially.

*According to Cisco VNI (2016), "Annual global IP traffic will reach 3.3 ZB (ZB; 1000 Exabytes [EB]) by 2021 and Global IP traffic will increase nearly threefold over the next 5 years, and will have increased 127-fold from 2005 to 2021"*

The evolution of social media, ubiquitous computing, IOT and smartphones has not only increased the bandwidth requirements but also the complexity of the networks. This leads to massive increase in east west traffic (i.e. data center to data center) as well as north south traffic (data center to client machines). According to Cisco VNI (2016) 63 percent of the total IP traffic will be generated by portable devices such as mobile phones, tablet PC.

The Current Network technologies and approaches will not able be to scale up according to the present and future needed of flexible, dynamic scalable and high bandwidth networks. This inflexibility lying in the current technology leads to a new approach i.e. SDN which seems promising to solve the existing and future requirement of the ICT. Some of the points that drive the motivation behind moving towards the SDN networks are:

1.    Simplified Switch Design
2.    Loose coupling to provide better evolution
3.    Ease of network application development
4.    Open Network Protocols leads to cost effective devices
5.    Better and easy network management
6.    Better support to tackle the exponentially growing network and data
7.    Better Network Security Solutions

## Traditional Network

In the traditional networking approach, most of the networking functionalities are implemented in a dedicated appliance and hardware i.e. the switches, routers etc. Operating and maintaining today's network is an arduous task because of the many complexities and the various policies implemented on it. To maintain a network from global perspective, it is required to express global network policies but to configure this network operators have to configure each individual network devices separately. Today's network is a heterogeneous collection of switches, routers and middle boxes, which uses vendor specific and low-level commands, which is a very complicated, expensive and error-prone process. So implementing new global policy or changing a small set of device need each device to configure separately using the command line interface provided by the vendor. This modification or scaling of networks is a complex and time taking task.

In addition to the configuration complexities, handling network dynamics and automation is also missing to provide event based triggering of necessary actions. As the network grows, the number of policies defined on the application layer also grows rapidly, and it becomes extremely difficult to manage. To make changes in the networking layer is almost an impossible task. This makes the traditional network stagnant and ossified (Chowdhury & Boutaba, 2009) and therefore, the need for a general management paradigm increases, in order to provide common management abstractions that hides the details of the physical infrastructure, and enables flexible network management.

## Software Defined Networks (SDN) vs. Traditional Networks

Software-Defined Networking (SDN) has the potential to reduce many of these traditional network problems because of its support to dynamic nature of network, centralized control plane and direct programmability. As given by the Open Networking Foundation (ONF)

*SDN is the physical separation of the network control plane from the forwarding plane, and where the control plane controls devices, i.e., the control and data planes are decoupled, network intelligence and state are logically centralized in the SDN architecture and the underlying network infrastructure is abstracted from the applications. (ONF White Paper (2012))*

Figure 1 shows the difference between the traditional network and SDN networks. The traditional network carries a distributed control whereas the software defined network contains the centralized network. According to Nunes, Mendonca, Nguyen, Obraczka, Turletti, (2014), the SDN architecture decouples control logic from the forwarding hardware, and enables the consolidation of middle boxes, simpler policy management, and new functionalities. The solid lines define the data-plane links and the dashed lines the control-plane links.

*Figure 1. Traditional Networks vs SDN Network (Nunes, Mendonca, Nguyen, Obraczka, & Turletti, 2014)*

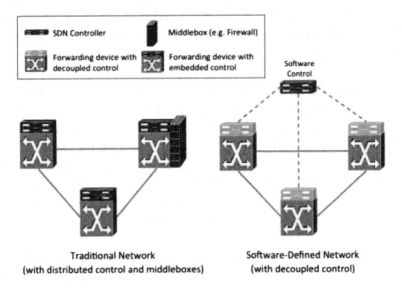

Traditional Network
(with distributed control and middleboxes)

Software-Defined Network
(with decoupled control)

## History of SDN

Although the origin of SDN dates back to decades ago, as early as 1980s, the implementation started just few years back, the first being the GSMP project developed by IPSILON in 1996, Tempest in 1998, and SS7 networks in 1993. The OpenFlow project is one of the most used implementation protocol, developed by the ONF in 2009.

*SDN is an emerging architecture that is dynamic, manageable, cost-effective, and adaptable, making it ideal for the high-bandwidth, dynamic nature of today's applications.(ONF SDN)*

The idea of centralized control plane and open protocol has traveled a long journey to finally evolve as SDN and Open flow. The few projects are worth mentioning that has nurtured the idea of centralized control plane and programmable networks. These projects have laid the foundation of SDN networks that are described below.

1.  **Open Signaling:** This project has been started as an attempt to improve the ATM, internet and mobile networks. The Project OPENSIG (Campbell,

Katzela, Miki & Vicente, 1999) is focused on creating open, extensible and programmable networks. The concept they proposed was separation of control logic from hardware circuitry so that better deployment of services can be done using open interfaces. The Proposed project emphasized on making the protocols open. Based on this, IETF developed General Switch Management Protocol GSMP (rfc 3292) (Doria 2002).

2. **Active Networking:** The Active Networking concept comes up with the idea of programmable networks. They proposed two concepts - a programmable switch and capsules which is useful in sending control codes along with the data codes. This project didn't get success due to security concerns.

3. **DCAN:** DCAN project focused on the concept of designing new infrastructure for the ATM networks. This infrastructure is supposed to provide scalable control and management of ATM networks. The DCAN also focused on that the infrastructure contains separate management switches that controls the ATM switches.

4. **4D Project:** The 4D project presented a clear view of separating the routing decision logic and protocols used in interaction of networking devices involved in forwarding the packets. It proposed giving the "decision" plane a global view of the network, serviced by a "dissemination" and "discovery" plane, for control of a "data" plane for forwarding traffic(Nunes et al. 2014). Nox (Gude, Koponen,Pettit, Pfaff, Casado, McKeown, & Shenker, 2008) an Open flow controller is motivated from the 4D project. Nox is also known as Operating system for networks.

5. **NETCONF:** NETCONF is project proposed by the IETF network configuration working group. The project is based on development of protocol for management which is designed to modify the configuration of switches and routers. The proposed protocol is supposed to have an API that will provide extension of configuration of network devices. SNMP simple network management protocol which is widely deployed network management protocol has several flaws such as security. NETCONF is supposed to remove these flaws and it's in active development phase.

6. **ETHANE:** Ethane (Casado, Freedman, Pettit, Luo, McKeown, 2007) is one project that can be termed as a true predecessor of OpenFlow. Ethane provided concept of ethane switches and controller to provide a new way of new management for enterprises. Ethane has used the flow table in ethane switches and separate channel for communication between the controller and switches.

## FEATURES AND BENEFITS OF SDN NETWORKS

The most charming points of SDN are centralization of the control logic and simplification network management, which will enable networks to keep in pace with the fast changing today's networks. SDN enables the current networking to address the high-bandwidth, dynamic nature of today's applications, adapt the network to ever changing business needs and significantly reduce operations and management complexity. One of the primary advantages of SDN is the support for more data-intensive applications like big data, network virtualization, and the Internet of Things (IOT).

### Features

1.  **Environment:** The Software defined network can work in all types of network environment. It can work as a part of carrier grade services, campus network, enterprise or a cloud data center.
2.  **Services:** The SDN network can provide its services to residential customers, non-residential customers; intent based services as well as non-intent based services.
3.  **Resources:** SDN services can be implemented over any kind of resource physical, virtual, compute or storage.
4.  **Policy:** It enables global policies for management, security and access rules over the whole network.
5.  **Scalability:** It can scale from local to global service span.

### Benefits of SDN Networks

Some of the main benefits that SDN enterprises can achieve include:

1.  **Centralized Control Plane:** Centralization of control plane will ease the management, control and monitoring of whole network from one central location. Global policy management, Event based triggering and centralize information base will help the network to cope with fast changing scenarios. Since the whole topology information is available at one central location the congestion and fault information will move very quick to all devices so corrective measures can be taken as once such a rerouting.
2.  **Automation:** The automation is provided by the application running over the control plane i.e. controller by using the northbound interface. The automation can be event triggered by some predefined rule or due to some exception to

take accordingly. As in a monitoring application a rule can be set so that if the link utilization exceeds a certain value the traffic can be redirected using automated rules.

3. **Flow Programming:** SDN provides the network managers an interface where they can configure, manage, secure and optimize network resources with easy and efficiency with the help of automated SDN program with a dashboard.

4. **Higher Rate of Innovation:** SDN is evolved as concept of open protocols. The Northbound API provides a programming interface which allows application to be developed and new functionalities are added in the networks. The Open flow protocols provides an open box concept, source is in public domain and open for research and development.

5. **Reduced Overall Network CAPEX and OPEX:** It works on simplified switch so it reduces the hardware cost involved in the development of the network infrastructure. Virtualization and automation reduces the cost of maintenance.

6. **Increased Network Reliability:** The centralized management interface contains all the network information such as topology, devices and links. So if any part of the network malfunctions the necessary action can be taken rapidly such as rerouting or blocking. As compared to current network with distributed control plane error information takes lot of time to propagate through the network so SDN networks are considered more reliable.

## SDN Architecture

The inflexibility of the traditional network is due to the tightly coupling of control plane and data plane. These inflexibilities of traditional network hides the adaptation

*Figure 2. Features of Software defined networks*

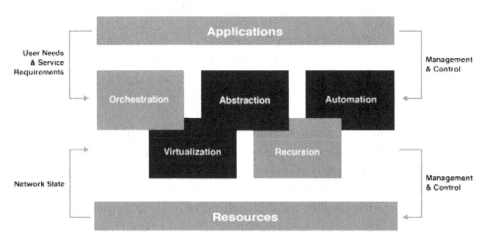

of changing network infrastructure needs. The network infrastructure component such as router and switches used in current network are closed system. The Vendor specific implementation of the control logic is implemented in the routers which are provided with a limited user interface.

The SDN architecture distributes the tightly coupled control and forwarding logic into different layers. Open Network Foundation has given three layered reference architecture for the SDN networks. The Reference SDN architecture shown is Figure 3:

1.  **Data Layer:** The Data/Forwarding layer comprises the network elements, which are merely forwarding devices. They are exposed to the control layer through the South-bound communication interface.
2.  **Control Layer:** The Control Layer lies in the middle of the architecture and is responsible for translating the applications' requirements thus putting a more granular control over the network elements, while providing relevant information up to the SDN applications. This layer is logically centralized to manage all the connected OpenFlow elements in executing out the policies defined on them.
3.  **Application Layer:** The Application Layer has all the SDN applications residing over it. This layer communicates the SDN applications through the North-bound communication interface.

*Figure 3. SDN Reference Model*

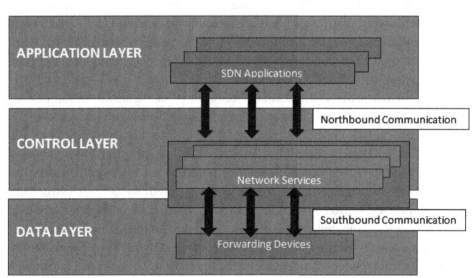

## Components of SDN

The main components of SDN are Controllers, SDN switches and the infrastructural backbone networks.

1. **SDN Application:** SDN provides a programmable network by an API called Northbound API on which applications can be developed using different high level language such as java, php or python. REST API's are used to fetch the data from the controller to develop web based application. The Types of Application that can be developed are:
   ○ **Network Engineering Applications:** These set of applications include applications for Network Management, Security Policy Enforcement, Traffic Engineering and QoS Policy Enforcement.
   ○ **Service Management Application:** These set of applications include applications for Automated (multi-layer, multi-vendor) Network Provisioning, Virtual Private Cloud Provisioning and SLA Monitoring.
2. **Revenue Generating application:** These set of applications include applications for Software-Defined Data Center (SDDC), Big Data Applications (based on L4-L7 data) and End-to-End QoS Management.
3. **SDN Controller:** As mentioned earlier, the controller is the brain of the network. It can be either distributed, centralized or hybrid. In centralized type, a controller manages all the forwarding elements in the system, and retains a global view of the entire network. Controllers such as ODL, ONOS etc. are centralized controllers. Whereas in distributed type, more than one controllers are used and are distributed over the entire network. Hybrid type controllers are those that have both the centralized as well as the distributed concepts. Most widely used SDN controllers are Floodlight, OpenDaylight, OpenContrail, Ryu, FlowVisor, BEACON, NOX and POX.
4. **SDN Switches:** SDN switches or devices are non-intelligent forwarding devices that follow the rules installed on them by their controllers. Most common SDN switches are the OpenFlow switches that work on the OpenFlow protocol, defined by ONF. An OpenFlow switch has a flow table that gives provision for lookup and then packet forwarding based on the rules on the table. The switches are connected to the controller by a secured channel. Each switch has a unique DPID, also known as the data path identifier. When a packet arrives at the switch and the switch finds no matching rules for the particular data packet i.e., a *packet miss* is encountered, then about 200 bytes of the data is sent to the controller, which then decides what appropriate actions need to be taken as given by the network administrator or operators. The controller then install

the defined flows on the switch, so that when the next data packet arrives at the switch, and the matching rules are fulfilled, the data is routed according to the corresponding rules for that match, instead of sending it again to the controller. Therefore, by removing the complexities on the switches and routers, and instead managed and controlled from a logical centralized controller, the performance and flexibility are increased on the networks.

5. **SDN Data Path:** The SDN Datapath is basically logical network device. The Datapath or logical device may contain all or a subset of its physical counterpart. An SDN Datapath consists of data forwarding engine, zero or more data processing engine and a controller to Datapath interface. These engines and functions may include simple forwarding between the data path's external interfaces or internal traffic processing or termination functions. A single physical device may contain more than one SDN data path or a single SDN Datapath may span across multiple physical network elements.

6. **SDN Control to Data Plane Interface (CDPI):** The SDN Control to data plane interface provides the communication between an SDN Controller and an SDN Datapath. This interface provides
   ◦ Programmatic control of all forwarding operations
   ◦ Capabilities advertisement
   ◦ Statistics reporting
   ◦ Event notification
   CDPI is implemented in an open, vendor-neutral and interoperable way.

7. **SDN Northbound API:** SDN Northbound API are interfaces between SDN Applications and SDN Controllers. The Northbound API provides abstract network views and enables direct expression of network behaviour and requirements. This may occur at any level of abstraction (latitude) and across different sets of functionality (longitude). One value of SDN lies in the expectation that these interfaces are implemented in an open, vendor-neutral and interoperable way.

8. **Challenges in SDN Network:** A lot of research has been successfully conducted for SDN network on test bed networks and some successful implementation in real scenario. SDN still have challenges exists to its implementation in real scenario. SDN networks have been successfully implemented in many greenfield project but a network can't run in isolation if it is a part of an internet. Replacing traditional network with SDN network is not a practical approach. So the biggest challenge of SDN will be its interoperability with the existing legacy networks. Second is due to centralization, it also creates single point of failure. Single control point leads to excess load on a single point. Security is one more concern with the SDN network. If the control channels

have been compromised whole network can be hijacked. Control is also the most vulnerable point of attack for Dos and DDos attack. The protocols, API and Programming languages need to be standardized to provide a matured solution that will be universally accepted.

## RESEARCH CHALLENGES AND FUTURE DIRECTIONS

Considering these challenges towards the growth of SDN networks the future works that needs to be done in the SDN can be categorize in 3 types.

1.  **Protocols Standardization:** The SDN protocols, API's i.e. South-bound and North bound API need to standardize so that it will have wide-spread use. The device manufacture will use these standard protocols to build devices that support this protocol. Since SDN is working on Open Standard parallel development may lead to different version of the protocols that may create compatibility issues. Open Flow is one of standard protocol that is being used to develop open flow switches. There is also a need of development or selection of programming language that will used to develop 3$^{rd}$ party apps running over the controller.

2.  **Replacement of Traditional Networks:** Traditional network has been used for long time since its evolution and lot of work has already been done. There is a huge installation of switches as enterprise and backbone networks. It's neither feasible nor practical approach to attempt a replacement of traditional network in one go. SDN needs to start as running parallel to the traditional network. As an approach we have to develop devices that support both protocols from the traditional network as well as Open flow protocols. Second the protocols needs to be developed in such a way that it fully supports the interoperability of both types of network.

3.  **Controller:** The issues existed related to placement of controller, number of controller, hierarchical vs distributed controller, security, performance, fault tolerance and load balancing. Since controller can be implemented on X86 server so performance and load balancing is a major challenge. Failure of the controller may lead to disruption of the whole service so we need to optimize fault tolerant solution for the same. Although lot of research has been done on the same still no fully agreed solution is available.

4.  **Deployment:** Lot of works needs to be done if we want SDN to be fully fledged deployed. Wireless Network, Mesh Network and Wireless Sensor Network are the area where SDN solutions have not been fully developed.

## CONCLUSION

Software defined networking seems a promising technology that can cope with the changing network technology. It not only gives benefits to the network operators, but it also creates scope for the researchers, mainly due to its flexibility to design, build and operate networks according to the needs. The centralized management interface, programmability and open protocols helps in removing the Ossification of the network. Although it still has some challenges, industries and researchers are moving towards SDN from the traditional networking due to its more advantages.

## INTRODUCTION TO NFV

According to European Telecommunications Standards Institute (ETSI), "Network Functions Virtualization is a network evolution that utilizes the technologies of IT virtualization to deploy the network node functions onto industry standard high volume servers, storage and switches, or even cloud computing infrastructure" (NFV-ISG, White paper 2015).

In the current network scenario, for setting up a particular network infrastructure we have to implement each network functions by separate hardware called middle boxes such as firewall, NAT or load balancer. This multiplicity of devices increases the cost of network setup and maintenance. Further adding new service or network expansion requires replacement and addition of new devices. For solving this problem of network ossification (i.e. inflexibility) ETSI industry specification group has formalized NFV that utilizes the virtualization to provide network functionalities of any middle box in the form of software running on commodity server. Different software code can run simultaneously, so by using Virtualized Network Function, different devices are converged to one single device serving all the network functions.

The main characteristics of NFV in the current network are:

1. It exploits the concepts of virtualization to virtualize network function.
2. It decouples the network functionality from the hardware and implements it over the commodity server.
3. Reduces number of devices to be installed for setting up a network.
4. Breaks the ossification and provide the flexibility to modify the network infrastructure easily.
5. Reduces the Capex and Opex of deployment of new networks services.
6. Restrains the use of different H/W devices for different network services.

By following the aforementioned points it can be concluded that NFV will transform the current network by removing the ossification, convergence of Network Functions on single devices, fast deployment and expansion of infrastructure and reduced Capex of Opex in network management.

## DIFFERENCE AND SIMILARITIES BETWEEN SDN AND NFV

If we compare NFV with SDN the only difference is that SDN separates the data and control plane from the routers whereas NFV decouples the application software from hardware to run different application on single server and run it as a multi-tenant application. The network functions (NF) are abstracted into a software that can run on a range of industry standard server hardware, that are highly scalable and flexible, which can be instantiated or moved to any locations, without the need for new hardware or equipment installation.

NFV and SDN are independent entities but they are complementary to each other, and can be used together giving greater mutual benefits. Many use cases of SDN overlap with those of NFV. Network Functions Virtualization goals can be achieved using non-SDN concept, relying on the techniques currently in use in many datacenters. But using SDN approaches i.e., separation of data plane and forwarding plane can enhance performance, simplify compatibility with the existing deployments, and facilitates operation and maintenance procedures. NFV can support SDN by providing the infrastructure upon which the SDN software runs. The objectives of both the concepts align closely with each other to use commodity servers and switches.

*Figure 4. NFV replacing middle boxes with commodity server and virtual appliance*

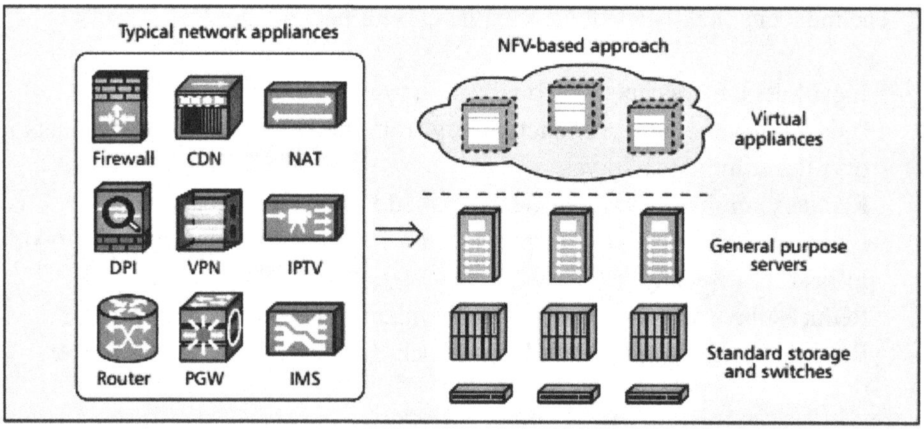

*Figure 5. Relationship of SDN and NFV*

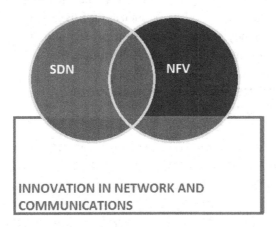

*Figure 6. Working Together SDN and NFV*

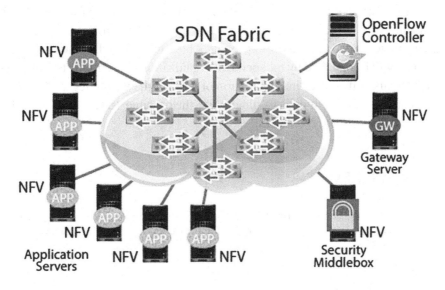

## NFV AND TELECOM INDUSTRY

The telecommunication industry has been following rigorous standards for stability, protocol adherence and quality, since time immemorial. Although the concept of virtualization worked well in the past, there was reliance on the proprietary hardware and slow development pace, which led to long product cycles. The rise of significant competition in communication services from fast-moving organizations operating at large scale has accelerated the growth and momentum across the industry.

15

NFV is supposed to have great impact on the architecture and function of telecommunication and support systems such as OSS/BSS. Virtualization also helps self-managed redundancy and failover scenarios. Using high automation with the help of NFV we can achieve high gain in OSS and BSS.

## Network Functions Virtualization Industry Specification Group (NFV ISG)

Network Functions Virtualization Industry Specification Group (NFV ISG) which is a part of the European Telecommunications Standards Institute (ETSI) published a white paper on NFV in October 2012, at a conference in Darmstadt, Germany on SDN and OpenFlow. NFV ISG was formed of representatives from the telecommunication industry across Europe and beyond. Since the launch in 2012, the NFV ISG has grown to 235 companies.

The main focus of NFV ISG is to provide interoperability for NFV solutions coming from different vendors in an open ecosystem. The key requirement for the interoperability is to provide standard interface so that they different standard can be amalgamated. Second focus is to provide a hierarchy of orchestrators which in many cases will be operated by independent organization and in multi-tenant mode. The third focus of this is to find interaction of NFV with existing legacy OSS/BSS components. The fourth thing is to standardize the possible service models such as NFVIaaS, NFVPaaS and NFVSaaS.

## HISTORY OF NFV

The concept of logical network started way before formal NFV was proposed in 2012. The categorizations in which the history of NFV can be divided are:

1. Virtual LAN
2. Virtual Private Network
3. Active and Programmable Networks
4. Overlay Networks

## Virtual LAN

VLAN created a logical LAN so that all the devices which belong to the same VLAN lies in the same broadcast domain without considering their physical locations. The specialized switches are needed for VLAN to implement. All VLAN frames carry a VLAN ID so that a frame should reach all the devices belonging to the same VLAN. The configuration and management of VLAN are easier since a virtual network. Virtual LAN are also use to divide the broadcast domain of a switch in different VLANs.

## Virtual Private Network (VPN's)

VPN are a way to provide the secure connectivity to a private network using the public network. VPN works on tunneling by creating a path through the public network to provide access to private networks. Virtual private networks either provide site to site secure connectivity or remote access to intranet.

## Active and Programmable Networks

The concept of active and programmable networks came into picture with a requirement of flexible network for easy configuration and management. It comes with two different approaches one was open signaling and the other was active networks approach. The open signaling approach works on abstraction of logical layer from physical layer where as Active network approach supports dynamic deployment of the services.

## Overlay Networks

Overlay networks are logical network created over a physical network. Peer to peer networks is an example of an overlay networks. Overlay networks creates new kind of network services over an existing network removes the need of changing of the underlying physical networks.

## Evolution of NFV

The foundation of NFV started in 2012 when the telecom service providers selected ETSI as the standard body for the development of NFV specification. ETSI is now a collaboration of more than 200 companies working together to provide standard, specification and development approach towards NFV. The specification published in 2013 covers infrastructural overview, framework for architecture, management and orchestration and security.

# NFV FRAMEWORK

As described by the NFV ISG, Network Functions Virtualization framework has three main components:

## NFV Infrastructure (NFVI)

"NFVI is the totality of the hardware and software components which build up the environment in which VNFs are deployed."(ETSI GS NFV INF 001 V1.1.1 (2015-01) To support the various use cases and the applications fields already identified by the NFV ISG, a common infrastructure consisting of software and hardware components that can provide the environment for the VNFs to build up and evolve is required. The various field of application are content delivery networks CDN, Fixed access networks, Mobile core and IMS, Mobile base station home environment and platform such as NFVIaaS, NFVPaaS, NFVSaaS.

On this NFVI, VNFs are deployed thus providing the ecosystem for multiple use cases and fields of application simultaneously. NFVI domain can be categorized as follows:

1.  **NFV Compute Domain:** Includes the functional elements such as processors, accelerators, network interfaces and storage. It also identifies the interfaces between the compute domain and other elements of the NFVI as well as other external interface, which are supported by NFV.
2.  **NFV Hypervisor Domain:** A hypervisor is a virtual machine monitor that allows virtual machines, called hosts to be deployed. Hypervisors allocate resources to these hosts. NFV Hypervisor Domain primarily focuses on the use of hypervisors as an implementation technology.
3.  **NFV Infrastructure Network Domain:** This domain identifies the external interfaces of the domain as well as the functional blocks within the domain. The functional blocks include virtual networks, network resources, other virtualization layer options, control and administrative agents. It also includes interfaces to the other NFVI domains, and other features of the networking domain that impact the aspects of NFV.

## Virtual Network Functions

Virtual Network Functions are software implementations of network functions previously implemented as proprietary hardware appliances, which now can be deployed on the network functions virtualization infrastructure. The concept of VNF component (VNFC) has been developed as a general approach to virtualizing

*Figure 7. High level ETSI NFV framework*

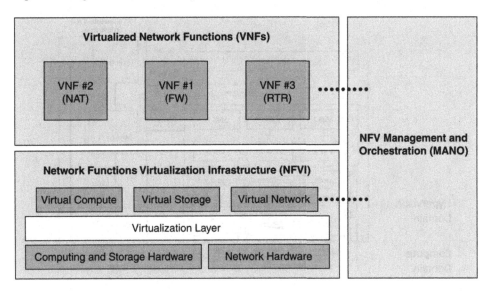

a network function and identifying a common software design patterns. A VNFC is defined as an internal component of a VNF that can be mapped to a single container interface to provide a subset of the VNF's functionality.

## NFV Management and Orchestration (MANO)

The management of network functions deployment on the standard hardware through virtualization, interoperability of interfaces and information models and mapping of these models to data models are done by NFV Management and Orchestration layer.

NFV Management and Orchestration functions are categorized into three: virtualized resources, virtualized network functions, and network services. MANO provides all resources that VNFs and network services require, which includes the virtualization containers that are identified within the NFVI such as compute, storage and network services.

## BENEFITS OF NFV

Network Functions Virtualization offers potentially a number of benefits which overlaps with some of the benefits of SDN. Some of the major benefits include:

*Figure 8. NFV Management and orchestration*

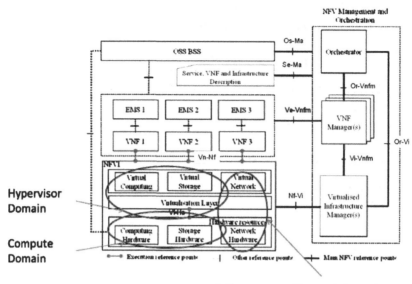

1. Reduced equipment costs and reduced power consumption through consolidating equipment and exploiting the economies of scale of the IT industry.
2. Increased speed of Time to market by minimizing the typical network operator cycle of innovation.
3. Availability of network appliance multi-version and multi-tenancy, which allows use of a single platform for different applications, users and tenants. This allows network operators to share resources across services and across different customer bases.
4. Targeted service introduction based on geography or customer sets is possible. Services can be rapidly scaled up/down as required.
5. Enables a wide variety of eco-systems and encourages openness. It opens the virtual appliance market to pure software entrants, small players and academia, encouraging more innovation to bring new services and new revenue streams quickly at much lower risk.

## CHALLENGES

Though Network Functions Virtualization has many benefits, there are many challenges as well in this current scenario:

1.  Achieving high performance virtualized network appliances which are portable between different hardware vendors, and with different hypervisors.
2.  Achieving co-existence with bespoke hardware based network platforms whilst enabling an efficient migration path to fully virtualized network platforms, which reuse network operator OSS/BSS. OSS/BSS development needs to move to a model in-line with Network Functions Virtualization and this is where SDN can play a role.
3.  Managing and orchestrating many virtual network appliances, particularly alongside legacy management systems, while ensuring security from attack and misconfiguration.
4.  NFV will only scale if all of the network functions can be automated.
5.  Ensuring the appropriate level of resilience to hardware and software failures.
6.  Integrating multiple virtual appliances from different vendors. Network operators need to be able to mix and match hardware from different vendors without incurring significant integration costs and avoiding lock-in.

## RESEARCH AREAS AND FUTURE DIRECTIONS

The future directions in which NFV has to move forward check the performance of virtualization in real time environment, placement of virtual appliances, instantiation and migration of Virtual appliances.

1.  **Network Performance of Virtualized NF:** Although virtualization seems promising to reducing the Capex and Opex and provide flexibility to the network but performance will be a point of concern due to unpredictability in real time load. Some studies show that running the virtual appliances on a multiprocessor environment leads to poor throughput of TCP/UPD packets.
2.  **Placement of Virtual Appliances:** Placement of middle boxes is another aspect to be looked at. Placement of virtual appliances cannot be at the same place where original middle boxes are placed. Moving middle boxes to the data center will increase unnecessary traffic which causes delay. Many appliances in the network are placed according to the topology so as to minimize delay. Since the VA are usually run as VM, putting these VMs on the edge network will be more beneficial.
3.  **Instantiation and Migration of Virtual Appliances:** VNF are meant to increase the network flexibility by providing the network functions as per the dynamic requirements. These dynamic instances are the VM that need to be instantiated and also migrated to provide flexibility. The process using native VM is not efficient, so different solution is required to be suitable for NFV.

4. **Energy Efficiency:** In the telecom industry the energy bills are one of the most significant portions of the expenditure. NFV promises to reduce the energy cost by virtualization. The number of devices can be increased or decreased as per the need but this makes the telecom services dependent on the cloud computing. So the energy efficiency of NFV will be become dependent on the cloud computing.

5. **Security, Privacy, and Trust:** Implementing the Virtualized NF over the public cloud will incorporate the security issues that are already present in the cloud computing (Mijumbi, Serrat, Gorricho, Bouten, Turck, & Boutaba 2016).

## CONCLUSION

To remove the network ossification and provide solutions for the changing network needs, the TSP are looking forward to create an environment that will transform the OSS/BSS component of a telecom sector towards virtualized services. Surely NFV will provide the flexibility and ease of deployment with lower Capex and Opex but NFV is in infancy state so it will take time to be implemented fully. On moving the NF function over the cloud all issues inherit from the cloud computing. The discussed challenges need to tackle so that it will become standard technology used in the telecom industry.

## REFERENCES

Bogineni, K., Davidson, D., Slauson, A., Molocznik, L., Martin, C., McBean, K., . . . Smith, K. (2016). SDN-NFV reference architecture. New York: Verizon.

Campbell, A. T., Katzela, I., Miki, K., & Vicente, J. (1999). Open signaling for ATM, internet and mobile networks (OPENSIG'98). *Computer Communication Review*, 29(1), 97–108. doi:10.1145/505754.505762

Casado, M., Freedman, M. J., Pettit, J., Luo, J., McKeown, N., & Shenker, S. (2007, August). Ethane: Taking control of the enterprise. *Computer Communication Review*, 37(4), 1–12. doi:10.1145/1282427.1282382

Casado, M., Freedman, M. J., Pettit, J., Luo, J., McKeown, N., & Shenker, S. (2007, August). Ethane: Taking control of the enterprise. *Computer Communication Review*, 37(4), 1–12. doi:10.1145/1282427.1282382

Chiosi, M., Clarke, D., Willis, P., Reid, A., Feger, J., Bugenhagen, M., & Benitez, J. (2012, October). Network functions virtualization: An introduction, benefits, challenges and call for action. In *SDN and OpenFlow World Congress* (pp. 22-24). Academic Press.

Chowdhury, N. M. K., & Boutaba, R. (2009). Network virtualization: State of the art and research challenges. *IEEE Communications Magazine, 47*(7), 20–26. doi:10.1109/MCOM.2009.5183468

Chowdhury, N. M. K., & Boutaba, R. (2009). Network virtualization: State of the art and research challenges. *IEEE Communications Magazine, 47*(7), 20–26. doi:10.1109/MCOM.2009.5183468

Chowdhury, N. M. K., & Boutaba, R. (2010). A survey of network virtualization. *Computer Networks, 54*(5), 862–876. doi:10.1016/j.comnet.2009.10.017

Cisco, V. N. I. (2016). *Cisco visual networking index: Global mobile data traffic forecast update, 2016–2021*. Retrieved from https://www.cisco.com/c/en/us/solutions/collateral/service-provider/visual-networking-index-vni/complete-white-paper-c11-481360.html

Doria, A., Hellstrand, F., Sundell, K., & Worster, T. (2002). General Switch Management Protocol V3. *RFC 3292*. Retrieved from https://tools.ietf.org/html/rfc3292

Enns, R. (2006). *NETCONF Configuration Protocol*. Retrieved from https://tools.ietf.org/pdf/rfc4741.pdf

Feamster, N., Rexford, J., & Zegura, E. (2014). The road to SDN: An intellectual history of programmable networks. *Computer Communication Review, 44*(2), 87–98. doi:10.1145/2602204.2602219

Fundation, O. N. (2012). Software-defined networking: The new norm for networks. *ONF White Paper, 2*, 2-6.

Gens, F. (2012). *IDC Predictions 2013: Competing on the 3rd Platform. Int*. Data Corporation.

Gude, N., Koponen, T., Pettit, J., Pfaff, B., Casado, M., McKeown, N., & Shenker, S. (2008). NOX: Towards an operating system for networks. *Computer Communication Review, 38*(3), 105–110. doi:10.1145/1384609.1384625

Haleplidis, E., Pentikousis, K., Denazis, S., Salim, J. H., Meyer, D., & Koufopavlou, O. (2015). *Software-defined networking (SDN): Layers and architecture terminology* (No. RFC 7426).

Han, B., Gopalakrishnan, V., Ji, L., & Lee, S. (2015). Network function virtualization: Challenges and opportunities for innovations. *IEEE Communications Magazine*, *53*(2), 90–97. doi:10.1109/MCOM.2015.7045396

Hernandez-Valencia, E., Izzo, S., & Polonsky, B. (2015). How will NFV/SDN transform service provider opex? *IEEE Network*, *29*(3), 60–67. doi:10.1109/MNET.2015.7113227

Jain, R., & Paul, S. (2013). Network virtualization and software defined networking for cloud computing: A survey. *IEEE Communications Magazine*, *51*(11), 24–31. doi:10.1109/MCOM.2013.6658648

McKeown, N., Anderson, T., Balakrishnan, H., Parulkar, G., Peterson, L., Rexford, J., & Turner, J. et al. (2008). OpenFlow: Enabling innovation in campus networks. *Computer Communication Review*, *38*(2), 69–74. doi:10.1145/1355734.1355746

Mijumbi, R., Serrat, J., Gorricho, J. L., Bouten, N., De Turck, F., & Boutaba, R. (2016). Network function virtualization: State-of-the-art and research challenges. *IEEE Communications Surveys and Tutorials*, *18*(1), 236–262. doi:10.1109/COMST.2015.2477041

NFV-ISG. (2015). *White paper on Network Functions Virtualization, whitepaper3*. Retrieved September 2017, from https://portal.etsi.org/Portals/0/TBpages/NFV/Docs/NFV_White_Paper3.pdf

Nunes, B. A. A., Mendonca, M., Nguyen, X. N., Obraczka, K., & Turletti, T. (2014). A survey of software-defined networking: Past, present, and future of programmable networks. *IEEE Communications Surveys and Tutorials*, *16*(3), 1617–1634. doi:10.1109/SURV.2014.012214.00180

ONF SDN. (n.d.). *Open networking foundation*. Retrieved from https://www.opennetworking.org/

ONF White Paper. (2012). *Software-defined networking: The new norm for networks*. Retrieved from http://www.bigswitch.com/sites/default/files/sdn_resources/onf-whitepaper.pdf

Riera, J. F., Escalona, E., Batalle, J., Grasa, E., & Garcia-Espin, J. A. (2014, June). Virtual network function scheduling: Concept and challenges. In *Smart Communications in Network Technologies (SaCoNeT), 2014 International Conference on* (pp. 1-5). IEEE.

Xia, W., Wen, Y., Foh, C. H., Niyato, D., & Xie, H. (2015). A survey on software-defined networking. *IEEE Communications Surveys and Tutorials*, *17*(1), 27–51. doi:10.1109/COMST.2014.2330903

## KEY TERMS AND DEFINITIONS

**Control Plane:** In the SDN architecture the second layer in which the decision making is done. This plane is centralized and the SDN controller lies in this plane.

**Data Plane:** In the SDN architecture the lowest layer from which the actual data movement takes place. The SDN switches lies in this layer which uses the flow rules to forward a packet provided by the controller.

**Network Function Virtualization:** The functions such as firewall, NAT which are provided by the middle boxes is virtualized in the form of software to be run on standard X86 server or data center.

**OpenFlow:** It is the standard protocol for SDN given by ONF. The Open Flow specifications are used to develop open flow switches.

**Programmable Networks:** To remove the ossification existing in the network the concept of programmable networks comes into picture in which the control logic is programmable and can be changed as per requirement.

**Software-Defined Networking:** It is a networking paradigm based on decoupling the control plane from the data plane and putting the control plane on a centralized location (i.e., controller that provides a centralized management and control over the network).

**Virtual Network Functions:** The virtual network functions are the NF (i.e., network functions running as a piece of software over a server).

# Chapter 2
# Virtualizing Network Functions in Software–Defined Networks

**Vishal Kaushik**
*University of Petroleum and Energy Studies, India*

**Ajay Sharma**
*SRM University - Haryana, India*

**Ravi Tomar**
*University of Petroleum and Energy Studies, India*

## ABSTRACT

*Software-defined networking (SDN) is an emerging network architecture that facilitates the network administrator to control and manage network behavior dynamically. Different from traditional networks, software-defined networks support dynamic and scalable computing. The dynamic behavior is achieved by decoupling or disassociating the system. The swing of control from tightly bound individual networks to assessable computing devices enables infrastructure abstraction. Due to the abstraction, the network can be considered as a logical or virtual entity. In this chapter, relation between network function virtualization (NFV) and software-defined networking (SDN) has been outlined. This chapter focuses on describing the pros and cons of NFV technologies. network functions virtualization (NFV) was founded under the work of the European Telecommunications Standards Institute (ETSI).*

DOI: 10.4018/978-1-5225-3640-6.ch002

# INTRODUCTION

## CDN: Content Delivery Network

The term Network Function Virtualization (NFV) was initially announced in October 2012. A consortium formed by some leading telecommunication companies such as AT&T, BT, China Mobile, and Deutsche Telekom introduced the NFV Call to the Active document (Chiosi et al., 2013). Another new committee established under the European Telecommunications Standards Institute (ETSI) focused on improving the speed and operating standards. They worked on constructing the NFV standards and their work results as a white paper on Software-defined Network (SDN) and is entitled as "Network Functions Virtualization (Simone et al., 2015). This had been published by a specification group in Darmstadt, Germany. NFV, being a part of that work e ETSI and comprised of representatives from European telecommunication industry from Europe. They produced a standard terminology definition & use guiding the vendors and operators to facilitate better management and implementation of NFV. Herewith, a traditional standard for stability, quality and protocol adherence came into existence in a more refined manner (Borcoci, 2015).

## Understanding Relationship Between NFV and SDN

The construction of NVF revolves around the key features of SDNs such as control/data plane separation, virtualization, SDN controllers, and data center concept. The NVF and SDF shares similar goals but both have different working strategies.

The statement that "Due to recent network focused advancements in PC hardware, any service that is able to be delivered on proprietary, application-specific hardware should be able to be done on a virtual machine" summarizes the entire evolution of Network Function Virtualization. Nowadays, a number of network devices viz. Routers, Firewalls, Load Balancers and so on are running virtualized on commodity hardware (Noble, 2017).

With a clear objective of reducing equipment costs and decreasing time to market, NFV achieves elasticity and scalability along with strong ecosystem. The SDN also breaks the bond that relates the control/application software with the hardware. Both the architectures- NFV and SDN need optimization at carrier scale of the dynamic cloud environment (Benington, 2014).

For achieving greater agility, SDN and NFV aim to control automation and virtualization. Whereas optimizing the deployment of network functions (such as DNS, load balancers, firewalls etc.) was the main intention of NFV. The physical as well as the virtual layers that enable to interconnect virtual network function

*Figure 1. SDN and NFV Relationship*

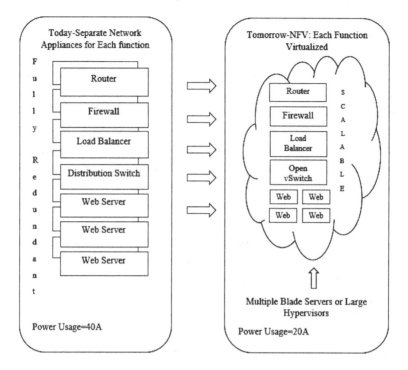

endpoints require large-scale dynamic network connectivity to be deployed (Nunes et al., 2014)

Network Function Virtualization finds its roots in several previously described network operations problems, especially the implications of bundling services by network equipment manufacturers within their platform Operating Systems. NFV can also be applied to appliance vendors in a way that does not take advantage of the processing scale/innovation seen by many customers in their data centers.

Different from NFV, SDN involves different control modules, interfaces and the applications that are mandatory for its proper working. NFV just needs shifting of network applications based on dedicated hardware to virtual containers on Commercial-off-the-shelf (COTS) hardware. More illustratively, SDN is present whereas NFV is future (Matias et al., 2015).

NFV unites forwarding devices and middle-boxes shaping a common control framework. Use of NFV enables network policies to get implemented by the operators irrespective of the placements viz. placement of functions etc. and also it provisions no need of thinking about the steering which includes how to route traffic through these functions. The network services are deployed on generic x86 hardware facilitating flexible resource allocation, scale-out architectures, bare metals or virtual machines etc. (Kolias, 2014; McKeown et al., 2008).

The network services and functions can be further categorized into three major categories- simple virtualized services, service chaining, and services virtualization or platform virtualization.

## Requirements of Networking Through NFV

Today's environment where networks are static and quite expensive to manage imposes a number of challenges in supporting NFV:

- Real-time and dynamic provisioning: The automatic deployment of VNFs, VNF FGs and their management in the NFV infrastructure.
- Provisioning of physical and virtual infrastructures with seamless control.
- Carrier-grade should allow robustness and scalability.
- Openness and interoperability: The network elements and VNFs from different vendor must co-exists. The NFV allows the interoperability and co-existence through open interface. NFV allows network elements and VNFs from multiple vendors interoperate and co-exist through API and open interfaces (i.e., Open Flow).
- Global scope and cross-administration of NFV: Connectivity distributing over multiple administration dominions and geographies is imperative.
- Acceleration in innovation: The demands of NFV require a substantial complex forwarding plane, combining virtual and physical applications in cooperation with extensive control and application software; on the contrary, SDN lay down on the principles which are based on Open Flow as the cornerstone and tend to change the control plane to be software-centric, programmable and open which is an ideal foundation for innovation in SDN.

## MODEL ARCHITECTURAL FRAMEWORK FOR NFV

### Model Architectural Framework of Network Function Virtualization

The architectural framework of NFV is organized into three layers and these are Virtualized network function (VNF), Network Function Virtualization Infrastructure (NFVI), and Network Functions Virtualization Management and Orchestration Architectural Framework (NFV-MANO).

*Figure 2. Demonstration of Network Function Virtualization Intersection*

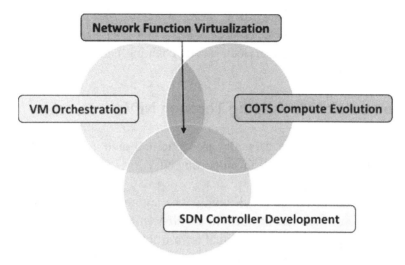

*Figure 3. NFV Networking Requirements*

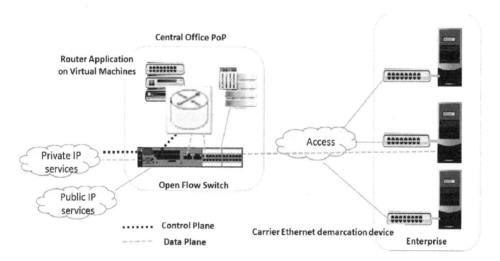

## Virtualized Network Function (VNF)

The VNF can be considered equivalent to the accelerator, which is responsible for implementation and handling of profound network functions that are developed on the Network function virtualization infrastructure. They act as an aid in delivering full-scale networking communication services.

# Network Function Virtualization Infrastructure (NFVI)

NFVI can be defined as a set of resources which is comprised of all the hardware and software components distributed over several locations. Moreover, it acts as a platform for the deployment of VNFs.

# Network Functions Virtualization Management and Orchestration Architectural Framework (NFV-MANO)

The objective behind this third layer, NFV-MANO is to manage NFVI and VNFs. As a whole, it could be viewed as the collection of all functional blocks and reference interfaces. The functional blocks consisting of data repositories are used to communicate data/information via the defined interfaces. (NFV Report Series Part I, SDNCentral LLC, 2017; Bogineni et.al, 2016)

## Requirements for Implementation of NFV Framework

The requirements for NFV Framework implementation has been suggested by Lorena et al. (2017). These requirements are

- **General:** Predictable performance, fractional or complete virtualization.
- **Portability:** Decoupled from underlying architecture.

*Figure 4. Model Architectural Framework for NFV*

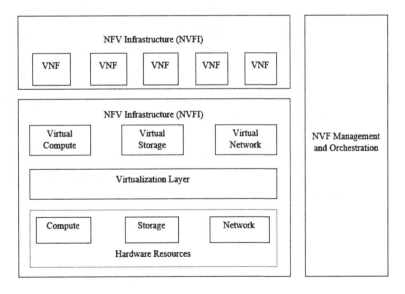

- **Elasticity:** Movable to other services and scalable to meet SLAs.
- **Performance:** Facilities to monitor.
- **Resiliency:** This can be specified by packet loss rate, calls drops and time to recover, etc. Ability to recreate after failure.
- **Security:** Roll-based authentication, authorization.
- **Service Continuity:** Smooth and continuous service after failures or migration.
- **Service Assurance:** Detecting fault using Time stamp and forward copies of packets.
- **Energy Efficiency Requirements:** Saving energy by placing a subset of VNF in a power conserving sleep state.
- **Transition:** Coexistence with legacy and interoperability among multi-vendor implementations.
- **Service Models:** When required, an operator may use NFV infrastructure which is operated by other operators.

## Performance Indicators of Network Function Virtualization

It is possible to create a number of services and applications on flexible network architectures using NFV as a platform. The lack of proper software architecture on servers with the transferal to new generation architecture leads to loss of competitive advantages and time-to-market with the consequences of performance issues.

With this, equivalent or better performance can be realized using virtualization as with legacy physical equipment. The usage of hypervisors, virtual switches ad virtual machines for cloud application foundation results into addition of layer of software overhead and associated complexity. (Yang et al., 2016)

Hypervisors, virtual switches and virtual machines building the cloud application foundation add layers of software overhead and associated bottlenecks. There are some common NFV performance bottlenecks in designing the physical appliances and these bottlenecks can even multiply when migrating to virtualization. As a result, transition from VM to VM communications lead to expansion of performance issue. (LeBlan, 2014)

To bypass NFV performance bottlenecks before there occurrence, packet processing software are highly applicable in software transition with technology.

The evaluation of packet processing software requires certain metrics that enables cost-effective value proposition and smooth transition to future requirements. These metrics includes:

- Equivalent physical and virtual performance.
- Transparency.

- No major changes required to OS, hypervisor, virtual switch, and management.
- Accessibility across multi-vendor processors, hardware platforms and NIC.

## Typical Performance

- 3-4 Gbps per CPU core assuming very light per-packet processing
- An order of magnitude less than what the hardware could do (more than 10 Gbps per core,40+ Gbps per x86 server)

## Bottlenecks

- TCP stack and Linux kernel in NFV virtual machines
- Hypervisor virtual switch
- NIC TCP offload works only with VLANs

## Solutions

- Optimized virtual switches (ex: INTEL DPDK)
- Dedicated virtual NICs (hypervisor bypass)

*Figure 5. Performance Indicators of NFV*

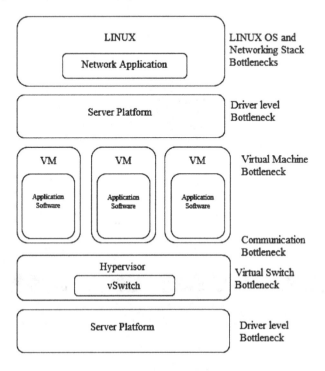

- Dedicated packet processing CPU cores
- User-mode packet processing (viz. PF_RING)

## VIRTUALIZATION OF NETWORK SERVICES

### Various Ways to Achieve Virtualization of Network Services

The virtualization of network services can be achieved through a number of ways; however, they all use the same form of architecture what is defined in Network Attached Storage (NAS) or shared form of other storage/memory architecture. One of the most popular methods of virtualization of network services includes the use of Linux virtual containers. Moreover, other methods include:

- A- Separate portioned hypervisor
- B- Use of multiple/compartmentalized operating systems
- C- Use of bare metal machines
- D- Embedded hypervisor
- E- Composite, distributed or clustered services/functions
- F- Shared storage

*Figure 6. Methods of Network Services Virtualization*

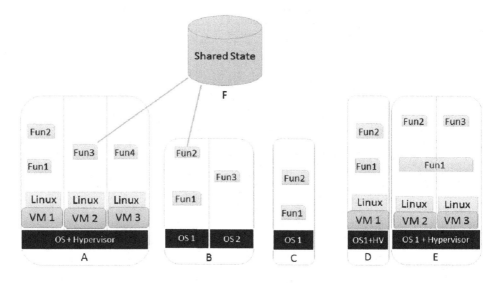

## Virtualizing Network Functions in Blade Server and Virtualization Environments

Some of the major features of using Blade Server and virtualization for NFV are:

- Less complex standard hardware
- Use of lower CapEx
- Use of lower OpEx
- Increased flexibility
- Reduction in risk
- Availability of open market to software suppliers
- Less power consumption
- Testing of new apps
- Reduced TTM

## NFV Practices and Recommendations for Network Services Virtualization

Though virtualization of network services has featured a lot of advantages, they give rise to some major concerns regarding NFV practices and recommendations as listed below:

- NFV orchestration evaluates the degradation of individual services/functions resulted due to the introduction of the 0hypervisor and multiple virtualized services on the same physical hardware. It also supervises the hypervisor and host resources to troubleshoot, and hereby resolving the contention of physical resources.

*Figure 7. NFV using Blade Server and virtualization*

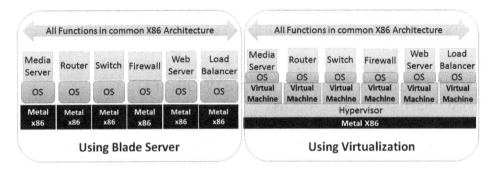

- An introduction of hypervisor results into a Single Point of Failure (SPOF) which may affect the working of virtual machines on a host and other defined chains of network services.
- Hypervisor comprising a virtual switch has the ability to control traffic in order to avoid application failure while serving multiple vNICs of various virtual machines.
- The hypervisor also provisions the feature of management awareness that distributes and isolate the applications when the failure of a physical machine state like NIC port takes place. Moreover, the management awareness by hypervisor is bridged by SDN controller and Orchestration cooperation.

## Benefits of Network Services Virtualization

Though virtualization of network services has featured a lot of advantages, they give rise to some major concerns regarding NFV practices and recommendations as listed below:

- NFV orchestration evaluates the degradation of individual services/functions resulted due to the introduction of the 0hypervisor and multiple virtualized services on the same physical hardware. It also supervises the hypervisor and host resources to troubleshoot, and hereby resolving the contention of physical resources.
- An introduction of hypervisor results into a Single Point of Failure (SPOF) which may affect the working of virtual machines on a host and other defined chains of network services.
- Hypervisor comprising a virtual switch has the ability to control traffic in order to avoid application failure while serving multiple vNICs of various virtual machines.
- The hypervisor also provisions the feature of management awareness that distributes and isolate the applications when the failure of a physical machine state like NIC port takes place. Moreover, the management awareness by hypervisor is bridged by SDN controller and Orchestration cooperation.

## CHALLENGES IN SUPPORTING NETWORKING THROUGH VIRTUALIZATION

Today's environment where networks are static and quite expensive to manage imposes a number of challenges in supporting NFV:

- **Real-Time and Dynamic Provisioning:** The automatic deployment of VNFs, VNF FGs and their management in the NFV infrastructure.
- Provisioning of physical and virtual infrastructures with seamless control.
- Carrier-grade should allow robustness and scalability.
- **Openness and Interoperability:** The network elements and VNFs from different vendor must co-exists. The NFV allows the interoperability and co-existence through open interface
- NFV allows network elements and VNFs from multiple vendors interoperate and co-exist through API and open interfaces (i.e., Open Flow).
- **Global Scope and Cross-Administration of NFV:** Connectivity distributing over multiple administration dominions and geographies is imperative.
- **Acceleration in Innovation:** The demands of NFV require a substantial complex forwarding plane, combining virtual and physical applications in cooperation with extensive control and application software; on the contrary, SDN lay down on the principles which are based on Open Flow as the cornerstone and tend to change the control plane to be software-centric, programmable and open which is an ideal foundation for innovation in SDN.

## Mitigation Software Hardware Strategies

Since virtualization and abstraction incur money, a number of additional mitigation hardware and software strategies have been designed few of them are discussed as ahead.

## Data Plane I/O Accelerator

Data Plane I/O is an accelerator which enables to run services on COTS hardware. The use of hypervisor vSwitch, primarily designed for NFV/service virtualization increases the performance overhead for I/O. The I/O techniques can be software based which may include operating system or hypervisor. The two mostly used I/O acceleration techniques are: (Aditess, 2016)

- **Virtio:** I/O benefits are mainly provided by defining a layer of abstraction over devices in a paravirtualized hypervisor VMM. It also acts as a platform for disk and network I/O virtualization in Linux, FreeBSD, and other operating systems.
- **SR-IOV:** It is defined as PIC-SIG Single-Root I/O Virtualization (SR-IOV) which acts as an extension to PCI Express specification. The major role of SR-IOV is in splitting physical functions into lighter-weight virtual functions. i.e. it allows a network adaptor, to separate access to its resources

among various PCIe hardware functions where PCIe specification splits a device into multiple PCI Express Requester IDs. It can distinguish between individual traffic streams via I/O MMU. The other functions of SR-IOV are to perform delivery directly to a virtual machine and apply memory/interrupt translations. It works with I/O hardware built around PCIe technology. It has both hardware and software support requirements.

## Concept of Services Engineered Path

In 2010, Jim Guichard, principal architect in the CTO Office at Juniper Networks gave a proposal to decouple the Service and Network infrastructure.

Tunneling or switching is a technology that provides a path to specific service function and enables selective traffic redirection based upon short lived classifiers. In this, signaled path is requested via pre- path computation element.

The Service Engineered Path (SEP) concept was introduced as a very strong new means of service delivery for the Service Provider community—a Juniper-specific solution and many more, but one that solved the problem prior to any standardization of such a concept. (Albert Greenberg et.al, 2005)

The main problem due to the SEP was that service providers were constrained in making new service offerings by the need to deploy the service appliances (or dedicated services blades) comprising of the service offerings which includes Intrusion Detection Systems (IDS), Intrusion Prevention Systems (IPS), firewall, load balancers, and SSL offloaders that were run within the edge routers that would serve their projected markets.

*Figure 8. Services Engineered Path*

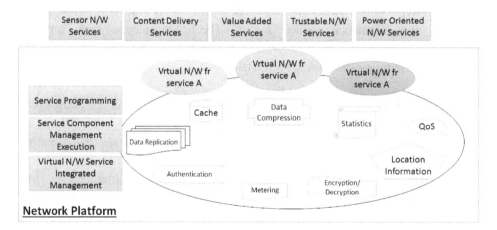

But this operation resulted service introduction as laborious and disruptive network functions. By this path, too many subscribers came into existence and hence, requiring the installation of more appliances/blades.

Consequently, different motivations were required for SEP to optimally stitch the path of a subscriber service through multiple sites in a WAN and many more operations. These includes mainly:

- Network devices providing Service Enabling Technologies (SETs) would be transparent to the general network infrastructure.
- Upgradation to one or more service instances wouldn't affect routing in the network, providing flexible service SET.
- Last but not the least, providing the ability to link together services of different types by enabling new and innovative bundled services.

The construction of service consisting of different components in hierarchies includes:

- **Service:** A service function, application, or content used in collaboration with other SETs to enable a service.
- **SET Sequence:** Predetermined sequence of SETs that form the service using which it gives defined outcomes.
- **Set Sequence Path:** Several combinations of Service Nodes that could form part of the SET sequence. The SET sequence path is a list of combinations available that could be used to satisfy the service.

With the passage of time, SDN and NFV started using technologies which include PCE and OPENFLOW, using service orchestration.

With the introduction of SEP concept, Virtualization techniques began to evolve; making wholesale virtualization of the service plane on COTS – Commercial-Off-The-Shelf wasn't an essential part as it is now with ETSI NFV.

In case of MPLS fabric from a prior post, the working of service chaining set of stacked labels onto the packets at the network ingress (such as the first leaf node the packet encounters, or even the edge of the network itself, or at the data center border router). The way that Service chaining works in the case of the MPLS fabric from a prior post, a set of labels is stacked onto the packet at the network ingress (at the data center border router, or the first leaf node the packet encounters, or even the edge of the network itself). The first label is responsible for traffic forwarding to the first service in the chain where it drops its label and thereafter packet is forwarded without label. In the same way, second label is responsible for forwarding packets to the second service and again packet drop its label there. (Rick McGeer, 2013)

This is a straightforward and powerful approach which help us to virtualize services into a generic data center fabric. These services can be executed on standard computer and storage. It facilitates easy addition and removal of service just by including VMs and pushing the stack of labels accordingly at the network entrance. At last, it also enables us to scale services by spinning VMs and using a scale out rather than scaling up by principles.

Moreover, the concept of service chaining should not assume always that the service elements would be located in a data center (or that all the service elements are virtualized), even though that can be a long-term goal of service providers for their edge/access deployments. It may be possible that services may get associated with network boundaries, for e.g. a security policy can be attached to the network boundary or a load balancer can be inserted at a network boundary. The figure describes network boundary, which can be:

- The borderline separating a tenant network from an external network (such as the Internet or the VPN to the enterprise network)
- The borderline that separate one tenant network from other tenant from different networks.
- The boundary that separate multiple networks of the same tenant

Here, moving of a network functions into software results that building a service chain won't require acquiring hardware anymore.

*Figure 9. Multiple Network Functions Over Framework*

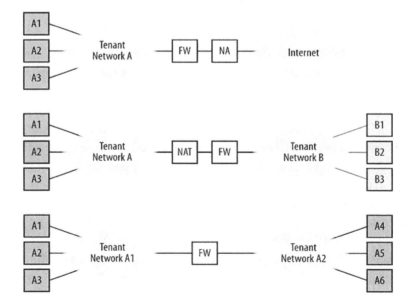

## Metadata

Metadata can be used in sharing information about user's traffic with network functions making up a processing path and is important to service chaining concept.

The standardization of the overlay encapsulation and the traffic matching protocol(s) used in creating service chains/paths raises a number of queries which may get complicated by the consideration of whether some sort of metadata is needed to be implanted in the flow. The answer to the above-cited question may depend on the vision of the role of the controller and its service chaining application, specifically whether they will be charged with creating a chain that precludes any inter-block knowledge. It may also depend on whether the virtualization point of view limits function decomposition to the same virtual device or composite and thus separates an internal chain that uses some IPC mechanism allowing internal embedded metadata from the external chain.

Metadata can be both- the implicit or the explicit. The explicit alternative, to embed the metadata, may result in extensions in packets to pass metadata from one chain member to another that will almost certainly require standardization to promote an open environment and may bring on collateral concerns about the transparency of such augmented flows to the existing network infrastructure.

## Networking an Application Level Approach

A solution can be explored, by using application–based protocol. The network construct view requires tunneling because data flows have intrinsic routing that needs to be obscured. This view assumes manipulation of the network protocols to direct the flows as well as to manage metadata, with the aid of a controller.

Data flow in treated as application input and output in the application construct view. Applications are made to run on servers using discrete sockets where servers have resolvable names (DNS). The service instance name to IP address binding identifies the load balancer (or an any cast address for a bank of ADC/load balance capacity—the assumption of a load balancer is quite common) for a set of components that run the service and potentially multiple input and output ports representing different application personalities (i.e., configurations or behaviors). Bidirectional flows use two personalities. (Monge et al., 2015)

The mapping from internal service ports to external transport ports is specified by the service path for each service and connectivity between the transport ports where these service paths are generated from a data model expressing the relationships between a service component, services, and service paths; and are propagated/applied from a management system to the service instances (through a yet-to-be-determined API).

Such approach to chaining via a series of familiar application-keyed technologies viz. DNS and ADC/LB along with some new application management technologies viz. controllers and their API may become interesting if the number of chains (and thus, tunnels) becomes overwhelming. Alternatively, the functional elements on the same device might use IPC mechanisms via shared memory to improve performance in cases where a mixture of application interaction via an external protocol and internal IPC form the chain.

## Scalability

One cannot ignore the consideration around the scale and complexity even if the current state of SDN makes the network construct acceptable, given that it is already an available entity with which one can experiment and build. However, scale and complexity also cannot drive the application-level approach conversation.

Placement of the service nodes and constraints that may restrict the service paths are the major components which the complexity discussion revolves around –

- How many chains will there be, and what are the constraints on the path selection of service chains (e.g., overall latency of the delivered service, administrative boundaries, and tariffs)?
- How do those constraints affect the HA policy for a service (e.g., should individual SETs be added to or from the chain if their placement causes trombone flows in the network, or should the flow fail over to an entirely new chain)?

*Figure 10. Application Level Networking via NFV*

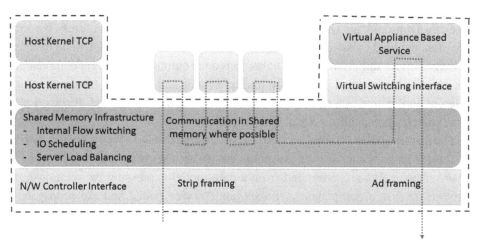

- How often will the chain topology change, and how dynamic/elastic is the loading of the elements in the chain?
- Is there a benefit to service placement algorithms that minimize the potential for network bottlenecks and contribution to overall delay in a serviced flow?
- What role does policy play in the service chain embedded within the chain as a decision/branch point or when expressed as multiple different chain topologies?

## Goals and Objectives

- Pre-standardization of the work in such a way that satisfies current as well as the future technical specifications and standards in ad hoc Standards Development Organizations (SDOs).
- In the form of an ETSI Industry Specification Group (ISG).

Objectives:

- It includes specifying requirements and architecture. Analyzing the gap in virtualization of network functions.
- It ensures that the overall network operator's platform is simple and easy.
- It tends to achieve virtualized network functions with high performance.
- It must provide assurance of appropriate levels of resilience to hardware and software failure
- It enables the management and orchestration of VNFs.
- The integration of new virtualized appliances into existing management systems must be simple.

## Software Architecture of Network Function Virtualization

Software Architecture (NFV SWA) – It defines use cases and how solutions should be structured and possibly decomposed into functional blocks.

What services can be virtualized and in what method is one of the interesting questions for NFV; with regard to which, there is a spectrum of potential solutions, from the fully virtualized service running as a single VM through a multipart (a service comprised of functional sub-blocks), to the service that must run on bare metal. Note that the latter could still benefit from orchestration from an operations perspective.

The virtualized functions must have the capability to directly interact with INF or indirectly through MANO so that the operation requirements (e.g. computation, storage, security, QOS, memory resources) and support requirements (monitoring, metering, and billing) can be identified.

- Their proposed Control Signal Processing Function Group will focus on authentication/authorization, policy, state management, mobility, and mobility-related support functions, including call record collection and lawful intercept.
- Their proposed User Data Processing FG will focus on packet forwarding, duplication, counting, processing, load balancing, and application layer steering (i.e., proxy).
- Their proposed Data and Storage FG will focus on data storage and management.

## Network Function Virtualization vs. Cloud Implementations

A demonstration was hosted at Telefónica's NFV Reference Lab, Madrid which provides two different deployment environments:

- An NFV-ready NFVI pool, with a Telefónica, developed NFV ready VIM implementing the requisite Enhanced Platform Awareness (EPA) and a Cyan NFV-Orchestrator which supports advanced VNF deployment using enhanced NFV information models.
- A standard cloud infrastructure pool ala classic cloud computing, with the same Telefónica VIM, connected to the same Cyan NFV-Orchestrator but not using the enhanced information model as the basis for the deployment.

## Optimized Deployment of Network Function Virtualization

The correct NFV TOSCA model is used in the primary deployment whereas the VNFD models are used in secondary deployment. The information in the model facilitates the Planet Blue orchestrator to optimally deploy Brocade configuration through the Telefónica VIM. The result is the achievement of full line rate performance of 23 Mbps (40 Gbps @ 192 Bytes). The deployment of an intelligent NFV through the EPA aware delivery stacked onto underlying NFVI with correct extended information model having deterministic VNF attributes is easy to demonstrate using deployment scenario.

The benefits of doing an "intelligent" NFV deployment through the EPA aware delivery stack onto underlying NFVI using the correct extended information model which contains the attributes required for deterministic VNF performance can easily be demonstrated using this deployment scenario. Brocade vRouter with the correct

EPA parameters exposed via VNF Descriptor and en- forced by the Cyan NFVO and the VIM is deployed. The Brocade vRouter can achieve the high performance as expected by design correctly implementing the PCIe pass through, the NUMA awareness, CPU pining, and huge page requirement as required by the Brocade VNF.

## Non-Standardized (Non-ETSI) in Network Function Virtualization

The existence of the ETSI workgroup shouldn't imply that it is the place where service virtualization is studied and standards are conducted for the production service virtualization offerings. This is far from the case, e.g.

- The academic community is starting to study some of the questions around NFV as part of the burgeoning SDN research they are performing.
- The service chaining has been targeted by many existing controller/framework vendors as one of their applications and a few startups viz. LineRate, Embrane are positioning controllers for layer 2 through layer 7 that use their own virtualized services while working.
- Existing vendors of highly integrated network elements are delving into intermediate or total virtualization of their platform/solutions.
- Though it is too early for a complete section in this revision, the IETF has already begun soliciting interest in the area of service chaining. A proposed workgroup named Network Service Chaining [NSC] is currently collecting drafts in its BoF (birds of a feather) stage which includes drafts proposing formalized packet headers for expressing service context and metadata as well as the need for a standardized generic service control plane.

## Standardized (ETSI) NFV: ISG Works

- **Use Cases:** Initial application field and technical challenges.
- **Requirements:** Technical and business requirements for an NFV framework, including service models.
- **Architectural Framework:** High level functional architectural and design idea for VNFs and underlying virtualization infrastructure.
- **Terminology:** Repository for common terms used within ETSI NFV documents.
- **Use Cases:** Initial application fields: Four main service-oriented use cases.
- Construction of NFV infrastructure as a Service.
- VNF implementation as a Service.
- Virtual Network Platform construction as a Service.

- VNF Forwarding Graphs for Specific targets
- Mobile core network (EPC) and IP Multimedia Subsystem (IMS).
- Mobile base station.
- Virtualized home environment
- Static access network
- Virtualized Content Delivery Network (CDN).

## Virtualizing Network Platform

Current service provider networks have evolved into a collection of purpose-designed, integrated elements or platforms e.g. the fundamental design of a core routing platform is to forward packets at an extremely high speed and low latency with packaging sensitive to physical footprint, power consumption, and associated heat. Without an entirely different set of forwarding blades and service blades, the placement of this platform at the network/provider edge where a tradeoff is required between forwarding rate, session state management, protocol session scale, and other services may be difficult.

Some vendors have gained proficiencies in packaging certain types of platforms over time. The most common examples are the Broadband Network Gateway and Evolved Packet Core components.

As SDN began to be explored by network operators, competitors to the entrenched "big three or four" vendors of these platforms began to explore new packaging models while provisioning the reduced cost and leveraging some of the principles of service virtualization.

The general designs put forward were to use an SDN Controller e.g. an OpenFlow controller to program forwarding state into a (much simpler and lower cost) switching element and create application specific state (protocol or user session state) on an associated server-based application. There are also the projects to replace or centralize the functions of the current generation of routers with cheaper components like Route Flow (BGP and IGP on OpenFlow) or Flexinet (BGP on OpenFlow) and more recent work with IP Infusion (ZebOS BGPD). Traditional vendors are responding by virtualizing low-hanging fruit in traditional network operations viz. the BGP Route Reflector (vRR).

These devices can be easily converted to running in a VM as they are purposely not in the data plane by design. vRR becomes a potential SDN control centralization point if it has a standardized programming interface and standardized controller/agent control session. Then, existing Provider Edge deployments start to look like SDN deployments (even if they continue to leverage the existing distributed control plane for the most part) bridging present operations and a more virtualized future operation.

## Challenges With Network Function Virtualization

In the current era, major operators desire to adapt cloud technologies to NFV in the carrier environment. An operator need to overcome major network challenges such as:

- **Fixed Configurations:** The hardware-based network appliances are configured at a system with fixed IP locations which continued unchanged for years.
- **Manually Intensive Management:** The installation and configuration of network appliances is a complex and time consuming task. Thus, we need to reduce the time. The automated provisioning for virtual appliances in the NFV environment decrease provisioning and configuration cost and times. Automated configuration also reduces the possibility of manually introduced configuration errors.
- **Rapid Growth of IP End Points:** Virtualization of fast network appliances concludes into increased number of network endpoints in the NFV environment. Millions of endpoints for residential and mobile applications obviously increase the pressure on existing network mechanisms such as Layer 2 VLANs, or additional complexity for bi-sectional bandwidth scaling such as TRILL and SPB.
- **Network Endpoint Mobility:** Physical appliances are found to be stationary and typically provisioned once in their lifetime. The migration of VNFs to different physical servers in different sub-networks or physical locations use tunneling addresses and protocols that dictate how they will reached.

VNFs can migrate readily to disparate physical servers which may appear in different sub-networks or even physical locations, and hence, use different tunneling addresses, or even have different protocols that dictate how they will be reached. Moreover, NFV decompose traditional linkage into IP location and identity.

- **Elasticity:** The VNFs can be on demand created, adjusted and destroyed in real time in the NFV environment, thus, the networks must be enriched with the ability of elasticity. They must have the capability to reconfigure rapidly with optimized resources in the dynamic NFV environment.
- **Multi-Tenancy:** Generally, NFV use cases are similar to the cloud-like "as a service" offerings. The feasibility of such services rely on efficient multi-tenancy. Thus, granular policy management is desirable for assigning services and flows, but decoupled from the physical infrastructure.

## VIRTUALIZED EPC: CHALLENGES/OPPORTUNITIES

1. Network function scaling should be independent, e.g., data vs. control plane functions.
2. Deployment of EPC, e.g., single data center over multiple DCs…
3. Efficient resiliency schemes by utilizing VNF instance migration.
4. Alternative migration/co-existence paths: single vs. coexistence of separate mobile cores

Orchestration and automation

- Service decomposition
- Provisioning and configuration automation
- Auto-scaling
- High-availability
- Service insertion for stateful services
- On-demand service chaining
- Integration with or orchestration/provisioning systems
- No standard deployment process or API

Licensing challenges

- Vendors like to license boxes (instances), not throughput

## CONCLUSION

The introduction of SDN, orchestration techniques and virtualization advances have materialized the comparatively older idea of Network Function Virtualization which when first brought up was not really capable of being realized.

NFV that brings structural change in the telecommunication infrastructure that will definitely result into cost efficiencies, market expansions and improvement to telecommunication industry infrastructure and applications. The disaggregation of the traditional roles and technology in telecommunications applications results into NFV. However, virtualization alone is not the perfect solution to all service deployment problems; but, actually presents new reliability problem vectors that a service orchestration system or architecture has to mitigate.

The researchers has already working in decomposing existing services into their functional elements with varying opinions on the granularity of this decomposition.

The decomposition will certainly influence service chaining resiliency and availability of overall services and individual elements.

Simply, NFV is a killer use-case for open stack.

At last, it is explicit that traditional vendors are pursuing low-hanging fruit transformations of their integrated service platforms via virtualization with an eye on when the price/performance characteristics of doing so may be feasible for more complex integrations at the Provider Edge (vCPE/vBNG/vPE). These will certainly include early offerings of virtualized firewall, DPI, and load balancing functions since these are fundamental to almost every chain in production. Ultimately, Intrusion Detection Systems (IDS), Intrusion Prevention Systems (IPS), caches, SSL off-loaders, and WAN optimizers will be targeted particularly for the Enterprise networking/ tenant space. However, the very prominent question to be answered is whether or not these transformations will be soon enough to allow traditional hardware device vendors to keep pace with these trends, or if newer non-incumbents will have the ability to take a foothold. (ETSI, 2013b)

# REFERENCES

Aditess. (2016). *Tailoring the needs for NFV-to-SDN convergence: An opportunity for the ARCADIA framework.* Retrieved from http://www.arcadia-framework.eu/ tailoring-needs-nfv-sdn-convergence-opportunity-arcadia-framework/

Aleplidis, E., Pentikousis, K., Denazis, S., Salim, J. H., Meyer, D., & Koufopavlou, O. (2015). *Software-defined networking (SDN): Layers and Eugen Borcoci.* InfoSystems Conference, Rome, Italy.

Barona López, L. I., Valdivieso Caraguay, A. L., Monge, M. A. S., & García Villalba, L. J. (2017). *Key Technologies in the Context of Future Networks: Operational and Management Requirements.* Retrieved from http://www.mdpi.com/1999-5903/9/1/1

Casado, M., Koponen, T., Shenker, S., & Tootoonchian, A. (2012, August). Fabric: a retrospective on evolving SDN. In *Proceedings of the first workshop on Hot topics in software defined networks* (pp. 85-90). ACM. doi:10.1145/2342441.2342459

Chua, R. (2017). *2017 NFV Report Series Part I: Foundations of NFV: NFV Infrastructure and VIM Report Available Now.* Retrieved from https://www.sdxcentral. com/articles/announcements/nfv-infrastructure-vim-report-avialable/2017/04/

ETSI. (2012). *Network Functions Virtualisation: An Introduction, Benefits, Enablers, Challenges & Call for Action.* Retrieved from https://portal.etsi.org/nfv/ nfv_white_paper.pdf

ETSI. (2013a). *Network Functions Virtualisation: Network Operator Perspectives on Industry Progress*. Retrieved from https://portal.etsi.org/nfv/nfv_white_paper2.pdf

ETSI. (2013b). *ETSI NFV 001 V1.1.1, 2013-10, NFV Use Cases*. Retrieved from http://www.etsi.org/deliver/etsi_gs/NFV/001_099/001/01.01.01_60/gs_NFV001v010101p.pdf

ETSI. (2013c). *ETSI GS NFV 004 v1.1.1 2013-10, NFV Virtualization Requirements*. Retrieved from http://www.etsi.org/deliver/etsi_gs/NFV/001_099/004/01.01.01_60/gs_NFV004v010101p.pdf

ETSI. (2014a). *Network Functions Virtualisation (NFV): Network Operator Perspectives on Industry Progress*. Retrieved from https://portal.etsi.org/Portals/0/TBpages/NFV/Docs/NFV_White_Paper3.pdf

ETSI. (2014b). *Network Functions Virtualization (NFV); Terminology for Main Concepts in NFV*. Retrieved from http://www.etsi.org/deliver/etsi_gs/NFV/001_099/003/01.02.01_60/gs_NFV003v010201p.pdf

ETSI. (2014c). *ETSI GS NFV 002 v1.2.1 2014-12, NFV Architectural Framework*. Retrieved from http://www.etsi.org/deliver/etsi_gs/NFV/001_099/002/01.02.01_60/gs_NFV002v010201p.pdf

Greenberg, A., Hjalmtysson, G., Maltz, D. A., Myers, A., Rexford, J., Xie, G., & Zhang, H. (2005, October). A clean slate 4D approach to network control and management. *Computer Communication Review*, *35*(5), 41–54. doi:10.1145/1096536.1096541

Kolias, C. (2014). Bundling NFV and SDN for Open Networking. Proceedings of NetSeminar at Stanford.

Matias, J., Garay, J., Toledo, N., Unzilla, J., & Jacob, E. (2015). Toward an SDN-enabled NFV architecture. *IEEE Communications Magazine*, *53*(4), 187–193. doi:10.1109/MCOM.2015.7081093

McKeown, N., Anderson, T., Balakrishnan, H., Parulkar, G., Peterson, L., Rexford, J., & Turner, J. (2008). OpenFlow: Enabling innovation in campus networks. *ACM SIGCOMM Computer Communication Review, 38*(2), 69-74.

Metzler, J., & Metzler, A. (2015). *The 2015 Guide to SDN and NFV*. Retrieved from https://www.a10networks.com/sites/default/files/resource-files/2015Ebook-A10-all.pdf

Monge, A. S., & Szarkowicz, K. G. (2015). *MPLS in the SDN Era: Interoperable Scenarios to Make Networks Scale to New Services*. O'Reilly Media, Inc.

Noble, S., (2017). *Building Modern Networks*. Birmingham: Packt Publishing.

Nunes, B. A. A., Mendonca, M., Nguyen, X. N., Obraczka, K., & Turletti, T. (2014). A survey of software-defined networking: Past, present, and future of programmable networks. *IEEE Communications Surveys and Tutorials*, *16*(3), 1617–1634. doi:10.1109/SURV.2014.012214.00180

Open Networking Foundation. (n.d.). *OpenFlow-Enabled SDN and Network Functions Virtualization*. Retrieved from https://www.opennetworking.org/images/stories/downloads/sdn-resources/solutionbriefs/sb-sdn-nvf-solution.pdf

Reid, A. (n.d.). *Network Functions Virtualization and ETSI NFV ISG*. Retrieved from http://www.commnet.ac.uk/documents/commnet workshop networks/CommNets EPSRC workshop Reid.pdf

Yang, H.H., & Quek, T.Q.S. (2016). *Massive MIMO Meets Small Cell: Backhaul and Cooperation*. New York: Springer.

Zimmerman, M., Allan, D., Cohn, M., Damouny, N., Kolias, C., Maguire, J., . . . Shirazipour, M. (2014). *ONF SOLUTION BRIEF - OpenFlow-enabled SDN and Network Functions Virtualization*. Retrieved from https://www.opennetworking.org/

## KEY TERMS AND DEFINITIONS

**CDN:** Content delivery network (CDN) is spatially distributed clusters of services over geographical regions to ensure high availability and performance.

**NFV:** Network function virtualization (NFV) is an initiative to demoralize the need of proprietary and dedicated hardware in networks via virtualization.

**SDN:** Software-defined network (SDN) is the dynamically programmable network functionality via open interfaces.

**Virtualization:** Virtualization techniques refer to create a virtual version of any hardware, platform, storage, and networking devices.

# Chapter 3
# Introduction to OpenFlow

**Mohit Kumar Jaiswal**
*University of Petroleum and Energy Studies, India*

## ABSTRACT

*The SDN controller is interfaced with the hardware of the network (i.e., with switches and routers) using OpenFlow. Basically, OpenFlow is an open interface used for configuring the forwarding tables of network switch according to the desired path derived by the SDN controller. OpenFlow enables more innovation in controller platforms and applications, and describes a solution for each frame or packet flow. OpenFlow is based on an ethernet switch with an internal flow-table and a standardized interface to add and remove flow entries of forwarding table of the system. The control mechanism from each one of the switch and router up to SDN controller are encrypted with the transport layer security (TLS) and secure socket layer (SSL) OpenFlow protocols to provide the additional security inside the network.*

## HISTORY

The SDN approach towards networking comes into demand after six year research collaboration between Stanford University and the University of California at Berkeley. The OpenFlow interface is a key component of SDN approach and was introduced in 2008 to offer an alternative to proprietary solutions which restrict flexibility and inspire vendor lock-in. The initiative was intended to pace innovation through simple software which is open source, controlled and managed locally. (Erickson, 2011)

The Open Networking Foundation (ONF) is a profitless trade organization established on March 21, 2011, the organization is supported by six companies i.e., Deutsche Telekom, Facebook, Google, Microsoft, Verizon, and Yahoo! intended towards encouraging networking through software defined networking (SDN) and

DOI: 10.4018/978-1-5225-3640-6.ch003

calibrating the OpenFlow protocol and corresponding technologies. (Melno Park, Calif., 2017)

The first version of the OpenFlow protocol i.e. version 1.1 was released on 28 February 2011, and further new evolution of the standard was managed by the Open Networking Foundation (ONF)(Jain, 2014). Version 1.2 of OpenFlow was approved on December 2011 by the ONF board and published it in February 2012 (Goransson, Black, Culver, 2016). The latest version of OpenFlow is 1.5. (McKeown; et al., 2008)

## INTRODUCTION

Open Network Foundation (ONF) defines OpenFlow as

*OpenFlow is the first standard communication interface defined between the control and forwarding layers of an SDN architecture. OpenFlow allows direct access to manipulation of the forwarding plane of network devices such as switches and routers, both physical and virtual (hypervisor-based). (Noyes, 2009)*

OpenFlow is the initially institutionalized interface and the most commonly used protocol outlined particularly for SDN. It is an open convention used for the communication between controllers and switches. In other words, it is an open interface used for configuring the forwarding tables of network switches and routers according to the desired path of network packets derived by the SDN Controller. In an OpenFlow, surrounding devices which want to communicate to an SDN Controller should support the OpenFlow protocol. OpenFlow uses Transmission Control Protocol (TCP) means that a controller can interact with switch over a network and need not to be co-located at the side of switches. Across this convention, the SDN Controller drops changes to the flow-table of switches/routers which helps network administrator in controlling the flow of packets, splitting the traffic for optimum performance, and are convenient for testing new configurations and applications. Through this, routing paths can be updated time-to-time or *ad hoc* by the controller and converted into rules and actions with a configurable lifespan, which are then updated to the switches forwarding table, jilting the actual flow of matched packets to the buffer of switch for the time span as per those rules.

The major component of OpenFlow which shares common objective with SDN are:

- Decoupling of the control and data planes of the switches, the control plane is managed by the centralised controllers which may be one or more in number but synchronized.

- Using an institutionalized interface communication between SDN controller and the switches for updating the forwarding table of switch over the network.
- The centralised controllers will be programmed via modern, extensible API's over the network.

The control mechanism of OpenFlow are encrypted with the Transport Layer Security(TLS) and Secure Sockets Layer(SSL) OpenFlow Protocols from SDN Controller to each switch and router to provide the auxiliary security inside the Network. Also, Open Flow allows the controller to remotely manage switches. These switches may have origins from different vendors, with each one of them having its own proprietary interfaces and scripting languages.

## ARCHITECTURE

The key components of the OpenFlow model, as shown in Figure 1, have become at least part of the common definition of SDN, mainly:

- Separation of the control and data planes (in the case of the ONF, the control plane is managed on a logically centralized controller system).
- Using a standardized protocol between controller and an agent on the network element for instantiating state (in the case of OpenFlow, forwarding state).
- Providing network programmability from a centralized view via a modern, extensible API.

For instantiating flows, OpenFlow provides a standardized southbound protocol i.e., controller to element agent, while there is no standard for either the northbound API i.e., application facing, or east/west API.

The distribution of east/west state on the primary controller is based on a database distribution model, which permits federation of one vendor's controllers but restricts the interoperable state exchange.

The Working Group of Architecture is indirectly attempting to address the architecture of OpenFlow as a general SDN architecture. The ONF has also attempted to merge the definition of SDN and OpenFlow. Without these standardized interfaces like OpenFlow, there is a question mark on the openness of the ONF definition of SDN.

Application services (Figure 2) provided by most of the OpenFlow controllers are: path computation, topology (determined through LLDP, which limits topology to layer 2), and provisioning. To support Of-Config, they need to support a NETCONF driver.

*Figure 1. Architecture of OpenFlow*

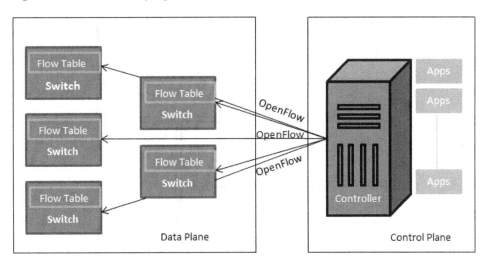

There is still question going on about the SDN architecture and OpenFlow whether the type of services provided by an OpenFlow controller are sufficient to fulfil all the potential needs of the SDN applications.

The main research on the macro topics of OpenFlow model are being conducted specifically at the Open Network Research Center (ONRC), and in many different academics and research facilities like (troubleshooting, the expression of higher level policies with OpenFlow semantics, and on protocols for verification layer between controllers and elements).

OpenFlow is a set of protocols and an API; it is just a program and not a product in itself and not a single feature of a product. Without the application programs (single or many) and protocols the controller is useless for giving instructions on which flows goes on which elements i.e., switches and routers (for their own reasons).

Presently OpenFlow protocol is splits into two parts:

1. A wire protocol which is responsible for establishing a control session, describing a message structure for interchanging flow modifications and collecting statistics, and clarifying the elementary structure of a switch (ports and tables). Version 1.1 added the functionality to support more than one tables, stored action execution, and metadata passing—eventually developing the logical pipeline processing within a switch for supervising flows

2. A configuration and management protocol. of-config based on NETCONF (using Yang data models) to assign physical ports of a switches to the respective controllers, outline high availability (active/standby) and response of controller

*Figure 2. Components of OpenFlow Controller*

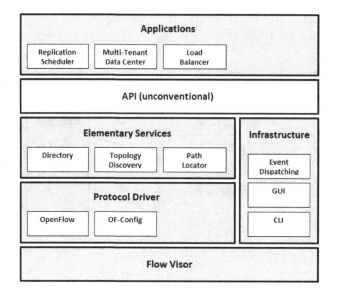

during connection failure. However, OpenFlow can build the elementary operation of OpenFlow command/control, it cannot boot or sustain an element i.e., switches, routers.

In 2012, The ONF moved from "plugfests" by examining the interoperability and acceptance to a further formalised test (outsourced to Indiana University). This was motivated by the complexity of the post-OpenFlow wire version 1.0 primitive set.

OpenFlow protocols indirectly provide the network slicing (It is an attractive feature which allows to split an element into independently controlled groups of ports or a network into different administrative domains). Although tools like FlowVisor (similar to network virtualization, which behaves like transparent proxy across elements and multiple controllers) which will introduce some intermediary delay to manage the packets flow across controller and switches, some other tools like specific vendor implementations which behaves like agents that allows the formation of numerous virtual switches with independent controller sessions make network slicing possible in OpenFlow.

## WIRE PROTOCOL

In computer networking, a wire protocol refers to a process of obtaining the data from point to point. A wire protocol is required for the interoperability of more than one application. It generally refers to protocols higher than the physical layer (Open Networking Foundation Formed to Speed Network Innovation, 2011). They often refer to diffuse object protocols, or they use applications that were dedicated to work together.

In contrast to transport protocols of fourth layer of OSI model (like TCP or UDP), a wire protocol is used to outline a common way to demonstrate the data at application level. It refers only to a common application layer protocol.

In OpenFlow firstly, it instigates the idea of replacing ephemeral state (flow entries are not stored in permanent storage on the network element) for the stiff and unstandardized semantics of various vendor's protocol configuration (the potential to design ephemeral state along with programmatic control may be a short-term advantage of OpenFlow, as there are proposals to add this functionality existing programmatic methods like NETCONF). Ephemeral state also enhances the slower configuration commit models of past attempts at network automation.

The result of such configuration is to create forwarding state (although distributed and learned in a distributed control environment). For many network engineers, the testing of proper configuration is to validate forwarding state i.e., examining at routing, forwarding, or bridging tables. Obviously, this leads to increase in burden to the controller(s) in the form of managing and maintenance of this state (if we need to be dedicated and always have certain forwarding protocols in the forwarding table) versus the distributed management of configuration stanzas on the network elements (Although this is not a new theory in that PCRF/PCEF/PCC systems have already done this with mobile networks on a per-subscriber basis in past) Standard organizations have been working on a clear definition and standardized processing of Interchanged messages and interoperability of different vendor's components of the overall system. In future, the mobile policy systems could also evolve into SDN systems and have SDN characteristics due to the flexibility of the OpenFlow.

Second, in an OpenFlow flow entry, the header of entire packets (layer 2 and layer 3 is must) are available for match and update actions, see Figure 3. Numerous of the field matches can be masked i.e., the supported type of match (offset or contiguous based) is another platform-dependent capability. These have been refined over the different releases of OpenFlow versions. Figure 3 demonstrates the complication of implementing the L2+L3+ACL forwarding functionality (with next hop concept for fast connection) can be the integration of primitives supported from table to table leads to a very broad combination of contingencies to support.

There is noticeable difference in broadness of operator control in contrast to the distributed IP/MPLS model (OpenFlow has an 11-tuple match space). This includes:

- The network can imitate IP destination forwarding behaviour, because of its masking potential in the match instructions.

*Figure 3. Structure of wire protocol of OpenFlow*

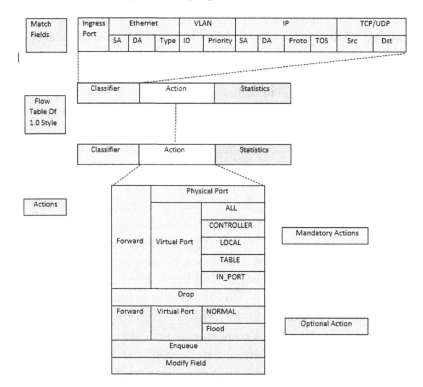

- At present, there is no standardized identical to the packet matching strengths of OpenFlow, which makes it very strong alternative for Policy Based Routing or other match/forward mechanisms in the diffuse control environment.
- The network can unveil source/destination routing behaviour at both the layers i.e., Layer 2 and Layer 3.

Eventually, there is commitment of the modify action. The actual concept about switch was that it could be made to act like a service appliance with services like firewall or NAT. This capability of switches is highly reliant on vendor implementation which may or may not noticeable in hardware-based forwarding systems. Although, with the labelled control actions made it possible to the OpenFlow controlled element to imitate integrated platform behaviours similar to MPLS LSR or other conventional diffused platform functions, which was added to the version 1.3 of the wire protocol.

Entries of the table can be prioritized according to our need in case of entries are overlapping, along with the expiry time of the entries. It can perform and save clean-up operation in some cases and can set and perform drop dead efficacy for flows during the failure of any controller.

The OpenFlow protocol is extended with the extension "experimenter" (it can be public or private) for statistics, flow match fields, control messages, meter operation, and for vendor-specific extensions (which can be public or private).

TABLE was required to build a multi-table pipeline, OpenFlow supports up to 255 untyped tables with random GoTo ordering. OpenFlow supports 'Physical', 'Logical', and 'Reserved' port types. These ports are used as ingress, egress, or bidirectional structures. IN_PORT and ANY are self-explanatory 'Reserved' ports.

The rest RESERVED ports possess important and interesting behaviours. CONTROLLER is the only reserved port which is required in this particular set, others are optional. The other ports are ANY, IN_PORT, ALL, and TABLE which all are required. These all combinations are captivating for their potential interactions in a hybrid.

- **Local:** This Logical port is an egress-only port which allows OpenFlow applications to access and processes the ports of the element host operating system (OS).
- **Normal:** This Logical port is also egress-only ports which allow the switch to function like a conventional Ethernet switch with associated flooding/learning behaviours. According to protocol functional specification, this port is only supported by a Hybrid switch i.e., which behaves like both OpenFlow switch and Layer 2 switch.
- **Controller:** This Reserved port allows the flow rule to forward the packets from the data path to controller and vice versa over the control channels. This also enables the behaviour like PACKET_IN and PACKET_OUT.
- **Flood:** This logical port is an egress-only port which uses the replication engine of the network element for sending the packet out with all non-reserved standard ports. FLOOD supports the element packet replication engine which makes it vary from the another reserved port ALL which includes the ingress ports.

There are two modes which are offered by the forwarding paradigm namely, proactive (pre-provisioned) and reactive (data-plane driven). In the proactive mode, the driven program locates the forwarding entries before its demand. While in the reactive mode, if flow fails to match the existing entries, the driver has two possibilities i.e., either to drop the flow or to apply PACKET_IN option to make decision to create a flow entry which is capable of accommodating the packets.

The control channel is used to configure, supervise and provide the path for packets between the switch and controller/applications. This channel was initially described as a symmetric TCP session which is secured by the Transport Layer Security (TLS).

Statistics support covers table, port, flow, queue and vendor-specific hardware's.

In the case of reliances between the successive messages, OpenFlow supports the BARRIER message to develop a pacing mechanism for creating flow control e.g. in PACKET_OUT operation which requires packet to be matched that allows forwarding before the flow of packets.

Multiple auxiliary connections are introduced (TCP, UDP, TLS, or DTLS) in version 1.3 of OpenFlow protocol, which are capable of controlling nay type or subtype of OpenFlow messages.

## REPLICATION

OpenFlow provides numerous techniques for packet replication. The reserved virtual ports ANY and FLOOD are mainly used for the replication of the packets e.g., LLDP used to assemble topology for the controller, often uses FLOOD as its output port.

Group tables permits the grouping of ports into an output ports sets for enabling multicasting, fast-failover, indirection and multipath. There are four group tables in a list of the action buckets where apparently egress port is specified and one of the actions is output, but only two are necessary:

- **All:** It is used for multipath its nature is more related with live/live video feeds or in the multipath where reformation is needed at the end nodes. This multipath is different from the IP forwarding perceptions. In this all action buckets in the list have to be performed.
- **Indirect:** It is used to encourage the concurrence behaviour of the next hop in IP forwarding for rapid convergence.

Consecutive replication is permitted by Action lists in Apply action by constructing using a list of output/port actions.

## FORWARDING ABSTRACTION WORKGROUP (FAWG)

OpenFlow switch works effectively with software-based switch which are highly versatile in scaling and packet manipulation characteristics or with a hardware-forwarding entity that follows

to some simplifying presumptions e.g., large, wide, deep, and multi-entrant memories like a TCAM. However, each switches functionality dependent on their vendors which results in a remarkable variation within the support of all packet manipulations enabled by the set of OpenFlow multi-tables, primitives, and alternative features which provide strength to the OpenFlow protocol.

The potential combinatorial complexity of OpenFlow version 1.1 'see Figure 4' and further versions don't work properly with ASIC-based forwarders due to that question arises on the capability of concept picked for OpenFlow, as has its appropriateness for ALL applications.

From version 1.3 of OpenFlow, it started supporting few ancient table capability descriptions by adding the concept match type for every match fields e.g., exact match, LPM, and wildcard.

Drawbacks which were cited for the existing theory (OpenFlow) are:

- Combinatorial state explosion
- Control events which were operated by Data-plane
- Fragile Indirection Infrastructure
- Loss of Information
- Leakage of Information
- Deficient concept of Control plane to Data plane
- Weak extensibility
- Numerous control engines
- Time-sensitive periodic messaging

*Figure 4. OpenFlow pipeline model in v1.1 and above (n = no. of tables, a = no. of actions and l = match field width size)*

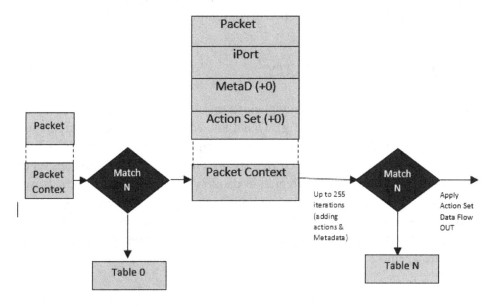

FAWG is a discrete workgroup, which is trying a first-generation, negotiated switch model through Table Type Patterns (TTPs). FAWG has created a method of constructing, uniquely identifying, and sharing TTPs. To determine agreed TTPs between controller and the network elements has developed a negotiated messaging and algorithm which is built on a Yang model in version 1.4 of of-config.

A TTP is a predetermined switch behaviour model, represented by match/mask, action table profiles and table linkage through a pipeline which represents the personality. According to the task of elements in the service flow, these table profiles may vary e.g., for the Hierarchal Virtual Private LAN Services (HVPLS) forwarder position of elements matter whether element is head-end, mid-point, or exit-point. To achieve TTP, moreover modifications are required as per the current need.

As FAWG get success in developing, negotiated switch model through Table Type Patterns, it provides awareness about elements potential to the applications placed above the controller, at least from a behaviour profile aspects.

Example of the need for TTP or FPMOD (Forwarding Plane Models) (OpenFlow, n.d.). Hardware tables can be shared when they have similar data with low key variation e.g., logical tables with two views: MAC forwarding and MAC Learning. This table can be implemented many different ways including as an individual hardware table. OpenFlow controller must have different tables for MAC learning and MAC bridging in order to implement MAC learning/bridging. Currently, there is no method to tie these two differing views. See Figure 5, for elementary example which shows the situation where synchronization of table of flow mods from the two different OpenFlow table entities may be required i.e., MAC forwarding before MAC learning is not possible. In Figure 5, IPv4 and IPv6 tables directed to group tables emulate the use of next hop abstraction in conventional FIBs for rapid convergence.

## CONFIG AND EXTENSIBILITY

The of-config protocol was initially planned to set OpenFlow related information on the network element (of-config). OpenFlow Management and Configuration (of-config) is a unusual set of protocols that defines a mechanism for OpenFlow. OF-Config was developed under Open Network Foundation which provides set of rules to access and modify configuration data on an OpenFlow switches. It was designed for OpenFlow implementation on both physical and logical switches. (DiffServ --The Scalable End-to-End QoS Model. Retrieved March 30, 2017)

The OF-Config protocol shows the following components of the controller-switch management:

*Figure 5. Example of Complexity behind TTP model for L2 + L3 + ACL/PBR TTP*
*Source: D. Meyer and C. Beckmann of Brocade.*

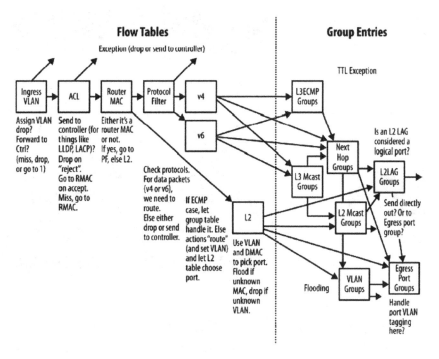

- **OpenFlow Configuration Point:** OF-Config spots OF-Config commands related issues.
- **OpenFlow Capable Switch:** It is a switching device that composed of numerous ports and queues, which can be physical or logical.
- **OpenFlow Logical Switch:** It consists under OpenFlow capable switch itself, which assigns a part of ports and queues that make up an OpenFlow capable switch, see Figure 6.

According to OF-Config version 1.1, it separates itself from any presumptions that an operator would run FlowVisor to attain numerous logical switch abstractions inside physical switch.

The OF-Config Point can be positioned in the same server like OpenFlow controller or within conventional network management products. This point is capable of managing more than one OpenFlow-capable physical or virtual switches. The OF-Config Point can handle many OpenFlow capable switches and vice-versa see Figure 6. It can communicate with OF Logical switches. The control point provide IP addresses and port numbers of OpenFlow controller to every single OF logical switches for controlling packet flows through the switches. It also describes along

*Figure 6. Relationship between config and wire protocols*

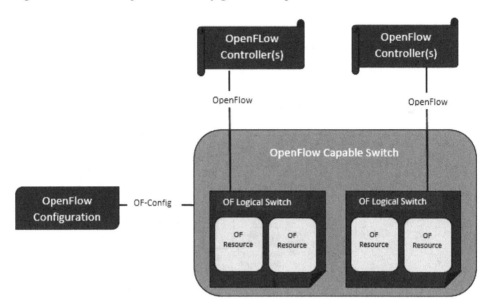

with configuration certificate, whether TCP or TLS will be used during interaction between controller and switch. Every single logical switches works differently within the same OpenFlow capable switches.

OF-Config Point is capable of spotting all the resources allotted to a logical switch, retrieve switch status along with error codes during the configuration operation failure. It can configure tunnels and set parameters of the port on the switch.

The specification OF-Config 1.1.1 contains UML diagrams, examples of XML; this protocol is designed around XML schemas, NETCONF protocol for delivery and Yang data models. Configuration information is sent to, and retrieved from, switches remotely. Netconf can send or retrieve full information about configuration and can communicate asynchronous notifications from the switch.

Proposals exist for the further expanding of OF-Config in the areas of bootstrapping and the abilities to support many more switches/native functionality.

## Evaluation in Capability OF-Config Protocol Based on Different OpenFlow Versions

1.  OF-Config version 1.0 based on OpenFlow version 1.2
    a.  Assigning controllers to logical switches
    b.  Extracting assignment of resources to logical switches
    c.  Configuring some properties of ports and queues

2. OF-Config version 1.1 based on OpenFlow version 1.3
   a. Added resource type "table" and controller certificates
   b. Extracting capabilities of logical switch signed to controller
   c. Configuration of tunnel endpoints.
3. OF-Config version 1.2 based on OpenFlow version 1.3
   a. Retrieving capable switch capabilities, configuring logical switch capabilities
   b. Assigning resources to logical switches
   c. Topology detection
   d. Event notification

NETCONF may also be expanded to mark its presence in the call home scenarios i.e., connections which is initiated by switches, but the nomination of BEEP (Blocks Extensible Exchange Protocol is a feature which permits you to enable either the NETCONF server or the NETCONF client for initiating a connection inside OF-Config) to a conventional protocol may require some changes in the specification or cooperative work with the IETF.

## EVOLUTION OF OPENFLOW

1. Features of OpenFlow version 1.0
   a. Single table
   b. Fixed 12 tuple match field
   c. Ingress Port
   d. Ethernet: source, destination, type, VLAN
   e. IPv4: source, destination, protocol, ToS(Type of Service)
   f. TCP/UDP: source port, destination port
2. Features of OpenFlow version 1.1
   a. Multiprotocol Label Switching (MPLS)
      i. Multi-label support
      ii. Match on MPLS label, traffic class
      iii. Actions on TTL (Time to Live) i.e., to set, copy-inward, copy-outward, decrement
      iv. PUSH, POP actions on MPLS shim headers
   b. VLAN and QinQ tunnelling, Metadata
      i. Supports multiple levels of VLAN tagging
      ii. Actions to set VLAN ID, priority
      iii. PUSH, POP actions to VLAN headers

*Figure 7. Evolution of OpenFlow versions*

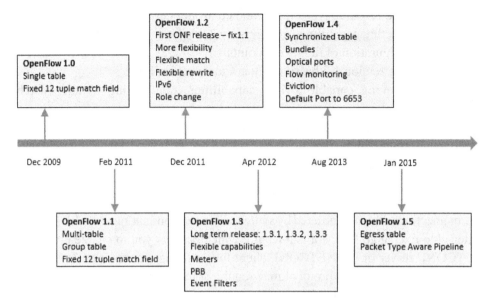

c.  Groups
    i.  Group properties; Group ID, Group Type: all, select, indirect, fast-fallover, Counters
3.  Features of OpenFlow version 1.2
    a.  OpenFlow Extensible Match (OXM)
    b.  IPv6: source, destination, flow label, ICMPv6
        i.  Match on source and destination address of IPv6 (prefix/arbitrary bitmask, IP DSCP, IPv6 flow label, IP ECN, IP protocol)
        ii. Match on ICMPv6 type, code, ND target, ND source, and destination link layer
    c.  Actions on TTL i.e., to set, copy-in, copy-out, decrement
4.  Features of OpenFlow version 1.3
    a.  IPv6 Extension Headers
    b.  Provider Backbone Bridging (PBB)
    c.  Per flow meters
        i.  Meter properties: Meter ID, Meter Flags (bps, pps, burst size, statistics), Counters (packets, bytes, duration), list of meter bands
        ii. Meter band properties: Type (drop, DSCP remark, experimenter), Rate, Burst size, Counters (packets, bytes)
        iii. Special meters (slow-path, to-controller, and all-flows)

5. Features of OpenFlow version 1.4
   a. Synchronized Table, synchronization of flow tables in bidirectional or unidirectional way (OpenFlow. Retrieved March 27, 2017).
   b. Concept of Bundles for grouping related states, to convert multiple operations into an atomic operation.
   c. Optical ports
   d. Flow monitoring
   e. Eviction
   f. Default Port to 6653
6. Features of OpenFlow version 1.5
   a. Egress Table, it involves matching and processing of packets at output port also.
   b. Packet Type Aware Pipeline
   c. Extension of bundle with Scheduled bundle by including an execution time property.

OpenFlow switch consists of three components (OpenFlow Table Type Patterns. Retrieved April 20, 2017):

- Flow table
- Secured Channel
- OpenFlow protocol

OpenFlow switch may contain more than one flow tables, a secure channel for connection with controller, and OpenFlow protocol which is used for the communication with controller.

Flow table contains flow entries, The Schema of flow entry of OpenFlow version 1.5 looks like that shown in Table 1.

Flow entry comprises of:

- **Match Fields:** Match against packet
- **Priority:** Flow entries of matching precedence
- **Instruction:** Instruction set which are executed after the packet matching
- **Timeout:** Maximum amount of idle time

*Table 1. Schema of flow entry of OpenFlow version 1.5 n*

| Match Fields | Priority | Counters | Instruction | Timeouts | Cookie | Flag |
|---|---|---|---|---|---|---|

Opennetworking, 2017.

- **Cookie:** Indeterminate data value chosen by the controller
- **Flags:** Modifying the management way of flow entries

As soon as packets arrive from switch port, flow entries compare the packets with match fields. If the packet match found, then only packets will be processed according to the given set of instruction.

Major Obstacles faced by OpenFlow are:

- **Performance:** This can be improved by pre-occupying the flow tables at the boot time or at the time of policy creation in a proactive manner as an alternative for reacting packets in events.
- **Scale:** This can be improved by defining Flow Rule Allocation.
- **Risk:** This can be reduced by introducing Hybrid Architecture which supports both OpenFlow enabled devices and legacy network devices.

## HYBRID MODELS

Hybrid Working Group is created by Open Network Foundation. This group only focuses on developing Hybrid model. Ships in the Night (SIN) model architecture is proposed by this group and was approved by the ONF board.

Assumption of controlled points between the native controllers and OpenFlow is the new invention in networking elements, the security is the major issue about how the reserved ports could be utilized, so that, to allow access to native processes on the native network or on the hybrid applications of controller side or OpenFlow ports spoofing IGP peers and other protocol sessions to insert or to attain states.

### Ships in the Night (SIN) Model

The SIN model theory presumes that a physical or logical port can only be used either for native or OpenFlow, but not for both simultaneously. Since, switches conventionally have control plane, so OpenFlow controller manages only trunked links port or VLANs. The local control plane can perform the large tasks periodically like running LACP, LLDP and BFD, and passes link only to the OpenFlow controller, which also resolves the communication problem between controllers and switches.

The SIN mainly focuses on:

- Vaulting the resources which are allocated to the OpenFlow process and such that they could not obstruct the native side operations and vice versa.

- Inflexible rules for the processing of flows which uses the LOCAL, FLOOD, and NORMAL reserved ports.
- Dodging the need to synchronize state or notifications of event between the control planes.

The SIN model permits the segregation of the ports by VLANs or logical port and suggested the use of MSTP (Multiple Spanning Tree Protocol) for spanning tree in such an environment.

The SIN approach suits well in academic environments where OpenFlow is running simultaneously with the production network.

## Benefits of Hybrid Model

There are many benefits of supporting hybrid mode in SDN controller:

- It minimizes the complexity and scope of the forwarding decisions made by the controller. All OpenFlow hybrid switches have many root conventional forwarding logic in their ASICs and firmware. The controller will make use of those embedded logics which are available, for routing rather than re-implementing the same logic. SDN's value is in integrating new features to the networks. If all SDN does is centralize the same forwarding decision, then there is no reason for administration to move to SDN (Wackerly, 2014).

*Figure 8. Architecture of SIN*
*Source: ONF Hybrid SIN WorkGroup.*

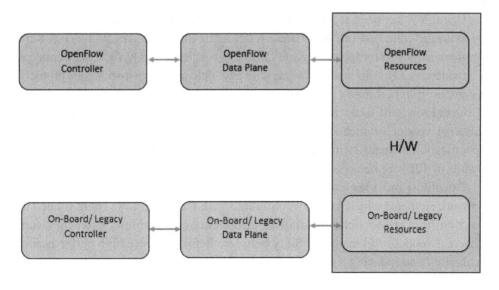

- It reduces traffic of control plane. Since, with the reduced traffic controller has to make forwarding decision for specific packet types/flows, which results in reducing the PACKET_IN messages that are being sent to the controller from the controlled switches. This results in increasing the overall performance of the controller (Wackerly, 2014).
- It also lowers the obstacle to SDN adoption, because it allows administrators to adopt SDN in different stages, as per requirement. This gradual emigration helps in adoption of SDN and in completely replacing all forwarding decisions in their conventional network with those made by the centralized controller (Wackerly, 2014).
- Lastly, it scales much more gracefully in terms of the number of OpenFlow rules it pushes to switches (Wackerly, 2014).

## CONCLUSION

OpenFlow along with ONF is mainly responsible for the concept of SDN in the today's world of computer networking, by providing the first legacy of SDN control:

- Methods in determining path of the packets
- Centralized control point
- Provides Northbound API which reveals the topology
- Presents Standardized Southbound API for instantiating the forwarding state on multivendor infrastructure
- Allocating services to the application of the controller

OpenFlow has been around from several years results in adopted and deployed by many different vendors, but it needs lot more modifications regarding Hardware Implementation, Interoperability and Conformance. Regrettably, there is no concept of standardized Northbound API along with any standardized east-west state protocol for application portability and controller vendor interoperability.

OpenFlow still faces challenges in the interoperability between switches of different vendor's which implements different features. Additionally, OpenFlow specification changes swiftly and some of the feature are not well-defined, which results in different behaviour of switches and controllers.

OpenFlow provides advance protocols for flow/traffic control, only for those network elements which are fully configured with the OpenFlow. There is need to work on the hybrid model which allows configuration of OpenFlow on switches from different vendors and interoperability between them to achieve high performance, scalability and reducing risk.

## REFERENCES

Cisco. (2005). *DiffServ --The Scalable End-to-End QoS Model*. Retrieved March 30, 2017, from https://www.cisco.com/en/US/technologies/tk543/tk766/technologies_ white_paper09186a00800a3e2f.html

Darabinejad, B., Rasoul, S., & Fayyeh, M. (2014). An introduction to software defined networking. *International Journal of Intelligent Information Systems*, *3*(6), 71-74.

Erickson, D. (2011). *Open Networking Foundation Formed to Speed Network Innovation*. Portland, OR: Open Networking Foundation.

Goransson, P., Black, C., & Culver, T. (2016). *Software Defined Networks: A Comprehensive Approach*. Burlington: Morgan Kaufmann.

Jain, R. (2014). *OpenFlow, Software Defined OpenFlow, Software Defined Networking (SDN) and Network Networking (SDN) and Network Function Virtualization (NFV)*. Tutorial at 2014 IEEE 15th International Conference on High Performance Switching and Routing, Vancouver, Canada.

McKeown, N., Anderson, T., Balakrishnan, H., Parulkar, G., Peterson, L., & Rexford, J. (2008). OpenFlow: Enabling Innovation in Campus Networks. *ACM Communications Review*. Retrieved 2017-01-11 from https://dl.acm.org/citation. cfm?id=1355734.1355746

Melno Park. (2017). *Open Networking Foundation Unveils New Open Innovation Pipeline to Transform Open Networking*. Open Networking Foundation.

Noyes, K. (2009). *Google and other titans form Open Networking Foundation*. Retrieved January 15, 2017, from https://www.computerworld.com.au/article/380663/ google_other_titans_form_open_networking_foundation/?fp=4&fpid=78268965

Open Networking. (2017). *OpenFlow Table Type Patterns*. Retrieved April 20, 2017 from https://www.opennetworking.org

Open Networking Foundation. (2011). *Open Networking Foundation Formed to Speed Network Innovation*. Retrieved January 18, 2017 from https://www.opennetworking. org/news-and-events/press-releases/onf-formed-to-speed-network-innovation/

OpenFlow. (n.d.). Retrieved March 27, 2017, from https://www.opennetworking. org/sdn-resources/

PC Mag. (n.d.). *Definition of: Wire Protocol*. Retrieved March 29, 2017, from https:// www.pcmag.com/encyclopedia/term/54750/wire-protocol

# Chapter 4
# SDN Controller

**Sujitha S.**
*Thiagarajar College of Engineering, India*

**Manikandan M. S. K.**
*Thiagarajar College of Engineering, India*

**Ashwini G.**
*Thiagarajar College of Engineering, India*

## ABSTRACT

*Designing and organizing networks has become extra innovative over the past few years with the assistance of SDN (software-defined networking). The software implements network protocols that undergo years of equivalence and interoperability testing. Software-defined networking (SDN) is a move toward computer networking that allows network administrators to programmatically initialize, manage, alter, and direct network behavior dynamically through open interfaces and abstraction of lower-level functionality. SDN controller is an application in software-defined networking (SDN) that manages run control to permit clever networking. SDN controllers are based on protocols, such as OpenFlow, that permit servers to inform switches where to send packets. This chapter explores SDN controllers.*

## INTRODUCTION

Software Defined Networking (SDN), frequently referred to as a innovative new idea in computer networking, promises to dramatically simplify the network control, management and innovation through network programmability. Computer networks are typically construct from a huge number of network components such as routers, firewalls, switches, hubs with a lot of protocols like software, which are

DOI: 10.4018/978-1-5225-3640-6.ch004

implemented and fixed on them. The origins of software-defined networking began in associate passing minute once Sun Microsystems free Java in 1995. SDN model permits network administrators to achieve the network lightness required by a lot of and a lot of virtualized and dynamic applications. SDN has potential use cases and benefits for just about every district of the network in every Layer 2 and Layer 3 segments. SDN allows network administrators to handle network services through idea of lower level utility and to be cost-effective, and adaptable, seeking to be apt for the high-bandwidth, dynamic nature of today's applications. Besides the Network abstraction, the SDN architecture will provide a set of Application Programming Interfaces(APIs)that simplifies the implementation of common network services for example multicast, routing, security, access control, traffic engineering, Qos, energy efficiency and various forms of policy management. In SDN, the network intelligence is understandably centralized in software-based controllers at the control plane, and network devices develop into the simple packet forwarding devices (the data plane) that can be programmed through an open interface. One of the early on implementations of this open interface is called OpenFlow. The forwarding hardware consists of the following:

- A flow table contains flow entries consisting of equal rules and procedures that take on active flows.
- A transport layer protocol that strongly communicate with a controller regarding new entries that are not at present in the flow table

This lead to a formalization of the principle elements that define SDN today:

- Centralization of control
- Separation of control and forwarding functions
- Capability to program the performance of the network with well-defined interfaces (Pate, 2013).

# INTERNET PROTOCOL VS. SOFTWARE-DEFINED NETWORK

There is constant discussion in far more than that approach of network is improved; software-defined networking or net protocol (IP) networking, Whereas they each have their compensation and drawbacks, overall have established the software-defined system to be desirable. Key attributes of associate degree SDN surroundings get in its user friendliness, value potency, and reduced issue. However, whereas it's predominately superior to scientific discipline networking, there are a unit variety of cases during which scientific discipline networking may be extra advantageous.

Software-defined networking may be in an exceedingly line associated with ease, flexibility, and quantifiability in many network atmosphere (Costanzo). Scientific discipline networks area unit unable to equal these qualities and since of this associate degree increasing amount of net suppliers and business area unit begin to swear extra on SDNs. Not solely is that this vogue adjustable however it's conjointly user friendly to system directors.

Unlike informatics networks, systems administrator not got to flip switches, bear physical configuration policies, or have straight right to use to the hardware. In its place, SDN systems directors area unit ready to have central programmable management over network transfer while not the desired to possess straight access to the hardware (Costanzo). Also, SDNs offer singular management over the network infrastructure and in doing therefore decrease quality of processes through mechanization (Costanzo). This is often helpful to firms WHO should be ready to run time period changes at not solely the applying stage however conjointly the user purpose. Systems directors at any purpose will create these necessary changes in time in spite of their place. Remote access and changes to the network area unit created potential through the completion of a role-based access system; this technique is gifted to convey the security to remain hackers and different attackers from accessing the business's system (Koldhofe et al). Sadly, these on the fly and remote changes aren't probable through the employment of internet-protocol networks. Within the informatics networks systems directors should have straight access to the board and bear manual style policies so as to form any changes. Any network rule amendment needs creating hardware changes that makes the system rigid. SDN permits for limitless policies and alter to those policies for intrusion finding, firewalls and cargo reconciliation by means that of changes to code, that makes running networks abundant additional versatile.

One more way in which software-defined networking outmatches and outperforms internet protocol networks is the information that it allows administrators to designate network services with no conglomerating interfaces and condition together (Costanzo). Not only does it permit administrators to decide exact services, it also permits them to control the two planes. Software-defined networking is able to divide the control plane and data plane. Software-defined networking is documented for how advanced and user friendly it is but an advantage a small number of seem to realize is how able it is and how less likely it is to experience technical difficulties.

Due to the ability of systems directors to interrelate directly with the package, they will produce changes to knowledge flow passages, that ensures that knowledge packets don't get queued and degrade system performance. By making certain the data doesn't block the pathways or overload them in anyway, it's less seemingly that the networks can malfunction or information technical difficulties. Another key advantage to package outlined networking is that the value of it. It's cheaper than internet-protocol networks since it doesn't want as many folks performing on it (Costanzo). Firms may doubtless cut out the bulk of their system engineer expenses and solely got to suppose slightly variety of systems directors instead of a entire cluster of them.

## SOME OF THE SPECIFIC ADVANTAGES OF SOFTWARE DEFINED NETWORKING

- **Central Network Provisioning:** Software outlined networks offers a centralized viewpoint of the whole network, formation it easier to integrate enterprise management and provisioning. By abstracting the management and information planes, SDN will speed up service unleash and create accessible a lot of speed in provisioning along virtual and physical network devices from a middle location.
- **Holistic Endeavor Management:** Enterprise networks got to came upon newest applications and virtual machines on demand to produce somewhere to remain new process requirements like those for large information. SDN permits IT managers to experiment with network set up with no impacting the network. SDN additionally supports management of equally physical and virtual switches and network devices on or following a central controller; slightly can't do with SNMP. SDN provides a solitary set of genus APIs to create one management console for physical and virtual devices.
- **More Granular Security:** One of the compensation of security outlined networking to appeals the bulk to that managers is central security. Virtualization has created network management further difficult. With virtual machines forthcoming and going as a part of physical systems, it's further exhausting to perpetually apply firewall and content filtering polices. The SDN Controller provides a central position of management to produce out security and policy data systematically throughout the enterprise. Integrative safety management into one entity, just like the SDN Controller, has the disadvantage of making a central purpose of attack; however SDN will with efficiency be accustomed run security throughout the enterprise if it's enforced powerfully and properly.
- **Lower Operating Costs:** Administrative effectiveness, enhancements in server operation, higher management of virtualization, and different edges ought to result in operational savings. Though it's still close to the start to indicate actual proof of savings, SDN ought to lesser overall in operation prices and lead to body savings since several of the routine network management problems is centralized and automatic.

- **Hardware Savings and Reduced Capital Expenditures:** Adopting SDN too provides innovative life to existing network devices. SDN makes it easier within the direction of optimize commoditized hardware. Getable hardware skills to be repurposed victimization commands from the SDN controller and less pricy hardware may be deployed to superior result since new devices essentially become "white box" switches with all the cleverness focused at the SDN controller.
- **Cloud Abstraction:** Cloud computing is at this point to attend and it's developing into a united infrastructure. By abstracting cloud resources exploitation software system outlined networking, it's easier to unify cloud resources. The networking mechanism therefore on structure large knowledge center platforms will all be managed as of the SDN controller.
- **Guaranteed Content Delivery:** The capability to shape and control data transfer is one of the main advantages of software defined networking. Being capable to straight and automate data transfer makes it easier to execute quality of services (QoS) for voice over IP and multimedia transmissions. Streaming high quality video is easier because SDN improves network responsiveness to ensure faultless user knowledge (Ingram Micro Advisor, n.d.)

## Other Benefits of SDN

- SDNs enable enterprise safety in businesses with high throughput yet low down latency necessities by domain separation within a solitary data center.
- SDNs permit for central control plane commands over multiple end-devices, which can make stronger network firewall capability.
- The SDN controller can be configured to act as a alternative on behalf of applications to prevent and control network mechanism accesses
- SDNs might exploit "service chaining" as a method of inserting services into the run of network interchange as it moves among network devices. Commands and give access control lists (ACLs) as a means of enforcing network safety.

## BUILDING BLOCKS

The SDN Switch, the SDN controller and the interfaces there on the controller for communication with forwarding devices, usually southbound interface in adding up to network applications interface are the unique building blocks of an SDN deployment. Switches in an SDN are frequently represented as an essential forwarding hardware accessible through an open crossing point, as the control logic plus algorithms are offloaded to a controller. OpenFlow switches approach in two varieties: pure (OpenFlow-only) and mixture (OpenFlow-enabled). Most gainful switches presented nowadays are hybrids. An OpenFlow switch consists of a flow table, which performs packet research and forwarding. Each flow table in the Switch holds a set of flow entries that consist of:

- Header field or equal fields, with information bring into being in packet header, ingress port, and metadata, used to match received packets.
- Counters used to collect statistics for the particular flow, such as number of received packets, number of bytes and length of the flow.
- A set of commands or events to be applied after a match that decides how to handle matching packets. For example, the action might be to forward a packet out to a exacting port.

## SDN ARCHITECTURE

The architecture of SDN, contains

- **Directly Programmable:** Network control is in a directly line programmable
- **Agile:** Abstracting control as of forwarding lets administrators dynamically adjust network-wide travel flow to meet altering requirements.
- **Centrally Managed:** Network cleverness is (logically) centralized in software-based SDN controllers to maintain a global outlook of the network, which appears to applications and policy engines as a solitary, logical button.
- **Programmatically Configured:** SDN lets network managers organize, run, safe, and optimize network assets very fast through dynamic, routine SDN programs, which they can write themselves since the programs do not depend on proprietary software.
- **Open Standards-Based and Vendor-Neutral:** When implemented through open standards, SDN simplify system plan and procedure as commands are provided by SDN controllers instead of a variety of, vendor-specific plans and protocols (Open Networking Foundation, n.d.).

## DIFFERENT PLANES OF SDN

Traditionally, a network device can be divided into three different planes as shown in Figure 1.

*Figure 1. Three planes of SDN*

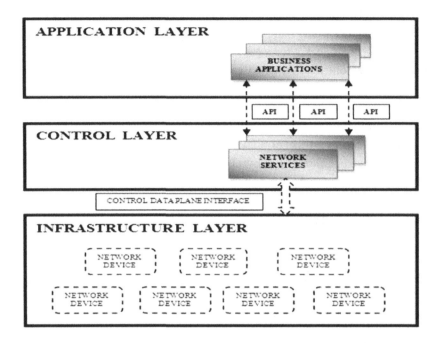

The diagram explains the three layers of SDN such as application layer, Control layer and infrastructure layer

The Control Plane is one and only in charge for building the decisions as to how a exact packet is handle. This is often done on traditional devices with static routes or through dynamic routing protocols. The control plane is generally distributed and is in charge mostly for the configuration of the forwarding plane by means of a Control-Plane Southbound Interface (CPSI) with DAL as a position of reference. CP is in charge for instructing FP regarding how to handle network packets. Communication between control-plane entities, colloquially referred to as the "east-west" border, is typically implemented during gateway protocols such as BGP [RFC4271] or other protocols such as the Path Computation Element (PCE) Communication Protocol (PCEP) [RFC5440]. These equivalent protocol messages are usually exchanged in-band and subsequently redirected by the forwarding plane to the control plane for additional processing. Control-plane functionalities typically include:

- Topology detection and preservation
- Packet way selection and instantiation
- Path failover mechanisms

The CPSI is usually defined with the following characteristics:

- Time-critical border that require low latency and sometime high bandwidth in order to execute many operations in short order
- Oriented towards wire competence and device representation instead of human readability

The Management Plane or Application Plane is in charge for the running of a device; an paradigm of this would be by means of telnet or SSH to link to a device that is then managed throughout the CLI.

The Data Plane or Infrastructure Plane is where the collection of the device's action is finished; this includes the genuine forwarding of data in an exact port and out an exact port based on a forwarding table or base (FIB) (Wilkins, 2014).

## A Simple Device and Centralized Control

Building on the thought of division of forwarding and management planes, consecutive quality is that the generalization of devices, that are then management led by a centralized theme running management and control software package. In its place of many thousands of lines of difficult management plane software package running on the device and permitting the device to perform autonomously, that software package is detached from the device and placed in an exceedingly centralized controller. This software-based controller manages the network mistreatment higher-level policies. The controller then provides primitive directions to the essential devices once applicable so as to permit them to form quick selections relating to a way to deal by suggests that of inward packets. (How SDN Works, n.d.)

Table 1 shows the difference between the control plane and data plane.

*Table 1. Difference between control and data plane*

| Control Plane | Data Plane |
|---|---|
| The control plane functions have the system design, management, and exchange of routing table information | Forwards traffic to the next hop alongside the path to the chosen target network according to control plane logic |
| Control plane packets are *designed to* or nearby *originate through* the router itself | Also called as Forwarding Plane |
| Control plane packets are processed via the router to bring up to date the routing table information. | Data plane packets go *via* the router |

*Figure 2. Taxonomy diagram for SDN layers*

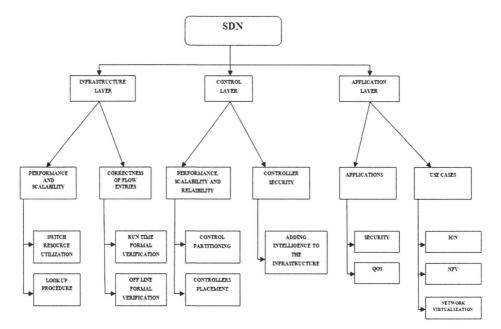

## TWO TYPES OF APPLICATION PROGRAMMING INTERFACES IN SDN

### Southbound API

The communication between the controller and therefore the sent device is oft said as south application programming interface (API). A typical, open customary SDN protocol and a standout among the foremost renowned alternatives for south APIs is OpenFlow. OpenFlow is one possibility that's unremarkably accustomed send commands from the controller to the deployed device. It's not the sole protocol out there (for example, Cisco's OpFlex really supplement OpenFlow) however it's the foremost documented and therefore the one that has extremely peaked the importance of the broader networking community.

### Northbound API

The contradictory of the south API is that the northward API, it involves the communications as of a business application to the controller. The SDN application itself are often written to hold out a really massive set of potential activities; the foremost basic of that might be to inform a deployed device to forward a packet with an identical set of contents out a particular interface. However, the northward API are often terribly tough, like only if a high quality of Service provisioned path from one finish of a system to a different dynamically, then tear it go into reverse once the applying was accomplished with its network communication. An added common example would be a firewall or Intrusion interference System (IPS) application that performs the normal functions of those hardware devices entirely in software package and uses the controller to hold out the acceptable action on the deployed piece of apparatus (Wilkins, 2014).

# FLOW TABLES

Flow tables area unit the basic knowledge structures in associate degree SDN device. These flow tables allow the device to estimate inward certain packets and take the appropriate action supported the contents of the packet that has simply been established. Packets have sometimes been received by networking devices and evaluated supported sure fields. These actions might absorb forwarding the packet to a precise port, dropping the packet, or flooding the packet on all ports, within the middle of others. Associate degree SDN device isn't essentially completely different except that this basic operation has been rendered additional general and additional programmable through the flow tables and their associated logic. Flow tables comprises variety of prioritized flow entries, every of that characteristically consists of 2 mechanisms: match fields and actions. Match fields area unit accustomed assess against inward certain packets. Associate degree inward certain packet is compared against the match fields in priority order, and also the 1st whole match is chosen. Actions area unit the commands that the network device ought to perform if associate degree inward certain packet matches the match fields specific for that flow entry. Match fields will have wildcards for fields that aren't applicable to a specific match. As an example, once corresponding packets based mostly simply on science address or subnet, all different fields would be wild carded. Similarly, if corresponding on solely waterproof address or UDP/TCP port, the opposite fields area unit unsuitable, and consequently those fields area unit wild carded. Betting on the appliance necessities, all fields are also vital, within which case there would be no wildcards. The flow table and flow entry constructs allow the SDN application developer to own a good vary of potentialities for corresponding packets and taking appropriate actions. (How SDN Works, n.d.)

# SWITCHES IN SDN

There are two types of switch models were available in SDN, they are:

- Hardware based switch models
- software based switch models

## Hardware Based Switch Models of SDN

OpenFlow reference standard is the main and early SDN enabling technologies being currently implemented in the commodity-networking hardware. Table 2 lists commercial switches that are at present available, along with their producer, and the version of OpenFlow they have implemented.

This hardware functionality permits the device together match packets and then takes actions at a extremely high rate. However, it also presents a sequence of challenges to the SDN device developer.

Specifically:

- How best to decode from flow entries to hardware entries; for example, how most excellent to use the CAMs, TCAMs, or hardware-based hash tables?
- Which of the flow entries to switch in hardware versus how many to drop back to using software?

*Table 2. Hardware implementations*

| Manufacturer | Switch Models | OpenFlow Version |
|---|---|---|
| Brocade | NetIron CES 2000 Series, CER 2000 | 1.0 |
| Hewlett packard | 3500/3500yI,5400zI,6200zI,6600,8200zI | 1.0 |
| IBM | Rackswitch G8264, G8264T | 1.0 |
| Juniper | EX9200 Programmable switch | 1.0 |
| NEC | PF5240,PF5820 | 1.0 |
| Pica8 | P-3290,P-3295 | 1.2 |
| Pronto | 3290 and 3780 | 1.0 |
| Broadcom | BCM56846 | 1.0 |
| Extreme networks | BlackDiamond 8K, Summit | 1.0 |
| Netgear | GSM7352Sv2 | 1.0 |
| Arista | 7150,7500,7050 series | 1.0 |

Most implementations are able to use hardware to handle some of the lookups, but others are handed off to software to be handled there. Clearly, hardware will handle the flow lookups much faster than software, but hardware tables have limits on the number of flow entries they can hold at any time, and software tables could be used to handle the overflow.

- How to deal with hardware action limitations that may impact whether to put into practice the flow in hardware versus software? For example, certain actions such as packet alteration may be incomplete or not accessible if handled in hardware.
- How to track statistics on individual flows?

In using devices such as TCAMs, which might equal multiple flows, it is not probable to use those devices to count individual flows separately. Furthermore, meeting statistics across the various tables can be difficult because the tables may count something two times or not at all (How SDN Works, n.d.).

## Software Based Switch Models of SDN

There square measure several OpenFlow software system switches procurable that may be used as an example, to run Associate in Nursing OpenFlow take a look at-be or to expand and test OpenFlow-based network applications. a listing of current software system switches with a short description, as well as implementation language and therefore the OpenFlow customary, square measure as follows

- **OpenVSwitch:** It is a multi layer and production quality virtual switch licensed under the Apache 2.0 license. It is designed to allow network automation through programmatic extension, while still supporting standard management interfaces and protocols
- **Indigo:** It is runs on physical switches and uses the hardware features of Ethernet Switch ASICs to run OpenFlow at line rates. It is based on the OpenFlow Reference Implementation from Stanford University
- **LINC:** It is an open source project led by Flow Forwarding effort and is an apache 2 license executions based on OpenFlow 1.2/1.3.1. LINC is architected to use generally-available commodity x86 hardware and runs on a multiplicity of platforms such as Linux, Solaris, windows, MacOS, and FreeBSD where Erlang runtime is presented.
- **PANTOU:** This turns a profitable wireless router/ access point to an openflow-enabled switch. Pantou is based on the BackFire OpenWrt free. The openflow modules are based on the stand ford direction implementation.

- **OF13SOFTSWITCH:** This is an OpenFlow 1.3 compatible user-space software switch execution based on the Ericsson Traffic Lab 1.1 softswitch. The latest version of this software switch includes the switch implementation, a safe channel for linking the switch to the controller, a library for conversion from to OpenFlow 1.3 and a design device.

## Existing SDN Device Implementations

A number of SDN device implementations are offered nowadays, each business and open supply. Software system SDN devices are principally open supply. Currently, 2 major alternatives are available: OpenvSwitch (OVS) as of Nicira and Indigo as of massive Switch. Incumbent network instrumentation makers (NEMs), like Cisco, HP, NEC, IBM, Juniper, and Extreme, have supplemental OpenFlow delay to a number of their gift switches. Generally, these switches could operate in each gift mode additionally as OpenFlow mode. there's conjointly a replacement category of devices known as white-box switches, that are modest in this they're engineered primarily from mercantile atomic number 14 shift chips and a goods mainframe and memory by a cheap distinctive device manufacturer (ODM) missing a widely known brand. One amongst the building of SDN is that the physical shift infrastructure could also be engineered from OpenFlow-enabled white-box switches at weigh less straight value than switches from established NEMs. Most inheritance management plane software system isn't gift from these devices, since this practicality is basically inevitable to be provided by a centralized controller. Such white-box devices of times use the open supply OVS or Indigo switch code for the OpenFlow logic, then chart the packet-processing a part of those switch implementations to their exacting hardware.

## Scaling the Number of Flows

The coarseness of flow definitions can typically be additional fine because the device holding them approaches the sting of the system and can be additional general because the device approaches the core. At the sting, flows can permit completely different policies to be applied to individual users and even different travel styles of constant user. This can mean, in some cases, many flow entries for one user. This level of flow coarseness would merely not scale if it were applied nearer to the network core, wherever nice switches touch upon the traffic for tens of thousands of users at the same time. In those core devices, the flow definitions are going to be typically additional course, with one mass run entry matching the traffic from an oversized variety of users whose traffic is mass in how, like a tunnel, a VLAN, or a MPLS LSP. Policies applied deep into the system can doubtless not be user-centric policies however rather policies that apply to those mass flows. One optimistic result's that there'll not be associate explosion within the variety of flow entries within the core switches because of managing the traffic emanating from thousands of flows in border switches. (How SDN Works, n.d.)

## THREAT VECTORS IN SDN

Software-defined networks have two properties which can be seen as good-looking honey pots for malicious users and a basis of headaches for less ready network operators. First, the capacity to control the system by means of software (always subject to bugs and a score of other weakness). Second, the centralization of the network intelligence in the controller(s). Anyone with access to the servers can potentially control the entire network.

### Threat Vector 1

Forged or faked traffic flows, which can be used to assault switches and controllers. This risk can be triggered by defective (non-malicious) devices or by a malevolent user. An attacker can use system elements (e.g., switches, servers, or personal computers) to start on a DoS attack next to OpenFlow switches (e.g., targeting to exhaust TCAMs) and controller resources. A simple authentication machine could mitigate the difficulty, but if an attacker assumes the control of an application server that stores the particulars of numerous users, it can easily use the same authenticated ports and source MAC addresses to insert authorized, but forged into the network.

### Possible Solutions

The use of intrusion detection systems with hold up for runtime root-cause investigation could assist recognize abnormal flows. This could be joined with mechanisms for dynamic manage of switch performance (e.g., rate bounds for control plane requests).

### Threat Vector 2

Attacks on vulnerabilities in switches, which can with no trouble wreak havoc with the system. One single switch could be used to go down or slow down packets in the system, replica or deviate network transfer (e.g., for data theft purposes), or even insert traffic or forged requests to overload the controller or adjacent switches.

## Possible Solutions

The use of mechanisms of software evidence, such as autonomic trust management solutions for software mechanism, is a possible mitigating factor. Mechanisms to check and detect irregular behavior of network devices can also be useful to beat this kind of threats.

## Threat Vector 3

Attacks on control plane communications, which can be used to make DoS attacks or for data stealing. As is well-known in the safety community, using TLS/SSL does not per se assurance secure communication, and that compromises the controller device link. A variety of papers report the weaknesses of TLS/SSL communications and its main anchor of trust, the PKI infrastructure. The security of those communications is as strong as its weakest link, which could be a self-signed certificate, a compromised Certificate Authority, or vulnerable applications and libraries. For instance, there are many man-in-the-middle weak implementations of SSL being used in world-wide dangerous systems. Moreover, the TLS/SSL representation is not sufficient to set up and assure trust between controllers and switches. Once an attacker gains right of entry to the control plane, it may be capable of aggregating sufficient power force (in terms of the number of switches under its control) to start on DDoS attacks. This lack of trust guarantees could even allow the creation of a virtual black hole system (e.g., by using OpenFlow-based slicing techniques) allowing data leakage while the usual production traffic flows.

## Possible Solutions

The use of oligarchic faith models with several trust-anchor certification authorities (e.g., one per sub-domain or per controller instance) is a possibility. An- other is securing communication with entry cryptography across controller replicas (where the switch will need at smallest amount n shares to get a suitable controller message). Additionally, the use of lively, automated and assured machine association mechanisms may be considered, in order to guarantee hope between the control plane and data plane devices.

## Threat Vector 4

Attacks on and vulnerabilities in controllers, which are almost certainly the most severe threats to SDNs. A faulty or malicious controller could compromise a whole network. The use of a common intrusion detection organization may not be sufficient, as it may be tough to find the correct grouping of events that trigger a exacting behavior and, more importantly, to tag it as malicious. Likewise, a malicious application can potentially do anything it pleases in the network, as controllers simply offer abstractions that translate into issuing configuration commands to the fundamental communications.

## Possible Solutions

Several techniques can be used, such as reproduction (to detect, remove or mask irregular behavior), employing diversity (of controllers, protocols, programming languages, software images, etc.), and recovery (periodically refreshing the system to a clean and reliable state). It is also important to secure all the sensitive elements inside the controller (e.g., crypto keys/secrets). Furthermore, security policies enforcing correct behavior might be mapped onto those techniques, restricting which interfaces an application can use and what kind of rules it can generate to program the network (along the lines of security-based prioritization).

## Threat Vector 5

Be short of mechanisms to make sure trust between the controller and organization applications, whereby equally to threat number 3, controllers and applications lack the skill to put up trusted relationships. The main difference from the referred threat would lie in the way the certification is completed. The techniques used to confirm network devices are different from those used for applications.

## Possible Solutions

Mechanisms intended for autonomic trust management could be used to security that the application is trusted during its life span.

## Threat Vector 6

Attacks on and vulnerabilities in administrative stations which, as it is also common in traditional networks, are used in SDNs to access the network controller. These machines are already an exploitable target in current networks, the difference being that the threat surface as seen from a single compromised machine increases dramatically in SDNs. It becomes easy to reprogram the network from a single location.

## Possible Solutions

The use of protocols requiring twice credential confirmation (e.g., requiring the qualifications of two different users to right of entry a control server). Also, the use of assured revival mechanisms to guarantee a reliable state after reboot.

## Threat Vector 7

Lack of trusted capital for forensics and remediation, which would permit to understand the cause of a detected problem and proceed to a fast and secure mode recovery. In order to investigate and set up facts about an occurrence, require reliable information from all components and domains of the network. Furthermore, this data will only be useful if its trustworthiness (integrity, authenticity, etc.) can be assured. Likewise, remediation requires safe and consistent system snapshots to assurance a quick plus right recovery of network basics to a familiar working state.

## Possible Solutions

Logging and tracing are the normal mechanisms in use, and are needed both in the information and control planes. Though, in order to be efficient, they should be impossible to remove (a log that is guaranteed to be absolute and safe). In addition, logs should be stored in distant and safe environments.

## SDN CONTROLLER

The controller maintains a outlook of the whole network, implements policy decisions, controls all the SDN devices that involve the network infrastructure, and provides a northbound API for applications. When have said that the controller implements policy decisions concerning routing, forwarding, redirecting, load balancing, and the similar to, these statements referred to both the controller and the applications that create use of that controller. Controllers frequently come with their individual set of common application modules, such as a learning switch, a router, a basic firewall, and a easy load balancer. These are really SDN applications, but they are over and over again bundled with the controller. The control plane in SDN and OpenFlow in particular is logically centralized and net apps are on paper as if the network is solitary organization.

With a Reactive control representation, the OpenFlow switches have to consult an openflow controller every time a result must be made, such as what time a new packet flow reaches an OpenFlow switch. In the case of flow based control granularity, there will be a little presentation delay as the first packet of each original flow is forwarded to the controller for result, after which future interchange within that flow will be forwarded at line rate inside the switching hardware. While the first packet delay is insignificant in many cases, it may be a concern if the middle OpenFlow controller is geographically remote or if the majority flows are short-lived. An alternative proactive approach is also probable in OpenFlow to push policy rules out from the controller to the switches.

## The Role of Controller in SDN Approach

Multiple controllers may be used to decrease the latency or add to the scalability and fault tolerance of the OpenFlow (SDN) deployment. OpenFlow allows the link of several controllers to a switch, which would permit backup controllers to get over in the event of a failure. Onix and HyperFlow get the thought further by attempting to keep a logically centralized, but physically circulated control plane. This decreases the lookup overhead by enabling message with local controllers, while still allowing applications to be written by means of a simplified central vision of the system. The possible major downside of this approach is maintaining the reliable state in the overall distributed system. This may cause Net Apps, so as to believe they have an correct outlook of the network, to proceed incorrectly due to inconsistency in the worldwide network condition.

Recalling the operating system similarity, an OpenFlow controller acts as a system operating system and be supposed to implement at least two interfaces: a southbound interface so as to allows OpenFlow switches to converse with the controller, and a northbound interface that presents a programmable application programming interface (API) to system control and management applications (that is, Net Apps).

## Existing Implementations in Controllers

Currently, there are dissimilar OpenFlow (and SDN) controller implementations, Open Source Resources, as part of existing open source projects.

Table 3 shows the list of controllers in SDN.

## POX CONTROLLER

The major component of a Software Defined Networks is the SDN controller, called a network operating system. The controller is what defines the environment of the SDN paradigm. It is the in charge component for intent communication with all programmable basics of the network, providing a united view of the system. POX

*Table 3. List of controllers*

| Controller | Implementation | Developer |
|---|---|---|
| POX | Python | Nicira |
| NOX | Python/C++ | Nicira |
| MUL | C | Kulcloud |
| Maestro | Java | Rice university |
| Trema | Ruby/C | NEC |
| Beacon | Java | Standford |
| Jaxon | Java | Independent developers |
| Helios | C | NEC |
| Floodlight | Java | BigSwitch |
| SNAC | C++ | Nicira |
| Ryu | Python | NTT, OSRG group |
| Nodeflow | Javascript | Independent developers |
| Ovs-controller | C | Independent developers |
| Flowvisor | C | Standford/Nicira |
| Routeflow | C++ | CPqD |

is an open source development stage for Python-based software-defined networking (SDN) control applications, such because OpenFlow SDN controllers. POX, which enables fast growth and prototyping, is becoming additional commonly used than NOX

## POX Features

- "Pythonic" OpenFlow border.
- Reusable example mechanism for pathway selection, topology detection, etc.
- Specifically target Linux, Mac OS, plus Windows.
- Topology detection.
- Supports the same GUI and dream tools as NOX.
- Performs well compared to NOX applications on paper in Python.

## NOX CONTROLLER

NOX is an unlock source development stage for C++ - based software-defined networking (SDN) control applications. NOX has two divide lines of development:

- NOX-Classic
- NOX, too known as new NOX

## NOX Features

- Provides a C++ OpenFlow 1.0 API.
- Provides quick, asynchronous IO.
- Is targeted at new Linux distributions (mainly Ubuntu 11.10 and 12.04, other than also Debian and RHEL 6).

   Includes sample components for:

- Topology detection
- Knowledge switch
- Network-wide switch

## OPENMUL CONTROLLER

OpenMUL Controller provides a bottom controller platform for all SDN/Openflow. It is a lightweight SDN/Openflow controller written almost entirely in C (from scratch) and provides a very stable platform with top performance in terms of flow handling (download rate and latency). It is designed for performance, reliability and availability which is the need of the hour for deployment of SDN in mission-critical networks.

   It is also extremely flexible, modular and simple to learn. Mul means "base or root" in Sanskrit. Mul is marked "mool" as in "school". OpenMUL provides multi-level in addition to multi-language APIs to hold up different application requirements. The `C` language bindings can be used for presentation and latency responsive apps as RESTful APIs can be used by web apps. It be able to control system devices behind Openflow, OVSDB as well as Netconf. The following are the major components of OpenMUL controller:

## MUL Director/Core

- Major part of Mul
- Handles all low down level switch connections plus does Openflow processing

- Provides application programming border in form of MLAPIS (mid-level APIs)
- Provides Openflow (or any south bound protocol) agnostic right of entry to devices
- Supports hooks for high speed low-latency learning (reactive) processing infrastructure
- Makes sure all flows, groups, meters and other switch specific entities are kept in sync across switch, controller reboots/failures.

## MUL Infrastructure Services

- These give essential infra services built on top of mul director/core
- Currently obtainable: Topology discovery service, path judgment service, path connector service

## MUL System Apps

- System apps are built using a ordinary api provided by mul-director plus mul-services
- These are hardly aware of Openflow and therefore designed to work across different openflow versions provided switches hold up common obligation of these apps
- Currently presented: L2switch, CLI app, NBAPI web server

## MAESTRO CONTROLLER

Maestro is an extensible Java-based OpenFlow Controller at large by Rice University. It has hold up designed for multi-threading and targets researchers. Maestro is a platform for achieving routine and programmatic network control functions by means of these modularized applications.

The programming framework of Maestro provides interfaces for:

- Introducing new customized control functions adding modularized control components.
- Maintaining network state on behalf of the control components.
- Composing control components by specifying the execution sequencing and the shared network state of the components.

# TREMA CONTROLLER

Trema is more a software stage for OpenFlow developers/researchers/enthusiasts than a manufacture controller. Trema structural design includes center modules such as packet-in filter, switch plus switch manager, OpenFlow application border, essential libraries, network DSL for configurations, an emulator designed for included development, and Tremashark to hold up debugging. Trema employs a multi-process model, in which a lot of functional modules are insecurely coupled through a messenger. The functional modules might be any of the user modules (applications) or the center modules. The modules act together through messenger using the six important APIs — the first three are for in receipt of and last three are for distribution messages

# BEACON CONTROLLER

Beacon is a quick, cross-platform, modular, Java-based OpenFlow manager that supports both event-based plus threaded process. This allows it to be run on dissimilar platforms, even in Android-based stylish phones. One of the main benefits of beacon is its active nature. This controller permits applications to be in progress, stopped up and installed on run time.

## Key Features

- **Stable:** Beacon has been in development as early 2010, and has been used in more than a few research projects, networking classes, plus test deployments. Beacon currently powers a 100-vswitch, 20-physical switch investigational data center and has run for months with no downtime.
- **Cross-Platform:** Beacon is printed in Java and runs on a lot of platforms, as of high end multi-core Linux servers to Android phones.
- **Open Source:** Beacon is accepted under a grouping of the GPL v2 license and the Stanford University FOSS License Exception v1.0.
- **Dynamic:** Code bundles in Beacon can be in progress/stopped up/refreshed/installed at runtime, with no interrupting additional non-dependent bundles (i.e. replace your running Learning Switch application with no disconnecting switches).
- **Rapid Development:** Beacon is simple to get up and running. Java plus Eclipse simplify development and debugging of your applications.
- **Fast:** Beacon is multithreaded, make sure out performance benchmarks.

- **Web UI:** Beacon optionally embed the Jetty enterprise net server and a custom extensible UI framework
- **Frameworks:** Beacon builds on mature Java frameworks such as Spring and Equinox (OSGi) (Erickson, 2013).

## JAXON CONTROLLER

Jaxon is a Java-based OpenFlow Controller so as to provide a slim border to NOX to bridge Java applications in addition to the NOX controller.

## HELIOS CONTROLLER

The HELIOS repair Controller monitors all processes which contain been in progress on the server. In case a process be supposed to fail, the HELIOS Service Controller restarts this process following a short time.

- Automatic service restart 10 seconds after failure
- Automatic disable following 10 failures; every failure inside a minute
- Automatic preliminary order of the services.

## FLOODLIGHT CONTROLLER

Floodlight Controller is associate SDN Controller offered by huge Switch Networks that works with the OpenFlow protocol to orchestrate traffic flows in an exceedingly software-defined networking (SDN) setting. The Floodlight Controller realizes a collection of common functionalities to regulate associated inquire an OpenFlow network, whereas applications on prime of it understand totally options to resolve different user desires over the network. The figures below show the link among the Floodlight Controller, the applications engineered as Java modules compiled with Floodlight, and therefore the applications engineered over the Floodlight REST API.

### Features

- Offers a module loading scheme that make it easy to expand and improve.
- Easy to set up by means of smallest dependencies
- Supports a wide range of virtual- plus physical- OpenFlow switches

- Can handle varied OpenFlow and non-OpenFlow networks – it can direct several "islands" of OpenFlow hardware switches
- Planned to be high-performance – be multithreaded from the position up
- Hold up for OpenStack (connection) cloud orchestration stage

## SNAC CONTROLLER

It is an Open source OpenFlow controller by means of graphical user interface. It uses web-based policy manager to direct the network. It is a unit of NOX plus requires suitable version of NOX. Allows admission control, shows system components, system usage, and proceedings. Reports a lot of flow-level traffic particulars using REST API. New hosts combination the network is automatically heading for to SNAC for verification

## RYU CONTROLLER

Ryu is a component-based software definite networking framework. Ryu provides software components by means of well defined API that create it simple for developers to make new network management and control applications. Ryu supports a variety of protocols for organization network devices, such as OpenFlow, Netconf, OF-config, etc. Regarding OpenFlow, Ryu supports completely 1.0, 1.2, 1.3, 1.4, 1.5 and Nicira Extensions. The Ryu Controller provides software components, by means of well-defined application program interfaces (APIs), so as to make it simple for developers to make new network management and control applications. This component move toward helps organizations modify deployments to meet their specific requirements; developers can rapidly and simply modify existing components or put into practice their own to make sure the underlying system can meet the changing stress of their applications. The Ryu Controller can use OpenFlow to cooperate with the forwarding plane (switches and routers) to change how the network will handle interchange flows. It has been tested and specialized to work with a number of OpenFlow switches, counting Open vSwitch and offerings from Centec, Hewlett Packard, IBM, and NEC (SDX Central, n.d.).

Most controller platforms representation some native features to permit these key features:

- Skill to listen to asynchronous actions (e.g., PACKET_IN, FLOW_REMOVED) and to view events using Ryu. controller. handler. set_ev_cls decorator.

- Ability to parse inward bound packets (e.g., ARP, ICMP, TCP) and make packets to send out keen on the network

## NODEFLOW CONTROLLER

Node is a fast, lightweight, and proficient server-side java script platform based on Google's V8 runtime.

## FLOWVISOR CONTROLLER

FlowVisor is a new software-defined networking (SDN) controller so as to enables network virtualization by in-between a physical network keen on several logical networks. FlowVisor ensures so as to each controller touches simply the switches and possessions assigned to it. FlowVisor slices a physical network keen on abstracted units of bandwidth, topology, exchange and network machine central processing units (CPUs). It operates as a see-through proxy controller between the physical switches of an OpenFlow network and other OpenFlow controllers and enables several controllers to function the similar physical infrastructure; much similar to a server hypervisor allows several operating systems to use the same x86-based hardware. (Rouse, 2013)

### Purpose of FlowVisor

- FlowVisor is a particular purpose OpenFlow controller so as to acts as a transparent proxy between OpenFlow switches and several OpenFlow controllers
- FlowVisor creates rich "slices" of network resources and delegates manage of each slice to a dissimilar controller
- FlowVisor enforces separation between each slice, i.e., one slice cannot control another's interchange. (Flowvisor, 2014)

## ROUTEFLOW CONTROLLER

RouteFlow is an unlock source project to give virtualized IP routing services in excess of OpenFlow enabled hardware. OpenFlow controllers such as POX and Ryu, which are used to attach the switches to the RFServer.

The major components of the RouteFlow answer are:

- RouteFlow Client (RF-Client)
- RouteFlow Server (RF-Server)
- RouteFlow Proxy (RF-Proxy)

The communication between the components is definite by a set of RouteFlow protocol communication (Route Flow, 2015)

RouteFlow relies on technology such as:

- OpenFlow-enabled switches that be able software-based (such as Mininet) or hardware-based (such as NetFPGAs)
- OpenFlow controllers such as POX and Ryu, that be used to join the switches to the RFServer
- The Quagga routing engine can be used in the virtual equipment to give routing services
- Open vSwitch is used to attach the virtual machines
- MongoDB is used to give a centralized database for the system and also to implement an IPC service
- LXC containers as virtual machines intended for running the RFClient and Quagga (CPqD, n.d.).

## CONCLUSION

The idea of a programmable network in the beginning took shape as dynamic networking, which espoused many of the same visions as SDN but lacked both a clear use case and an incremental deployment path. After the era of active-networking do research projects, the pendulum swung from vision to practicality, in the form of sorting out the data and control planes to make the set of connections easier to manage. This work focused for the most part on better ways to route network traffic—a much narrower vision than earlier work on active networking. Ultimately, the work on OpenFlow and network operating systems struck the right sense of balance between vision and expediency. This work advocated network-wide control for a wide range of applications, yet relied only on the accessible capabilities of switch chipsets. Backward compatibility with existing switch hardware appealed to many tools vendors clamoring to compete in the rising market in data-center networks. The balance of a broad, clear vision with a practical strategy for widespread adoption gained traction when SDN found a compelling use case in network virtualization. As SDN continues to develop, its the past has important lessons to teach. First, SDN technologies will live or die based on "use pulls." Although SDN is often heralded as the solution to all networking problems, it is worth identification that it is just a tool for solving network-management problems more easily. SDN simply gives developers the power to create new applications and find solutions to ancient problems. In this respect, the work is just beginning. If the past is any suggestion, the development of these new technologies will require novelty on multiple timescales, from long-term bold visions (such as active networking) to near-term innovative problem solving (such as the operationally focused work on separating the control and data planes). Second, the balance between visualization and practicality remains tenuous. The bold vision of SDN advocates a variety of control applications; yet OpenFlow's control over the data plane is confined to ancient match-action operations on packet-header fields. The initial design of OpenFlow was driven by the aspiration for rapid adoption, not first principles. Supporting a wide range of network services would require much more complicated ways of analyzing and manipulating traffic (e.g., deep-packet inspection, as well as compression, encryption, and transcoding of packets), using product servers (e.g., x86 machines) or programmable hardware (e.g., FPGAs, network processors, and GPUs), or both. Fascinatingly, the renewed interest in more complicated data-plane functionality, such as NFV, harkens back to the earlier work on active networking, bringing the story full circle. Maintaining SDN's bold vision requires more thinking outside the box about the best ways to program the network without being controlled by the restrictions of current technologies. Rather than simply designing SDN applications with the current OpenFlow protocols in mind, developers should think about what variety of control they want to have over the data plane, and balance that vision with a practical strategy for deployment.

## REFERENCES

Advantages of Software Defined Networking. (2014). Retrieved from http://www.ingrammicroadvisor.com/data-center/7-advantages-of-software-defined-networking

Algarni. (2013). Software-Defined Networking Overview and Implementation. Academic Press.

Build SDN Agilely. (2017). Retrieved from https://osrg.github.io/ryu/

CPqD. (n.d.). *What is it?* Retrieved from http://cpqd.github.io/RouteFlow/

Erickson, D. (2013). *What is Beacon?* Retrieved from https://openflow.stanford.edu/display/Beacon/Home

HowSDN Works. (n.d.). Retrieved from http://cdn.ttgtmedia.com/rms/editorial/HowSDNWorks-SoftwareDefinedNetworks-Ch4.pdf

Ingram Micro Advisor. (n.d.). *7 Advantages of Software Defined Networking*. Retrieved from http://www.ingrammicroadvisor.com/data-center/7-advantages-of-software-defined-networking

NFV and SDN. What's the Difference? (2013). Retrieved from https://www.sdxcentral.com/articles/contributed/nfv-and-sdn-whats-the-difference/2013/03/

Open Networking Foundation. (n.d.). *Software-Defined Networking (SDN) Definition*. Retrieved from https://www.opennetworking.org/sdn-resources/sdn-definition

OpenFlow Controllers. (n.d.). Retrieved from https://www.packtpub.com/books/content/openflow-controllers

Pate, P. (2013). *NFV and SDN: What's the Difference?* Retrieved from https://www.sdxcentral.com/articles/contributed/nfv-and-sdn-whats-the-difference/2013/03/

Road to SDN. (2013). Retrieved from http://queue.acm.org/detail.cfm?id=2560327

Rouse, M. (2013). *What is FlowVisor?* Retrieved from http://searchsdn.techtarget.com/definition/FlowVisor

RouteFlow. (2015). Retrieved from https://sites.google.com/site/routeflow/home

SDN Controller. (n.d.). Retrieved from http://searchsdn.techtarget.com/definition/SDN-controller-software-defined-networking-controller

SDX Central. (n.d.). *What Is Ryu Controller?* Retrieved from https://www.sdxcentral.com/sdn/definitions/sdn-controllers/open-source-sdn controllers/what-is-ryu-controller/

Stanford. (2014). *Flowvisor*. Retrieved from https://openflow.stanford.edu/display/DOCS/Flowvisor

What Are SDN Controllers (or SDN Controllers Platforms)? (n.d.). Retrieved from https://www.sdxcentral.com/sdn/definitions/sdn-controllers/

What Is Ryu Controller? (n.d.). Retrieved from https://www.sdxcentral.com/sdn/definitions/sdn-controllers/open-source-sdn-controllers/what-is-ryu-controller/

Wilkins, S. (2014, November 25). *A Guide To Software Defined Networking (SDN) Solutions - Software Defined Networking: What It Is And Isn't*. Retrieved from http://www.tomsitpro.com/articles/software-defined-networking-solutions,2-835.html

# Chapter 5
# The Heart and Brain of SDN:
## SDN Controllers

**Pranav Arora**
*University of Petroleum and Energy Studies, India*

## ABSTRACT

*The chapter explores the various types and functionalities of controllers present in the field of software-defined networking. It is responsible for providing a bridge between various application interfaces. It enables smart networking and is solely responsible for having an authority over the network. It takes input from one API, processes it, and returns output for the high-level interface or API. They instruct the switch as to what functions to perform and can be of two types: either pure or hybrid. The controller at the central layer performs all the functions of the "evergreen" existing switches. The data plane of the router is solely the foreground for the switch to apply all its powers, while in hybrid switch software-defined networking and existing technologies work hand in hand. An administrator can build up the SDN tools to manage the traffic, whereas the existing network protocols progressively move the various incoming packets onto the network. This engenders hybrid network. Here the existing and SDN technologies or switches, work under the similar conditions.*

## INTRODUCTION

The need of the present scenario is to give a general overview of the industry-specific as well as open source SDN technologies. As the IT industry is still thriving and is ambiguous of the role of software defined networking in the market, the solutions which are presented by different vendors won't all be compared. But the discussion holds in stock a great fathomed discussion about various popular SDN controllers

DOI: 10.4018/978-1-5225-3640-6.ch005

like NOX, POX, Flood Light, RYU etc. A closer look would be given to the free side of the market i.e. open source side. Being the vortex of the software defined architecture; the controllers belonging to this category have also developed with a period of time.

## BACKGROUND

The rise of this concept was given when the data centers saw that the network devices had to reconfigure. This was a tedious task as they had to manually do it and keep any eye on every device if something goes wrong. The evolution of networks overtime gave birth to software defined networking and network virtualization. The control and data plane of the router are separated and instead of control plane being in charge a controller agent is in charge there in SDN architecture. The controller agents communicate with the SDN controller which in return provide dynamic path allocation to devices depending on the network load. Giving the past, present and future scenarios it is time to focus on the agenda of the chapter. The SDN controllers which form the key component of this macrocosm.

## DEFINITION

*A SDN controller is software's piece in software-defined networking (SDN) that controls or manages the flow control of the network to initiate smart networking. SDN controllers are prepared to function on various protocols, most popular being Open Flow, that allows servers to tell, switches where to send packets.*

Before diving into the basics of what a SDN controller is, what their types are and how do they all differ from each other, the very miniscule thing to look at is what it comes to our mind whenever we hear controller. Yosr, Madi, and Debbabi (2014) specified in the taxonomy of Software defined networking about the role of controllers. We have heard about remote controllers, air conditioner controllers and various others. The problem is we have heard about them but never tried to figure out what is their purpose internally. Here we are not going to talk about Controllers in general but a specific kind of controller that is SDN Controller.

Not to worry if the talk starts to get tech savvy, everything would become vivid as you go on to read the entire unit. Each and every question about this technology will be handled with utmost simplicity and ease as we move into the fathoms.

In this chapter we will look at the following major topics:

1. **Controllers:**
   a. Their functions
   b. Usage and benefits of Controllers as a single entity.
   c. Criteria to evaluate a Controller
   d. Types of Controllers.
   e. Benefits of different types of Controllers
   f. Comparing each controller with the previous and finding the optimal one for a particular scenario.

Now, what does it comes to your mind when you read the word control? Probably to manipulate someone, or have an authority over someone.

## Similarly, a Controller Has an Authority Over the SDN Network

A Controller is at the core of the SDN network. It acts as a middle man and connects the switches and the routers at the lower end to the applications or the business logic at the upper end. This helps in providing an abstraction to the application layer about the inner functioning of the system.

Wibowo, Gregor, Ahmed and Chavez (2017) clearly state the importance of a controller over a network.

Controller manages flow control to enable a kind of a network which manages situations on its own, somewhat intelligent by nature. There are numerous protocols on which a controller can be based on. One of the most popular is Open Flow.

In effect, It somewhat plays a role of an Operating System. You must have used a computer and know for a fact that the entire system runs over an OS. What does an OS do? It provides an interface between the hardware of the system and the user applications thus making it convenient to talk to the hardware in human terms.

Well, to be extremely precise OS's main building block is kernel. So, to go down in the abstraction level Controller is the kernel for OS and OS for the computer system.

Let's not get side-tracked, coming back to the topic. By taking the control plane off the network hardware and running the software instead, the controller facilitates automated network management and eases the process to integrate and administer business applications.

For a lucid view of the SDN architecture, look at the Figure 1 and focus on the position of the controller. For now, forget about the Agents or drivers. The controller is the central entity responsible for taking in the requirements from SDN application layer a.k.a Northbound Interface down to SDN data path and providing Application Layer with an abstract view of the system.

A lot of technical terms? No problem. Let's decompose it in very simple terms.

*Figure 1. Layer-wise architecture of SDN (overview)*

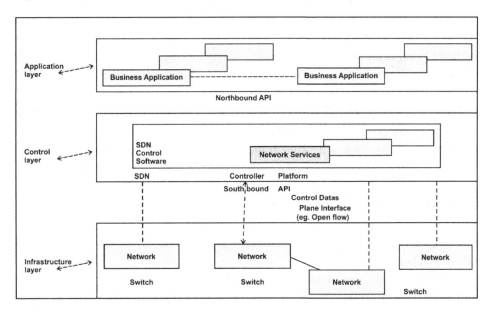

A controller sits in between the 2 layers of the SDN system. It takes the input from upper layer, does the processing in the lower layer, and passes the result back to the upper layer.

The northbound or southbound interface conceptualize the lower level details which primarily includes data or any functions. Normally northbound interface is drawn at the top and southbound in the bottom. They are generic terms and can be used over all layers of computer systems.

## FUNCTIONS OF CONTROLLERS

The job of the controller is to instruct the switch as to what action they should perform or take using an interface also known as southbound Application Programming Interface. CBench (2008) mentioned the proximity of controllers to the future needs. As mentioned above, Open Flow is pervasively taking on the SDN market for controllers to communicate with the switches. Now the switches can be either pure or hybrid switches. The function of pure switch is to forward packets straight-forward while the hybrid one supports both features of Open Flow forwarding and traditional switch bridging and routing.

## Uses and Benefits of Controllers

Now comes the fun part, WHY use them anyway? What is wrong with the current method? What is the hype all about?

Consider Figure 2 and focus on the central part of the image which shows control plane inclusive of agent, logic and driver.

Heller, Sherwood and McKeown (2012) clearly mentions that the thing is, if we only have an integrated control and data plane of a router, to make any configuration changes we have to it manually in each and every network centre's routers separately. This is a very tedious and mundane job. To avoid this commotion, Controllers come into play. Once we logically segregate the planes of the routers, controller abstracts the network from the hardware and makes it possible to control the entire network from a single console. They typically contain a collection of "pluggable" modules, meaning they can be detached or attached when the need be, that can perform different network tasks.

Some of the basic tasks include gathering network statistics, what all devices are within the network and how to enhance the functionality and support more advanced capabilities such as running algorithms to perform analytics throughout the network.

*Figure 2. Controller architecture (detailed)*

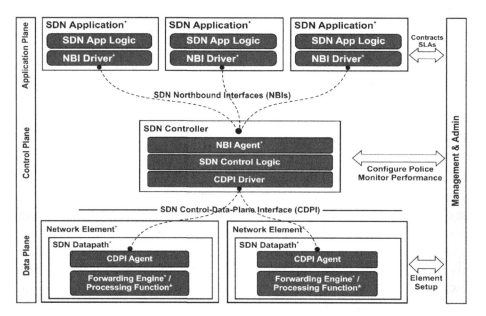

## Criteria to Evaluate a Controller

Here comes the most significant portion of the chapter. What are the factors that are taken into account when we need to evaluate a controller? Consider this analogy; you go to an electrical shop to buy a Television. Now when you decide to buy a television, the shopkeeper asks which all remote controllers you want. He shows you three different types. As a normal person you would choose the remote of the same company of which you bought the television of. Right?

So, when any organization which sets out to invest, looks for a set of features in its products. The same is the case for SDN Controllers.

It might be a little lengthy but read along, it is highly significant if you are inclined towards making a career in SDN.

According to the research by Ashton and Metzler (2012) the following are the major 10 salient features or let's just say 10 characteristics that a Controller must have to be identified as a "Usable/Implementable Controller".

### Network Virtualization

This stands to be the most crucial aspect of SDN. It is not a part of SDN though; it is a separate technology which focuses on converting every deployment of network products remotely rather than installing them by hand-on. It is nothing new that came along, it has been there for a long time. VLANs (Virtual Lans) have been in production networks for decades. Another type of network virtualization is VRF. VRF is a network layer protocol where there is presence of physical routers running on their own protocols and transforming and building their own forwarding tables along with providing many sublime router instances.

These methods or ways or techs may seem helpful, they are limited in their scope. In order to make their values shoot up rocket sky-high, NFV needs to abstract the network resources alongside maintaining end-to-end connection .Which simply means that virtual topology is decoupled from the physical topology .The benefits which entails to the organisations using this method is that now developers can amend the layer 1 schemes . Example is to enhance the network without affecting the already built up streams.

### OpenFlow Support

As soon as message in form of segment or packet reaches the switches, the prefilled entries in the table flow are matched with the header of the message. It is the job of the controller to make a decision on what to do with the packet either make a separate entry in the table flow or else drop it.

There are some basic requirements that must be fulfilled by an OpenFlow Controller which mainly are:

1.  Field Comparison
2.  Changing/Transforming the header structure for supporting basic OpenFlow methods.
3.  Finding out a new area of network using LLD mechanism.

Choosing/Opting for a particular controller, a firm must clearly know the features of the controller and what all it can specifically do along with vendor's future requirements if they wish to acquire or build advanced models for that controller. The aim behind this is, many functionalities like Ipv6 is integrally present in 1.0 version of OpenFlow but not in the 3.0 version.

## Scalability

Scalability refers to the process of expanding the system as the requirements starts to grow .The LAN as we all know it, is present in many layers of the OSI or TCP/IP model(practically implemented) in which network layer's features and methods of routing are used to form a connection with many data link layer networks . The thing is, you can't use these old LAN cables for humungous network connection which are poles apart. The reason being, they lack scalability, primarily because at least one network layer device is required to ensure a connection between these small scaled layer 2 network devices.

Software Defined Networking plays a key role here, it gives the power to an organization to create a scalable model/view of network where the team can add extra functionalities whenever required and Controller takes the full authority over the network managing as it was a single workable device.

An important factor to look here while designing of the system is the number of switches the Controller holds the capability to handle.

The present situation demands the firms to think high of the controllers and believe that a single controller can handle at least 200 switches at once. The factor which "the present situation" fails to put forward is that the amount of switches which a controller can support completely relies on the fact the Software Defined Networking (SDN) use cases which can be supported at once.

Thus, organization should ensure that controllers can manage and moreover lessen or retrench the impact of broadcast over the network while evaluating them.

One another factor that encumbers the scaling of SDN is the high increase in the amount of flow table entries which occurs while applying certain optimization algorithms, which as a result increases a hop-by-hop entry for each flow (Ashton and

Metzler, 2012). Thus, Organization should look into this factor that the controllers can mitigate this vast increase while evaluating them. One easy solution to this problem is, allowing SDN controllers to implement transcribing in the heart of the network. It basically means that is the controller could override the already written data over the header then there would be a need to handle only 2 unique entries which would be the starting and going out point for the messages in the network . Another point of view here to mention is the capacity of a controller to create a network that can redistribute over many sites/destinations. This will be beneficial to the virtual boxes to communicate amongst them. In order to optimise this utility, controller must provide automation of network propagandas to migrated servers and storage.

## Network Functionality

To ensure that security is not compromised at any aspect, it is prevalent for providers of cloud-based services like AWS, ZOHO, and Tata, to isolate one tenant from another. Network functionality is a topic for the open source service providers for the cloud but with time it has been taking the enterprise firms in its storm cloud (pun intended). Like we have to accept the terms and conditions of any service/product we download or purchase on the internet, to ensure the data of our agreement is secure, the firms need to keep one client data hidden from the other ones. Generally there are 2 environments to run a product in, production and testing. The IT firms nowadays prefer programmers to develop their apps in production environment without the disruption of the network flow. In order to fulfil the above mentioned conditions in an effective manner .Software Defined Networking should make sure that the VNs are completely air-gapped from each other and should be controlled from a central main server rather than being distributed and should make sure that the system settings are by default applied and not to be applied manually .

It is like creating an air-gap between the clouds of information which one user to another.

To allow the flows to be routed, it is extremely necessary for the controller to handle any decisional scenario while considering multiple header fields. Like power path software available for EMC networking traffic modulation, it is also relative for controller to find out multiple ways for traffic flow amongst various links from source to destinations. This ability also solves the issue in STP and enhances the availability of the network by making it readily available 24 *7. The controller should also define Quality of Service functionalities on a flow-to-flow basis.

## Network Programmability

The basis on which SDN concept was developed is Network programmability. In previous days, network was configured from device to device. This manual approach was time consuming and was predicted to errors. The conditional changes don't affect the config in any way because the system is static. "All Hail" the controller as it gives an interface to the system in form of a UI sort of environment. What does it mean by programmable interface? The controller actually redirects traffic. Example is building a shielded network that makes the traffic inbound to the server. Now if the sources trying to fetch the network are clean then the firewall should not consume all the resources and the IT firm should make sure that traffic should not go through this shield and should be outsourced or rather outbound. It is monotonous when it comes the old style networks. Few other areas of concern are that organisations must look for generally include masking of packets when the arrive at the controller.

But the job of controller is not easy at all as it must mask tedious combinations of multiple packet header fields. Dynamic deployment of these filters should be opted for on VMs and being the intermediaries' i.e. the controllers they must forward the table entries to the switch. Who wants static programming of network? No one right? So the controller allows for short slate like temporary plates to configure that enables scripting Command Line Interfaces to be renewed.

To mention another fact that how does controller enables such tremendous programming capabilities is by implementation of the upper layer's Application Programming Interfaces. (Ashton and Metzler, 2012). This upper layer or "Northbound" Application Interface has a small trick up its sleeve. It passes the information of control to any other potential candidate that holds the key to dynamically transform the network like moving packet to greater bandwidth path or more suitable way or improving the Quality of Service settings on the basis of how much free the network is .

## Reliability

At the prefatory note, it was mentioned that SDN controller provides an intelligent network that does design validation while configuring the network and hence eliminates manual errors. What all capabilities a controller can provide, it is still degraded in the market for one of the main and important reason and that is, it is a single point failure and hence the controller decreases overall network availability. Therefore, while evaluating controllers, organization has to understand the functionality of controllers in terms of reliability.

One popular example for reliable source is the power path software used by DELL EMC to transfer the network to multiple paths if one of them fails. Similar is the scenario for any SDN Controller that is to discover multiple paths between start and destination, the availability of the solution is not impacted by the outage of the link. On the other hand, SDN Controller if sets up a single path between start and end point of the network, if the path fails for whatever reason, should be able to route the traffic to an active link. This can only be satisfied if the controller is monitoring the network continuously.

In terms of the availability of the controller itself, it is critical that the controller be built using both hardware and software redundancy features. It is also imperative that the SDN controller enable clustering. For example, clustering two SDN controllers in active/hot standby mode increases reliability and clustering three or more SDN controllers, with one in hot standby mode, increases the availability, scalability and performance of an SDN controller. However, in order for the clustering to provide for very fast failover times, it is important that the solution is capable of maintaining the synchronization of the memory between the active and standby controllers.

## Network Security

Security plays a key role when it comes to any field of computer science or technology. If the data can't be protected, what is the need of storing it anyway? SDN controller is expected to provide organization class authorization and authentication of the administrators. Not only this, the administrators must try to encumber/limit down the network bandwidth in a fungible way as they lock down any other traffic on the internet. As discussed earlier, the controller should maintain an air gap or isolation between all tenants. DoS, DDoS attacks are quite common on a network, so the controller should have the ability to limit the control communications and tell the administrator of any future attacks prior to happening.

## Centralized Monitoring and Virtualizations

Most of the times, what happens is that when the network start to degrade i.e. the network performance starts to degrade, it is noticed by the user first rather than the organization. For example, if the wifi speed plunges drastically who comes to know that first, the user or the ISP? Definitely the user. Thus, the primary reasons for degraded performance are the lack of visibility into the end-to-end network flows.

Let's consider a scenario; SNMP is a very well-known tech for managing communications and networks like the MAC of the message sender. The problem of this protocol persists in scaling the network when it uses the concept of quantisation and sampling. This creates a situation where a fixed rate of sampling defines every

1 out of N packet, thus reducing the rate of it when the traffic or network speed takes a notch up. The technique cannot offer the deep knowledge for running apps which answers the WHY of every problem i.e. troubleshoots, neither it provides firms with a compliancy factor for the large scaling regulations sets.

The benefits of Software Defined Networking come only into picture when the problem becomes messy. It gives firms clarity of the network flow from moiety of one half to the other. Unlike SNMP, OpenFlow is used to gather number flags on any network. The job the controller is to recognise the data gathered by the protocol to find issues in the network and simultaneously make it take another path for file transfer during a damaged network. The controller should keep any eye on the various branches of hierarchies of traffics they are answering to. Consider a scenario where an IT firm like Oracle does not choose to eye over repeated message over the network. To picture out a map of the pre-existing network in your head might be daunting but crucial. But as the abstraction world is taking over the nations it is essential that we visualize the milieu where many virtual networks run over the physical one.

So to see and present the physical network in a visual format, SDN controller comes to the rescue for any organisation. Not only the physical network but simultaneously visualising the virtual network over the top of physical network is done by the controllers. To summarise in extremely simple terms of what the above lines mentioned is that the controllers should provide a lucid perspective or view of the network flow both from physical and virtual angle to get insight view of each network separately.

IT firms should enquire that is it easy to manage and handle the controller using standard methods and ways? Like the Simple Network Management Protocol manages the condition of the controller in terms of MTTF or MTBF. The firms should possibly enquire for the fact that whether the controller manages a huge range of support for management information bases for managing the entities in the information network elements.

## Performance

The primary job of the controller is to build a network flow. The performance of the controller is majorly judged on 2 factors which include the number of flows that the controller can setup in a second and the time taken for setting up the flow. The factors mentioned above are extremely under the bulge when extra controllers are to put into action. Consider when routers in production Software Defined Networking throws out more flows than the capacity of the controller, the number of controller's requirement must be increased (Ashton and Metzler, 2012). The setting up of the flow can be done in two major fashions, either before or during the course i.e. proactively or reactively. The former occurs before the message is pinged at the switch, this means that the switch is already aware of where to or what to do with the packet once it arrives. This gives an unprecedented advantage in setting up the network and there is no restriction on the number of packets that can be handled by the controller per minute or second. In the perfect world, then controller should popularize the flow tables to the highest capacity possible. But that happens in perfect world, not in a real one. The latter set up fashion of reactive setting up happens when the switch (which runs on OpenFlow protocol) gets the message that fits no match with any of the entries in the flow table and hence it is sent to the controller which decides what will be the fate of the packet. Once the controller. Which is the Supreme Court in this scenario gives its orders, to the high court, i.e. the switch as to how to process the flow it is entered into the cache of OpenFlow switch and the Supreme Court also decides the lifetime of the cache. The major ornaments governing the affect the time of slow setup are the power of processing of the OpenFlow switches and alongside the input output performance and processing of the controller itself. Consider a controller that is written in low level programming language will be much faster than a high level programming language because there is no overhead of converting into low level or say bytecode (in case of Java) . Today's scenario should atleast pose a challenge in front of these controllers to not become a blockage in the way of OpenFlow switches which are responsible for adding or deleting flow entries in the flow table.

## Controller's Vendors

As the demand and the need of SDN is increasing day by day, a lot of vendors are on the verge of entering the market or have entered. Vendors are those exact people which can be pictured in the mind right now. The only minuscule of difference is that these vendors are much more sophisticated in the product they sell and are highly efficient in their production process of controllers. Now as there are many similar products in the market, similarly this field has equal number of competitions too. This is creating volatility in the market and creating a pandemonium in the controller market too. The major owners to these products are not general public but multi-million dollar organizations or big tech giants who have a lot of funds to invest. But when it comes to bargaining, no one has the guts to settle for a saddle point. Everyone wants to earn themselves high profit or prevent themselves for huge loss. Thus, Organizations evaluating controllers should not only focus on the technical attributes of the controllers but also on the vendors as to what are their credibility percentage, where do they stand in market, what are their past sales ratio, number of defects produced per set of products etc.

The above factors are a look upon but a major factor that cannot be missed by any IT organization is to see that "Whether the vendor has technical and financial capability to handle ongoing research and development in the field of SDN?" Agility plays a key role in defining how strong and for how long is the vendor going to stay in market.

## TYPES OF CONTROLLERS

Now after discussing and having a better understanding of the criteria selection of the controllers and why should we separate the data and the control plane, let's have a look at the many different options at the SDN Controllers. Jarschel, Lehrieder, Magyari and Pries(2012); Kotani, Suzuki, and Shimonishi (2012) enlightened in their research, with a number of Open Flow controllers.

There are a number of Controllers that exists including:

1.   NOX
2.   RYU
3.   Floodlight
4.   Pyretic
5.   Frenetic
6.   Procera
7.   RouteFlow
8.   Trema
9.   Open Daylight (controller baseline project over which many controllers are built)
10.  ONOS
11.  Beacon
12.  Cherry
13.  Faucet (Python based on Ryu for production networks)
14.  Open Contrail

and the list goes on .

Let's explore the merits and take a closer look at the following 4 controllers:

1.   NOX
2.   POX
3.   Floodlight
4.   Ryu

We will be handling the rest of the sub-topics together, which primarily includes, comparing the Controllers to each other and finding the best one for any given scenario.

Let's dive in!

The first controller to feast upon is:

## NOX

It is a first generation Open-Flow Controller. It is open source, stable and widely used.

It majorly has two flavours:

1.  **Classic:** It is written in C++/Python and is NO LONGER SUPPORTED.
2.  **New Nox:** It is written in C++ only. It is fast, clean and has wide community support.

The NOX architecture contains two major components:

1.  Switches
2.  Network Attached Servers

The controller maintains a network view and the controller may maintain several applications that might run on the network view. The abstraction is at the switch control level where OpenFlow is the major governing protocol. The control depends upon the granularity of the flow which is dependent on the 10 tuple structure. Voellmy, Ford, Hudak, and Yang (2012) presented their ideas in a pellucid form in their paper on scaling of SDN controllers for multicore servers.

The controller may make forwarding decisions for packets that belong to different parts of flow space. A flow is defined by the header or by the 10 tuple. A counter which maintains statistics and actions that must be performed on these packets that match these flow definitions.

These actions might include forwarding the packet, dropping it or sending it to the controller.

The basic programmatic interface is based on EVENTS.

A controller knows how to process different types of events like, which switches should join it or leave, which set of packets should ingress or egress and various statistics maintenance. The controller also keeps track of a network view which includes underlying network topology and also speaks a control protocol to the switches in the network. The control protocol actually allows updating the state in the networks switches. The NOX Controller implements The OPEN FLOW Protocol.

## Characteristics of NOX

1. Implemented in C++
2. Supports Open Flow v1.0
3. A fork of NOX -> CPQD supports open flow till v1.3.

NOX provides good performance but it requires programmer to write the control application in C++ which can be slow for development and debugging.

## There Comes the Role of POX

POX has a really high demand, support from various tech communities and is very well managed in its own way. It is very easy to use and easy to write the control programmes. It can be used to quickly prototype a brand new control application. But being written in python it does not provide that level of performance which is provided by NOX.

You can use POX for class projects or University Research Programmes but it is refrained to be used in Large Internet Data centres because of Low Performance.

Well, welcome to the World of Comparison, the researchers believe that you have been dwelling in one for a long time now.

Let's get started and compare the different types of controllers and which is better and in which situation.

## 1. NOX

Nox is the tyro or the building block in the phase of OpenFlow controller. It provides the network control platform facility that actually gives a level notch programmable interface for the development control network apps and for managing purposes. The abstractive nature of NOX turns network into a software conundrum.

Before getting deeper, let's clarify what is NOX really:

The work was initiated by a company known as Nicira Networks which has now been acquired by VMware; alongside OpenFlow. There has been an introduction of multiple flavors and advancements in the NOX environment particularly giving rise to 3 separate lines:

1. **Classic:** It is widely used free software which was introduced in the year 2009 under the GNU General Public License.
2. **Original:** It can be said as the advancement of classic in a unique way. It is great performance in the metrics of speed and maintains excellent base for the

codes but has only support of C++ programming language and provides few applications support.

3. **POX:** It is considered a brother to the NOX family (or even sister, not to be offended in any manner). Python language is readily available source for coding here.

To be clear in the language, the reference of the term NOX only refers to the original one and not the Classic (though they both are NOX) because there lies a certain amount of differences between both of them. Refer to Table 1 for clarity among the differences amongst the mentioned.

## NOX Architecture

Figure 3 elucidates the architecture of NOX controller. Research by Sridhar Rao (2014) supports that the central core of NOX gives helper methods, like threading and event engine, along with network packet process apart from the OpenFlow API for communicating with the switches and input output support.

The first layer of the architecture has Core, Net, Web apps. With the advancement of NOX architecture there are only 2 core applications, which include switch and OpenFlow. The network and web apps have been discontinued or let us say removed. The central layer has in-built components of NOX. The managers and dispatchers in the central layer are self-explanatory while the DSO i.e. the dynamic shared object scans the directory structure of any components being implemented as it is.

## Initiating NOX

The presumptions are that you run on a terminal in a linux machine. To start or to initiate NOX, the command ine should be within "build/src" directory. The statement to initiate the NOX is somewhat like below mentioned:

*Table 1. NOX versions comparisons*

|  | **NOX Classic** | **NOX** |
|---|---|---|
| Internal Applications | Simple Network Management Protocol | OpenFlow, Switch |
| Network Apps | Authorising, Routing, Managing | --- |
| Web Apps | Web server and various internet services | --- |
| Language(s) Available | C++ and Python | C++ Only |
| GUI | YES | NO |

*Figure 3. Architecture of NOX controller*

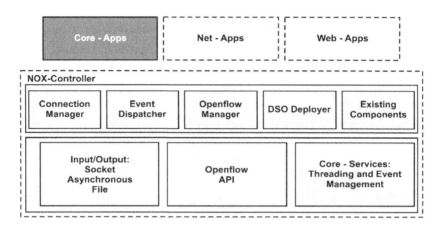

```
./nox_core [OPTIONS] [APP[=ARG[,ARG]...]]
[APP[=ARG[,ARG]...]]...
```

Now the upper code shows a generic way of initiating the controller, but if specifically you need to listen to incoming connections from suppose port 8080 refer to below code:

```
./nox_core -v -i ptcp:8080
```

No the central part of the controller is in place and the switches are also allowed to built a network with it but the NOX won't put on any implications on them till now. It is just to show how connection is established.

NOX provides a humungous amount of central traffic handling solutions. It provides control logic for traffic engineering, authenticating, accessing, and creation of virtual network, monitoring and report generation for diagnostics of the network. The irony of the facts is that it itself does not do one of those things instead it embarks it with a programmable view to these tiny pieces that can easily do there required functions. The only thing left out is in the scenario is that what all components should NOX use, to run on.

Consider the below code: 6633(It refers to OpenFlow protocol port)

```
./nox_core -v -i ptcp:6633 switch
```

Will make the switches act as regular MAC learning switches.

## Developing Application in NOX (Developed in C++)

For creating the extension of this controller we will write the below switch code. What we mean by creating a switch explicitly refers to:

- Get the grip over Media access control referral
- Shows the path to the address if it is known where to reach
  So the app we develop would be rather inclined to know the below scenarios:
- As soon as a switch connects
- As soon as a switch disconnects
- Message-Ins.

The Object oriented features being exploited rigorously here uses the class of switch to show a simple component. Every component is designed in the same manner.

```
Class Switch: public Component
```

A mapping is required in form of table to store the media access control's addresses.

```
Mac-table-map  mac-tables;
```

The mac-table-map is actually a hashing that maintains the media access control addresses, which maps to the paths identities.

The job of a particular component is to instill properties that are present in the classes', include a constructor in similarity with the hub's one and insert a macro named REGISTER_COMPONENT by the support of outside bonds to get dynamic linkage .

```
REGISTER_COMPONENT (Simple-components-factory<Switch>, Switch);
```

While making directory structure, which is statutory task while building a controller requires it to have meta. Json file right in the place where it itself is. (Sridhar Rao, 1994).As the system boots the controller first determines the location of the json file and uses it to find out which fields are active and about their relative dependencies. It is exactly same as system looks for operating system in the ROM during the boot up process.

There are two main methods which are called up at load time of the controller and those are configured and install and in that particular order only. Consider a simple analogy as to why configure first and install second. E.g. A person bought a new router and new mobile phone. The man believes that his Internet service provider is a great well-wisher of his and will definitely provide him with high speed internet. Man starts his android phone and goes to play store and looks at a CCNA preparation app and thinks to install it. Just look back a moment and analyze. The router was bought but never configured by the official of ISP. The router is first configured and then only can we move further in the process of installing apps or installing anything for that matter. So the configure and install methods initializes the events and event handlers over the network.

The apps developed all consists of the below methods:

1.   void configure();

The method below is generally used when we want to indulge for specific events. The OpenFlow switch registers itself for the 3 scenarios (as said above):

```
registers_handlers("Openflow_datapaths_join_event", handle_
datapaths_join);
registers_handlers("Openflow_datapath_leave_event",  handle_
datapath_leave);
registers_handlers("ofp_packet_in", handle_packet_in);
```

The appropriate stand is taken by the event handlers methods. The first two methods modify the mac-table entries accordingly. The message-in (appropriately packet-in) does the function of grasping the media access control address and inserting it into the flow table. Table 2 is the table that deals with application programming interfaces used in this particular event handler.

*Table 2. API for NOX operations*

| Operation | API |
|---|---|
| Packet from the Event Message | assert_cast<const v1::ofp_packet_in*>(ofe.msg) |
| Obtain Packet Information | v1::ofp_match flow; flow.from_packet(pi.in_port(), pi.packet()); |
| Create Flow mod | v1::ofp_flow_mod()..buffer_id(pi.buffer_id()) .cookie(0).command(v1::ofp_flow_mod::OFPFC_ADD).timeouts… |
| Set action in the flowmod | v1::ofp_action_output().port(out_port); |
| Send packet | Openflow_datapath& dp = ofe.dp; dp->send() |

2.    void install();

What all is to be done by the install function is completely related to the app which is going to utilize it. The switch app mentioned earlier has no function in the install operation. Otherwise any other app could start up a process or build internal structure directories etc.

To be precise and clear, this controller is free (open source), which gives a comfortable, easy as well as an uncomplicated platform for building network control software in C++.

## 2. RYU

The discussion of certain characteristics of the Controller is a must before knowing its functions:-

1.    Ryu is written in Python
2.    It supports OpenFlow v1.0, v1.2, v1.3 and various Nicira modules.
3.    It also supports OpenStack (It is a set of software tools which are used for cloud computing i.e. think of it as the future of Cloud)
4.    The disadvantage stands at its performance, being written in python, it is not much faster, though light to implement but not highly scalable. Being written in python is actually not a disadvantage when seen through a single perspective. But as soon as comparison is made between the various parameters of a controller. RYU falls back because of the less scalability and swiftness.

In similarity to other SDN controllers, the RYU controller also can form and forward packets memos, can hear over any conversations made through asynchronous events like flow_removed, handle incoming and outgoing packets over the web and parse them simultaneously. Figure 4 clearly indicates the simple architecture of RYU.

## Working of RYU

In this module, a Ryu application is written, that makes OpenFlow switches work as a data link layer.

Ryu application being a module of Python has the property of defining a sub-class 'ryu.base.app_manager.RyuApp', (Sridhar Rao,1994). The app manager chooses the first module by name if there are more than two such classes defined in a module. There is a concept of singleton classes which says that a class can only have a single object. Hence assistance is provided to only one object of this controller.

*Figure 4. Architecture of RYU*

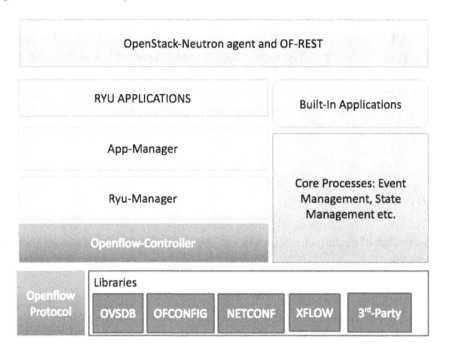

It inherits from the base class app_manager.RyuApp. The name of switch which we will refer further is HeySwitch.

```
from ryu.base import app_manager
from ryu.controller import ofp_event
from ryu.controller.handler import MAIN_DISPATCHER
from ryu.controller. Handler import set_ev_cls
class HeySwitch(app_manager.RyuApp):
def __init__(self, *args, **kwargs):
super(HeySwitch, self).__init__(*args, **kwargs)
```

Like a ticket is raised in a service station for getting our work done, similarly this app raises or gets an event. To raise event, apt base.app_manager function is called. A particular function controller.handler.set_ey_cls is used if the app wants to register to listen about particular events. This particular function is referred as decorator. A decorator deals with decorated function only. Primary parameter shows the most awaited event, starting the function call in return. The latter one also indicates the state but somewhat it is like a log to the switch. Consider a simple scenario where the controller and switch are under heated discussion or doing some interaction and the app wishes to ignore certain packet messages. So it calls the MAIN_DISPATCHER function as the latter parameter that specifies to be called after the interaction between the app and the switch is completed. What the example below is focusing on is app wants to know about message events, at each instance the controller receives a message, and a handler method is fired up. The below app is capable enough to forward a message to any port number regardless of the protocol instate.

Consider the below code:

```
set_env_cls(ofp_event.EventOFPPacketIn, MAIN_DISPATCHER)
def packet_in_handler(self, ev):
msg = ev.msg
dp = msg.datapath
ofp = dp.ofproto
ofp_parser = dp.ofproto_parser
actions = [ofp_parser.OFPActionOutput(ofp.OFPP_FLOOD)]
out = ofp_parser.OFPPacketOut(
datapath=dp, buffer_id=msg.buffer_id, in_port=msg.in_port,
actions=actions)
dp.send_msg(out)
```

Engage yourself on to packet_in_handler method . The set_env_cls application programming interface has the job to call in packet_in_handler which internally is called when a message/packet is received. The two parameters msg.datapath refers to the switch while the ev.msg refers to the packet_in data structure. Therefore the dp.ofproto presents the OpenFlow protocol negotiated between controller and switches. The incoming packet is parsed with ofproto_parser.

After attaining the packet_in msg, the job is to present it to all the working port using packet_out msg. A class named OFPAcionOutput works alongside packet_out message to mention the port number of the Layer 2 device from where you want to send your packet from. OFPP_FLOOD is used under the circumstance of giving it all or rather call broadcasting as the name suggests. OFPPAcket_Out class is responsible for the building of packet_in message from scratch. Now the switch and msg everything ready, all is left is to provide the path on which to carry using send_msg function with OpenFlow msg object, that enables controllers to create a packet and move it forward to the switch.

This finishes the process of writing a Ryu application. (Sridhar Rao, 1994). As Ryu application is nothing more than a python script which runs on interpreter, the file can be easily saved with any name and extension. This hypothesis is put forward in the assumption that above code is named HeySwitch.py, the code to run this particular app is: %ryu-manager HeySwitch.py.

Considering the open-source controllers like Ryu, it is comparatively a great piece as it has a huge set of features to choose from which is continuously in a growing state. Developers are instilling much more components and giving it high amount of abstractions and this area has been under research and is like a gold mine if highly researched. Ryu has also been used by commercial vendors, such as Pica8, in their solutions. Extremely big names in the face of controller business use Ryu.

## 3. POX

1.   It is also written in python.
2.   It supports OpenFlow v1.0 .
3.   It is very easy to program and building prototypes of control programs.
4.   The drawback is that it has low performance level.

### Working of POX Controller

- Fire up Mininet on a terminal window using the following command. This starts a network emulation environment to emulate 1 switch with 3 hosts. The switch tries to connect to port 6633 on localhost. Initially, there is no controller listening.

```
$ Sudo mn --topo single,3 --mac --controller remote --switch
ovsk
```

- Since POX does not support OpenFlow 1.3 yet, it is best to statically set the OpenFlow version of the OVS

```
$ sudo ovs-vsctl set bridge s1 protocols=OpenFlow10
```

- Next, start the POX Controller. Assuming that the main folder where POX is installed is /home/ubuntu/pox, the command below starts the controller by initiating the OpenFlow Protocol Handler.

```
$ cd /home/Ubuntu/pox && ./pox.py log.level
```

- The above command runs POX controller. This prints additional output of messages exchanged with the switch

```
POX 0.1.0 (betta) / Copyright 2011-2013 James McCauley, et al.
DEBUG:core:POX 0.1.0 (betta) going up...
DEBUG:core:Running on CPython (2.7.3/Sep 26 2013 16:35:25)
DEBUG:core:Platform is Linux-3.5.0-30-generic-x86_64-with-
Ubuntu-12.10-quantal
INFO:core:POX 0.1.0 (betta) is up.
DEBUG:openflow.of_01:Listening on 0.0.0.0:6633
INFO:openflow.of_01:[00-00-00-00-00-01 1] connected
```

- Next, check if the hosts in the mininet topology can reach each other

```
mininet> h1 ping h2
PING 10.0.0.2 (10.0.0.2) 56(84) bytes of data.
64 bytes from 10.0.0.2: icmp_req=1 ttl=64 time=49.1 ms
64 bytes from 10.0.0.2: icmp_req=2 ttl=64 time=46.3 ms
64 bytes from 10.0.0.2: icmp_req=3 ttl=64 time=29.1 ms
64 bytes from 10.0.0.2: icmp_req=4 ttl=64 time=42.9 ms
64 bytes from 10.0.0.2: icmp_req=5 ttl=64 time=26.2 ms
```

## 4. FLOODLIGHT

Flood light is an SDN Controller platform. It is apache-licensed, Java based, enterprise class controller and currently running on its version 4 . The underlying functionality of this controller includes Topology discovery, installation and deletion of a switch and statistical counting like packets or flow counting or port statistical query etc. It supports REST API's and therefore communicates with switches using the same. Being in Java, it has a great performance level .

The only drawback is, it is pretty hard to learn and comprehend as compared to other controllers.

*Table 3. POX: Packets parser*

| Events Generated From Messages From Switch | Packets Parsed by pox/lib |
|---|---|
| FlowRemoved, FeaturesReceived ConnectionUp, FeaturesReceived RawStatsReply, PortStatus PacketIn, BarrierIn, SwitchDescReceived, FlowStatsReceived, QueueStatsReceived, AggregateFlowStatsReceived, TableStatsReceived, PortStatsReceived | arp, dhcp, dns eapol, eap ethernet, icmp igmp, ipv4 llc, lldp, mpls rip, tcp, udp, vlan |

Now well we could have gone into the Frenetic and Pyretic controllers too but they are not only controllers but languages and controllers independently.

## FUTURE TRENDS

Automation could never cause any harm to an industry but the level to which it grabs labour opportunities is tremendous . What it implies is, SDN has a vast field of growth in data centres for managing traffic . Specific controllers which are more to open-source side can be developed for their usage, as many controllers are still on the enterprise and paid sides . In this growth, the plunging takes place in the jobs sector. Being more inclined to machines, people would be less needed. The pros and cons of any substance are present right in front . It is a matter of, how are they implemented in use . For e.g. A new SDN controller is developed which implements Haskell (Function oriented language) and runs great on a piece of hardware . The problem is it might not work for other hardware's. So in order to build a more sophisticated environment, usage of controller which is universal would be great instead of building so many separate controllers. Apart form it, their use should be focused on a closed domain so that they don't eat up all the job opportunities for the people. In order to use this architecture B2B security needs to be established from ground up .

## CONCLUSION

Definition as a logically centralized entity neither prescribes nor preludes implementation details of the controllers such as federation of multiple controllers, the hierarchical connection of controllers, communication interfaces between controllers, nor virtualisation or slicing network resources but it still gives a general idea as to where the controller stands in an SDN environment.

The upcoming days or TTL (time to live) in nerds language, for SDN completely depends on the level of understanding network managers and programmers and administrators are able to build. If given a chance in the industry like Google did, and succeeded with SDN, this technology can go berserk and take on the entire Tech industry. It is just a matter of time when people try to understand its utmost importance and give its privileges it deserves.

Not to worry if certain sections remained unclear while reading through, it might take some time to sink in. Going through the unit again would clear your views. Whenever you feel to drop out, remember this quote by Bruce lee,

*I am not scared of a man, who has practiced 10,000 kicks a single time, I am afraid of that man who has practiced a single kick 10,000 times.*

The more you read, the better you grow.

## REFERENCES

A & M. (2012, April). *Ten Things to look for in an SDN Controller*. Retrieved April, 2017, from http://www.webtorials.com/content/2012/08/2012-application-service-delivery-han

Controller Benchmarker. (2008). Retrieved from https://www. openflow.org/wk/index.php/Oflops

Franciscus, W. X., Gregory, M. A., Khandakar, A., & Gomez, K. M. (2017). Multi-domain Software Defined Networking: Research status and challenges. *Journal of Network and Computer Applications*. doi:10.1016/j.jnca.2017.03.004

H. (2012). Software Defined Networking (SDN): A Revolution in Computer Network. *IOSR Journal of Computer Engineering, 15*(5), 103-106. Retrieved from http://ict.unimap.edu.my/images/doc/ SDN%20IBM%20WhitePaper.pdf

Heller, B., Sherwood, R., & McKeown, N. (2012). The controller placement problem. *HotSDN, 12*, 1–6.

Jarraya, Y., Madi, T., & Debbabi, M. (2014). A Survey and a Layered Taxonomy of Software-Defined Networking. *IEEE Communications Surveys and Tutorials, 16*(4), 1955–1980. doi:10.1109/COMST.2014.2320094

Jarschel, M., Lehrieder, F., Magyari, Z., & Pries, R. (2012). A flexible OpenFlow-controller benchmark. *Software Defined Networking,* 48-53. doi:10.1109/EWSDN.2012.15

Kotani, D., Suzuki, K., & Shimonishi, H. (2012). A Design and Implementation of OpenFlow Controller Handling IP Multicast with Fast Tree Switching. *Applications and the Internet (SAINT), 2012 IEEE/IPSJ 12th International Symposium,* 60-67. doi:10.1109/SAINT.2012.17

OpenFlow Switch Consortium. (2017). Retrieved August 3, 2017, from http://www.openflow.org/

Rao, S. (2014, March). *SDN Series Part Four: Ryu, a Rich-Featured Open Source SDN Controller Supported by NTT Labs*. Retrieved May, 2017, from https://thenewstack.io/tag/sdn-series/

Voellmy, A., & Wang, J. (2012). Scalable Software Defined Network Controllers. *SIGCOMM, 12*, 1–2.

## KEY TERMS AND DEFINITIONS

**Floodlight:** It is slightly different in its demeanor in a way that it is a branch of the beacon controller and written in Java; hence, it supports object orientation and is platform independent and robust in nature. It supports only 1.0v of open flow and provides all the possible facilities as any other controller.

**NOX:** The very first of its kind in the open source controllers. It is a platform for traffic control over the network with a superior level of interface for the handling of the network control applications. It majorly had C++ support and came out in classic and original versions.

**OpenFlow:** An open source network protocol which is programmable in nature and directs and handles the traffic flow of the network. The SDN controller can run on multiple protocols but it is one of the most popular ones. It segregates the programming of the layer 2 and 3 devices from the hardware they are running over.

**POX:** This is equally important when it comes to defining the taxonomy of SDN controllers. Being the elder brother of NOX, it was written in python and was insanely helpful in building programs and code for controlling flow of packets.

**RYU:** An advancement to the *OX series of controllers. Though it also works on python but it supports all the versions of open flow and supports the open stack which is a set of software used for building cloud applications.

**SDN Controller:** Being the vortex of the SDN architecture, all the controller agents present in the devices answer to the controller which in turn enables intelligent networking by managing and handling the traffic flow of the network.

**Software-Defined Networking:** Architecture rather than a protocol. The purpose of this system is to provide dynamic path allocation to various network devices connected into the network.

# Chapter 6
# SDN Practical Orientation

**Lalit Pandey**
*Independent Researcher, India*

## ABSTRACT

*This chapter is focused on SDN practical approach with Cisco controllers APIC, APIC-EM, and the application programming interfaces with real-world benefits and challenges. The chapter uses Cisco SDN way of managing, administering, maintaining, and implementing platforms using an external tool. This chapter will also discuss the controller API structures, management model of the controller, and using POSTMAN tool to push API requests and talk to the APIC controller. The chapter also discusses some of the important APIC EM applications like PnP, Easy QoS, IWAN, etc.*

## INTRODUCTION

SDN is an Innovative technology that enables us to control, manage, Automate & Orchestrate the underlying resources by abstracting the management and Control plane from the Individual devices to the Controllers and by introducing an abstraction that decouples the control from the data plane.

Controller (Intelligent Software/Application) has the visibility of the complete network with decision making authority and all the hardware simply forwards the packets based on the controller's Instructions.

Software Defined Networking is changing the way we design and manage our networks. Data Plane has been completely separated from the Control & Management Plane of the controller (Darabinejad, Rasoul, Fayyeh, 2014). This open source controller can be managed with our own customized software on the well defined Application Programming Interfaces (APIs) called as Northbound APIs (Xia, Wen,

DOI: 10.4018/978-1-5225-3640-6.ch006

Foh, Niyato, & Xie, 2015). These are the specific APIs that are opened from the controller to be managed with the customized software and it pushes the configuration further to the devices that the controller manages with its southbound APIs.

Devices will no longer be configured or Managed with their local management. It is all done by the controller in a programmatic way, not prone to human errors. Time to Provision Applications, Configurations, deployments tasks have been reduced from days to minutes. SDN is also an answer to the Rapid changes to the network configurations through the predefined scripts and with the customized scripts for our customized tasks (Programmatic Approach to configurations).There is a lot of administrative overhead to the overall datacenter and still there is a chance to configure at least one of the datacenter device incorrectly as the configuration & Implementation need proper planning of the overall network.

## SOME OF THE SDN REAL WORLD BENEFITS IN TODAY'S IT

1. Rapid reconfiguration of the devices.
2. Abstraction of the Infrastructure.
3. Automation & Orchestration.
4. Devices Programmability.
5. Application level Enhanced visibility.
6. Handling unpredictable traffic Patterns.
7. Centralized management approach to the system using Controllers.
8. Reduced Capital & Operational Expenses.
9. Traffic Optimization.
10. Management of the Open Source system with Northbound & Southbound API (Application Programming Interfaces).
11. Better Granular Security.
12. Extensibility
13. Inbuilt Security because of the White List Model.

The programmatic approach is used to simplify operations with automation & Orchestration of the dynamic network & Application oriented Infrastructure.

## TRADITIONAL APPROACH

Network architectures that combine control plane and data plane functions in a single device like a Router or a Switch. It is an element of a device that defines the Interaction with Its neighbors (Haleplidis, Pentikousis, Denazis, Salim, Meyer,

& Koufopavlou, 2015). There are a number of Control Plane Protocols like OSPF -Open Shortest Path First, BGP - Border Gateway Protocol and Layer 2 Protocols like Spanning Tree Protocol. These protocols are like a brain to the network that gives much stability to the network and pose limitations at the same time due to its dependency on the static metrics defined like Bandwidth, Hop Count and do not provide the application level visibility. Security is another concern in the traditional network architecture which depends on the Black List Model which says that everything is allowed by default and we configure the network as per our security requirements and allow/deny specific ports/protocols between different IP Subnets through access lists. Maintenance of the static access list entries on Individual router & switches is not that easy and isolating issues/troubleshooting network by investigating through a list of entries on every Individual device is another challenge now a days.

Many data plane functionality & features like QOS (Quality of service), ACL (Access-list), NAT (Network Address Translation), Vlan (Virtual Lan) are static in nature and depends on the device specific configurations. Additionally the configuration has to be done manually on individual devices which limit the scalability. Configurations & management are more prone to human errors which results in network down situations. Isolating issues is becoming more complex in bigger & complex networks due to the lack of visibility into the Infrastructure & Applications.

## OPERATIONAL CHALLENGES

1.  Human Errors.
2.  Provisioning & de-provisioning.
3.  Manual Configurations on devices.
4.  Integration with L4-L7 Devices.
5.  Lack of Application Level Visibility.
6.  Verification of the configurations takes a lot of time.
7.  Rapid Reconfigurations of the device for frequent changes in the network.
8.  Isolation of operational Issues.
9.  Layer 2 Protocols configurations, management & troubleshooting.
10. No Inbuilt security availability – Everything is allowed by default.
11. Limitations posed by the existing features & Protocols due to their static behavior.
12. Les Granular Control over the network.

Every vendor has its own way of automating & orchestrating most of the frequent operational tasks with their own controllers and eventually reducing the operational expenses. Different vendors are creating their own overlay solution to minimize network overhead and have the visibility of the architecture at the same time. Some of the vendors have their own underlay solution as well.

Cisco defined the datacenter Automation & Orchestration with ACI (Application Centric Infrastructure) with application level visibility as well as built-in tools for more granular policy, micro segmentation & Security.

This solution has a tight Integration between the underlay and the overlay solution built around 9K Series of Cisco nexus switches connected in a mesh fashion (Leaf Spine architecture). Management plane is abstracted from the fabric (Leaf Spine Nodes) to the controller known as Application policy Infrastructure controller (APIC).

APIC is software on UCS C Series Server with a locked down completely encrypted image. Application policy Infrastructure controllers are configured in cluster always. These controllers are synchronized controllers in cluster that provides the visibility, application deployment, fabric management, health monitoring, and policy management for the multitenant ACI environment.

Multitenant concept has been introduced in most of the IT Solutions to segregate the policies, configurations etc. For a provider environment, different tenants can be created for different organizations. Different tenants can be created for different departments for enterprise environment based on security zone. Tenant is more of a unit of Isolation and this is configured as per the organizational requirement and practices.

ACI has four types of tenants:

1. **User Tenant:** Configured by the administrator as per the organization's requirement for segregating policies that govern the operations of web, database & Applications.
2. **The Management Tenant:** This is system provided tenant however this tenant can be configured by the fabric administrator.
3. **Common Tenant:** This is also a system provided tenant and can be configured by the fabric administrator.
4. **Infrastructure Tenant:** System provided but can be configured by the fabric administrator. This tenant governs the operation of Infrastructure resources such as VXLAN overlay network etc.

Two types of policies within the ACI fabric:

1. **Fabric Policies:** Policies that govern the operation of the fabric ports including the fabric configuration like Border Gateway Protocol (BGP), Network Time Protocol (NTP), Intermediate System-to-Intermediate System Protocol (IS-IS) etc.

2. **Access Policies:** Policies that govern the operation of the access ports which gives the connectivity to the underlying resources like compute, storage, virtual machines, Hypervisors, Network, End Points etc.

## APPLICATION CENTRIC INFRASTRUCTURE

The transformation from the traditional methods to cloud approach increases the requirements for flexible, programmable & scalable Infrastructure (Jain & Paul, 2013). ACI changes the way we use our datacenter/Infrastructure. Conventional approach was based upon the Imperative Model which means that we manage/support what our network devices do and we expect them to follow as per the configurations. ACI uses a declarative Model where we mention our expected result and the fabric does the work to provide that end expected result.

ACI is a combination of Application Policy Infrastructure Controller (APIC) & 9K Platform. ACI is a centralized approach to the fabric (Leaf & Spine Fabric) including automation & Orchestration with application level visibility, policy driven approach and security. APIC is the centralized controller where the management has completely been abstracted from the fabric (Leaf & Spine 9K Switches) and gives the complete visibility with inbuilt tools. ACI is built around the white list Model which

*Figure 1. Application centric infrastructure*

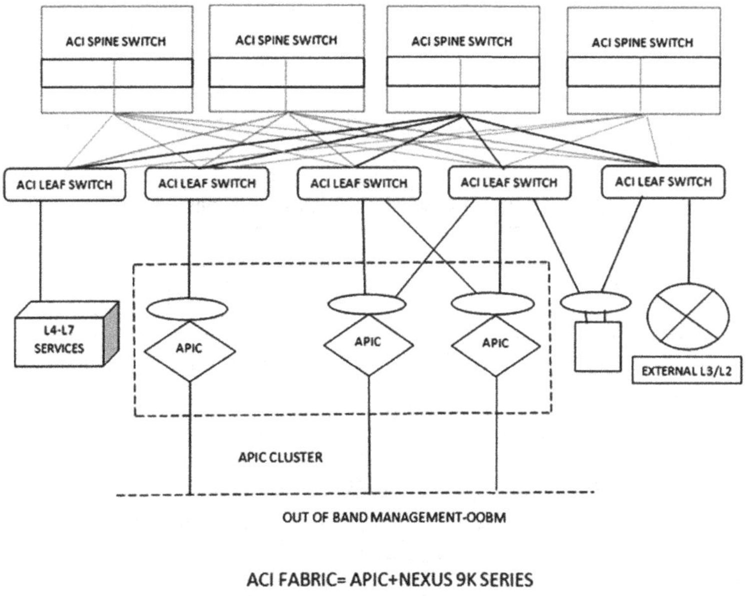

says that everything is denied by default and we have to have a contract between the two EPGs (End Point groups) to allow all traffic or specific port/protocols between two End Point Group (EPG).

ACI provides a scalable, multi-tenant, programmable & policy driven Infrastructure where the end point connectivity is governed & controlled by the Application centric policies on a stateless hardware. ACI views the leaf & spine architecture from application's standpoint and connect various end point groups using contracts over non-blocking penalty free overlay network.

Application centric Infrastructure Controller do not operate in the data path of the fabric which means that even in the absence of the controllers the data path will not be affected. The fabric consists of 40 Gbps. High bandwidth links between leaf & Spine Switches with no link connecting between Leaf to Leaf or Spine to Spine. 9k platform switches – 9500 & 9300 Series Nexus Switches that operates either in NXOS Mode or ACI mode.

## Features That Define APIC

1. APIC is the controller for the ACI Fabric.
2. APIC is not under the data path of the fabric.
3. APIC is not the control plane of the ACI Infrastructure.

*Figure 2. Application policy infrastructure controller*

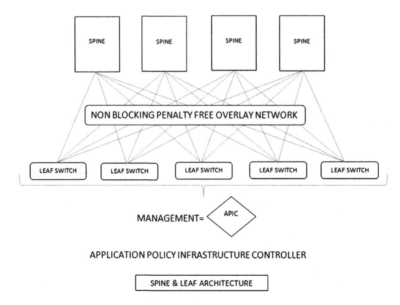

*Figure 3. Spine leaf topology*

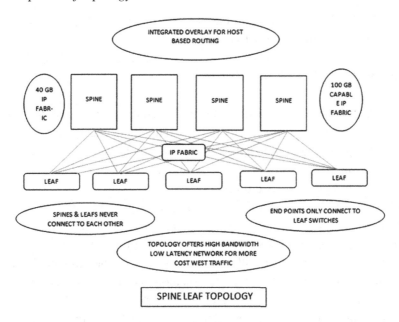

4.   APICs are minimum set of 3 synchronized, replicated and highly redundant cluster controllers on UCS C Series server.
5.   APIC is the controller where the entire management of the fabric is abstracted.

ACI policy model approach automatically provides the policies in the ACI Infrastructure so when the change occurred to the fabric APIC applies that change to the ACI Policy Model, the policy model afterwards initiates the change to the managed endpoint. It also gives the ability to integrate the Layer4 –Layer7 services either in unmanaged or managed way with device packages available.

There are three primary ways to access the APIC Controller:

*Figure 4. Policy based provisioning on stateless hardware*

**Policy Based Provisioning On Stateless Hardware**

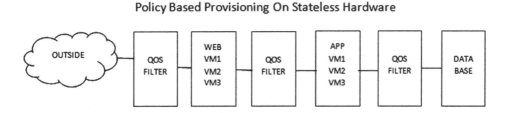

1. Graphical user Interface(GUI)
2. Application Programming Interface(API)
3. Command line Interface (CLI)

## Fundamental ACI Terminologies

1. **End Point Groups:** Container for application end points that allow the separation of policy, forwarding & security not based upon the vlan or subnets but based upon the grouping of the application endpoints instead.
2. **Bridge Domain:** Layer 2 container within the ACI fabric, Bridge domain may contain multiple subnets unlike vlan.
3. **VRF:** Private network or a Routing Instance.
4. **Tenant:** Logical Container for different organizations, security Space, Departments or as per the Infrastructure Isolation requirements.
5. **Contracts:** Stateless firewall policies that defines the inbound & outbound permit & deny rules. Contracts are analogous to access control list in the conventional infrastructure with several advantages.
6. **Application Network Profile (ANP):** Group of EPGs with a contract between them that defines the connectivity and how the EPGs communicate.

Bridge domain is analogous to vlan in traditional concept but BD is a like a container for subnets. It can be defined to define a Layer 2 boundary and are Vxlan which

*Figure 5. Application network profile ANP*

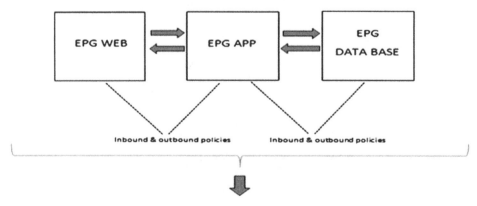

Group of EPGs and the policies that define the communication between end point groups is called as Application Network profile.

allows a device on subnet A to communicate directly to device on subnet B using vxlan bridging. And also allows device on subnet A to communicate to the device on subnet B in a different vxlan using vxlan routing so the IP address is irrelevant as the routing is host based.

In Figure 6, Within ACI Fabric there are two customers, Customer A & Customer B. Customer A and Customer B are two tenants in application centric Infrastructure. Development and Production are two different VRFs as a part of the customer A environment. There is a Development bridge domain under VRF A and has a single subnet A. There is also a Production BD under VRF B which has two subnets part of the same bridge domain under the same VRF.

Customer B is Tenant B in ACI and has only one VRF C which is application VRF. There are two applications BD with only a single subnet.

Cisco ACI enables to integrate physical and virtual workloads in highly programmable and multi- hypervisor environment and multi-Tenant environment. It behaves as a single big switch with spines as the fabric modules and leafs as the line cards of a single big modular chassis switch. Adding more leaf is like adding more line cards for end points connectivity and adding more spines is like adding more backplane bandwidth to the switch.

## ACI Fabric Inside

ACI fabric has IS-IS as the routing protocol which helps to advertise VTEP IDs and loopbacks to create tunnels from every leaf switch to all other nodes within the fabric.

Infrastructure VRF is used by the management network for in-band communication between Controller APIC and Switches. Out of band management OOB is through the management ports to access the APIC cluster.

*Figure 6.*

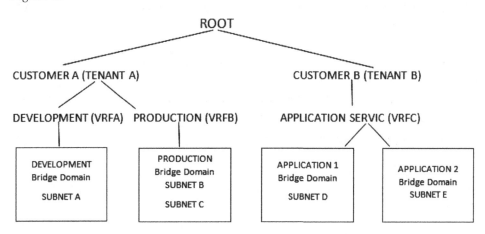

## ACI REST APIs

Representational state transfer (REST) architecture is based on a set of principles that supports cloud platforms which is simple, fast & light weight approach. ACI API is REST based. As APIC is designed for the programmability, It accepts & returns HTTP/HTTPS messages that contain JSON - JavaScript Object Notation or XML- Extensible Markup Language documents. Any programming language can be used to generate messages however like python.

REST Application Programming Interface is the programmatic Interface to the management Information tree (MIT), a hierarchical tree structure of managed objects. Rest methods like GET, POST, and DELETE are supported through APIs.

GET – Nullipotent Method (Does not make any changes even If It is called multiple times) – Read only method

POST, DELETE - Idempotent Method (No additional Effect even If It is called more than once with the same input parameters)

## MANAGEMENT INFORMATION MODEL

Hierarchical tree structure of managed objects which can be physical or a logical component of the ACI Fabric that are arranged in parent & child nodes fashion.

Every managed object in the Management Information tree are not created by the users, some are automatically created by the ACI Fabric.

Application programming Interface exposes full access to the APIC for management, automation, operation, deployment, configuration & a lot more with the REST based approach that Interacts with the APIC which further Interacts with the fabric.

There are lot of tools & application available to allow interaction with the Application programming Interface of the controller. We will be using POSTMAN to Interact with APIC APIs (Google Chrome Application to push messages to the controller).

Postman is a REST Client that runs as an application inside the Chrome browser and useful application to Interacts with REST APIs of the controller.

Format representation of REST commands, some of the calls may not need the payload and we are using either Java Script Object Notation (JSON) or XML for the body or payload of the REST API call:

```
<HTTP verb (GET, POST, PUT, DELETE)> <URI>
{
```

```
    JSON or XML Body If Required
}
```

Rest Call to the controller IP address using method Post to login into the APIC

```
POST https://<IP-of-APIC>/api/aaaLogin.json
{
    "aaaUser": {
        "attributes": {
            "name": "Username of the APIC",
            "pwd": "APIC Password"
        }
    }
}
```

POSTMAN Tool is used to send API requests. In the below method POST method has been used highlighted in Orange, based on Java Script Object Notation (JSON) as its body. Once the "Send" is clicked, It returns a response code that confirm If the REST Call is successful.

If the response code is a well known value of 200, It indicates the REST call is received and processed and a response is returned.

Common status codes in REST Architecture:

1. Status okay (200).
2. 201 Created
3. 202 Accepted
4. 400 Bad Request
5. 404 Not Found

*Figure 7.*

137

6.   408 Request Timeout
7.   500 Internal Server Error
8.   503 Service Unavailable
9.   502 Bad Gateway
10.  501 Not Implemented

Refresh messages are required to maintain the authenticated session with the APIC Controller before the timeout period. In order to send the refresh message, following execution is needed:

```
GET    https://<IP-of-APIC>/api/aaaRefresh.json
no payload
```

This should send the status back as status okay (200).

## Create a Tenant and VRF

After we have logged into the APIC (Controller), with the following API request, VRF named "VRFSales" will be created with the Tenant name as "TenantSales". VRF is also called as Private Network in ACI environment.

```
POST https://<IP-of-APIC>/api/node/mo.json
{
    "polUni": {
        "attributes": {}
          "children":[{
              "fvTenant": {
                  "attributes": {
                      "name": "TenantSales"
                  }
                  "children": [{
                      "fvCtx": {
                        "attributes": {
                            "name": "VRFSales "
                        }
                      }
                  }]
              }
```

```
        }]
    }
}
```

Tenant is actually a child of the overall ACI system known as the 'Policy Universe' (polUni).

## Authentication

REST API username and password based authentication uses following subset of request URIs:

DN Targets with a POST operation

1.   aaaLogin
2.   aaaLogout
3.   aaaRefresh

Payload contain XML or JSON body & the response to the POST operation will contain an authentication token as a cookie header and and an attribute to the **aaaLogin (Subset of URI)** object in the response named token. Subsequent operations on the REST API can use this token value as a cookie named APIC-cookie to authenticate all future requests.

*Figure 8.*

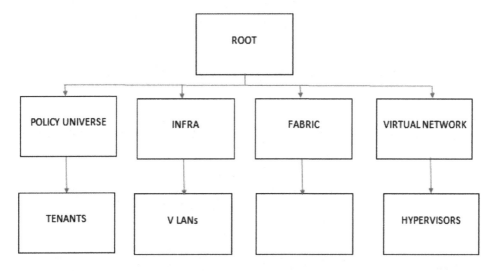

# APPLICATION CENTRIC INFRASTRUCTURE CONTROLLER: ENTERPRISE MODULE

APIC-EM is for the user centric Infrastructure for Enterprise Module – ISR, ASR, Catalyst, Nexus 7k, Nexus 5K, WLAN etc.

APIC-EM is based upon the Cisco DNA – Digital Networking Architecture which delivers the automation & orchestration to the enterprise branch campus & Wide area network WAN.

APIC-EM is software defined networking way to automate the network deployments, Configurations & providing the traffic control optimization at the same time. Controller is the centralized management where we mention what end result we expect and controller does the rest of the work. APIC-EM is neither the control nor the data plane of the devices (Switches, Routers etc).It is more of management of the end devices that collects the topology Information, Visibility of the entire network and can be used to manage the hardware, push configurations to the devices and automates the enterprise Infrastructure.

*Figure 9.*

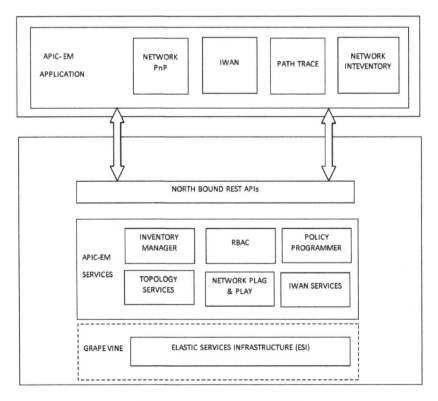

CISCO APIC EM (SDN CNTROLLER) - ENTERPRISE

APIC-EM has its APIs exposed as northbound APIs – Application programming Interface to get the controller controlled by the Cisco or third party software / applications and Its south bound Application programming Interfaces that controls the devices managed by the APIC-EM such as ISR Routers, ASR, Nexus 7K, Nexus 5k, Wireless Access Points etc. Deployments, Implementations, Configurations & most of the production frequent operational tasks is automated, efficient & programmable and time to perform the activities has been reduced from days to hours to minutes.

Controller not only automates our Infrastructure but it also gives the complete visibility into our network.

## Operational Challenges

1. Human Errors.
2. Provisioning & de-provisioning.
3. Manual Configurations on devices.
4. Lack of Network Visibility.
5. Verification of the configurations takes a lot of time.
6. Rapid Reconfigurations of the device for frequent changes in the network.
7. Isolation of operational Issues.
8. Les Granular Control over the network.
9. Keep the consistent configuration.
10. Dynamic policies as per the requirement.
11. Simplifying the overall network.
12. Network deployment automation.

APIC EM deployment can be Single host deployment or Multi Host deployment:

- **Single Host:** Virtual IP will not be configured in this case. All ingress requests into controller APIC EM will be through host IP. Deployment model can be changed from single host to multi host in future.
- **Multi Host:** Virtual IP will be configured and this IP will be the cluster IP of the controller (APIC EM Cluster) and all inbound requests into controller will not be through the host IP, this will be rather through the virtual IP.
- **APIC EM Support for Northbound and Southbound Application Programming Interfaces:** The REST based Northbound APIs can be used to control and manage the network through HTTPS with HTTPs methods (GET, PUT, POST, DELETE). This also ensures secure and programmatic control over the network.

Southbound APIs uses CLI, Telnet, SSH, SNMP as a protocol to communicate to the devices (Hardware) and manage the end network downstream.

## APIC-EM APPLICATIONS

- **Plug-and-Play (PnP):** The APIC-EM Controller's PnP (Plug and Play) application delivers on ZTD (Zero Touch Deployment) for Cisco Enterprise Network routers, switches and wireless controllers.
- **Easy QoS:** The APIC-EM Controller's Easy Quality of Service application provides a simple way to classify and assign application priority.
- **Intelligent WAN (IWAN) Application:** The APIC-EM Controller's Intelligent WAN (IWAN) application automates the configuration of advanced IWAN features on Cisco 4000 Series Integrated Service Routers.

## PATH TRACE

The APIC-EM Controller's Path Visualization application greatly eases and accelerates the task of connection troubleshooting.

### Plug-and-Play (PnP)

To deploy 200 new Cisco devices including routers, switches, access points etc., every Cisco device needs to be configured with a base configuration & the software needs to be upgraded. Task would take at least a week to get this done manually on every router, switch, Wireless Access Point .

Plug & Play (PnP) Application of Cisco APIC-EM will reduce the time to configure the above task from a week to hours by uploading the Image & the base configuration to APIC-EM & pushing this configuration to the network devices with PnP Server and agent communication.

Network Plug and Play is fast, consistent and secure method of device management. This gives us the leverage for Zero touch deployment and provisioning of the enterprise Infrastructure. It uses secure HTTPS method to manage the network and push configurations and manages the network throughout for Routers, Switches, Access Points Etc. Administrator gets the visibility to continuously monitor the progress of the Installation, configurations, status Etc.

Network Plug n Play can be used for both Greenfield and Brownfield deployments. It uses a very simple Agent-Server communication concept for deployment.

## Communication Working Model

PnP agent runs on Cisco devices like on Router Switches and Wireless APs which helps to automate the deployment. Agent is embedded in IOS and it requests for IP and APIC EM address which it gets via DHCP. Communication is completely secure as it operates over https/tcp.

PnP Server runs on the controller – APIC-EM which is the centralized server for the entire enterprise Infrastructure. It manages the configuration files, Images files, devices licenses Etc. PnP is the protocol that runs between the PnP agent and PnP Server.

APIC EM is the controller which is communicating to the end Cisco devices like Catalyst switches, ASR, ISR, Access Points etc with southbound APIs like CLI, PnP Protocol, SNMP etc. APIC EM northbound APIs can be used by the third party apps to manage APIC EM controller. Codes in programming languages like python, JSON can be used to manage the end network and communicate to the controller.

DHCP Option 63 and 43 is used for discovery.

Management of the devices with PnP is through the login to the APIC EM Controller and click on Network Plug and Play at the left hand side of the Dashboard.

## Easy QoS

APIC-EM can configure end-to-end QoS by providing the Cisco validated design features so that the provisioning & configuring QOS can be reduced from weeks to minutes without any human error or Involvement.

One of the options to configure the QOS end to end is with APIC-EM to categorize the applications as Business Relevant, Business Irrelevant and Default. QOS best practices are used to generate specific Network configuration

The other option is with the help of REST Application programming Interface.

## How Easily Does QOS Work?

Network Administrator initiated the intent to APIC EM QOS, the applications are continuously interacting with APIC EM-SDN Controller for Enterprise through northbound APIs and convey the application specific requirements and dynamic QOS requirements to the Controller (APIC EM).

Southbound application programming Interfaces converts the application/ platform dynamic QOS requirements to specific platform configuration to the existing Infrastructure.

## Intelligent WAN (IWAN) Application

IWAN Application can simplify the WAN deployments that has centralized policy automation engine which fully automates the provisioning of the WAN along with the rapid deployment of large number of datacenters or Sites. APIC-EM is built in with Cisco best practices for hybrid WAN leads to software defined WAN.

Using Cisco IWAN provides greater bandwidth to the branch office without using the expensive hardware and maintaining the security and efficiency at the same time. The two proposed primary IWAN Models are Dual Internet & Hybrid Deployment. IWAN is Software Defined WAN of Cisco which uses combination of two technologies DMVPN and PFR.

## DMVPN

Dynamic Multipoint VPN is a solution for building IPSec and GRE VPNs in a scalable and dynamic way.

## DMVPN Features

1.   Support for dynamic tunnel creation.
2.   Multipoint GRE Tunnel Interface.
3.   NHRP (Next Hop Resolution Protocol).
4.   One GRE link for the support of multiple GRE tunnels.
5.   Simplify the complexities of the configuration.

## Working of DMVPN

It works on the concept of Hub and Spoke technology. Hub is the NHRP Server of Hub-Spoke Concept and All the Spokes register with the HUB as their Clients. Spokes build a dynamic GRE tunnel with the hub only but not to the other spokes. When the packet has to be sent from one of the spoke to the other spoke. Spoke sends a packet to the private subnet behind another spoke. It gets the response from the NHRP Server (Hub) for the outside address of the destination spoke and then It creates a dynamic IPsec/GRE tunnel to the destination spoke and initiates the tunnel with the peer outside address. Now the dynamic spoke to spoke tunnel is built over mGRE (Multipoint Generic Routing Encapsulation Tunnel).This tunnel is entirely removed when the communication stop happening between the spokes.

# PFR (PERFORMANCE ROUTING)

There are lots of WAN challenges in today's WAN environment:

1.  Reliability of the available WAN links.
2.  Troubleshooting is getting more and more complex day by day.
3.  Lack of visibility into the entire Network Infrastructure and application level visibility.
4.  Bandwidth management.
5.  Degraded performance.

PFR can measure and select the best available path as per real time user defined policies and application level visibility into the network. It gives additional visibility into the traditional routing in addition to path selection. It helps PFR to identify the best path and selecting the best path and make routing adjustment by analyzing the real time performance metrics. Traffic load-balancing across different links by utilizing different link differently is one of the greatest feature of performance Routing PFR.

Performance Routing has two major components:

1.  Master Controller (MC): Apply verification, policy etc.
2.  Border Router (BR): Visibility into forwarding Path.

Optimized by some of the following factors:

1.  Jitter
2.  Delay
3.  Loss
4.  Throughput
5.  Cost

## Path Trace

Flow Analysis of APIC-EM or Path Trace allows path trace from one host to the other giving real time visibility into the entire path the packet takes to reach out to the destination and reverse path to see If It takes the same path to reach out to the source. This inbuilt tool gives the extra advantage to the network support team to troubleshoot the issue with more granular visibility into the network.

## Features

1.  It gives the ability to trace path to the destination IP address.
2.  Support for DMVPN
3.  Support for VRF Leaking & VRF Lite.
4.  Monitor performance for the application traffic.
5.  Path trace gives the trace result with the device health status (Memory, CPU etc)of every device along the path.
6.  Source and destination IP address can be provided along with the optional information like source and destination protocols and port numbers for path trace.
7.  It gives the enhanced flow visibility from the source to the destination.
8.  APIC EM continuously collects the network elements information through SNMP traps and stores in its database.

Cisco SDN Controllers like APIC and APIC EM are controllers to manage Datacenter and Enterprise architectures respectively. It also gives the leverage to manage these controllers through third party applications via northbound APIs. The tasks which used to take weeks to get implemented are deployed within minutes now. The overall benefit of using these controllers is to programmatically controlling the Infrastructure, centralized management and complete visibility along with quickly making the entire network ready for the applications to be deployed.

## CONCLUSION

This chapter primarily focusses on software defined network theoretical and practical approach. In order to take the practical approach we had proposed Cisco Controllers APIC, APIC-EM and the application programming Interfaces with real world benefits and challenges and their comparison with the traditional approach so adopted. This chapter focusses on managing, administering,maintaining & Implementing platforms using an external tool. This chapter also explain the structure and management model of API controller using POSTMAN tool to set up the communication

## REFERENCES

Chowdhury, N. M. K., & Boutaba, R. (2009). Network virtualization: State of the art and research challenges. *IEEE Communications Magazine*, *47*(7), 20–26. doi:10.1109/MCOM.2009.5183468

Chowdhury, N. M. K., & Boutaba, R. (2010). A survey of network virtualization. *Computer Networks*, *54*(5), 862–876. doi:10.1016/j.comnet.2009.10.017

Cisco. (2010). *Cisco visual networking index: Global mobile data traffic forecast update, 2009–2014*. Author.

Darabinejad, B., Rasoul, S., & Fayyeh. (2014). An introduction to software defined networking. *International Journal of Intelligent Information Systems, 3*(6), 71-74.

Erickson, D. (2011). *Open Networking Foundation Formed to Speed Network Innovation*. Portland, OR: Open Networking Foundation.

Feamster, N., Rexford, J., & Zegura, E. (2014). The road to SDN: An intellectual history of programmable networks. *Computer Communication Review*, *44*(2), 87–98. doi:10.1145/2602204.2602219

Fundation, O. N. (2012). Software-defined networking: The new norm for networks. *ONF White Paper, 2*, 2-6.

Gens, F. (2012). *IDC Predictions 2013: Competing on the 3rd Platform. Int*. Data Corporation.

Haleplidis, E., Pentikousis, K., Denazis, S., Salim, J. H., Meyer, D., & Koufopavlou, O. (2015). *Software-defined networking (SDN): Layers and architecture terminology* (No. RFC 7426).

Jain, R., & Paul, S. (2013). Network virtualization and software defined networking for cloud computing: A survey. *IEEE Communications Magazine*, *51*(11), 24–31. doi:10.1109/MCOM.2013.6658648

NFV-ISG. (2015). *White paper on Network Functions Virtualization, whitepaper3*. Retrieved from https://portal.etsi.org/Portals/0/TBpages/NFV/Docs/NFV_White_Paper3.pdf

## ADDITIONAL READING

Chowdhury, N. M. K., & Boutaba, R. (2009). Network virtualization: State of the art and research challenges. *IEEE Communications Magazine*, *47*(7), 20–26. doi:10.1109/MCOM.2009.5183468

Chowdhury, N. M. K., & Boutaba, R. (2010). A survey of network virtualization. *Computer Networks*, *54*(5), 862–876. doi:10.1016/j.comnet.2009.10.017

Feamster, N., Rexford, J., & Zegura, E. (2014). The road to SDN: An intellectual history of programmable networks. *Computer Communication Review*, *44*(2), 87–98. doi:10.1145/2602204.2602219

Jain, R., & Paul, S. (2013). Network virtualization and software defined networking for cloud computing: A survey. *IEEE Communications Magazine*, *51*(11), 24–31. doi:10.1109/MCOM.2013.6658648

Xia, W., Wen, Y., Foh, C. H., Niyato, D., & Xie, H. (2015). A survey on software-defined networking. *IEEE Communications Surveys and Tutorials*, *17*(1), 27–51. doi:10.1109/COMST.2014.2330903

## KEY TERMS AND DEFINITIONS

**ACI Controller:** A controller for ACI architecture.

**APIC-Enterprise Module:** A controller for enterprise network.

**Application Programming Infrastructure Controller:** A unifying point of automation and management for the application-centric infrastructure (ACI) fabric. It is Cisco propriety.

**Application-Centric Infrastructure:** An architecture with centralized automation and policy-driven application profiles.

**Dynamic Multipoint VPN:** It provides a secure network that is used for exchange of data between sites without passing the traffic through headquarter of VPN server or router.

**IWAN:** IWAN is an intelligent provided by Cisco for providing security and traffic control for WAN network.

**Virtual Routing Forwarding:** Technology that allows multiple instances of a routing table to exist in a router and work simultaneously.

# Chapter 7
# Simulation on SDN and NFV Models Through Mininet

**Premkumar Chithaluru**
*University of Petroleum and Energy Studies, India*

**Ravi Prakash**
*University of Petroleum and Energy Studies, India*

## ABSTRACT

*Mininet is a stage for working extensive systems on the assets of a finest single little framework or virtual machine. Mininet is made for initiating research in software-defined networking (SDN) and OpenFlow. Mininet permits executing predefined code intuitively on virtual equipment machine on a basic PC. Mininet gives an accommodation and authenticity at less cost. The auxiliary to Mininet is equipment test beds, which are quick and precise, yet extremely costly and shared. The other alternative is to utilize Mininet test system, which is low cost, yet some of the time moderate and requires code substitution. Mininet gives convenience, execution precision, and versatility.*

## INTRODUCTION

Mininet gives an immaculate virtual system, running genuine bit equipment and switch and application creating code on a solitary center machine (incorporates Virtual Machine and cloud or local) in division of seconds, with a little charge of amount should be focus on actual virtual System.

Mininet is utilizing for advancement of genuine applications, inventive educating and research and improvement as it offers simple connection with the system channel

DOI: 10.4018/978-1-5225-3640-6.ch007

*Figure 1.*

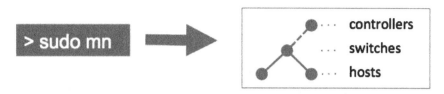

through the Mininet CLI (Command Line Interface) (and API), customization, speaking with others and execution on the genuine equipment to the current clients (Orfanidis C, 2016).

Mininet has been demonstrated an incredible approach to create, offer and explore different avenues regarding OpenFlow and Software-Defined Networking frameworks. It is legitimately created and upheld and is discharged under a lenient BSD Open Source permit. Clients are urged to contribute their code and bug/blunder reports fixes, documentation and whatever else which can enhance the framework equipment (Luo, Tie, Hwee-Pink Tan, and Tony QS Quek, 2012).

## DOWNLOAD/GET STARTED WITH MININET

Working with Mininet can be started by means of downloading a pre-bundled Mininet or Ubuntu Virtual Machine. The VM incorporates Mininet itself, all OpenFlow doubles and devices pre-introduced and modifications to the portion equipment design to help bigger/mass Mininet systems. One can continue by making any of the accompanying (De Gante, Alejandro, Mohamed Aslan, and Ashraf Matrawy, 2014):

**Choice 1:** Mininet VM Installation (simple or prescribed).
**Choice 2:** Native or latent Installation from Source.
**Choice 3:** Installation from Packages of Mininet bolstered for Ubuntu.
**Choice 4:** Upgrading a current Mininet Installation to framework.

### Option 1: Installation of the Mininet Virtual Machine (Easy, Recommended)

Mininet VM establishment is a very simple and he simplest and the most blame flexible technique for introducing Mininet. VM establishment should be possible by the following means (Sherwood, Rob, et al, 2009):

1. Download the Mininet VM picture and load that bundle into Machine.
2. Download and introduce a virtualization framework.
3. Among different potential outcomes, Virtual Box is prescribed in light of the fact that it is open source and takes a shot at OS X, Windows and Linux. In addition, there is advanced utilization of Qemu, also for the Workstation for Windows or Linux, so on for the VMware Fusion for Mac, or even the KVM for Linux OS.
4. Introduce a Sign up procedure for the Mininet-examine the list of mails, the hotspot for managing Mininet support services and dialog interface for the well-disposed Mininet group.
5. Using the VM Setup Notes sign into the VM and redo the coveted one.
6. Track the Walkthrough to get acquainted with the Mininet orders and its regular utilization.

## Option 2: Native Installation From Source

The choice functions admirably for nearby Virtual Machine or remote EC2 from amazon and local establishment as well. It expects the starting purpose of a new Ubuntu (or tentatively, Fedora) establishment.

It is emphatically prescribing running with later Ubuntu discharges as they bolster more up to date forms of Open vSwitch (Fedora likewise underpins late OVS discharges).

To introduce locally from source, the source code is required at first:

```
gite clone gite://gitehub.com/minnet/mininet
```

Note that the above gite order will look at the most recent and most noteworthy Mininet. On the off chance that the last labeled/discharged variant of Mininet or whatever other form is required particularly, it can be looked at unequivocally:

```
cd Minnet
gite tag # list available versions in the package
gite checkout -b 2.2.1 2.2.1  or use your installation version
cd..
```

After obtaining the source tree, the command for installation of Mininet is:

```
minnet/util/install.sh [options]
```

The regular install.sh options are as follows are:

- an: It introduces whatever is incorporated into the Mininet VM including the conditions such as Open vSwitch also the increases like the OpenFlow Wireshark dissector and POX. Of course, these devices are worked in catalogs made in the individual home registry.
- nfv: This option enables the Mininet, the OpenFlow reference switch, and Open vSwitch.
- s mydir: It is utilized before different alternatives to put source/assemble trees in a predefined index as opposed to in the concerned home registry.

Along these lines, any of the accompanying summons might be utilized:

- In order to have everything installed, type the command install.sh –a at the home directory
- Type the command install.sh -s mkdir –a to have everything installed using another directory for build
- install.sh -nfv command has to be keyed in for installing mininet + user switch + OVS from your home directory
- install.sh -s mkdir -nfv command has to be keyed in for installing install mininet + user switch + OVS from another directory.

The other accommodating alternatives e.g. introducing the OpenFlow Wireshark dissector can likewise be found, if it's not officially incorporated into the present rendition of Wireshark utilizing

```
install.sh -h | -o
```

Once the complete installation is done with, the basic Mininet functionality can be tested using:

```
$sudo mn --test pingall or #specific package to ping
```

## Option 3: Installation From Packages

In the event that another Ubuntu discharge is being run, one can introduce the Mininet bundles. Nonetheless, this may come about into a past adaptation of Mininet. Yet at the same time, it can be an exceptionally advantageous approach to begin.

On the off chance that, a more tested establishment of Mininet say 1.0 or Open vSwitch variation, which may have been executed and it put away in/usr/nearby is being updated and it must be guaranteed that any hints of more seasoned forms of Mininet and Open vSwitch from/usr/neighborhood/would have been evacuated:

```
sudo rm -rf /user/local/bin/mn /user/local/bin/mnexec \
/user/local/lib/python*/*/*minnet* \
/user/local/bin/ovs-* /user/local/sbin/ovs-*
```

Run the following command to confirm the Operating System:

```
lsb_release  -a | -l
```

Thereafter, only one of these commands and corresponding to the distribution has to be entered, to install the base Mininet package:

**Step 1:** For the Ubuntu 14.10 OS supporting Mininet 2.1.0, the command is:

```
sudo apt-get install mininet
```

or for the Ubuntu 14.04 OS supporting Mininet 2.1.0, the command is:

```
sudo apt-get install mininet
```

or for the Ubuntu 12.04 OS supporting Mininet 2.0.0, the command is:

```
sudo apt-get install mininet/precise-backports
```

After this has been completed, Open vSwitch-controller should be deactivated if it is installed and/or executing:

```
$sudo service OpenvSwitch-controller stop
$sudo update-rc.d OpenvSwitch-controller disable
```

Now, the Mininet has to be tested as follows:

```
$sudo mn --test pingall # or specific package to ping
```

In case, there is a complaint of Mininet about the Open vSwitch not working, there is a need to reconstruct its kernel module. So, it should be restarted with the following,

```
$sudo dpkg-reconfigure OpenvSwitch-datapath-dkms
$sudo service OpenFlow-switch restart
```

On the off chance that one wishes to experience the Mininet walkthrough and it is required to get the new extra programming introduced. To introduce the OpenFlow reference switch, reference controller and Wireshark dissector, there are some associated charges

```
gite clone gite://gitehub.com/minnet/mininet
mininet/util/install.sh -fw
```

## Option 4: How to Upgrade to Your Mininet Installation

There are numerous methods. You can run these commands, in case there are not any changes to the Mininet:

```
cd mininet
gite fetch
gite checkout master    # Or a specific version like 2.2.1
gite pull
sudo make install
```

As another contrasting option to sudo make introduce and sudo make create can likewise be attempted which can make typical connections from/client/python/... to the source tree.

It must be noted that this will cause Mininet to redesign itself; whatever other segments, for example, Open vSwitch and so forth can be overhauled independently according to the necessity.

## Mininet Sample Workflow

One can rapidly make, collaborate with, redo and share a product characterized organize model and gives a reasonable way to running on framework equipment using Mininet. The customary Mininet work process is being shown here,

In any case, in the Mininet walkthrough, the OpenFlow instructional exercise, and Mininet documentation, lot of extra subtle elements can be found

## Creating a Network

Using one command, the entire network can be can be formed, for example:

```
sudo mn --switch ovs --controller ref --topo tree, depth=4,
fanout=16 --test pingall
```

The over one begins a system with a tree topology of depth4 and fan-out 16 (i.e. 128 hosts associated with 12 switches or all the more relying upon organize territory) utilizing Open vSwitch switches under the control of the OpenFlow/Stanford reference controller, it runs the pingall test to check availability between each combine of hubs in the system.

## Collaboration With a Network

Mininet's CLI permits to control, and deal with the whole virtual system from a solitary comfort e.g. the accompanying CLI charge advises have h2 to ping the IP address of the host h2.

```
mininet> h2 ping h3 or # which host to ping
```

On a virtual host machine, any available Linux command or program can be executed. A web server can be easily started on one host machine and an HTTP request can also be made from the second host machine:

```
mininet> h2 python -m SimpleHTTPServer 80| or #which port no is
defined to system >& /tmp/http.log &
mininet> h3 wget -O - h2
```

## Involvement of a Network

Mininet is spread as a virtual machine (VM) iso picture having all the all conditions introduced some essential priori which can keep running on basic virtual machine screens, for example, VMware, Xen and Virtual Box. It's giving a super helpful holder to dissemination/sharing. Once a model is produced, the Virtual Machine iso picture might be conveyed to others to run, look at and adjust. A total and compacted Mininet VM is around at least 1 GB.

On the off chance that one is perusing about Software-Defined Network, he/she may get a kick out of the chance to have the capacity to click, download and run an absolutely real case of the machine/framework and in such cases to building up his very own Mininet variant framework can be performed to be imparted to others as well.

## Successively on Hardware

Once an outline/show is imitated effectively running on Mininet, it can be sent/executed on equipment for general/genuine utilize, testing and estimation on existing system topology.

To effectively executing port to equipment on the most readily accessible, each Mininet-copied segment/hub must be responding in an indistinguishable route from its closest genuine one. The virtual/contemporary topology should coordinate the genuine one. Virtual Ethernet arrange sets should and must be supplanted by interface level Ethernet network and number of Hosts copied as procedures ought to be supplanted by has with their own/self OS picture. What's more, each/every copied OpenFlow switch ought to be displaced by a physical one arranged to point to the controller and in addition, the controller requires no change. At the point when Mininet is being run, the controller "sees" a genuine system of switches are made plausible by an intercede with very much characterized state semantics is to be accessible.

## SDN Mininet Exercises

This activity shows most Mininet orders, and additionally its perplexing use working together with the Wireshark dissector.

The channel expects the base framework is the Mininet Virtual Machine or a local/detached Ubuntu establishment with the in introduction of all OpenFlow instruments and Mininet.

The whole procedure should take under 60 minutes.

Part 1:

- Every day the usage of Mininet execution is to be checked
- Display Startup Options to be executed
- Start Wireshark board
- Interact with Hosts and Switches in the system
- Test availability for checking in a system
- Run a straightforward web server and customer for network is built up or not.
- Cleanup/clear

Part 2:

- Prepare the Advanced Startup Options.
- Regression Test to be implemented in a board.
- Creating a new topology with size and parameters.

- Link varieties to be screened.
- Adjustable Verbosity in a both hosts.
- Custom Topologies to be delineate.
- ID = MAC is a character/check
- XTerm Display to be available.
- Other Switch Types must be checked.
- Mininet Benchmark must be accessible.
- Everything in its own Namespace (client switch for customer or server)

Part 3:

- The Command-Line Interface (CLI) of Mininet to be executed
- Showing the Options on screen.
- Execute the Python Interpreter.
- Confirmation of the network status.
- Execute the XTerm Display operations.

Part 4:

- Python API Examples can check.
- SSH daemon per each host.

## Part 1: Mininet Usage Daily

Firstly, make a note on charge language structure for this Exercise:

- $ Proceeds Linux orders that must be written as a shell script.
- Mininet> continues Mininet charges that must be specified at the Command Line Interface.
- # continues Linux orders that are written at a root/visitor shell incite

In each experiment, each charge ought to be written to one side of the provoke (and after that press return).

### *Display Startup Options*

The command line options for Mininet startup are to be followed.

Type the following commands for help message describing Mininet's startup options:

```
$sudo mn -h | -l
```

This command will give the typical usage of the listed options

## Start Wireshark

For viewing the control traffic using OpenFlow Wireshark dissector, first open Wireshark panel in the background:

```
$sudo Wireshark &
```

In the Wireshark filter box, enter this filter, and then click Apply:

```
Of
```

In Wireshark, click Capture, at that point Interfaces, at that point select Start on the loopback interface (lo).

For the present, there ought to be no OpenFlow bundles shown in the primary window.

Note: Wireshark stops as a matter of course in the Mininet Virtual Machine iso picture. Regardless of the possibility that it is not introduced in the framework alongside the OpenFlow module and one may introduce them two utilizing Mininet's install.sh script as takes after:

```
$ cd ~
$ gite clone https://gitehub.com/mininet/mininet#if it is not
there in the package
$ mininet/util/install.sh -w
```

On the off chance that Wireshark is introduced however the client neglects to run it (viz. he gets a blunder like $DISPLAY not set, please counsel the FAQ: https://gitehub.com/mininet/mininet/wiki/FAQ#wiki-x11-sending), setting X11 library up effectively empowers to run other Graphical User Interface codes and the xTerm terminal emulator which will be used later.

## Interact With Hosts and Switches

Begin an existing topology and execute the following the Command Line Interface:

```
$sudo mn
```

158

The regular topology is the insignificant/existed network topology, which allows one OpenFlow portion change associated with two has/numerous and incorporates the OpenFlow reference controller. The same ought to likewise be indicated on the order line with - topo=minimal is to be execute.

Other every topology is accessible out of the case which can be seen at the - topo segment in the yield of mn - h.

Other four elements, two host/hub forms, one switch process and one fundamental controller are currently executing in the Virtual Machine. The controller can be an external interface to the Virtual Machine. On the off chance that no particular test is passed as a parameter in the system, the Mininet Command Line Interface deals with.

In the Wireshark window, the switch of the kernel communicates with dependent controller.

Mininet Command Line Interface instructions to be exhibited through:

```
mininet> help
```

Command for exhibiting nodes:

```
mininet> nodes
```

Command for exhibiting links:

```
mininet> net
```

Command to exhibit dump information about all nodes:

```
mininet> dump
```

The switch and the two hosts listed can be seen here.

If the first character typed into the Mininet Command Line Interface is a host, switch or controller name, the command is executed on that node. Run a command on a host process:

```
mininet> h1 ipconfig -a
```

One can monitor the interface mechanism of the host h1-eth0 and loopback(lo). Because of being specific to the network namespace of the other node process, this interface (h1-eth0) is not observed by the default Linux system when ipconfig is executed.

In contrast, by default, the switch runs in the guest network namespace, so executing a command on the "switch" is the same as running it from a regular/ duplicate terminal:

```
mininet> s1 ipconfig -a
```

This shows when the switch has an interface along with the Virtual Machine's connection out with Ethernet (eth0) for host.

To emphasize the fact that the host have isolated network state, run Arp and route on both switch-s1 and host-h1.

There is a possibility to place in each host, the switch and controller in its own isolated home/root network namespace, but actually there is no benefit in doing so, unless one wants to duplicate a several number of multiple-controller networks. Mininet offers sustenance for this, which can be seen using the

```
        --innamespace option.
```

Only network virtualization is there, each host/node processes proof of the processes and directories e.g. display the list of processes which are running through a host process:

```
mininet> h1 ps -a | -h
```

This should be exactly same as master network namespace:

```
mininet> s1 ps -a | -o
```

Moreover, there is a possibility of using different process spaces with Linux containers, but at present Mininet does not do so. Having everything run in the "root" process namespace is flexible for debugging/executing, because it allows to see all of the running processes from the console using ps, kill, etc.

### Test Connectivity Between Hosts

To verify the ping from host 0 to host 1 the command is

```
mininet> h1 ping -c 1 h2
```

In the event that any string seems later in the order line with a hub name, the particular hub name is traded by its own particular IP address (which is going on here for have h2).

One may can watch OpenFlow control activity. The beginning host ARPs for the MAC address of the relating, which causes a packet_in message to go to the controller which thusly sends a packet_out message to surge the communicate bundle to different ports on the switch (just other information port here). The following host sees the ARP ask for and sends an answer which goes to the controller. The controller sends this to the underlying host and sends down a stream section.

As of now, the main host/hub has data of the MAC address of the following/comparing and subsequently, can exchange to ping through an Internet Control Message Protocol Echo Request. This ask for alongside its comparing answer from the following host goes to the controller board and result in a stream section pushed down (alongside the real bundles in general interims getting conveyed). Repeat the last ping command as follows.

```
mininet> h1 ping -c 1 h2 # or can change the hosts
```

One should see quite reduced ping time for the second attempt ($< 100\mu s$ or to some degree less too). A normal stream section covering Internet Control Message Protocol ping activity was already introduced in the switch, so there was not any creation of control movement, and the parcels instantly go through the switch.

A least complex approach to run this test is to utilize the Mininet Command Line Interface worked in pingall charge, which does an all-sets ping.

```
mininet> pingall # or specific host to ping
```

## Run a Simple Web Server and Client

In which order or application which are accessible to the basic Linux framework (or VM) and its record framework can be controlled by Mininet has. Indeed, one can likewise enter any bash charge, including work control (employments/occasion/undertaking, slaughter/fire, and so forth.)

Give us a chance to have a go at beginning a straightforward HTTP localhost server on h1, making a demand from have h2 and thereafter shutdown the localhost server:

```
mininet> h1 python -m SimpleHTTPServer 80 | # or in which port
assembled with host &
mininet> h2 wget -O - h1
mininet> h1 kill %python
```

Use the command below to exit from the Command Line Interface:

```
mininet> exit
```

## Cleanup

Suppose the Mininet crashes due to some cause, then clean it up:

```
$sudo mn -c
```

# Part 2: Advanced Startup Options

## Execution of Regression Test

One does not need to delete into the Command Line Interface, Self-contained regression tests can also get run by the Mininet.

Run a regression test is to be run, the command is as follows,

```
$sudo mn --test pingpair
```

The command has created a slight topology which set ongoing the OpenFlow reference controller, executed all-pairs-ping test, and keeps ongoing both the network topologies and the controller.

Additional valued test is iperf, which is as follows:

```
$sudo mn --test iperf
```

Same Mininet is created by this command which executes an iperf server on one host, executed an iperf client on the second host and linked the bandwidth realized.

## Changing Topology Size and Type

The regular topology of the system made contains a two changes associated with three hosts which can be effectively changed to an alternate/local topology with –topo and the particular parameters can be passed for the creation of the topology. For example, to check/run all-sets ping network with one switch and three hubs the following set of instructions are there:

Run a relapse test as per the following,

```
$sudo mn --test pingall --topo double,4
```

Additional exercise with a linear topology where every switch has a single host and entire switches connected in a line is as follows:

```
$sudo mn --test pingall --topo linear,4
```

Moreover, given parameterized topologies are one of Mininet's most valuable and dominant features.

## Link Variations

Mininet 2.0 permits a user to set link parameters which can be set routinely using the CLI:

```
$sudo mn --link tc, bw=20, delay=10ms
mininet> iperf
mininet> h1 ping -c10 h2
```

Assuming the rescheduling for every connection is 20 ms, at that point the round excursion time (RET) must be roughly 40 ms sometimes, since the Internet Control Message Protocol ask for crosses two connections (one to the change, one to the goal) and the Internet Control Message Protocol answer navigates two connections returning.

The connections can be improved utilizing Mininet's Python Application Program Interface. Be that as it may, until further notice we will most likely need to proceed with the activity.

## Adjustable Verbosity

The regular verbosity level is *info* which displays what Mininet is doing during the process of startup and shutdown. Comparing this with full debug output with the *-v param*.

```
$sudo mn -v debug
mininet> exit
```

Lots of irrelevant extra information will be displayed. Now make use of this command, it displays the Command Line Interface output and some more output:

```
$sudo mn -v output
mininet> exit
```

External to the Command Line Interface, additional verbosity levels can be made use of e.g. warning which is used with the regression tests to hide needless function output.

```
ID = MAC
```

Naturally, has begun with haphazardly appointed MAC addresses which makes troubleshooting/executing complex, on the grounds that each time the Mininet is made and the MACs has been changing, so corresponding the control movement with particular hosts/hubs to be extreme.

### XTerm Display

For more complex/regular debugging, Mininet is started which issues one or more xTerms.

To begin with an xTerm for every host as well as switch, run with the **-x** option:

```
$sudo mn -x
```

xTerms will be highlighted inside couple of moments with window/danger names set right away.

Besides, extra xTerms can likewise be raised on the other hand as demonstrated as follows.

As a matter of course, just the hosts are placed in a different namespace. The window for each change (proportional to a customary/root terminal) is superfluous, yet can be an advantageous place to run and leave up switch troubleshoot summons, for example, stream counter dumps.

Intelligent orders can likewise be go through xTerms e.g. In the xTerm labeled "switch: s1 (root/guest)" run is as follows (Costanzo, Salvatore, et al, 2012),

```
# dpctl dump-flows tcp: 127.18.0.1:8989) # or it varies
according to system topology.
```

Further, xTerm has made up with labeled "host: h1" to be executed follows,

```
#ping 10.2.0.0) # or it varies according to system topology.
```

Go to the previous switch-s1 and run it as follows:

```
# Dpctl dump-flows tcp: 127.0.0.1:6634 # or it varies according
to system topology.
```

One may see various stream sections now. Then again, the dpctl summon incorporated with the Mininet Command Line Interface can be utilized without requiring any xTerms, using the aid of IP and switch port.

By checking ipconfig value, it can be said whether an xTerm is in the root namespace. In the event that every supporter is demonstrated including Ethernet-eth0 as well, in the root namespace. Furthermore, its title must contain "(visitor)".

Exit from the setup, from the Mininet CLI as per the following command:

```
mininet> exit
```

The xTerm window will close routinely.

## Other Switch Types

Other switches can likewise be used e.g. to execute the usr-sparse switch:

```
$sudo mn --switch usr --test iperf
```

It must be noted that the below layers of the Transmission Control Protocol iperf announced transfer speed contrasted with what is seen before with the portion switch.

In the event that the ping test is made as demonstrated before, one may see a considerably higher postponement since the bundles must persevere through extra part to-client space moves. The ping time will be more factor, as the client space prepare speaking to the host might be planned in and out by the OS. Then again, the client space switch can be an extraordinary beginning stage for executing new usefulness, particularly where programming execution is not basic.

Another case of switch sort is Open vSwitch (OVS) is comes with the Mininet Virtual Machine. Additionally, actually iperf revealed Transmission Control Protocol data transfer capacity would be same to the OpenFlow bit module, yet perhaps quicker.

```
$sudo mn --switch ovsk --test iperf
```

## Mininet Standard

At the time of record work, the slash down in topology as follows:

```
$ sudo mn --test none
```

## The Self Name Space Includes (User/Root Switch)

By default, the nodes are put in their own namespace while switches and the controller are in the root/guest namespace. To put switches in their own namespace and pass the **--in namespace** option is as follows,

```
$sudo mn --innamespace --switch user
```

On behalf of using loopback, the switches can talk to the controller through a separately connected to control connection. However, this option is not very useful, but it does provide an example of how to isolate different switches (Yang, Fan, et al, 2014).

```
mininet> exit
```

## Part 3: Mininet Command-Line Interface (CLI) Commands

### Display Options

The list of Command-Line Interface (CLI) options can be verified by starting up a small/regular topology and leaving it executing.
Command to deploy the Mininet is as follows,

```
$ sudo mn
```

The commands to execute are as:

```
mininet> help
```

### Link Up/Down in a Network Is Like

Links can be brought up and down for fault tolerance testing.
To disable both halves of a virtual Ethernet-eth pair:

```
mininet> link s1 h1 down
```

One may observe here that an OpenFlow Port Status Change notification gets generated. To bring the link back up:

```
mininet> link s1 h1 up
```

## xTerm Display

To display an xTerm for h1 and h2:

```
mininet> xTerm h1 h2
```

# Part 4: Python API Samples

Different cases of how to utilize Mininet's Python Application Program Interface and in addition, perhaps the valuable code that has not been translated into the local code base are recorded in cases registry in the Mininet source tree.

Note: As noted at the beginning, this activity accepts either a Mininet Virtual Machine, which incorporates all that one may require or a local/inactive establishment with the majority of the related apparatuses, including the reference controller, a piece of the OpenFlow reference execution is being utilized or might be introduced utilizing install.sh - f on the off chance that it is not introduced.

## Secure Shell per Have

One example that may be especially useful executes a SSH daemon on each host is as follows:

```
$sudo ~/mininet/examples/sshd.py
```

Using any node, one can *ssh* into existing systems, and execute collaborating commands as follows:

```
$ssh 10.2.0.1 # or it varies according to system topology.
$ping 10.2.1.2 # or it varies according to system topology.
$exit
```

Exit Secure Shell example Mininet is as follows,

```
$exit
```

# Mininet Overview

Mininet is a function emulator that produces temporary hosts, switches and controllers and connections. Mininet has executed standard Linux to organize programming and its switches bolster OpenFlow for exceptionally adaptable custom directing and Software-Defined Networking (SDN).

Mininet put a fundamental part in examine, improvement, getting the hang of, prototyping, testing, troubleshooting, and encourages some other undertakings that could profit by having a total practical test arrange on a portable workstation or other Personal Computer.

## Mininet

- Mininet gives a smooth and cost-effective system testbed for actualizing OpenFlow applications.
- Activates numerous simultaneous technocrats to work smoothly on the same or different topology.
- It fortifies framework equipment - level relapse tests, which are reliable, repeatable and effectively gathered.
- It empowers troublesome topology testing, with no compelling reason to wire up an existed system.
- Has a Command Line Interface that is topology-mindful and OpenFlow-mindful for executing system tests.
- Enables self-assertive/circle commonplace topologies and consolidates an essential arrangement of default topologies.
- Is usable out of the crate without equipment programming, additionally gives an adaptable, client and extensible Python Application Program Interface for arrange creation/alter and experimentation.

Mininet gives a most straightforward approach to get right framework conduct to the degree upheld by framework equipment execution and to practice with various comparative/distinctive topologies.

Mininet systems run genuine code including standard Unix/Linux organize applications and in addition the genuine Linux piece and system stack including any portion expansions which one may have accessible as long as they are good with arrange namespaces. Because of this, the code being produced and tried on Mininet, for an OpenFlow controller, altered switch, or host, can move to a genuine framework with little changes for certifiable testing, execution assessment, and sending.

All the more illustratively, a plan that works in Mininet can ordinarily move specifically to equipment switches for line-rate packet sending (C. Kolias, 2014).

## How It Works

Each and every working framework virtualizes registering/running assets utilizing a procedure reflection. A procedure based virtualization to run various hosts/hubs and switches on a solitary Operating System bit is utilized by the Mininet. Since adaptation 2.2.26, Linux has upheld arrange namespaces, a lightweight virtualization include which gives singular procedures isolate organize interfaces, directing tables, and ARP tables. The complete Linux includes chroot () correctional facilities, process and client namespaces and CPU and memory points of confinement to give full Operating system virtualization, yet these extra elements are not required by Mininet. It can make bit or client space OpenFlow changes, controllers to control the changes, and has to convey over the imitated arrange. Besides, Mininet associates switches and has utilizing virtual Ethernet-eth sets.

Mininet's code completely runs in Python aside from C-Language.

Mininet at present needs a Linux bit, it might bolster other working frameworks with prepare based virtualization, for example, Solaris compartments or! FreeBSD imprisons sooner rather than later (J. Metzler, 2015).

## Why Mininet Is Better

A large portion of the best elements of equipment emulators, framework equipment testbeds and test systems are consolidated into Mininet (E. Haleplidis et al, 2015).

Mininet contrasted with full framework virtualization based methodologies:

- **Boots Speedier:** Speed is of the order of seconds rather than minutes in constant applications.
- **Scales Bigger:** A huge number of hosts/hubs and switches versus single digits.
- **It Gives More Data Transfer Capacity:** Commonly at least 2gbps aggregate transmission capacity on unassuming framework equipment.
- **Installs Effortlessly:** a total Virtual Machine is available that keeps executing on VMware or Virtual Box for Mac/Windows/Linux with OpenFlow v1.0 devices as of now introduced.

Mininet contrasted with equipment test beds like,

- Is less cost and constantly accessible 24 x 7(even preceding gathering due dates)?
- Is rapidly reconfigurable or reboot and restartable.

Mininet contrasted with test systems:

It runs unpretentious, unchanged code, including application code, Operating System bit code and control plane code (incorporates both OpenFlow controller code and Open vSwitch code).

- Easily/easily associates with genuine systems
- Offers intuitive execution - you can sort at it

## Limitations

- Mininet-based systems can't overhead the Central Processing Unit or transfer speed accessible on a solitary server.
- Mininet can't keep running on other non-Linux-perfect OpenFlow switches or applications. Be that as it may, this is not an issue end and end.

## FUTURE RESEARCH DIRECTIONS

The arrangement of the broad writing in the spaces of SDN, Mininet, and WSNs will give the potential chances to future research. Mininet arrangements can be used to lessen the working expenses through diminishing work costs, upgrading computerization, enhancing the following strategy, and keeping the material misfortune. Semantic Web is the expansion of the World Wide Web that indexes data on a website page and reprocesses it so that different machines including PCs can comprehend the data. An examination of linkages among SDN, Mininet, WSNs, NFV, and Semantic Web in worldwide operations would appear to be reasonable for future research endeavors.

## CONCLUSION

This part demonstrated the review of SDN; SDN controller and steering convention; OpenFlow-based SDN; the security worries for SDN; the outline of Mininet; the security worries for Mininet; the diagram of WSNs; WSNs and topology control; and the significance of WSNs. SDN includes a few categories of system novelty which are there for creating the system as flexible as the virtualized server and capacity framework of the present day server farm. SDN objective is to permit specialists and executives to quickly respond to the varying business necessities. In SDN, a system head can form the movement from a concentrated control reassure without touching the specific switches, and can convey directions to anywhere they are mandatory in the system.

Mininet is an independent accretion of portable clients that impart over moderately data transfer capacity bound remote connections. Since the nodes are portable, the system topology may alter rapidly and unpredictably after some time. The system is decentralized, where all system activities (e.g., finding the topology and conveying the messages) must be implemented by the nodes themselves. Mininets require the productive circulated calculations to decide arrange association, connect booking, and directing. Nodes like to stem as meagre power importantly and communicate as infrequently as could be permitted, along these lines diminishing the probability of location or block attempt. A slip by in any of these prerequisites may debase the execution and reliability of the system.

WSNs comprise in an arrangement of spatially appropriated self-ruling gadgets, more often than not battery-fueled and intended to work for a drawn out stretch of time. Limiting the vitality utilization is a vital plan thought. Many steering, control administration, and information scattering conventions have been intended for WSNs where vitality mindfulness is a basic plan issue. Every sensor node involves the processes of identifying, making, transmission, mobilizer, position determining framework, and power units. Sensor nodes are sent in true conditions and decide some physical practices. Sensors are minor gadgets, low costing, and having low preparing capacities. Sensors take into account detecting over bigger land areas with more prominent precision. Expanding the processing abilities of present day sensors have empowered the current WSNs to execute many inquiries inside the system.

SDN, Mininet, and NFV turn into the developing parts of ICT applications and can be successfully used in worldwide operations. SDN, Mininet, and NFV can possibly build the productivity of operations in different enterprises, they can enrich the resource ability to perceive and their traceability, reduce the dependence on manual techniques, decrease the operational budgets, and provide valuable information to business exploration.

## REFERENCES

Casado, M. (2012). Fabric: A retrospective on evolving SDN. *Proceedings of the first workshop on Hot topics in software defined networks, HotSDN '12*, 85-90. doi:10.1145/2342441.2342459

Costanzo, S. (2012). Software defined wireless networks: Unbridling sdns. *Software Defined Networking (EWSDN). European Workshop on*, 1-6.

De Gante, A., Aslan, M., & Matrawy, A. (2014). Smart wireless sensor network management based on software-defined networking. *Communications (QBSC), 2014 27th Biennial Symposium on*, 71-75.

Greenberg, A., Hjalmtysson, G., Maltz, D. A., Myers, A., Rexford, J., Xie, G., & Zhang, H. et al. (2005). A clean slate 4d approach to network control and management. *Computer Communication Review*, *35*(5), 41–54. doi:10.1145/1096536.1096541

Haleplidis. (2015). *Software-Defined Networking (SDN): Layers and Architecture Terminology* (RFC 7426). Retrieved from http://tools.ietf.org/search/rfc7426

Kolias.(2014).*Bundling NFV and SDN for Open Networking*. NetSeminar @ Stanford.

Kolias, C. (2014). *Bundling NFV and SDN for Open Networking*. Retrieved from http://netseminar.stanford.edu/seminars/05_22_14.pdf

Luo, Tan, & Quek. (2012). Sensor OpenFlow: Enabling software-defined wireless sensor networks. *IEEE Communications Letters, 16*(11), 1896-1899.

Marcondes, C. (2013). *A Survey of Software-Defined Networking: Past, Present and Future of Programmable for Wireless Mobile & Adhoc Networks*. Retrieved from https://www.google.ro/?gws_rd=ssl#q=ETSI+NFV+USe+cases++tutorial

Matias, J., Garay, J., Toledo, N., Unzilla, J., & Jacob, E. (2015, April). Toward (2015) an SDN-Enabled NFV Architecture. *IEEE Communications Magazine, 53*(4), 187–193. doi:10.1109/MCOM.2015.7081093

McKeown, N., & Anderson, T. (2005). *OpenFlow: Enabling Innovation în Campus Networks*. Retrieved from http://www.openflow.org/documents/openflow-wp-latest.pdf

Mendonca, M. (2005). *A Survey of Software-Defined Networking: Past, Present and Future of Programmable Networks*. Retrieved from http://hal.inria.fr/hal-00825087/

MetzlerJ. (2015). Retrieved from http://www.webtorials.com/content/2014/11/the-2015-guide-to-sdn-nfv.html

Nunes, B. A. A., Mendonca, M., Nguyen, X.-N., Obraczka, K., & Turletti, T. (2014). A survey of software-defined networking: Past, present, and future of programmable networks. *IEEE Communications Surveys and Tutorials, 16*(3), 1617–1634. doi:10.1109/SURV.2014.012214.00180

Olivier, F., Gonzalez, C., & Nolot, F. (2015). SDN Based Architecture for Clustered WSN. *Innovative Mobile and Internet Services in Ubiquitous Computing (IMIS), 9th International Conference on*, 342 – 347.

Reid, A. (2013). *Network Functions Virtualization and ETSI NFV ISG*. Retrieved from http://www.commnet.ac.uk/documents/commnet workshop networks/CommNets EPSRC workshop Reid.pdf

Sherwood, R. (2009). *Flow Visor: A network virtualization layer*. OpenFlow Switch Consortium, Tech. Rep: 1-13.

Yang, F. (2014). OpenFlow-based load balancing for wireless mesh infrastructure. *Consumer Communications and Networking Conference (CCNC), IEEE 11th*, 444-449.

Zeng, D. (2013). Evolution of software-defined sensor networks. *Mobile Ad-hoc and Sensor Networks (MSN), IEEE Ninth International Conference on*, 410-413.

## KEY TERMS AND DEFINITIONS

**BSD:** Frequently utilized non-particularly to allude to any of the BSD relatives which together frame a branch of the group of Unix-like working frameworks. Working frameworks got from the first BSD code remain effectively created and broadly utilized.

**CLI:** A method for collaborating with a PC program where the client (or customer) issues charges to the program as progressive lines of content (summon lines). A program which handles the interface is known as a summon dialect mediator or shell.

**Hotspot:** A physical area where individuals may get Internet get to, commonly utilizing Wi-Fi innovation, by means of a wireless local area network (WLAN) using a router connected to an internet service provider.

**KVM:** A virtualization framework for the Linux portion that transforms it into a hypervisor. It was converged into the Linux part mainline in bit form 2.6.20, which was discharged on February 5, 2007. KVM requires a processor with equipment virtualization augmentations.

**Linux OS:** A Unix-like PC working framework collected under the model of free and open-source programming advancement and dispersion.

**Mininet:** A system emulator which makes a system of virtual hosts, switches, controllers, and connections. Mininet has run standard Linux organize programming, and its switches bolster OpenFlow for exceedingly adaptable custom directing and software-defined networking.

**Open vSwitch:** A creation quality, multilayer virtual switch authorized under the open source Apache 2.0 permit. It is intended to empower monstrous system computerization through automatic expansion, while as yet supporting standard administration interfaces and conventions (e.g., NetFlow, sFlow, IPFIX, RSPAN, CLI, LACP, 802.1ag). Moreover, it is intended to help circulation over various physical servers like VMware's vNetwork disseminated vSwitch or Cisco's Nexus 1000V.

**OpenFlow:** An interchanges convention that offers access to the sending plane of a system switch or switch over the system.

**Python Interpreter:** Generally introduced as/usr/nearby/container/python3.6 on those machines where it is accessible; putting/usr/neighborhood/receptacle in your Unix shells.

**Software-Defined Network (SDN):** The physical detachment of the system control plane from the sending plane, and where a control plane controls a few gadgets.

**SSH:** A cryptographic network protocol for operating network services securely over an unsecured network.

**Virtual Machine:** An imitating of a PC framework. Virtual machines depend on PC structures and give usefulness of a physical PC. Their usage may include specific equipment, programming, or a blend.

**Wireless Sensor Networks:** The remote systems comprising of spatially disseminated independent gadgets utilizing sensors to screen the physical or ecological conditions.

**XTerm:** The standard terminal emulator for the X Window System. A client can have a wide range of summons of xterm running on the double on a similar show, each of which gives autonomous information/yield for the procedure running in it (ordinarily the procedure is a Unix shell).

# Chapter 8
# NFV Practical Implementation

**Lalit Pandey**
*Independent Researcher, India*

## ABSTRACT

*This chapter is focused on the traditional network architecture limitations with NFV benefits. Discussion of NFV architecture and framework as well as management and orchestration has been discussed in this chapter. Cisco VNF portfolio and virtual network functions implementation is included with software implementation of the architecture of NFV (network function virtualization). Management and orchestration functional layers as per ETSI standard. The challenges in NFV implementation is also a concern today, which is a part of this chapter.*

## NFV PRACTICAL ORIENTATION

Network functions virtualization (NFV) has changed the way we have traditionally thought about networking design, deployment & Implementation of the networking components within the IT Infrastructure through the approach of virtualization & not through the traditional hardware approach with predefined software within each component.

NFV decouples network functions from underlying hardware resources by virtualizing the storage, network and compute functions (Chiosi, Clarke, Willis, Reid, Feger, Bugenhagen, & Benitez, 2012). The Idea is to save the proprietary equipment cost by virtualizing network functions and creating on servers instead of their defined hardware.

This transition towards virtualization will take a period of time because providers & enterprises are not going to decommission their existing Infrastructure and replace everything by virtualized Individual components as this will be too expensive then.

DOI: 10.4018/978-1-5225-3640-6.ch008

*Figure 1. Changes with NFV with VNFs*

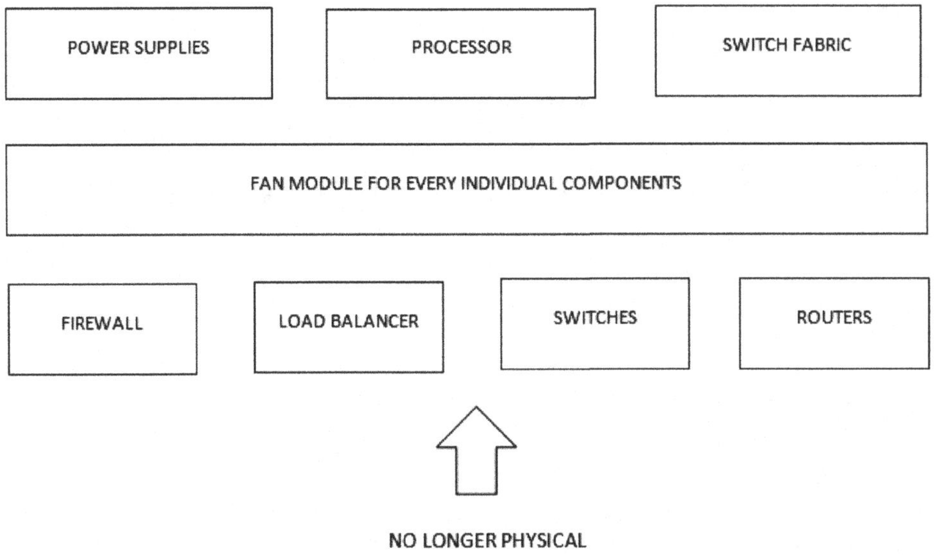

| POWER SUPPLIES | PROCESSOR | SWITCH FABRIC |

| FAN MODULE FOR EVERY INDIVIDUAL COMPONENTS |

| FIREWALL | LOAD BALANCER | SWITCHES | ROUTERS |

NO LONGER PHYSICAL

## TRADITIONAL NETWORK ARCHITECTURE LIMITATIONS

1. Scalability Limitations.
2. Vendor dependent predefined hardware & software components.
3. High operational cost due to the management of Individual hardware within datacenters.
4. More Space & Power Requirements.
5. Individual Hardware management Issues.
6. Huge Capital Expenditure.
7. Limitation in rapidly offering services to the users due to the time to build the infrastructure.
8. Additional hardware to deploy for High Availability.

## NFV BENEFITS

1. Service Elasticity.
2. Operational Efficiency.
3. Automated Network Operations.
4. Capital Expenditure Reduction.
5. Vendor agnostic.

6. Software Oriented Innovation.
7. Rapid Service Delivery
8. Reduced Space & Power Consumption.
9. Hardware Flexibility
10. Scalability & Multi-tenancy.
11. Reduction of number of network devices management.
12. Reduced complexity for HA (High Availability).
13. Reduction of network elements for deployment and management.

## NFV ARCHITECTURE AND FRAMEWORK

The relevance of NFV framework is to ensure standardization & compatibility between different vendor software pieces of share hardware resources.

Virtualized Network Function (VNF) – A software component that replaces the vendor specific hardware to perform the same function on share hardware, eventually reducing the capital & operational expenses.

*Figure 2. Network virtualization*

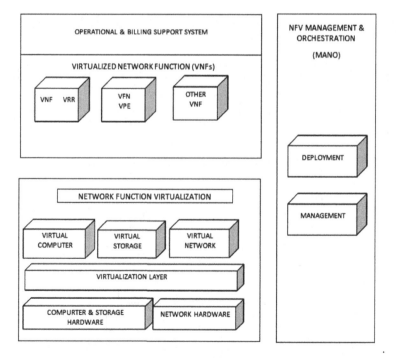

VNF can be any network functions such as a Switch, Router, Firewall, NAT, IPS/IDS, WAAS etc. (Chowdhury & Boutaba, 2009; Chowdhury, & Boutaba, 2010; Bogineni, Davidson, Slauson, Molocznik, Martin, McBean, & Smith 2016).

It involves the Implementation of Software functions that run on any Standard Industry Servers without the need of Installing the vendor hardware to install a new service within the networking Infrastructure.

Building Block for NFV Enterprise Virtualization:

1.  A transport network.
2.  Physical Hardware.
3.  Virtualized Network Function (VNF)
4.  Hypervisors.
5.  Orchestration & Management.

Different vendors are offering their own VNFs & organization may chose to implement different vendor VNF and Implement It on shared hardware.

This architecture is the basis of the standardization within NFV Architecture framework and is called as the ETSI NFV Framework. The categorization of the high level building block of the virtualized Infrastructure is divided into three major blocks:

*Figure 3.*

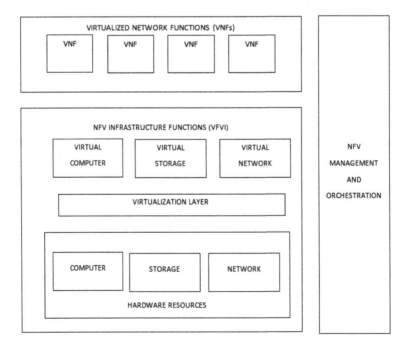

1.  **VNF – Virtualized Network Function Block:** Software function that perform the same task as the proprietary hardware in the form of virtual machines on top of the shared hardware resources.
2.  **Network Functions Virtualization Infrastructure (NFVI) Block:** The fundamental building block of hardware and software to make the VNF virtualization possible on shared hardware comes under this block.
3.  **Management and Orchestration (MANO) Block:** Management and Orchestration of Infrastructure resources & VNFs (virtual network functions).

## VIRTUAL NETWORK FUNCTIONS

Software Implementation of Individual network functions that can be deployed in a shared virtualized environment and decoupled from the underlying hardware.

The idea of NFV is to build these software functions instead of the traditional vendor hardware installations and reduce the overall expenditure for maintenance & capital Investment to purchase the Individual hardware. Implementation of VNFs like a virtual firewall or a virtual router behaves the same way as the vendor pre-integrated device.

## CISCO'S VNF PORTFOLIO

1.  IOSXRv
2.  CSR1000v
3.  ASAv
4.  Nexus 1000v
5.  vWAAS
6.  vWLC

*Figure 4. Efficient resource utilization through local balancing and scaling resources demand*

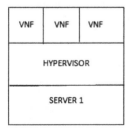
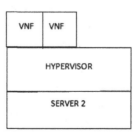
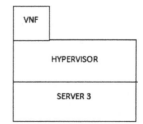

*Figure 5. Workstation accessing virtual resources within NFV infrastructure*

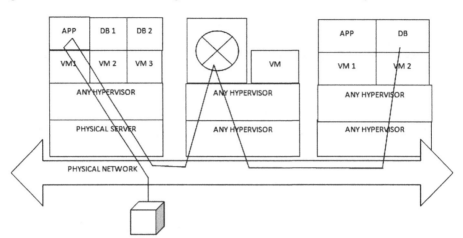

7.   vESA
8.   vWSA

## NETWORK FUNCTIONS VIRTUALIZATION INFRASTRUCTURE

NFVI is the underlying Infrastructure (compute, networking, storage) on which the VNFs are hosted. Shared hardware resources that VNFs uses to get the compute, connectivity & space as per the requirements.

*Figure 6.*

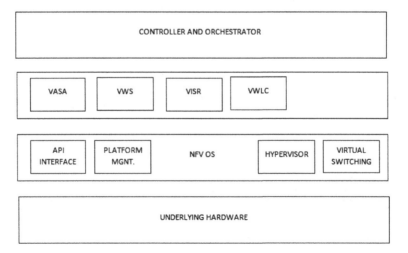

The hardware resources are logically divided into different virtual blocks and these virtual blocks are further presented as an Independent hardware for each virtual network functions.

## MANAGEMENT AND ORCHESTRATION (MANO)

ETSI MANO framework has been divided into three main functional layers:

### Virtualized Infrastructure Managers

VIMs handles the virtualization of the specialized hardware with VMM (virtual machine managers).It is used to manage the resources (compute, network & storage) of the NFV Infrastructure (NFVI).

*Figure 7.*

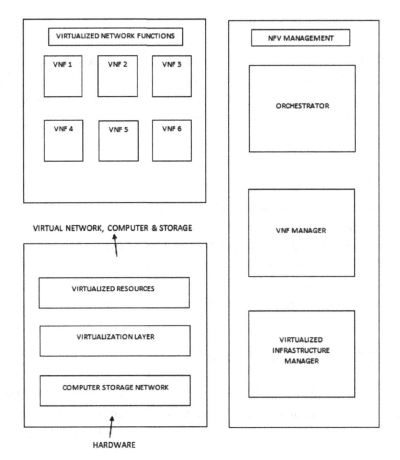

Component responsible for managing NFVI network, compute & storage (underlying) resources.

## VIMs Key Features

1. Management of the hardware/Inventory resources (compute, network, storage).
2. Management of the software resources like hypervisors etc.
3. It also collects the performance measurements of the virtualized environment and components.
4. Maintaining the Integration of vNF components and the underlying resources.
5. Orchestration of Infrastructure resources.

## Virtual Network Function Managers (VNFM)

Management, Support and configuration of VNFs (Complete lifecycle management of VNFs)

## NFV Orchestrator (NFVO)

NFV Orchestrator provides the lifecycle management of the network services & resources orchestration. NFVO is a key component of the MANO framework which provides the coordinated services around different software elements to work on shared Infrastructure. Key activities of NFVO include scaling, creating, deleting network functions.

## NFVO Provides

1. Lifecycle management of network functions:
2. Combining different vNFs together to achieve a more complex network function.
3. Instantiate vNF's and manage vNFs with VNFM (vNF Manager).
4. Support for multivendor VNFM.
5. Support of NFV MANO.
6. Support validation and resources request from VNFM.

## ELASTIC SERVICE CONTROLLER (ESC)

Elastic service controller is Cisco's VNFM (Virtual Network Functions Manager).
It simplifies operations with open standard architecture and fully controls virtual network functions.ESC is responsible for monitoring the vNFs state (alive, dead etc)

and vNF application health status (oversubscribed, underload etc.). It uses SNMP or ICMP to monitor the health status and keep track of it.

Cisco ESC (Elastic services controller) provides a single point of control to manage VNF lifecycle in a dynamic and multivendor environment. This also gives advance mgmt capabilities through open and standard ETSI VNF MANO (management and orchestration) architectures.

## Lifecycle Management of Elastic Service Controller

1. Onboarding of any new virtualized network function (vNF) if it is supported in VMWARE or Openstack environment.
2. Deployment and configuration of a new service, it includes the assignment of IP addressing, licensing, connectivity parameters etc.
3. Monitoring keep track of the state of the virtual machine within the virtual environment along with its resources status.
4. Healing of the vNFs component and services.
5. Support for Upgrades/downgrades of different vNFs.
6. Decommissioning of the vNFs when not in use.
7. Scalability of virtual network functions.

## Complete VNFs Lifecycle Management Summary

1. VNF license management
2. Monitoring
3. Deployment
4. Rollback
5. Recovery
6. Configuration
7. Scalability
8. Update

## CHALLENGES IN NFV IMPLEMENTATION

1. Compatibility Issues may be a concern between different vendor VNFs & different hypervisors.
2. Security should be considered.
3. Tight Integration of the underlay & Overlay is required for efficient functioning.
4. Verifying the virtual resources requirement before implementation.
5. Not a pre-Integrated Software & Hardware version.

## CISCO NETWORK SERVICES ORCHESTRATOR

Automation is the focused area for provider organizations and larger enterprises to reduce operational & capital expenses where competition is increasing exponentially to provide the same services at lower cost.

Network management standards like NETCONF & YANG are becoming very popular and abstracting the complete network management efficiently. Cisco NSO is multi-vendor service orchestrator for future network Infrastructure as well. It includes configuration management, validation, transaction Integrity & rollback. This is also the centralized pane of glass for L2-L7 networking, physical & virtual devices. Orchestration by Cisco NSO is YANG driven model for device data model as well as service data model.

## Business Challenges and the Need of Network Orchestration

1.  Higher operational expenses.
2.  Slow delivery of new services.
3.  Operational complexity.
4.  Integration of virtual & physical is challenging.
5.  Dynamic & Flexible management.
6.  Automation.
7.  Troubleshooting and testing end to end

Network administrators and Server provider operators are managing both the operational cost which is growing day by day and the revenue. because revenue from new services doesn't give faster growth most of the time but operational cost increases exponentially with each new service installed and arranging the compatible and upgraded adaptors to support that newly installed service or application. Adapters are expensive most of the time and hard to maintain.

NFV is changing the way we used to operate our network and to address these challenges.

The industry is moving towards service oriented way of network management. SDN is coming up with different ways to centralized manage the entire network, enabling unified set of Application programming interfaces and the services which can be controlled and operated in real time.

Configuration of the devices is one of the major costs driven factor in enterprise and provider network environment. There is still a lot of manual configuration to meet the day to day frequent changes in the network and preventing human error in the frequent changes is still a challenge. Frequent change of the physical equipment, replacement of the devices and changing needs of the customer are some major reasons for the changes in the network. These are also the reason for not implementing automated solutions as there are frequent changes in the network. Configuration changes are done manually in most of the provider environment or by writing a script as there are no well defined protocols or APIs. There is no such data or service model which can streamline the configuration management through well defined protocols or APIs.

There are lots of sources of the configuration changes. Network administrator are either modifying/adding the configuration manually time to time by planning a change window and many are writing a script to automate the configuration but these solutions are not scalable.

Cisco NSO is a multi vendor controller for service provider environment as well as enterprise platforms. Network Orchestrator supports virtual devices and provides a centralized way of management of the entire network Infrastructure. It also makes sure that the configuration has been pushed properly and there is no synchronization issue at frequent Internals.

## Cisco NSO Characteristics

1.   Support for multivendor environment.
2.   Centralized management of network services.
3.   Support for multiprotocol environment.
4.   Structured presentation of networking configurations and its state.
5.   Support for legacy devices as well which support telnet or ssh.
6.   Junos style CLI for configuration of network devices.
7.   Support for the abstraction of the configuration to reuse the same model to replicate to other devices.
8.   Support for the verification of the state of the existing components before deploying new services and components.
9.   Support for the rollback of the configurations.

## ETSI Management and Orchestration (MANO) Architecture: Cisco

Architectural layers:

1.   The NFV Orchestrator (NFVO) layer - to orchestrate NFV services using Cisco NSO.
2.   VNF Manager (VNFM) layer – to manage vNFs using Cisco Elastic Services Controller (ESC).

3. Virtualized Infrastructure Manager (VIM) – to manage the virtual and physical infrastructure. Where OpenStack, VMware, Cisco APIC can be deployed.
4. Physical & Virtual Network Infrastructure Layer for Physical & Virtual Network devices.

## Cisco NSO Solution to Network Orchestration and Management Challenges

1. It provides a centralized management and single application programming Interface to the entire Infrastructure.
2. Keeps accurate copy of network configuration.
3. Multi-vendor Orchestration platform.
4. Multi-vendor SDN Controller.
5. Supports traditional networking services.

*Figure 8.*

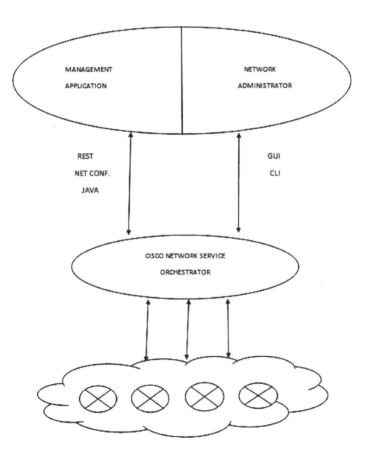

## Cisco Network Services Orchestrator Architecture

Lack of abstraction is a major drawback in networking environment. Due to lack of abstraction every configuration or policies are hard coded to the physical devices and it is removed completely as soon as the device is decommissioned. And this give rise to the same set of configurations and policies to a different set of hardware which can take time to build the physical device, configure it from the scratch. After building the configuration, testing is also mandatory where compatibility with the hardware is important with installed software and then finally testing it in the production environment.

NSO is a 3 layer architecture of forwarding (devices are responsible for forwarding traffic), Network operation layer and the abstraction layer which gives the ability to the architecture to not hardcode the configuration, policies to any physical entity.

Cisco NSO provides Operation layer, abstraction layer and communicate with the downstream forwarding layer using protocols like OpenFlow or by conventional methods like SNMP and CLI. With its northbound and southbound APIs It gives an abstracted view of the complete networking environment.

The power of NSO gives the ability to manage multivendor devices through a consistent southbound APIs which is not bound to any vendor product. It also helps to push the network configuration to the end devices vendor agnostically.

Cisco network services orchestrator (NSO) core engine is responsible for all management including upgradation /downgradation, synchronization when maintaining high availability etc. It enables policy oriented capacity management to setup the use of policies and use of resources as per the organizational requirements and best practices and provides standard northbound and southbound Interfaces to the environment.

NSO Core engines functionalities are summarized below:

1. It handles upgrades and downgrades of software components.
2. Maintain audit of the status changes and logs the changes in its database.
3. It stores the configurations rollbacks.
4. RBAC control can be enabled and used for more granular access to the infrastructure.
5. AAA centralized engines for authentication management.

## NORTHBOUND APPLICATION PROGRAMMING INTERFACES

- Northbound APIs – CLI – NSO Specific, Graphical User Interface

- Integration through Automation – REST(Representational state transfer), NETCONF etc.
- Monitor – NETCONF & SNMP Protocol (Monitoring of Cisco NSO).

## Primary Components of Cisco Network Service Orchestrator

1. **NETCONF:** Device management Protocol.
2. **YANG:** Service and device modeling

Traditional network doesn't have a well defined management protocol to manage the underlying resources and meets the demands of the most demanding IT Organizations. Protocols like SNMP can be used as south bound APIs to manage the Infrastructure. However they lack features from scalability standpoint and is not a defined solution to manage the order of the configuration which is again relevant from the configuration & management perspective.

SNMP can however be used for device polling, monitoring with Its MIB concept, It is not considered appropriate for configuration as SNMP Protocol has not been designed that way and Its cumbersome for configuration. Multivendor platform management approach is again a challenge as far as the compatibility with different vendor hardware & software.

## INTRODUCTION TO NETCONF

The challenges that we have in today's IT Infrastructure is multivendor platform compatibility with different hardware and software versions. This adds extra complexity and cost to the existing IT environment. Lack of consistency and visibility becomes a challenge in the multivendor platform environment.

SNMP (Simple network management protocol) is the standard for the monitoring & management of network devices but it was not used majorly for configuration management because of the lack of standardization among different vendors and order in which the configuration can be pushed which is again challenging. Due to the complex approach for the configuration, solution is expensive, complex & not scalable. SNMP has not been used extensively for other purposes except monitoring & polling.

NETCONF is a network management protocol which defines the management operations of the networking Insfrastructure.It is a IETF standard for programming of network elements.

# CURRENT NETWORK MANAGEMENT ENVIRONMENT CHARACTERISTICS

1.   Lack of programmatic approach to automate the frequently used daily operational tasks.
2.   Automation challenge.
3.   Not well defined protocol structures to support full fledge management of the devices.
4.   Cost & Complexity in multivendor environment.
5.   Lack of Integration between different environments.
6.   Complete visibility of the resources.
7.   SNMP was not designed for network configuration, it was created for the management of the network devices.
8.   SNMP is not for the new DevOps Model proposed.
9.   SNMP is cumbersome for the management of configuration of network devices.

This has resulted in the creation of new standard protocol for network management known as NETCONF.

NETCONF protocol gives the leverage to push, delete or manipulate configurations efficiently. It uses an Extensible Markup Language (XML) for configuration data and control messages. The protocol allows the device to expose a full application programming interface (API). A lot of vendor already support NETCONF to some extent and the list is growing with other vendors as well. Organizations are making their devices NETCONF understandable in their newer products & projects. It provides rich functions to manage configuration, operations & monitoring.

## NETCONF Properties

1.   Sessions use encrypted and efficient transport mechanism: XML content transported over SSH over TCP.
2.   Network Wide characteristics, a property to work parallel with different network element in the system.
3.   Messages use XML (Extensible Markup Language).
4.   Specially designed to provision & manage network elements within the Infrastructure.
5.   NETCONF uses a simple RPC-based mechanism.
6.   Designed for configuration.

*Table 1.*

|  | SNMP | NET CONF | SOAP | REST |
|---|---|---|---|---|
| STANDARD | IETF | IETF | W3C | |
| MANIPULATING/ACCESSING RESOURCES THROUGH | OIDs | PATHs | | URLs |
| DATA MODELING LANGUAGE | SMI | YANG | (WSDL, NOT DATA) | UNDEFINED,(WSDL) WADL, TEXT |
| MANAGEMENT OPERATION METHOD | SNMP | NET CONF | IN THE XML SCHEMA NOT STANDARDIZED | GENERIC HTTP OPERATIONS, POST, GET, PUT, PATCH |
| ENCODING USED | BER | XML | XML | XML, JSON |
| TRANSPORT STACK | UDP | SSH SSL TCP | SSH HTTP TCP | SST HTTP TCP |

# INTRODUCTION TO YANG

As per IETF RFC 6020

*YANG is a data modeling language used to model configuration and state data manipulated by the Network Configuration Protocol (NETCONF), NETCONF remote procedure calls, and NETCONF notifications. YANG is used to model the operations and content layers of NETCONF*

YANG over NETCONF is a way to translate a device oriented language to a human friendly language. NETCONF is giving a standardization to communicate to a wide range of devices. YANG data modeling language describes syntax and semantics more human understandable.

## YANG Characteristics

1. Designed for simplicity of the XML Code.
2. Designed for readability.
3. Designed to support any international character set by using UTF-8 encoding.
4. Data modeling language for defining payload (NETCONF Payload).

*Figure 9. SNMP vs. NETCONF*

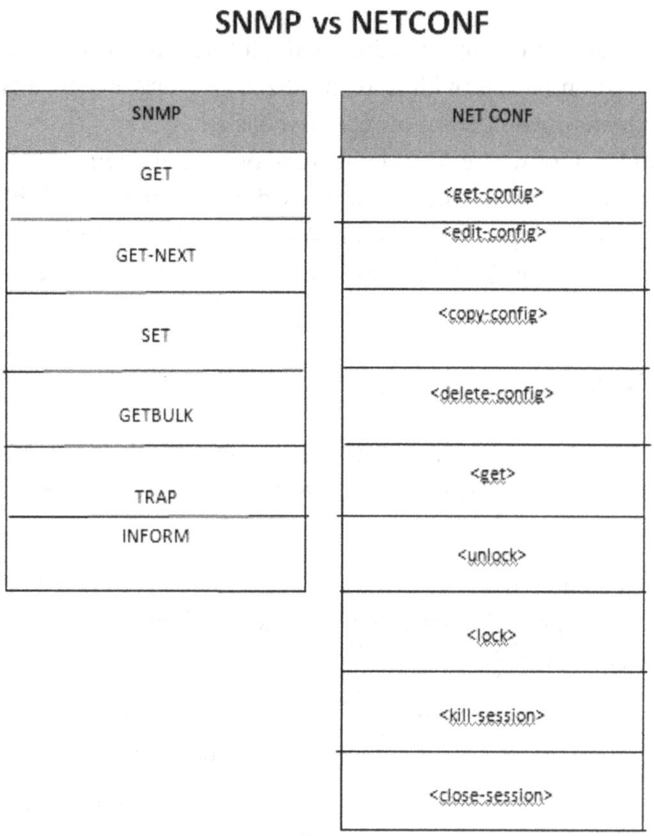

## SNMP vs NETCONF

| SNMP | NET CONF |
|------|----------|
| GET | <get-config> |
| GET-NEXT | <edit-config> |
| SET | <copy-config> |
| GETBULK | <delete-config> |
| TRAP | <get> |
| INFORM | <unlock> |
| | <lock> |
| | <kill-session> |
| | <close-session> |

5. YANG leverages an XML encoding of information.
6. Language is well defined for network devices and elements.
7. It makes the NETCONF language useful.

## Cisco Enterprise NFV Rest Application Programming Interfaces

Any command line tool such as curl can be used to push https requests. All REST APIs uses https protocol to push the data using the below HTTP Request Methods:

1. GET
2. POST
3. PUT
4. DELETE

# CONCLUSION

Evolving technologies from multivendor standpoint is trying to make the environment management less complex, providing a centralized view and management and invoke programming to automate the set of repetitive tasks.

In the era of DevOps where development and operations team are suppose to work together to handle modern datacenter and provider network traffic, NFV is playing a major role in virtualizing individual components to reduce the overall CAPEX and OPEX without worrying for the multivendor support and simplified management.

# REFERENCES

Bahnasse, A., & El Kamoun, N. (2014). Policy-based Management of a Secure Dynamic and Multipoint Virtual Private Network. *Global Journal of Computer Science and Technology, 14*(8).

Bahnasse, A., & Elkamoun, N. (2015). Study and evaluation of the high availability of a Dynamic Multipoint Virtual Private Network. *Revue MéDiterranéEnne Des TéLéCommunications, 5*(2).

Bogineni, K., Davidson, D., Slauson, A., Molocznik, L., Martin, C., McBean, K., & Smith, K. (2016). SDN-NFV reference architecture. Verizon.

Campbell, A. T., Katzela, I., Miki, K., & Vicente, J. (1999). Open signaling for ATM, internet and mobile networks (OPENSIG'98). *Computer Communication Review, 29*(1), 97–108. doi:10.1145/505754.505762

Casado, M., Freedman, M. J., Pettit, J., Luo, J., McKeown, N., & Shenker, S. (2007, August). Ethane: Taking control of the enterprise. *Computer Communication Review, 37*(4), 1–12. doi:10.1145/1282427.1282382

Chiosi, M., Clarke, D., Willis, P., Reid, A., Feger, J., Bugenhagen, M., & Benitez, J. (2012). Network functions virtualization: An introduction, benefits, challenges and call for action. In *SDN and OpenFlow World Congress* (pp. 22-24). Academic Press.

Chowdhury, N. M. K., & Boutaba, R. (2009). Network virtualization: State of the art and research challenges. *IEEE Communications Magazine, 47*(7), 20–26. doi:10.1109/MCOM.2009.5183468

Chowdhury, N. M. K., & Boutaba, R. (2010). A survey of network virtualization. *Computer Networks, 54*(5), 862–876. doi:10.1016/j.comnet.2009.10.017

Cisco. (2010). *Cisco visual networking index: Global mobile data traffic forecast update, 2009–2014.* Author.

Doria, A. (2002). General Switch Management Protocol V3. *RFC 3292.*

Foundation, O. N. (2012). Software-defined networking: The new norm for networks. *ONF White Paper, 2,* 2-6.

Gens, F. (2012). *IDC Predictions 2013: Competing on the 3rd Platform. Int.* Data Corporation.

Gude, N., Koponen, T., Pettit, J., Pfaff, B., Casado, M., McKeown, N., & Shenker, S. (2008). NOX: Towards an operating system for networks. *Computer Communication Review, 38*(3), 105–110. doi:10.1145/1384609.1384625

Haleplidis, E., Pentikousis, K., Denazis, S., Salim, J. H., Meyer, D., & Koufopavlou, O. (2015). *Software-defined networking (SDN): Layers and architecture terminology* (No. RFC 7426).

McKeown, N., Anderson, T., Balakrishnan, H., Parulkar, G., Peterson, L., Rexford, J., & Turner, J. (2008). OpenFlow: Enabling innovation in campus networks. *Computer Communication Review, 38*(2), 69–74. doi:10.1145/1355734.1355746

Nunes, B. A. A., Mendonca, M., Nguyen, X. N., Obraczka, K., & Turletti, T. (2014). A survey of software-defined networking: Past, present, and future of programmable networks. *IEEE Communications Surveys and Tutorials, 16*(3), 1617–1634. doi:10.1109/SURV.2014.012214.00180

Xia, W., Wen, Y., Foh, C. H., Niyato, D., & Xie, H. (2015). A survey on software-defined networking. *IEEE Communications Surveys and Tutorials, 17*(1), 27–51. doi:10.1109/COMST.2014.2330903

## KEY TERMS AND DEFINITIONS

**Elastic Services Controller:** Elastic services controller (ESC) provides a comprehensive lifecycle management platform for NFV.

**Load Balancer:** Used to distributes network and application traffic to number of servers to act as reverse proxy.

**Network Function Virtualization:** A network architecture which uses concept of IT virtualization to make connection among different networking nodes.

**NFV Infrastructure:** Set of resources that is used for hosting and connecting virtual connections.

**NFV Management and Organization:** Used for management and organization of NFV.

**Virtual Network Function:** A virtualized task that is used to moves network functions out of dedicated hardware devices and into software.

**VNF Manager:** A component of MANO architecture framework which is used to standardize the functions of virtual networking and increase the interoperability of software-defined networking elements.

# Chapter 9
# Quality of Service in SDN Technology

**Ankur Dumka**
*University of Petroleum and Energy Studies, India*

## ABSTRACT

*With the advancement in the requirement of data, the need for stringent quality of service guarantee is a demand of the current world, which brings the network programmers to design the network protocols that certify certain guaranteed performance in terms of service delivery. Here, focus is on the quality of service within the SDN network with its comparison and implementation using simulation. Types of quality of service are also discussed in this chapter with a focus on the ways of implementation of quality of service. The authors define a QoS management and orchestration architecture that allow them to manage the network in a modular manner. Performing the operation and results in such a network is shown as are the outputs for the same.*

## INTRODUCTION

Software defined network changes the networking in terms of type of configuration and managing the networks. SDN provides the abstraction of underlying network with the application reside in the upper layer. SDN provides an innovative approach to decouple the logic of control plane and data plane. Software-Defined Networking (SDN) is a latest technology that is dynamic, manageable, cost-effective, and adaptable, making it ideal for the high-bandwidth, dynamic nature of today's applications (Kannan Govindarajan, Kong Chee Meng, Hong Ong,(2013); Kim H., Feamster N., (2013)). SDN architecture decouples the control plane and data plane functions enabling the

DOI: 10.4018/978-1-5225-3640-6.ch009

control plane to become directly programmable and the underlying infrastructure to be abstracted for applications and network services (Akram Hakiria, Aniruddha Gokhalec, Pascal Berthoua, Douglas C. Schmidt, (2014); Kind M., Westphal F., Gladisch A., Topp S.,(2012)). The Open Flow protocol is a foundational element for building SDN solutions. The SDN architecture is:

- **Directly Programmable:** Control plane is directly programmable because it is decoupled from data plane (forwarding functions).
- **Agile:** Abstracting control from forwarding lets administrators dynamically adjust network-wide traffic flow to meet changing needs.
- Centrally managed
- Open standards-based and vendor-neutral

This means SDN control software sits at top of physical infrastructure layer composed of networking devices, with which it communicates via a control plane interface such as Open Flow (Kanaumi Y., Saito S., Kawai E., Ishii S., Kobayashi K., Shimojo S. (2013)). The idea is to turn networks into flexible, programmable platforms to optimize resource utilization, making them more cost effective and scalable. By providing APIs for business applications and services, SDN also promises to recast information technology by integrating cloud-based services and capabilities, and high-speed networking, into the computing fabric.

## SDN OPERATION

The SDN devices contain forwarding functionality for deciding what to do with each incoming packet. The devices also contain the data that drives those forwarding decisions. The data itself is actually represented by the flows defined by the controller, as depicted in the upper-left portion of each device. A flow describes a set of packets transferred from one network endpoint (or set of endpoints) to another endpoint (or set of endpoints). These endpoints may be defined as IP address-TCP/UDP port pairs, VLAN endpoints, layer three tunnel endpoints, and input ports, among other things. One set of rules describes the forwarding actions that the device should take for all packets belonging to that flow.

It can be understood from Figure 2 that flow is unidirectional, packets flowing between the same two endpoints in the opposite direction could each constitute a separate flow. Flows are represented on a device as a flow entry.

A flow table resides on the network device and consists of a series of flow entries and the actions to perform packet matching, when the SDN device receives a packet, it consults its flow tables in search of a match. These flow tables had been

*Figure 1. SDN architecture*

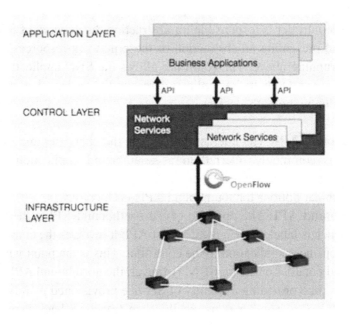

*Figure 2. SDN operation overview*

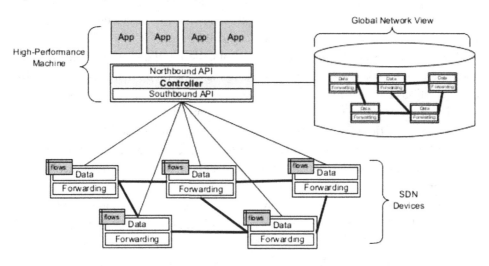

constructed previously when the controller downloaded appropriate flow rules to the device. If the SDN device finds a match, it takes the appropriate configured action, which usually entails forwarding the packet. If it does not find a match, the switch can either drop the packet or pass it to the controller, depending on the version of

OpenFlow and the configuration of the switch (Egilmez H. E., Dane, Gorkemli, Tekalp 2012).

The SDN controller is responsible for abstracting the network of SDN devices it controls and presenting an abstraction of these network resources to the SDN applications running above. The controller allows the SDN application to define flows on devices and to help the application respond to packets that are forwarded to the controller by the SDN devices.

- **Southbound API:** The interaction between the controller and the deployed device is commonly referred to as southbound application programing interface (API). A common, open standard SDN protocol, and one of the most popular options for southbound APIs is OpenFlow.
- **Northbound API:** The opposite of the southbound API is the northbound API, which is labeled in Figure 2 as just API; it involves the communications from a business application to the controller. This is the point where the real meat and potatoes exists for SDN. However, the northbound API can be very complex, like providing a Quality of Service provisioned path from one end of a network to another dynamically, then tearing it back down when the application was completed with its network interaction.

SDN applications are built on top of the controller. The SDN application interfaces with the controller, using it to set proactive flows on the devices and to receive packets that have been forwarded to the controller.

Proactive flows are established by the application; typically the application will set these flows when the application starts up, and the flows will persist until some configuration change is made. This kind of proactive flow is known as a static flow. Another kind of proactive flow is where the controller decides to modify a flow based on the traffic load currently being driven through a network device.

The flows that are defined in response to a packet forwarded to the controller. Upon receipt of incoming packets that have been forwarded to the controller, the SDN application will instruct the controller as to how to respond to the packet and, if appropriate, will establish new flows on the device in order to allow that device to respond locally the next time it sees a packet belonging to that flow. Such flows are called reactive flows.

There are also reactive flows that are defined or modified as a result of stimuli from sources other than packets from the controller. For example, the controller can insert flows reactively in response to other data sources such as intrusion detection systems (IDS) or the NetFlow traffic analyzer.

## SDN Devices

An SDN device is composed of an API for communication with the controller, an abstraction layer, and a packet-processing function. In the case of a virtual switch, this packet-processing function is packet-processing software, and in the case of a physical switch, the packet-processing function is embodied in the hardware for packet-processing logic. The packet-processing logic consists of the mechanisms to take actions based on the results of evaluating incoming packets and finding the highest-priority match. When a match is found, the incoming packet is processed locally unless it is explicitly forwarded to the controller. When no match is found, the packet may be copied to the controller for further processing. This process is also referred to as the controller consuming the packet.

In the case of a hardware switch, these mechanisms are implemented by the specialized hardware and in the case of a software switch (virtual switches), these same functions are mirrored by software. Since the case of the software switch is somewhat simpler than the hardware switch.

## OpenFlow

An SDN controller communicates with OpenFlow-compatible switches using the OpenFlow protocol running over the Secure Sockets Layer (SSL). Each switch connects to other OpenFlow switches and possibly to end-user devices that are the sources and destinations of packet flows (Civanlar S., Parlakisik M., Tekalp A. M., Gorkemli B., Kaytaz B., Onem E.,(2010)). Within each switch a series of tables typically implemented in hardware or firmware are used to manage the flows of packets through the switch.

## Working of OpenFlow

The OpenFlow specification defines three types of tables in the logical switch architecture.

1.  Flow Table matches incoming packets to a particular flow and specifies the functions that are to be performed on the packets.
2.  Multiple flow tables that operate in a pipeline fashion, as explained subsequently. A flow table may direct a flow to a Group Table, which may trigger a variety of actions that affect one or more flows.
3.  Meter Table can trigger a variety of performance-related actions on a flow.

*Figure 3. OpenFlow switch*

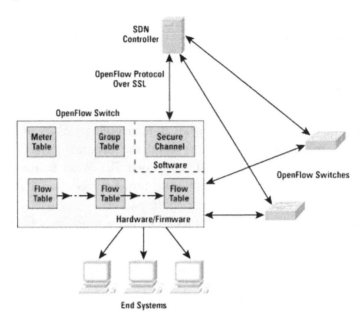

## Flow Tables

Flow tables consist of a number of prioritized flow entries, each of which typically consists of two components:

1.   Match Fields
2.   Actions

Match fields are used to compare against incoming packets. An incoming packet is compared against the match fields in priority order, and the first complete match is selected. Actions are the instructions that the network device should perform if an incoming packet matches the match fields specified for that flow entry. Match fields can have wildcards for fields that are not relevant to a particular match. For example, when matching packets based on just an IP address or subnet, then all other fields would be wild carded. Similarly, if matching on only MAC address or UDP/TCP port, the other fields are irrelevant, and consequently those fields are wild carded.

*Table 1. Header fields used for matching flows in the flow table*

| Ingress Port | Ether Source | Ether Desti | Ether Type | VLAN ID | VLAN Prior | IP Source | IP Desti | IP Proto | IP Tos | Source Port | Desti Port |
|---|---|---|---|---|---|---|---|---|---|---|---|

200

*Figure 4.*

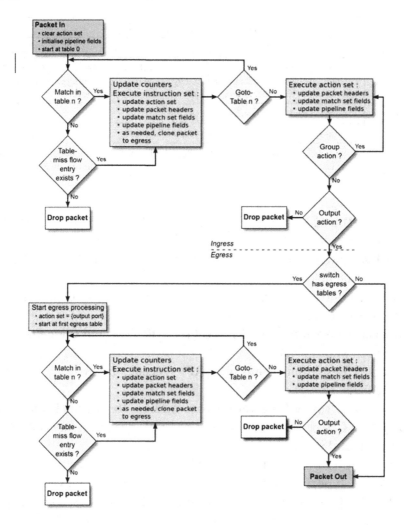

Each flow table contains entries consisting of six components as shown in Table 2.

The preceding match fields must be supported by any Open Flow- compliant switch. The following fields may be optionally supported:

- **Physical Port:** Used to designate underlying physical port when packet is received on a logical port.
- **Metadata:** Additional information that can be passed from one table to another during the processing of a packet.
- **Ethernet Type:** Ethernet Type field.

*Table 2. Flow table components*

| Match Fields | Used to select packets that match the values in the fields. |
|---|---|
| Priority | Relative priority of table entries. |
| Counters | Updated for matching packets. The OpenFlow specification defines a variety of timers. Examples include the number of received bytes and packets per port, per flow table, and per flow-table entry; number of dropped packets; and duration of a flow. |
| Instructions | Actions to be taken if a match occurs. |
| Timeouts | Maximum amount of idle time before a flow is expired by the switch. |
| Cookie | Opaque data value chosen by the controller. May be used by the controller to filter flow statistics, flow modification, and flow deletion; not used when processing packets. |

- **VLAN ID and VLAN User Priority:** Fields in the IEEE 802.1Q Virtual LAN header.
- **IPv4 or IPv6 DS and ECN:** Differentiated Services and Explicit Congestion Notification fields.
- **Stream Control Transmission Protocol (SCTP) Source and Destination Ports:** Exact match or wildcard value.
- **Internet Control Message Protocol (ICMP) Type and Code Fields:** Exact match or wildcard value.
- **Address Resolution Protocol (ARP) Opcode:** Exact match in Ether-net Type field.
- **Source and Target IPv4 Addresses in Address Resolution Protocol (ARP) Payload:** Can be an exact address, a bit masked value, a subnet mask value, or a wildcard value.
- **IPv6 Flow Label:** Exact match or wildcard.
- **ICMPv6 Type and Code Fields:** Exact match or wildcard value.
- **IPv6 Neighbor Discovery Target Address:** In an IPv6 Neighbor Discovery message.
- **IPv6 Neighbor Discovery Source and Target Addresses:** Link-layer address options in an IPv6 Neighbor Discovery message.
- **Multiprotocol Label Switching (MPLS) Label Value, Traffic Class, and Bottom of Stack (BoS):** Fields in the top label of an MPLS label stack (Ravi Tomar, Hitesh Kumar, Ankur Dumka, Abhineet Anand,(2015)).

## Flow-Table Pipeline

A switch may include more than one flow tables. If there is more than one flow table, they are organized as a pipeline as shown in Figure 5, with the tables labeled with increasing numbers starting with 0.

*Figure 5. Packet flow through open flow-compliant switch*

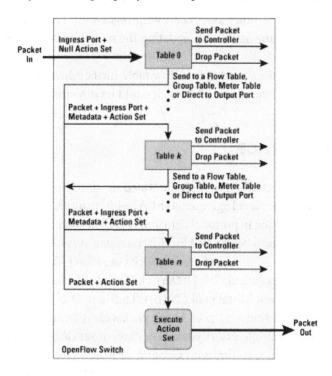

When a packet is presented to a table for matching, the input consists of the packet, the identity of the ingress port, the associated metadata value, and the associated action set. For Table 0, the metadata value is blank and the action set is null. Processing proceeds as follows:

Find the highest-priority matching flow entry. If there is no match on any entry and there is no table-miss entry, then the packet is dropped. If there is a match only on a table-miss entry, then that entry specifies one of three actions:

1. Send packet to controller. This action will enable the controller to define a new flow for this and similar packets, or decide to drop the packet.
2. Direct packet to another flow table farther down the pipeline.
3. Drop the packet.

If there is a match on one or more entries other than the table-miss entry, then the match is defined to be with the highest-priority matching entry. The following actions may then be performed:

1.  Update any counters associated with this entry.
2.  Execute any instructions associated with this entry. These instructions may include updating the action set, updating the metadata value, and performing actions.
3.  The packet is then forwarded to a flow table further down the pipeline, to the group table, or to the meter table, or it could be directed to an output port.

## QUALITY OF SERVICE

From customer perspective QoS can be defined as ability of service provider to maintain a level of service level agreement (SLA) with customer. To classify customer traffic, we use information in protocol data unit (PDU) at some layer. Once customer traffic is classified, it must be marked for differentiated services using protocol like 802.1P, precedence or IP differentiated services etc (Ravi Tomar, Hitesh Kumar, Ankur Dumka, Abhineet Anand,(2015); Derrick D'souza, Krishna Prabhu Sundharan, Savithru Lokanath, Vivek Mittal et.al,(2016)). Traffic in QoS is classified at access port and differentiated at network port. Using packet classification, you can partition network traffic into multiple priority levels or class of services. Committed Access Rate (CAR) is used for rate-limiting. Generic Traffic Shaper (GTS), Distributed Traffic Shaper (DTS) and Frame Relay Traffic Shaper (FRTS) are used for traffic shaper (Chui B., Yang Z.& Ding W., (2004); Kannan Govindarajan, Kong Chee Meng, Hong Ong,(2014); Egilmez A. T. H.E., Civanlar S., (2012)).

Quality of services is of two types:

1.  Differentiated services (Diffserv)
2.  Integrated Services (Intserv)

There are different methods to apply QoS

## IP Precedence

Class of service termed as CoS is allowed by IP precedence for a packet. 3 bits are used to determine type of service as:

1.  Using 3 bits, you can 8 CoS, these bits define how to treat a packet and what will be its priority.
2.  Weighted fair queuing (WFQ) and weighted random early detection (WRED) uses queue method.

*Table 3. Relationship between different services*

| Differentiated Services | Integrated Services |
|---|---|
| In differentiated service model a packet "class" can be marked directly in the packet. | In integrated service model Special QoS treatment to the flow of router is determined by signalling. |
| Differentiated service achieve better QoS | Integrated service QoS is used for real-time traffic |
| Diffserv model is RFC -2475 | Intserv model is RFC-1633 |
| Resources are allocated by dividing the traffic into small number of classes by the DiffServ architecture (Dongli Zhang and Dan Ionescu, (2007)). | Real time applications like remote video, multimedia conferencing, real time applications are motivated by IntServ architecture (Ankur Dumka, Hardwari Lal Mandoria, Vibudh Fore, Kanchan Dumka,(2015)) |
| No end-to-end signalling | It provide end-to-end QoS (Desire Oulai, Steven Chamberland & Samved Pierre, (2009)) |
| "Admission control" and "resource reservation" is not supported by DiffServ. | For establishing QoS, "resource reservation" and "admission control" is supported by IntServ. RSVP is used to signal explicitly the need for QoS of an application traffic in end-to-end path through network (Jyoti Tewari, Ankur Dumka, Gulista Khan, (2012)). |

3. Policy based routing (PBR) and Committed Access Rate (CAR) used to set precedence based on extended access-list classification.

Value of IP precedence numbers (3bits):

0 – routine
1 – priority
1 – immediate
2 – flash
3 – flash-override
4 – critical
5 – internet
6 – network

Using these classes you can define network policies in term of congestion and bandwidth allocation for each class using policy map and extended access list.

## Policy Based Routing (PBR)

It allow us to configure a defined policy for traffic flow by setting IP precedence. It also specify for certain traffic, such as priority traffic over high cost link.

PBR help us to perform following task:

1.  Classify traffic based on extended access-list. Access list then establish match criteria. (Access-list is used for policy with match route map and having match clause for specific routes to pass through)
2.  Set IP precedence bits, thus enable differentiated CoS
3.  Route packet to specific traffic engineered paths.

Policy can be based on IP address, port number and protocol or size of packets.

## Committed Access Rate (CAR)

It improved classification services and policing through rate limiting. Classification service of CAR is used to set IP precedence for packets entering the network.

Class Based Packet Marking User can differentiate packets by marking the packets based on designated marking. It allow user to perform following tasks:

1.  IP precedence bit or IP differentiated service code point termed as DSCP is used to mark packet by setting IP precedence bit in IP ToS byte.
2.  Packet can be marked by setting layer2 CoS value.
3.  A local QoS group value is associated with a packet
4.  Cell loss priority bit termed as CLP of ATM header is changed from 0 to 1.

## IP Precedence and IP DSCP Marking

1.  These marking can be used to identify traffic within the network. These marking used to decide how packet should be treated in Weighted Random Early Detection (WRED).
2.  First 6 bits of Type of service is used to determine IP DSCP value, Ip precedence value will become a part of DSCP itself, and therefore both the value cannot be set simultaneously. In case if both the value is set simultaneously then IP DSCP value will be the preferred one.
3.  IP DSCP preferred over IP precedence as it has more packet marking options but not supported by many whereas IP precedence is likely to support by all devices in network.
4.  User can set up to 8 different IP precedence marking and 64 different DSCP marking.

## CoS Value Marking

1.  By matching class of service value, mapping of layer 2 and layer 3 mapping can be configured. Router has to set the value of class of service in case in a packet need to be marked for differentiating QoS service based on different user, where packet leave a router and entering a switch, as switch can only process layer 2 class of service of packet. Thus, we can configured layer 2 and layer 3 mapping by matching class of service value.
2.  Maximum of 8 different class of service marking can be set up by user.

## QoS Group Value Marking

1.  To associate a group ID with a packet, packet will be associated with a local QoS group.
2.  Based on community string, autonomous system and prefix, user can classify packets into QoS group by using group ID.
3.  Traffic can be classified by using QoS group marking within a router, but the same classification cannot be made for the packets leaving the router.
4.  Total of 100 different QoS group marking can be set up by the user.

## Class Based Packet Marking

User can differentiate packets for providing QoS by using class based packet marking. This scheme provides efficient packet marking which can be used to differentiate packet based on these designated marking.

It performs following tasks:

1.  Packets can be marked by setting up of IP precedence bit or IP differentiated service code point termed as DSCP in IP ToS byte.
2.  Packet can be marked by setting up of layer2 CoS value
3.  A local QoS group value can be associated with the packet.

## Restrictions With Class-Based Packet Marking Feature

1.  It can mark only packets travelling on CEF switching paths. To use this, configure CEF in both interfaces receiving and sending the packets.
2.  Class-based packet marking feature can be configured on sub interface, interface or an ATM PVC, but not supported on following set of interface types:
    a.  fast Ethernet channel
    b.  Tunnel

c.    PRI

d.    ATM switched virtual circuit (SVC) that is data link connection identifier

e.    any interface that doesn't support CEF

## Policy Based Routing (PBR)

Functionality like protocol sensitive routing, equal access, source sensitive routing, routing based on dedicated links, routing based on interactive versus batch traffic services are provided by policy based routing. Policy based routing is done by means of BGP attributes that are set using route map.

## Random Early Detection (RED)

Random early detection congestion avoidance algorithm is used to drop incoming packets with increasing probability, as average utilization of buffer increases. Each time a packet arrive at the queue, the router determine the utilization at that time and associated with buffer utilization is a probability value. This value determines the probability that the incoming packets will be dropped by router. As current average buffer utilization increases, so does probability that the incoming packet will be dropped.

## Weighted Random Early Detection (WRED)

It works in same manner as RED; however it enables the distinction of packets with different marking like "in-profile", "out-of-profile" packets. Therefore, with WRED, a router can start to discard "out-of-profile" packets with greater probability than "in-profile" packets for a given average buffer utilization.

## Scheduling

Scheduling is another QoS feature implementation scheme, which determines when to serve and forward a packet in a given queue, relative to other queues. It also determines how allocation underlying link's capacity amongst various queues that share that link.

Common scheduling algorithms are:

1.    Strict priority
2.    Round robin and weighted/biased round robin
3.    Fair queuing and weighted fair queuing

Strict priority scheduling queues are ordered with relative priority. Schedulers serve queues in order of priority. It is useful for traffic with low latency requirements. In round robin and weighted/biased round robin, there is no priority between queues; scheduler services a packet from each queue in sequence. Thus, each queue gets an equal amount of servicing time. In weighted/biased RR scheduler certain queue can be provided with higher servicing rate by allowing a queue to receive more frequent visits from the scheduler. In fair queuing and weighted fair queuing, each number of queues contended for resources are allocated service opportunity based on an assigned weight. Weight may be derived from bandwidth allocation to queue. It determines scheduling sequence needed to service a queue so that it meets its long term bandwidth target.

## Shaping

Shaping is used for rate limiting, improves bandwidth utilization and minimizes packet loss. Shaping can take originally excessive non-conforming traffic and make it conforming. Traffic shaping is performed at ingress and egress of service provider network.

## Policing

Policing is used for limiting the rate and prevents excessive traffic from congesting the network and assuring that classified traffic conforms to Service level agreements. Traffic policing is performed at ingress to service provider's network.

There are three different mechanisms to implement policing:

1.  Single bucket, single policer
2.  Single rate, three colour
3.  Two rate, 3 colour

In single bucket, single policer, it allows traffic up to some degree of burst but will discard packets as soon as that burst tolerance exceeded. A simple example is a bucket filling with tap water. The water which can be in bucket will pass as servicing traffic rate while after bucket gets filled with water the water scattered will be discarded traffic . The size of bucket is termed as maximum buffering.

In single rate three colour marker, packet marked with green, orange or red based on one rate and two burst sizes. It is used when only burst size matters. In this the packet marked with green colour filled in bucket of committed burst and hence these packets are known as committed information rate. Whereas the packets marked with orange discarded over overflow from first bucket or queue will be in excess burst size bucket and can be used later whereas the packets marked with red are discarded packets.

In single rate three colour queue, there is only one source and colour of packets depends on their incoming value when compared with committed information rate(CIR) and peak information rate(PIR) packet marked with green, orange and red based on 2 rates and 2 burst size. It is used when peak rate must be enforced. In this if incoming packets is less than committed information rate(CIR) then that packet mark as green and if incoming traffic is between committed information rate and peak information rate (PIR) then first few packet marked green and then orange. If incoming traffic is above Peak information rate then that packets gets discarded and that packets colour as red.

## QOS OPTIMIZATION

The network bandwidth provided by a wired/wireless network link is limited. When a network flow passes through the network link, it consumes some or all of the limited network bandwidth. Usually, the network administrators do not manage the bandwidth usage of each flow because manually changing network devices setting on demand is error-prone and the response time to demands is usually too long to satisfy needs on time. In the case that several flows pass through the same link, consume all the limited bandwidth and each flow still needs more bandwidth, the bandwidth bottleneck occurs at the entrance of the congested link.

In the following simulation, eight traffic-source nodes from Internet generate eight traffic flows to those eight traffic-destination nodes, located at a local area network (LAN), separately (i.e., node 11 to node 1, node 12 to node 2, node 13 to node 3, and so on). Because the total link bandwidth from Internet is 80 Mbps (10 Mbps * 8 links) and the wired link bandwidth of the LAN is 1000 Mbps, no bandwidth bottleneck occurs at the entrance into the LAN. However, the wireless link bandwidth of the LAN is only 25 Mbps and is less than 80 Mbps. This causes the bandwidth bottleneck at the entrance into the wireless link. Because of the bandwidth bottleneck, the network packets sent from the eight traffic-source nodes are randomly dropped at the entrance into the wireless link (i.e., the access point device). As a consequence, the obtained receiving throughput of each traffic-destination node is unstable. The unstable receiving throughput may result in poor user experience on some real-time network applications, such as on-line video, video conference, etc In order to avoid the situation of unstable receiving throughput, one solution is to manage the bandwidth usage of each network flow. On an Open Flow switch device,

*Figure 6. Simulation of service implementation*

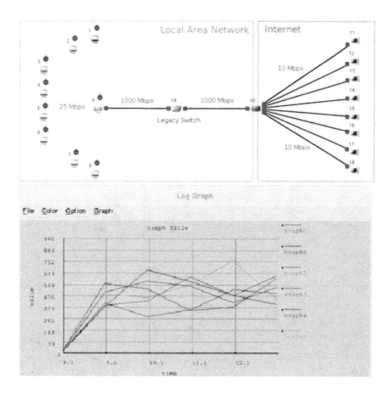

two ways can be used to control the bandwidth usage of each network flow. One is to use meter table and the other is to use the per-port output queues.

Here in this chapter, in Figure 7 we display an example case that has almost the same network topology as the one mentioned above. The only difference is that we replace the legacy switch in the LAN by an Open Flow switch, to which an SDN controller is connected. To provide a QoS service to the traffic-destination nodes, we classify them into three groups: the guaranteed group, the fairly-shared group, and the contended group (Chui, Yang & Ding, 2004). The total quantum of bandwidth of the wireless link (i.e., 25 Mbps) is assigned to these three groups: 10 Mbps for the guaranteed group, 12 Mbps for the fairly-shared group, and 3 Mbps for the contended group.

For those nodes belonging to the guaranteed group, we want to reserve fixed quantum of bandwidth to each one. In this example case, 6 Mbps is reserved for Node 1 and 4 Mbps is reserved for Node 2. For those nodes belonging to the fairly-shared group, we want them to fairly share the assigned quantum of bandwidth. In this case, Node 3, Node 4, Node 5, and Node 6 belong to this group and each of them

*Figure 7. Design of model for service implementation*

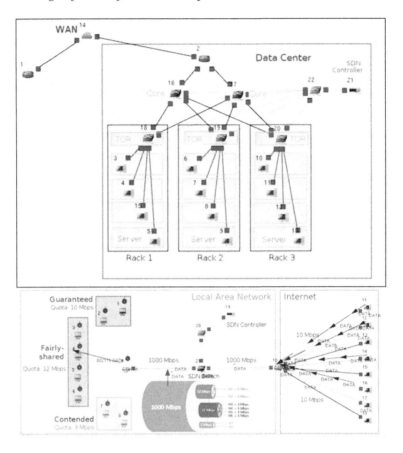

should obtain 3 Mbps (12/4). For those nodes belonging to the contended group, no bandwidth reservation is applied for everyone. In other words, all of them have to contend the allocated bandwidth of this group.

An SDN controller software (Ryu) is run up during the simulation with its restful north-bound interface being opened. We execute a script file to insert flow rules to the OpenFlow switch through the restful interface. We use one flow table and seven per-port output queues to realize the QoS service/scenario described above. From the simulation result, we can see that all those nodes applied with bandwidth reservation obtain the expected and stable receiving throughput (in KB/sec), and those nodes belonging to the contended group still obtain unstable throughput.

Thus by using SDN technology for implementation of QoS services with the SDN network the performance factor for the network will be increased as shown in Figure 8.

*Figure 8. Service implementation results*

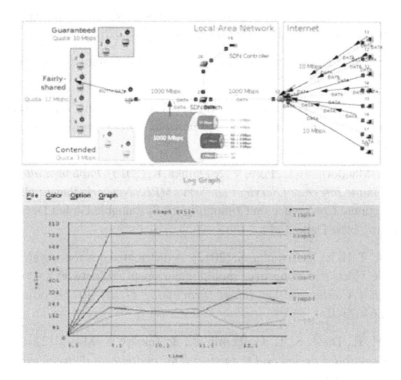

As mentioned at the beginning, manually changing network devices' setting on demand is error-prone and the response time to demands is usually too long to satisfy needs on time. These problems can be solved by developing an intelligent SDN controller APP. A network administrator just has to classify users and assign their allowed quantum of bandwidth usage on the APP in advance. This APP is able to automatically detect the target network flows and automatically configure the Open Flow switch to guarantee the bandwidth usage for each target flow.

## REFERENCES

Cao, Zhang, Huang, Zhang, & Gu. (2009). The design, Implementation and performance analysis of transport-MPLS network. *IEEE Journal*, 46-49.

Chui, B., Yang, Z., & Ding, W. (2004). A load balancing algorithm supporting QoS for traffic engineering in MPLS networks. *4th international conference on computer & Information technology*, 436-441.

Civanlar, S., Parlakisik, M., Tekalp, A. M., Gorkemli, B., Kaytaz, B., & Onem, E. (2010). *A qos-enabled openflow environment for scalable video streaming.* IEEE Globecom Workshops. doi:10.1109/GLOCOMW.2010.5700340

D'souza, Sundharan, Lokanath, & Mittal. (2016). Improving QoS in a Software-Defined Network. *Capstone Research Paper*, 1-9.

Doria, A., Salim, J.H., Haas, R., Khosravi, H., Wang, W., Dong, L., … Halpern, J. (2010). *Forwarding and control element separation (forces) protocol specification.* Academic Press.

Dumka, A., Mandoria, H. L., Fore, V., & Dumka, K. (2015). *Implementation of QoS Algorithm in the Integrated Services (IntServ) MPLS Network.* Paper published in 2nd International Conference on Computing for Sustainable Global Development (INDIAcom), New Delhi, India.

Egilmez, A. T. H. E., & Civanlar, S. (2012). A distributed qos routing architecture for scalable video streaming over multidomain openflow networks. *Proc. IEEE International Conference on Image Processing (ICIP 2012).* doi:10.1109/ICIP.2012.6467340

Egilmez, H. E., Dane, S. T., Gorkemli, B., & Tekalp, A. M. (2012). *Openqos: Openflow controller design and test network for multimedia delivery with quality of service.* NEM Summit.

Govindarajan, K., Meng, K. C., & Ong, H. (2013). A literature review on Software-Defined Networking (SDN) research topics, challenges and solutions. *Fifth International Conference on Advanced Computing (ICoAC)*, 293-299. doi:10.1109/ICoAC.2013.6921966

Govindarajan, K., Meng, K. C., & Ong, H. (2014). Realizing the Quality of Service (QoS) in Software-Defined Networking (SDN) based Cloud infrastructure. *2nd International Conference on Information and Communication Technology (ICoICT)*, 505 – 510.

Hakiria, A., Gokhalec, A., Berthoua, P., & Schmidt, D. C. (2014). Gayraud Thierry, "Software-defined Networking: Challenges and Research Opportunities for Future Internet. *International Council for Computer Communication, Elsevier, 2014*, 1–26.

Kanaumi, Y., Saito, S., Kawai, E., Ishii, S., Kobayashi, K., & Shimojo, S. (2013). Rise: A wide-area hybrid openflow network testbed. *IEICE Transactions, 96-B*(1), 108–118. doi:10.1587/transcom.E96.B.108

Kim, H., & Feamster, N. (2013). Improving network management with software defined networking. *Communications Magazine, IEEE, 51*(2), 114–119. doi:10.1109/MCOM.2013.6461195

Kind, M., Westphal, F., Gladisch, A., & Topp, S. (2012). Split architecture: Applying the software defined networking concept to carrier networks. In *World Telecommunications Congress* (pp. 1–6). WTC. Retrieved from http://www.fp7-sparc.eu/

Martini, B., Baroncelli, F, Martini, V., & Castoldi, P. (2009). ITU-T RACF implementation for application-driven QoS control in MPLS networks. *IEEE Journal*, 422-429.

Oulai, D., Chamberland, S., & Pierre, S. (2009). End-to-end Quality of Service constrained routing and admission control for MPLS network. *Journal of Communications and Networks (Seoul), 2*(3).

Tewari, Dumka, & Khan. (2012). Sync Preempted Probability Algorithm in the Integrated Services (IntServ) MPLS Network. *International Journal of Science and Research, 3*(6), 696-698.

Tomar, R., Kumar, H., Dumka, A., & Anand, A. (2015). Traffic management in MPLS network using GNS simulator using class for different services. *2015 2nd International Conference on Computing for Sustainable Global Development (INDIACom)*.

Zhang, D., & Ionescu, D. (2007). QoS performance Analysis in Deployment of DiffServ-aware MPLS Traffic Engineering. *8th ACIS International Conference on Software Engineering, Artificial Intelligence, Networking and Parallel/Distributed Computing, IEEE 2007*, 963-967. doi:10.1109/SNPD.2007.541

## KEY TERMS AND DEFINITIONS

**Class of Service:** Used to set up a priority to traffic in order to manage multiple traffic profiles over the network.

**Differentiated Service:** Architecture that is used to classify and manage traffic to provide quality of service within the network.

**Integrated Service:** Also an architecture that is used to classify and manage traffic for providing quality of service within the network.

**IP Precedence:** Of three bits that is used to set the priority of a packet on higher importance in case of congestion.

**QoS Optimization:** QoS optimization is concerned with measurement, modelling, characterization, and control of network traffic, and the application of techniques to achieve specific performance objectives.

**Quality of Service:** Quality of service can be defined as network ability to achieve maximum bandwidth by dealing with network performance parameters like latency, error rate, etc.

**Shaping:** A technique that is used to enforce lower bitrates than what the physical interface is capable of.

**Type of Service:** It specifies a datagram's priority and request a route for low-delay, high-throughput, or highly reliable service.

Chapter 10

# Analysis of Issues in SDN Security and Solutions

**Ankur Dumka**
*University of Petroleum and Energy Studies, India*

**Hardwari Lal Mandoria**
*G. B. Pant University of Agriculture and Technology, India*

**Anushree Sah**
*University of Petroleum and Energy Studies, India*

## ABSTRACT

*The chapter surveys the analysis of all the security aspects of software-defined network and determines the areas that are prone to security attacks in the given software-defined network architecture. If the fundamental network topology information is poisoned, all the dependent network services will become immediately affected, causing catastrophic problems like host location hijacking attack, link fabrication attack, denial of service attack, man in the middle attack. These attacks affect the following features of SDN: availability, performance, integrity, and security. The flexibility in the programmability of control plane has both acted as a bane as well as a boon to SDN. Like the ARP poisoning in the legacy networks, there are several other vulnerabilities in the SDN architecture as well.*

## INTRODUCTION

SDN provide user a functionality to program the network in easier manner and also creating dynamic flow policies. Distributed Denial of Service (DDoS) attack is one of the major factor which can cause the network as unreachable (Mohammad & Marc, 2015). By the means of spoofing which can cause the destination packet

DOI: 10.4018/978-1-5225-3640-6.ch010

unreachable as the source address will become unreachable in this case. Multiple types of attacks within the SDN networks can be categorized as:

1. Exploiting timers
2. CPU memory drainage
3. Reduction in computing power
4. Congestion within the network resources
5. Poisoning of the domain name translation

There can be multiple areas where the attacks can be done within the SDN network, such as hindering of the normal functioning of the service by attacking at the application layer. The attacks can also damage web browser, email application or media player. This type of disfunctioning can be caused by disruption of specific application and are termed as application level denial of service.

There can be permanent damage to the system which will completely destroy the hardware of the system through malicious attack which is termed as permanent denial of service or plashing. The permanent damage can be caused by attack on firmware which are the inbuilt code or program inside a system which runs the system (Lau, Rubin., Smith, et al., 2000). The permanent attack will change the firmware which is not acceptable by the hardware and the hardware gets crashed. The attack can caused harm to the routers or switches connected with the system. Thus, it is needed to check for signature of the trusted source before upgrading the firmware.

In terms of computing in SDN network, the denial of service attack is defined as (DoS attack) which is defined as when any host are getting resource temporary or permanently. This can be done by flooding a system with number of request so that the system gets interrupted with these request and will discard the genuine or legitimate requests (Needham, 1994; Tootoonchian & Ganjali, 2010). Denial of service can be categorized into two based on type of attacks. First is classified as those attack which crashes the service whereas second attacks are those which flood the services (Lau, Rubin, Smith, et al. 2000). IP spoofing is also a kind of attack where sender IP address will be forged in order to divert the packets as in this case, the location of attacking machines cannot be easily identified. Distributed Denial of service (DDos) is a cyber attack where perpetrator uses more than one unique IP address (Nakashima, Sueyoshi, Oshima, 2010). One more type of Dos attack is advanced persistent DoS attack, this is a type of cyber attack where cyber criminals uses multiple phases to penetrate the network and obtain valuable information over period of time. APDos attack involve network layer DDos attack through to focused application layer (HTTP) floods, followed by repeated SQLi and XSS attacks (Mirkovic, Reiher, 2004; Wang, Zheng, Lou, et al., 2014). APDoS attack can be categorized as:

1.  **Advanced Reconnaissance:** This include pre-attack open source intelligence (OSINT) and extensively decoyed scanning crafted to evade detection over long period.
2.  **Tactical Execution:** It refers to attack with a primary and secondary victims but focus is on primary
3.  **Explicit Motivation:** It refers to calculated end game or goal target
4.  **Large Computing Capacity:** It refers to attack on computer power and network bandwidth resources.
5.  **Simultaneous Multi-Threaded OSI Layer Attacks:** This focusses attacks on layer 3-7 of OSI model
6.  **Persistence Over Extended Periods:** It include well managed attacks over range of targets.

What do the attacker wants through DDoS attack? The question was very obvious as what will be the motive of the attacker while attacking on the network. The motive could be to bring down a specific webpage or website in order to keep it isolated from the business. Thus, causing harm to the company by losing all the online transactions of the company which ends up in failing all the transactions. The reason for such can be cited as business rivalries as one of the main reason (Mirkovic, Reiher 2004). There can be another reason to show grievance to the government by attacking the government websites and bring it down. There can be more reasons for this attack but main reason is to harm the company working in order to cause it harm. There are also the cases when any beginner could perform this attack effortlessly without having much technical expertise. Many attackers often put their tools and scripts online just to aid others who like to carry out similar operations. There are many other websites and forum which often provide tools and instructions manual to carry out such attacks. People who done attack to breach the security unknowingly are termed as "Script Kiddies".

## CASE STUDY

There are numerous types of attacks within the system that emerges day by day. One of the most happening attack held on 7 feb 2000 on the yahoo servers when they got crashed which causes unavailability of yahoo site for several hours leading to great loss to yahoo. There are others attacks to the companies like Buy.com, E-Bay and CNN to the very next day which causes a huge loss to the transaction of these companies where E-bay was a online bank which incurred a huge loss due to this attack. Other companies which suffers from these losses include ZDnet, Etrade an Excite, which crashes due to heavy bombardment of data with over 1 gigabit data per second which causes server to respond to the legitimate requests. These are some of the examples of DoS attacks on big giants.

Apart from the DoS attacks to these companies, there are several other cases where DoS attacks create a major havoc. The examples are the DoS attack on the revolutionary armed forces of Columbia on 2nd july, 2008. The attack was made by Columbian national forces to bring out their hostages. These intruders carried a series of DoS and Man in the Middle (MITM) attack. This attack lead to release of fifteen most crucial hostages. Thus, this attack was unique in its type where several hostages were freed without using of any arms or ammunition.

Confidentiality, integrity, availability of information, non-repudiation and authentication are some of the basic properties for a secure communication network. There is a need to secure a data from malicious attack or unintentional damage within the network in order to provide a secure communication transactions across the network. Gude, Koponen, Pettit, Pfaff, Casado, McKeown, and Shenker (2008) propose SANE architecture which was centered in a logical centralized controller which will be responsible for host authentication and enforcement of policy within the network. Ethane in his paper extended the work of Gude and proposes to control the network through the use of two components that are centralized controller and ethane switches. Where centralized controller are responsible for enforcement of global policies and ethane switches works as flow table which will forward the packet based on flow table.

Talking in terms of current SDN architecture, there are applications needed for providing various types of services. This can be resulted in breach of entire network which will be a serious threat in terms of security of the network. Talking of the SDN functional architecture, we can divide it into 3 parts as:

1.  **Application Layer:** This layer will be used for load balancing, traffic security monitoring etc.
2.  **Control Layer:** This layer is responsible for control commands by the means of controllers like NOX, Flood light etc. (Lau, Rubin, Smith, et al. 2000).
3.  **Data Layer:** This layer consists of routers, virtual switches etc.

The security threat can be considered within these three layers as well as interface connecting among these three layers.

Open flow vulnerability majorly focuses on transport layer security and Denial of Service (DoS) attacks.

1.  **Denial of Service Attack:** Based on the type of implementation we can divide our denial of service attacks as:

*Figure 1. SDN functional architecture*

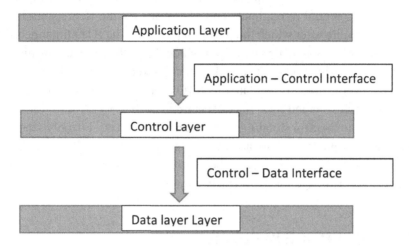

a.   **Distributed Denial of Service Attack:** As the name suggested distributed denial of service attack is combined strength of multiple systems work towards a single cause. In this type of attack, a platform is built with many systems which can work under remote commands. In this attack, the attacker hunt for the weakest part of the system within the network by scanning through the network. In this type of attack the attacker once complete the scanning and find the vulnerable host for attack and bring this host under control by software exploitation by means of buffer overflow, code injection etc. Once the sufficient host has been identified that can be brought under control, the attacker create backdoors which will allow special access for future entry. Attackers also update the host and tightens its security so that no other attackers can use the same host for attack. Thus, for future entry, the attacker will use the back entry that was specially crafted.

b.   **Low-Rate TCP Targeted Denial of Service:** Low-rate TCP targeted denial of service attack that employ number of packets for flooding the network. Thus, this attack exploits the working of TCP timer by bringing throughput of the system almost to zero. This attack generate packets only periodically in very minimal quantity. Thus the attacking packets can easily disguise with the legitimate packets and escape from the Anti-DoS traffic monitoring systems. This attack exploits the TCP timers and thus coined with the term "shrew attacks".

Thus due to flooding, the congestion occur which reduces the sender's rate and corresponding potential throughput. The TCP waits for the Retransmission Time Out (RTO) to expire after which the data is sent again. The RTO timer gets double as the congestion is more in this case after which the packets are retransmitted after timer out. Thus during a low rate attack, when packets are lost, TCP enters RTO. When an attacker is able to calculate this RTO time and sends attacking packets to create packet collision and loss, the attacker can push the TCP into waiting state. Hence, there is no need for flooding the network with packets, but only send packets when the timer is about to expire and push it again into the RTO waiting time. This type of attack can effortlessly escape the traffic monitors due to its low traffic rate and is a serious challenge for the security experts.

## DENIAL OF SERVICE IN DETAIL

When the user is denied access to resources of a particular machine, it may refer to as Denial-of-service (DoS) attack. In other words, it is the intentional block or interruption of services of a host accessing internet temporarily or permanently. Similarly, DDoS is the distributed denial of service which is intended suspension of computer and network resources in the machine of registered user. It causes the target system to stop responding to user's requests, resulting in long delays and outages. The user may be requesting to access a web browser, application, e-mail, voicemail, network etc. This is achieved by the attacker by creating a horde of network traffic in the target machine by the control of more than one remotely-controlled computer. When the target machine will flood with attacker's requests, it will lose time to send response to user's request.

DDoS attacks can be categorized into two groups:

1.  Semantic attacks
2.  Brute-force (flood) attacks.

Semantic attack works by taking advantage of a bug or glitch in the applications or protocols installed in the user's machine. It avails that ingredient of the application and consumes its resources in an inordinate amount. For instance, the attacker can deliver a series of packets across the server in order to inaugurate CPU time consuming operations. With large number of such requests, the target machine will be impotent to handle requests from authorized users. This attack can be abridged by regular updates of software and protocols in addition with implementation of exclusive filter mechanisms.

# ATTACK TECHNIQUES

## Network Based Attacks

### TCP SYN Flooding

DoS attacks are usually intended to employ stateful network protocols as they drain resources to maintain states. One such attack is TCP SYN flooding. It has an ample repercussion on many systems. On ensconcing a TCP connection to a server, a SYN message is send by the client to the server which acknowledges the message and sends a SYN-ACK message to the client. The connection is established when the user reciprocate with an ACK message. After successful connection establishment, client and server can exchange service-specific data. The debasement between client and server arises at half-open state when after sending the SYN-ACK message to the client, it does not receive the client's ACK message for a long duration. This information of the half-open connection needs to be stored by the server for which it has to allocate certain memory which is released either after the server receives the final ACK message or after the expiration of half-open connection state. Half-open connections are created by the attacking hosts through jesting source IPs in SYN messages or neglecting SYN-ACKs which results in the victim never receiving the final ACK message. An inordinate amount of half-open connections will flood the memory space as only a limited size of space is measured in its process table. The attacking hosts are capable of circulating imposture TCP SYN packets requesting connections at an exorbitant rate which is much higher than the expiration rate of half-open connections. Consequently, there will be no compliance of any new incoming connection which will incapacitate the victim to provide services.

### ICMP Smurf Flooding

ICMP is utilized to certify the response status of a computer in the Internet which is analyzed by sending an ICMP echo request packet to a computer. After receiving the request packet, the computer responds by returning an ICMP echo reply packet. The attacking hosts counterfeit ICMP echo requests by having the victim's address as the source address and the broadcast address of these outlying networks as the destination address during a smurf attack. The crafted packets are broadcasted to all computers on a network if the firewall or router of the outlying network does not filter any such packet. The ICMP echo reply packets are sent back to the victim by the computers in the request packets due to which the source network becomes clogged up.

## UDP Flooding

The current networks and systems have assimilated new security earmarks to prevent TCP and ICMP attacks. This is accomplished by plating and overhauling the implementation of TCP and ICMP protocols. Despite this, the attacker can impoverish the victim's connection resources by dispatching an inordinate amount of UDP packets towards a victim. This eventuates as the victim network is incapable of handling large volumes of traffic than the transport rate of transitional network. This horde of traffic can cause frazzle of victim's connection resources. All sorts of packets can be used to formulate pure flooding. Intermittently, attackers outpour service requests to restrain the victim from handling all requests with its constrained resources. When multiple users essay to access the same server synchronously, UDP flooding takes place which is quite analogous to flash crowds. The difference between DDoS attacks and flash crowds ensue in their intent and elicit procedure.

## Intermittent Flooding

Attackers measure their glutting actions to curtail the average flooding rate to a much subsided standard thereby attaining correspondent attack repercussion on authorized TCP connections. The attacking hosts can overflow the number of packets in a burst to choke and obstruct previous TCP connections in case of shrew attacks. All the obstructed packets go through downtime for a definitive period of time called retransmission-time-out (RTO) to readdress adrift packets. The attacking hosts can overflow the rate of transmission of packets at the consequent RTO to rupture retransmission. Hence, the exhaustion of authorized TCP connections with mesh of flooding actions can be carried out by the attacking hosts. This collusion of attacking hosts curtails the overflow traffic and also aids to evade detection. Guirguis et al. (2005) worked towards enhancing Quality of Service and successfully discovered analogous procedures contemplating services. On acquiring multiple requests, Quality of Service inhibit succeeding requests transiently until the processing of existing requests. Thus, DoS effect is actualized by attackers by flooding requests at a rate that will keep the server occupied by suppressing the approaching requests. It was discovered by Guirguis's study that a server will experience downtime for 200 seconds with a glut of 800 requests due to which the average burst rate could stoop down to 4 requests per second.

## Host Based Attacks

The attackers can commence DoS attacks by capitalizing on susceptibility in target's applications and systems in addition to exploitation of network protocols.

This attack is distinctive from other network based attacks in the sense that it is application specific. It includes employing particular algorithms memory structure, implementation, corroboration protocols etc. The attack can be carried out from a single host or multiple hosts depending on whether it is a customary intrusion or a network based DDoS attack respectively. The blemish and dearth in operations can crash applications or consume a formidable amount of computer resources easily though the traffic of host based attacks may not be as high as network based attacks.

## Attack Network

Distributed attacking hosts can commence multiple DoS attacks (also called DDoS attacks). The DDoS attack is put into motion following a two-step development procedure. The attack is initialized by developing a network with encroachment capabilities consisting of an inordinate surplus of jeopardizing computer systems (called zombies, bots, or attacking hosts) and distributing it across multiple host systems. After this, a colossal volume of traffic is send across the victim's machine either by the attacker or is self-regulated. Such attack network is a consequence of poorly structured and unimmunized computers of users. The impregnability of a vulnerable host can be jeopardized by following two proposals. The first one includes running malevolent programs namely, virus, Trojans, spyware etc. integrated in emails, web pages, files etc. The second proposal is carried through computerized programs namely, worms which can mechanically examine the vulnerable nature of remote computers. Taking undue advantage of this susceptibility, the attackers exploit user's system by rupturing into it and installing programs initiating DoS attack. Furthermore, heterogeneous other hosts are scanned and flood packets, backdoors are installed by the attacker. Hence, the attacker is referred to as the master of these compromised computers (zombies). The latter is capable of registering the vulnerable systems as an associate in the scenario of a complex network attack. It is a self-propagating network where the compromised systems repeat this procedure and exploit other computers with similar glitches. Thus, interruption or attack in one system can create a gigantic attack network consisting of thousands of computers.

## DDOS DETECTION USING ENTROPY

Entropy measures randomness. The main reason entropy is used for DDOS detection is its ability to measure randomness in the packets that are coming to a network. The higher the randomness the higher is the entropy and vice versa. There are two important types of DDOS detection using entropy:

1. Window size
2. Threshold

Window size depends on a time period or a number of packets. Entropy is calculated within this window to measure uncertainty in the coming packets. We require a threshold to detect an attack. Calculated entropy if passes a threshold or is below it, depending on the scheme, an attack is detected. Say n be the number of packet in a window and p is the probability of each element in the window then, entropy will be calculated as:

Entropy showcases packet headers as independent information symbols with distinct probability of occurrence. Selecting a window of some number, 10,000 for example, and moving the window forward, a pattern will emerge with probabilities for each type of packet header. Drastic changes in the bins of each header that varies from the average bin limits will alert the system of anomalies.

$$H = -\sum P_i \log P_i$$

Entropy is a, fairly, common method for DDOS detection. Qin et al. (2014) propose a technique with a window of 0.1 seconds and three levels of threshold. This method is concerned with maintaining a strategic distance from false positives and false negatives in the system. However, as the authors mentioned, the method is time consuming and uses more resources. This method also uses a time period window. For the threshold, the authors ran several datasets to find a suitable experimental threshold and it is a multiple of the standard deviation of the entropy values. In this method, the false negatives are higher than other methods and false positives are lower. No percentage of accuracy is indicated. There is also no mention of resources used for fast computation.

Nakashima, Sueyoshi, Oshima (2010) propose a short-term statistics detection method based on entropy computation. "Short-term" here refers to calculating entropy in small size windows. The study proposes a window size of 50 packets for gathering statistics. In this method, different window sizes were tested for optimal entropy measurement and a size of 50 was the lowest size that effectively detected attacks. Instead of a threshold, the authors used a one-sided test of significance to confirm whether an attack was in progress or not. In the DDoS detection case, the rate of attack traffic was increased by increments while the normal traffic rate was kept constant. The method proved to be effective the most when the attack traffic was 75% or higher than the normal traffic.

## Utilizing SDN Capabilities

When there comes an incoming connection, the controller will install a flow in the switch so that the rest of the incoming packets will be directed to the destination without further processing. Hence, any time a packet is seen in the controller, it is new. Destination host is within network of the controller while new packets come. This is induced on the basis of the fact that one of the hosts or a subnet of hosts in the network is being attacked. The network consists of the switches and hosts that are connected to it. Knowing that the packet is new and that the destination is in the network, the level of randomness can be quantified by calculating the entropy based on a window size. In this case, maximum entropy occurs when each packet is send by exactly one source. On the other side, minimum entropy occurs when all the packets in a window are send by single source. For example, if the window has 64 elements and all elements appear only once, then as per available equation the entropy will be 1.80. If one element appears 10 times, the entropy will be 1.64. This property of the entropy will be used for calculating the randomness in the SDN controller. Controller over the network has the central view that provides us the opportunity to evaluate the rate of incoming new packets to the controller and predicts whether an attack is in progress or not.

SDN enables to quantify randomness and have minimum and maximum based on the entropy making it a suitable method for DDOS detection. Using entropy, it is possible to see its value drop when a large number of packets are attacking one host or a subnet of hosts.

## Statistics Collection for Entropy

One of the functions of the controller is collecting statistics from the switch tables. The controller monitors the existing flows and if there is an inactive flow for a period of time, it will remove that flow. In this paper, we will make use of that property and add another set of statistics collection to the controller. Since the approximate number of hosts in the network is known, we added the destination IP address of the new incoming packets to be collected into windows of size 50. The entropy of each window is calculated and compared to an experimental threshold. If the entropy is lower than the threshold, an attack is detected. These functions are small (in terms of the amount of code added) and transparent to the other functionalities of the controller. These two properties make the solution applicable to different controllers with minimal changes.

## Window Size

The window size should be set to be smaller or equal to the number of hosts in order to provide accurate calculations. In this project, we set the window size at 50. The main reason for choosing 50 is the limited number of incoming new connection to each host in the network. In SDN, once a connection is established, the packets will not pass through the controller unless there is a new request. A second reason is the fact that a limited number of switches and hosts can be connected to each controller. Finally, a third reason for choosing this size is the amount of computation that is done for each window. A list of 50 values can be computed much faster than 500 and an attack in a 50-packet window is detected earlier. We also tested the entropy with three other window sizes and measured the CPU and memory usage. There is no difference in memory usage but the CPU usage slightly increases with respect to the window size. Considering the limited resources of the controller, this window size is ideal for networks with one controller and few hundred hosts.

## Attack Detection

For detecting an attack in the controller, we monitor the destination IP address of the incoming packets. A hash table of the arriving packets is developed by the addition of a function. In case of a new IP address in the table, it is added with count 1 which is incremented if its instance already exists in the table.

After 50 packets, the entropy of the window will be calculated and it shows the hash table where x is the destination IP address and y is the number of times it appeared. To compute the entropy as can be shown by given equation, we conclude with new equation where W is the window and p is the probability of each IP address.

Entropy becomes maximum when each IP address appears only once. If an attack is directed towards a host, a large number of packets will be directed to it. Entropy is reduced when these packets will fill most of the window and reduce the number of unique IPs in the window. We made use of this fact and set an experimental threshold. If the entropy drops below this threshold and that five consecutive windows have lower than threshold entropy, then an attack is in progress. Detection within 5 entropy periods is 250 packets in the attack, which gives the network an early alert of the attack. We tested with different values between one and five consecutive periods and, five has the lowest false positive for early detection. The other advantage of having five windows is the possibility of losing a switch or a broken link, which will cut off some hosts and reduce the number of new packets into the controller. This will cause a drop in the entropy and a false positive. Five windows can give the network admin enough time to act.

## SDN OPERATIONS

The SDN devices provides forwarding functionality for deciding what to do with each incoming packet. The devices also contain the data that drives those forwarding decisions. The data itself is actually represented by the flows defined by the controller, as depicted in the upper-left portion of each device. A flow describes a set of packets transferred from one network endpoint (or set of endpoints) to another endpoint (or set of endpoints). The endpoints may be defined as IP address- TCP/UDP port pairs, VLAN endpoints, layer three tunnel endpoints, and input ports, among other things. One set of rules describes the forwarding actions that the device should take for all packets belonging to that flow.

A flow is unidirectional in that packets flowing between the same two endpoints in the opposite direction could each constitute a separate flow. Flows are represented on a device as a flow entry.

A flow table resides on the network device and consists of a series of flow entries and the actions to perform when a packet matching that flow arrives at the device. When the SDN device receives a packet, it consults its flow tables in search of a match. These flow tables had been constructed previously when the controller downloaded appropriate flow rules to the device. If the SDN device finds a match, it takes the appropriate configured action, which usually entails forwarding the packet. If it does not find a match, the switch can either drop the packet or pass it to the controller, depending on the version of OpenFlow and the configuration of the switch.

## Southbound API

The interaction between the controller and the deployed device is commonly referred to as southbound application programing interface (API). A common, open standard SDN protocol, and one of the most popular options for southbound APIs is OpenFlow.

## Northbound API

The opposite of the southbound API is the northbound API, which is labelled as just API; connections from a business application to the controller are involved. Anybody with basic knowledge of programming can create an SDN application. The SDN application itself can be written to perform a very large set of potential activities; the most basic of which could be to tell a deployed device to forward a packet with a matching set of contents out a specific interface. However, the northbound API can be very complex, like providing a Quality of Service provisioned path from one end of a network to another dynamically, then tearing it back down when the application was completed with its network interaction.

The SDN controller is responsible for abstracting the network of SDN devices it controls and presenting an abstraction of these network resources to the SDN applications running above. The controller allows the SDN application to define flows on devices and to help the application respond to packets that are forwarded to the controller by the SDN devices. Since one controller can control a large number of network devices, these calculations are normally performed on a high-performance machine with an order-of-magnitude performance advantage over the CPU and memory capacity than is typically afforded to the network devices themselves. For example, a controller might be implemented on an eight-core, 2-GHz CPU versus the single-core, 1-GHz CPU that is more typical on a switch.

SDN applications are built on top of the controller. These applications should not be confused with the application layer defined in the seven-layer OSI model of computer networking. SDN application is part of network layers two and three so this concept is orthogonal to that of applications in the tight hierarchy of OSI protocol layers. The SDN application interfaces with the controller, using it to set proactive flows on the devices and to receive packets that have been forwarded to the controller. Proactive flows are established by the application; typically, the application will set these flows when the application starts up, and the flows will persist until some configuration change is made. This kind of proactive flow is known as a static flow. Another kind of proactive flow is where the controller decides to modify a flow based on the traffic load currently being driven through a network device (Lau, Rubin, Smith, et al. 2000).

In addition to flows defined proactively by the application, some flows are defined in response to a Packet forwarded to the controller. Upon receipt of incoming packets that have been forwarded to the controller, the SDN application will instruct the controller as to how to respond to the packet and, if appropriate, will establish new flows on the device in order to allow that device to respond locally the next time it sees a packet belonging to that flow. Such flows are called reactive flows. In this way, it is now possible to write software applications that implement forwarding, routing, overlay, multipath, and access control functions, among others.

Some reactive flows act or are modified as a result of stimuli from sources other than packets from the controller. For example, the controller can insert flows reactively in response to other data sources such as intrusion detection systems (IDS) or the Net Flow traffic analyser. The Open Flow protocol act as the means of communication between the controller and the device (Alsulaiman, Alyahya, Alkharboush, Alghafis, 2009; Su, Huang, Hu, 2013; Tootoonchian and Ganjali, 2010). Though Open Flow is the defined standard for such communication in Open SDN

## SDN DEVICES

An SDN device is composed of an API for communication with the controller, an abstraction layer, and a packet-processing function. In the case of a virtual switch, this packet-processing function is packet-processing software, and in the case of a physical switch, the packet processing function is embodied in the hardware for packet-processing logic,

The packet-processing logic consists of the mechanisms to take actions based on the results of evaluating incoming packets and finding the highest-priority match. When a match is found, the incoming packet is processed locally unless it is explicitly forwarded to the controller. When no match is found, the packet may be copied to the controller for further processing. This process is also referred to as the controller consuming the packet. In the case of a hardware switch, these mechanisms are implemented by the specialized hardware In the case of a software switch (virtual switches), these same functions are mirrored by software. Since the case of the software switch is somewhat simpler than the hardware switch.

## FLOW TABLES

Flow tables consist of a number of prioritized flow entries, each of which typically consists of two components: match fields and actions. Match fields are used to compare against incoming packets. An incoming packet is compared against the match fields in priority order, and the first complete match is selected. Actions are the instructions that the network device should perform if an incoming packet matches the match fields specified for that flow entry. Match fields can have wildcards for fields that are not relevant to a particular match. For example, when matching packets based just on IP address or subnet, all other fields would be wild carded. Similarly, if matching on only MAC address or UDP/TCP port, the other fields are irrelevant, and consequently those fields are wild carded. Depending on the application needs, all fields may be important, in which case there would be no wildcards. The flow table and flow entry constructs allow the SDN application developer to have a wide range of possibilities for matching packets and taking appropriate actions.

## OPENFLOW

OpenFlow is added as a feature to commercial Ethernet switches, routers and wireless access points – and provides a standardized hook to allow researchers to run experiments, without requiring vendors to expose the internal workings of their network devices. OpenFlow is a protocol that allows a server to tell network switches where to send packets. In a conventional network, each switch has proprietary software that tells it what to do. With OpenFlow, the packet-moving decisions are centralized, so that the network can be programmed independently of the individual switches and data center gear.

In a conventional switch, packet forwarding (the data path) and high-level routing (the control path) occur on the same device. An OpenFlow switch separates the data path from the control path (Lau, Rubin, Smith, et al., 2000). The data path portion resides on the switch itself; a separate controller makes high-level routing decisions. The switch and controller communicate by means of the OpenFlow protocol.

This methodology, known as software-defined networking (SDN), allows for more effective use of network resources than is possible with traditional networks. OpenFlow has gained favour in applications such as VM (virtual machine) mobility, mission-critical networks, and next generation IP-based mobile networks.

Several established companies including IBM, Google, and HP have either fully utilized, or announced their intention to support, the OpenFlow standard. Big Switch Networks, an SDN firm headquartered in Palo Alto, California, has implemented OpenFlow networks that run on top of traditional networks, making it possible to place virtual machines anywhere in a data center to reclaim stranded computing capacity. By early 2012, Google's internal network ran entirely on OpenFlow.

## Secure Channel

A brief look at the specification of OpenFlow shows the single point where the forwarding plane and control plane are connected. It is the secure channel between the controller and the switch. If the connection to the controller is lost, a pure Openflow switch will not be able to deal with unknown incoming packets. The secure channel is the lifeline of all Openflow switches in SDN. It is a TLS or TCP connection established between the controller and the switch. If the connection is lost, the switch will try to connect to a backup controller if there is one. This is the "fail secure mode" and all packets to the controller will be dropped. In an Openflow switch, all new packets will be processed in the switch and will not be sent to the controller. If the switch is capable of working both in SDN and in none SDN then, it is called Hybrid switch. In this case, the switch will not follow the Openflow protocol and the network loses its SDN architecture. The Openflow specification shows that without a controller in the network, we are dealing with a non-SDN network with no central control or separation of forwarding and control plane (Wang A, Guo Y, Hao F, et al.(2013)),. This section shows the importance of detecting any threat that can make the controller unreachable.

## Simulation

In order to find the output for the implementation and simulation of the model following command need to be executed in order to take ssh login.

```
ssh -X mininet@172.16.32.128sudo mn -top tree,3 -
controller=remote, ip=192.168.43.130, port=6653 -switch=ovsk,
protocols=OpenFlow13 pingall
```

In this case we had considered various cases while comparing our result. The first output will be for the normal traffic, where each host will have same probability of numbers of packets. This case was considered with total of 120 packets with a window. On simulating our result with such environment we will find the following window as output.

While considering the simulation with another case where each host is having different probability of number of packets to be send then in such a case we will be having total of 120 packets in a window with two attacker host (h3 and h4) simulation with such a situation will give output in manner shown in Figure 3-6.

Based on the results and simulation result when we check the analysis of normal traffic with attacked traffic we come up with a consolidated data in following format table which shows the consolidated result of the entropy with different scenario. Table 1 shows the traffic analysis with normal traffic pattern whereas Table 2 shows the entropy with traffic pattern with attacked traffic with different number of packets.

*Figure 2. Output screen for normal traffic*

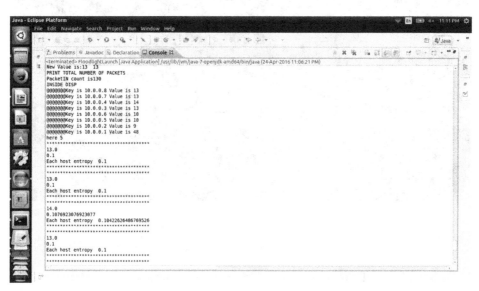

*Figure 3. Output with attacker host h3*

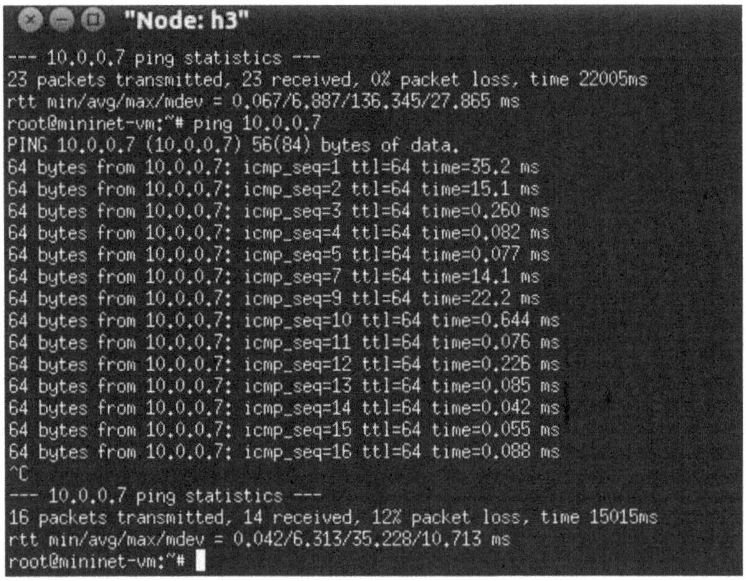

```
"Node: h3"
--- 10.0.0.7 ping statistics ---
23 packets transmitted, 23 received, 0% packet loss, time 22005ms
rtt min/avg/max/mdev = 0.067/6.887/136.345/27.865 ms
root@mininet-vm:~# ping 10.0.0.7
PING 10.0.0.7 (10.0.0.7) 56(84) bytes of data.
64 bytes from 10.0.0.7: icmp_seq=1 ttl=64 time=35.2 ms
64 bytes from 10.0.0.7: icmp_seq=2 ttl=64 time=15.1 ms
64 bytes from 10.0.0.7: icmp_seq=3 ttl=64 time=0.260 ms
64 bytes from 10.0.0.7: icmp_seq=4 ttl=64 time=0.082 ms
64 bytes from 10.0.0.7: icmp_seq=5 ttl=64 time=0.077 ms
64 bytes from 10.0.0.7: icmp_seq=7 ttl=64 time=14.1 ms
64 bytes from 10.0.0.7: icmp_seq=9 ttl=64 time=22.2 ms
64 bytes from 10.0.0.7: icmp_seq=10 ttl=64 time=0.644 ms
64 bytes from 10.0.0.7: icmp_seq=11 ttl=64 time=0.076 ms
64 bytes from 10.0.0.7: icmp_seq=12 ttl=64 time=0.226 ms
64 bytes from 10.0.0.7: icmp_seq=13 ttl=64 time=0.085 ms
64 bytes from 10.0.0.7: icmp_seq=14 ttl=64 time=0.042 ms
64 bytes from 10.0.0.7: icmp_seq=15 ttl=64 time=0.055 ms
64 bytes from 10.0.0.7: icmp_seq=16 ttl=64 time=0.088 ms
^C
--- 10.0.0.7 ping statistics ---
16 packets transmitted, 14 received, 12% packet loss, time 15015ms
rtt min/avg/max/mdev = 0.042/6.313/35.228/10.713 ms
root@mininet-vm:~#
```

*Figure 4. Output with attacker host h4*

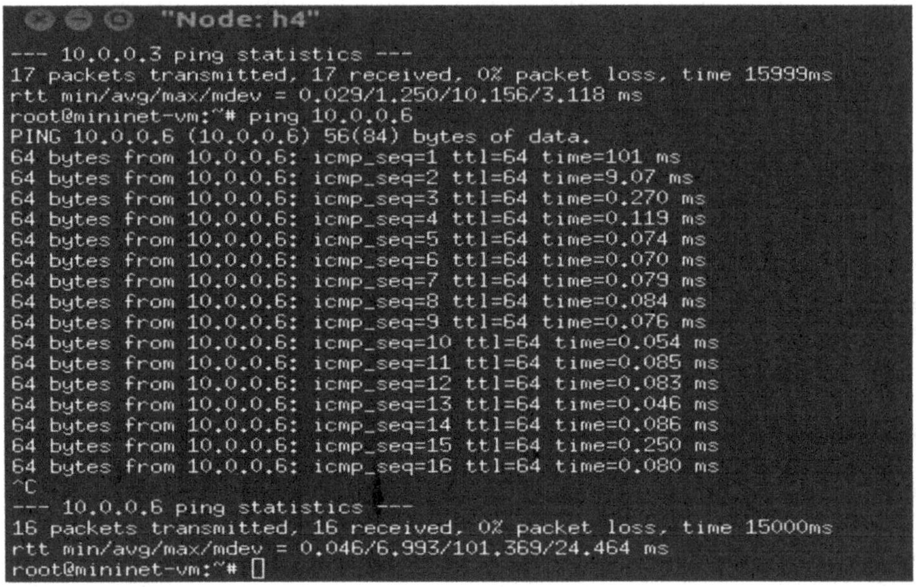

```
"Node: h4"
--- 10.0.0.3 ping statistics ---
17 packets transmitted, 17 received, 0% packet loss, time 15999ms
rtt min/avg/max/mdev = 0.029/1.250/10.156/3.118 ms
root@mininet-vm:~# ping 10.0.0.6
PING 10.0.0.6 (10.0.0.6) 56(84) bytes of data.
64 bytes from 10.0.0.6: icmp_seq=1 ttl=64 time=101 ms
64 bytes from 10.0.0.6: icmp_seq=2 ttl=64 time=9.07 ms
64 bytes from 10.0.0.6: icmp_seq=3 ttl=64 time=0.270 ms
64 bytes from 10.0.0.6: icmp_seq=4 ttl=64 time=0.119 ms
64 bytes from 10.0.0.6: icmp_seq=5 ttl=64 time=0.074 ms
64 bytes from 10.0.0.6: icmp_seq=6 ttl=64 time=0.070 ms
64 bytes from 10.0.0.6: icmp_seq=7 ttl=64 time=0.079 ms
64 bytes from 10.0.0.6: icmp_seq=8 ttl=64 time=0.084 ms
64 bytes from 10.0.0.6: icmp_seq=9 ttl=64 time=0.076 ms
64 bytes from 10.0.0.6: icmp_seq=10 ttl=64 time=0.054 ms
64 bytes from 10.0.0.6: icmp_seq=11 ttl=64 time=0.085 ms
64 bytes from 10.0.0.6: icmp_seq=12 ttl=64 time=0.083 ms
64 bytes from 10.0.0.6: icmp_seq=13 ttl=64 time=0.046 ms
64 bytes from 10.0.0.6: icmp_seq=14 ttl=64 time=0.086 ms
64 bytes from 10.0.0.6: icmp_seq=15 ttl=64 time=0.250 ms
64 bytes from 10.0.0.6: icmp_seq=16 ttl=64 time=0.080 ms
^C
--- 10.0.0.6 ping statistics ---
16 packets transmitted, 16 received, 0% packet loss, time 15000ms
rtt min/avg/max/mdev = 0.046/6.993/101.369/24.464 ms
root@mininet-vm:~#
```

*Figure 5. Output showing traffic attack*

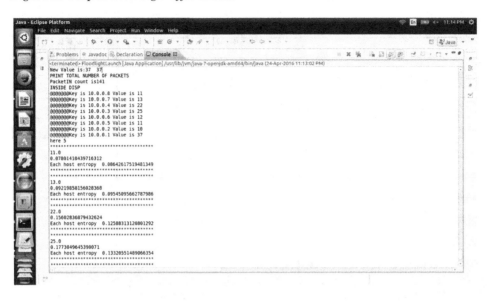

*Figure 6. Entropy screen for traffic attack*

*Table 1. Analysis of normal traffic*

| No. of Host | Source IP | No. of Pckts | Entropy |
|:---:|:---:|:---:|:---:|
| 1 | 10.0.0.8 | 9 | 0.0844 |
| 2 | 10.0.0.7 | 10 | 0.0899 |
| 3 | 10.0.0.6 | 14 | 0.0843 |
| 4 | 10.0.0.5 | 13 | 0.0899 |
| 5 | 10.0.0.4 | 9 | 0.1088 |
| 6 | 10.0.0.3 | 10 | 0.0457 |
| 7 | 10.0.0.2 | 9 | 0.0844 |
| 8 | 10.0.0.1 | 46 | 0.1596 |
| **Total** | **8** | **120** | **0.747** |

*Table 2. Analysis of attacked traffic*

| No. of Host | Source IP | No. of Pckts | Entropy |
|:---:|:---:|:---:|:---:|
| 1 | 10.0.0.8 | 7 | 0.0719 |
| 2 | 10.0.0.7 | 8 | 0.0784 |
| 3 | 10.0.0.6 | 7 | 0.0719 |
| 4 | 10.0.0.5 | 10 | 0.0899 |
| 5 | 10.0.0.4 | 25 | 0.1250 |
| 6 | 10.0.0.3 | 30 | 0.1259 |
| 7 | 10.0.0.2 | 10 | 0.0899 |
| 8 | 10.0.0.1 | 23 | 0.1218 |
| **Total** | **8** | **120** | **0.6021** |

When choosing a threshold for both the traffic pattern, we come across with the results shown in Table 3.

## CONCLUSION

During this research the threat detection to the controller is focused and based on that simulated the result. The quantification of early detection to first 250 to 500 packets as a range of traffic was considered. The proposed solution provides an efficient method of detection with minimal code of addition to the controller with no increase on CPU load in normal as well as attack condition. The proposed solution works particularly for SDN network. The solution detect any sort of threat

*Table 3. Threshold entropy result of normal and attacked traffic*

| Type of Traffic | Mini Entropy | Max Entropy | Mean Entropy |
|---|---|---|---|
| Normal Traffic | .211 | .245 | .222 |
| Attacked Traffic | .200 | .209 | .204 |

*Figure 7. Entropy result for normal and attacked traffic*

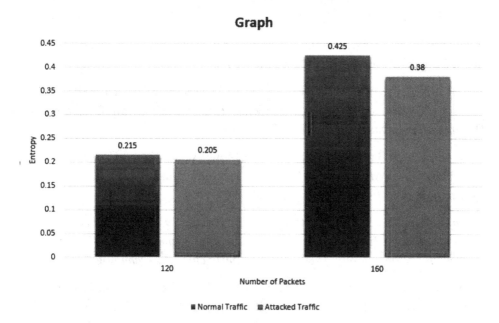

at the beginning stage. Entropy has been used as mechanism in DDoS detection in non-SDN network.

Thus from the above simulated result we came across with the result that the entropy for attacked traffic is lower than the normal traffic . We concluded the result with minimum entropy and maximum entropy. Based on the result obtained, we show the result in Figure 7 using graphical representation.

## REFERENCES

Alsulaiman, M., Alyahya, A., Alkharboush, R., & Alghafis, N. (2009). Intrusion Detection System Using Self-Organizing Maps. *2009 Third International Conference on Network and System Security*, 397-402. doi:10.1109/NSS.2009.62

Mirkovic, J., & Reiher, P. (2004). A Taxonomy of DDoS Attack and DDoS defense Mechanisms. *ACM SIGCOMM Computer Communications Review, 34*(2), 39–53. doi:10.1145/997150.997156

Mohammad, M. S., & Marc, S. (2015). *Early Detection of DDoS Attacks against SDN Controllers.* Department of Systems and Computer Engineering, Carleton University.

Nakashima, T., Sueyoshi, T., & Oshima, S. (2010). Early DoS/DDoS Detection Method using Short-term Statistics. *International Conference on Complex, Intelligent and Software Intensive Systems,* 168-173.

Needham, R. M. (1994). Denial of service: An example. *Communications of the ACM, 37*(11), 42–46. doi:10.1145/188280.188294

Su, W. L., Huang, W. Y. S., & Hu, K. Y. (2013). Design of Event-Based Intrusion Detection System on OpenFlow Network. *IEEE International Conference on Dependable Systems and Networks (SDN) 2013,* 1-2.

Tootoonchian & Ganjali, Y. (2010). HyperFlow: A Distributed Control Plane for OpenFlow. *Proceedings of 2010 Internet Network Management Conference on Research on Enterprise Networking (INM/WREN).*

Wang, A., Guo, Y., & Hao, F. (2013). Scotch: Elastically Scaling up SDN Control-Plane using vSwitch based Overlay. In *Proceedings of the 10th ACM International on Conference on emerging Networking Experiments and Technologies.* ACM.

Wang, B., Zheng, Y., & Lou, W. (2014). DDoS Attack Protection in the Era of Cloud Computing and Software-Defined Networking. *2014 IEEE 22nd International Conference on Network Protocols (ICNP),* 624-629. doi:10.1109/ICNP.2014.99

Zhijing, Q., Denker, G., Giannelli, C., Bellavista, P., & Venkatasubramanian, N. (2014). A software defined network for Internet of Things. *IEEE Network Operation and Management Symposium (NOMS).*

## ADDITIONAL READING

Anderson, T., Roscoe, T., & Wetherall, D. (2004). Preventing Internet Denial-of-Service with Capabilities. *Computer Communication Review, 34*(1), 39–44. doi:10.1145/972374.972382

Gude, N., Koponen, T., Pettit, J., Pfaff, B., Casado, M., McKeown, N., & Shenker, S. (2008). Nox: Towards an operating system for networks. *Computer Communication Review, 38*(3), 105–110. doi:10.1145/1384609.1384625

McKeown, N., Anderson, T., Balakrishnan, H., Parulkar, G., Peterson, L., Rexford, J., & Turner, J. et al. (2008). Openflow: Enabling innovation in campus networks. *Computer Communication Review*, *38*(2), 69–74. doi:10.1145/1355734.1355746

## KEY TERMS AND DEFINITIONS

**Denial of Service:** A type of attack on network where attackers prevents the legitimate users from accessing the service.

**Distributed Denial of Service:** Interruption of online services by overwhelming it with services from different sources.

**Entropy:** Entropy is randomness of an application in security aspect. A lack of entropy can have a negative impact on performance and security.

**Flooding:** Flooding is forwarding of packet from a router to every other router/node except the node from which the packet has been arrived.

**OpenFlow:** An open source network protocol which is programmable in nature and directs and handles the traffic flow of the network. The SDN controller can run on multiple protocols but it is one of the most popular ones. It segregates the programming of the layer 2 and 3 devices from the hardware they are running over.

**SDN Controller:** Being the vortex of the SDN architecture, all the controller agents present in the devices answer to the controller which in turn enables intelligent networking by managing and handling the traffic flow of the network.

**Software-Defined Network:** A technology that allow network administrator to programmatically initialize, control, change network behaviour dynamically.

# Chapter 11
# WSN Structure Based on SDN

**Premkumar Chithaluru**
*University of Petroleum and Energy Studies, India*

**Ravi Prakash**
*University of Petroleum and Energy Studies, India*

**Subodh Srivastava**
*Vallurupalli Nageswara Rao Vignana Jyothi Institute of Engineering and Technology, India*

## ABSTRACT

*In this chapter, a general structure for a product-characterized remote sensor is arranged where the controller is actualized at the base station and the SDN-WSN system by talking about and breaking down. The execution and vitality utilization of SDN-WSN system is superior to other vitality-effective conventions.*

## INTRODUCTION

As per the enhancements in the equipment hardware, innovations in the wireless channels and wireless detection, Wireless sensor Network (WSN) (Nunes, Bruno, et al., 2014) has pulled in comprehensively considerations of the entire world solace. WSNs are conveyed over the sensors with elements of remote detecting, information preparing/assembling and short way remote correspondence. In military safeguard, fiasco help, ecological checking, natural and business applications and other significant fields, WSNs is having wide sensor application prospects. WSNs have the custom/standard qualities of the remote system does not have, for example, more number of sensor nodes and high thickness, the sensors over all vitality, figuring/ requesting force and capacity limit are restricted. System topology changes as often

DOI: 10.4018/978-1-5225-3640-6.ch011

as possible happens and it makes them arrange capacity are limited. Software Defined Networking (SDN) was actualized to encourage over advancement and initiate the most effortless automatic control of the system information way (Luo, Tie, Hwee-Pink Tan, and Quek, 2012). The division of the sending equipment from the control rationale permits straightforward arrangement of new conventions, applications, organize representation and administration. In SDN arrange chairmen are permit to manage and organize the benefits through deliberation of lower level execution. This is finished by decoupling/isolating the framework that decides/requests about where movement is sent (control plane) from the existed frameworks that sending activity to the chose goal (data plane). System knowledge requests incorporated structure in programming based SDN controllers, which keep up a real perspective of the system. Besides, the SDN controller's unified knowledge, it is conceivable to changes to organize conduct and deploy/run new applications and system which benefits progressively. A novel bunched engineering for WSN in light of the SDN. We emphasize that the SDN controller's overall view will help beat the characteristic slacking of WSN.

## Architecture of SDN-WSN

The idea of SDN-WSN, clarifies the diverse advancements for the acknowledgment of SDN-WSN. The WSN may contains hundreds or even thousands of sensor nodes and cluster head (CH) and incorporate a base station and sink node. The sort of sensor nodes and their abilities changes as per their application field, for example, temperature sensors, dust storm sensors, and so on. Regularly, a thick/substantial system can't work productively without some sorted out structure. Thus, system has to bunch a game plan. There exists a cluster head (CH) in each group and alternate nodes are the basic sensor nodes (SN). In each bunch, the Cluster Head (CH) is an ace to preparing the operations of the sensor nodes. In this approach grouping gathered the data about the territory on the bunch by nodes will be sent to the CH. A product characterized sensor organize depends on a legitimately brought together controller. From the system perspective, the controller does not really require be a static node and the control-rationale be actualized as a piece of the base station or sink node. In the product characterized sensor arrange system, the sensor nodes don't need to settle on steering choices (De Gante, Alejandro, Mohamed Aslan, and Ashraf Matrawy, 2014). Or possibly, they forward packets to the subsequent group head or base station as indicated by the course table that is created by the base station. As it were, the courses which are viewed as optimal as per application-particular criteria are computed by the controller (in the base station). In this system, the controller utilizes the area data assembled by any confinement procedure when finding the best courses. In the base station engineering offered by Gante, the base station controller has to know the current topology of the whole system. SDN has a higher bore to produce the sending choices of SN in view of the guidelines set created by the Controller, allowing a superior collaboration among CH and SNs. In addition, SDN controllers, can limit the vitality utilization by various sensor nodes, settling on the best steering topology choice for the nodes. With the system administration which is controlled by the SDN, the steering choices and approaches have less meeting time in correlation with directing conventions. To deliver this design, CH needs to controls/send the bunch organize.

## WSN With SDN

The fundamental thought for overseeing WSN with SDN with the idea of Software-Defined Networking Wireless Sensor Networks SDN-WSN. In view of the likelihood that every sensor node underpins OpenFlow and sensors ought to have the capacity to perceive the stream table's entrances. This engineering gives a thought regarding, contrast amongst data and control plane. The Sensor OpenFlow (SOF) is a correspondence convention between the control plane and data plane. The data plane contains sensor stream parcel for sending, and the control plane is a controller for performing directing and QoS arrange control.

The present Evolution of Software-Defined Sensor Networks, for consolidating sensors nodes into distributed computing utilizing a Sensing-as-a-Service (SaaS). In this model, SaaS consolidates the detecting information with existing cloud administrations, for example, crush up administrations. The sensor controller having the SDN functionalities provides a nearby/essential database to store the information which is detected. Each sensor node can carry parcels to a sensor control server. In base station design for WSN in view of SDN with an audit of advantages of this innovative technology. The utilization of a SDN controller as a base station in WSNs, however did not present any insight about correspondence between sensor nodes. The controller can decide the ideal/possible directing is to be sending choices and embedding's these choices into sensor nodes stream tables. In others words, the sensor nodes don't settle on any directing choices, they just forward and drop bundles as per the standard information's set by the controller (base station) and break down the open doors and difficulties of SDN in IEEE 802.15.4 systems, executing a situation called SDN-WSN. The controller is implemented into sink nodes and so as to carry, every node must take in a way (as helpful as could be expected under the circumstances) to achieve the controller (Sherwood, Rob, et al. 2009). The controller occasionally produces a signal bundle to send it to the nodes. Likewise, the nodes store the rundown of nodes from which they got a guide parcel. Every single found neighbor will be connected much of the time to the sink node utilizing a parcel called a report bundle. A bunched WSN Architecture in light of

SDN, every node in WSN might be one of the three states: basic node, door node and group head node and the bunch head is called SDN – Cluster Head (SDN-CH). Each bunch is known as a SDN space. In each SDN area, the SDN-CH is the controller, responsible for dealing with the operation of the sensor nodes. The gathered data about nature is prepared on the space by nodes and will be steered to the SDN-CH and the entryway is occupied with blending and sending the information from whole sensor node areas to alternate spaces. The bunch head advances or drops the information from the sensor nodes as per whether mapping the run of the stream table, this will squander the node's vitality and a novel WSN engineering in view of SDN, Firstly, the controller makes the course table among group heads, when the CH gets information from sensors, it advances specifically in light of its course table. Furthermore, application would custom be able to the extent of information gathering for different sort sensors.

## Information Dissemination in SDN-WSN

The fundamental intention of this system design, CH node can be observed/controlled by the base station (BS), the particular transmitting methodology totally relies upon the controller and over all message connect is totally controllable, when CHs or SNs is having some unusual conditions, for example, vitality loosing and blame conditions, the controller node can modify procedure or change the sending way. The center of this structure is the data spread technique. The aggregate procedure can be separated into two phases.

## 1. Building Network

- Initially, the controller knows nothing about the system, so the nodes must transmit their state data including their address, position, remaining vitality and sorts to the controller and enroll themselves to the controller.
- According to the got data, the controller do three things. Right off the bat, the controller isolates the system into some uniform groups; besides, considering the node's position and remaining vitality artificially, the controller chooses a CH for each bunch; thirdly, the controller produces the course table for all the CHs, telling the CHs the following bounce for sending information to the BS.
- The controller sends the bunch results and course tables to the CHs. The bunch comes about incorporate the CH id and the part id in the group. The CH declares its own ID to the SNs in a group, and the SNs should reaction to the CH so that the CH can know the state in the bunch and answer to the controller later.

## 2. Collecting Data

- Firstly, the clients set particular trigger conditions for various SNs as indicated by the diverse needs.

- Secondly, The BS pushes the client's design to every one of the SNs, at that point every SN sets itself. Just when the condition is fulfilled, the SN begins to send information to its CH. The CH gathers and circuits the information, and advances it to the following jump CH delegated by the course table created by the controller, the CH need not coordinate the SN's information with stream table, on the grounds that the information the SN sent is fit for the client's need. Some of the time, the client may utilize diverse controller for various application, the BS to achieve the objective. The data from SNs to CH incorporates not just the gathered information, and also the leftover vitality of itself. After some time, intermediate, the system will change to building phrase once more, the distinction is that the nodes needn't send state data, on the grounds that the date gathered by SN incorporates the SN's remaining vitality, and the BS refreshes the node state data continuous, chooses new CHs and figures new course as indicated by the new system see, at that point distributes the new outcomes to the new CHs. The new CHs do arrangement in the bunch. On the off chance that the client alters the trigger conditions, the BS will push the new settings to relating nodes.

### Software Defined WSN and Related Challenges

Three-layer SDN design, one of its deciding elements is that system gadgets just forward movement, while sending choices are performed by the outside controller. Correspondence among various layers of the engineering is accomplished through the northbound and the southbound interfaces. The principal interface associates applications to the controller while the second interface handles correspondence amongst controller and information sending plane. OpenFlow convention is the most usually utilized southbound interface. It empowers the stream based activity control. The data plane gadgets separate and process activity streams as indicated by directions of the controller. To characterize a stream, controller can utilize any subset of L2-L4 bundle header fields upheld by OpenFlow, alongside the identifier of the interface with approaching parcel. This very granular control enables system to powerfully conform to the application and client prerequisites.

There is likewise an expanding enthusiasm for reception of SDN in remote space, where decoupling of the control and the data plane guarantees extra advantages. In remote systems, there is practically add up to accord about specialized arrangements that ought to be utilized at physical and connect layer of convention stack. Be that as it may, at higher layers' distinctive conventions are utilized, contingent upon particular situation. For instance, vitality obliged WSNs are typically in view of IEEE 802.15.4 convention, however the higher layers regularly utilize ZigBee or 6LOWPAN, which are not perfect. Likewise, there is no accord with respect to steering conventions to be utilized and numerous administration operations, which essentially constrains probability of sensor node relocation starting with one system then onto the next. In SDN systems these constraints are less articulated, in light of the fact that all administration operations are intelligently brought together and totally isolated from the sending operations. What is most vital, the system capacities are programming characterized and can be powerfully changed by the requirements.

Utilization of SDN idea in WSN systems is extremely testing because of restricted vitality, memory and computational assets of sensor nodes. One choice to decrease vitality utilization is to utilize obligation cycle systems, which suggest just intermittent action of radio interfaces. Another alternative is to perform data plane on a few nodes in the system. To the detriment of bigger deferral, the total expands vitality effectiveness on the grounds that excess information are disposed of inside the system. The third alternative, which we for the most part broke down, is to uniformly appropriate movement stack with unified directing calculation. Nonetheless, execution of these instruments requires southbound interface that will permit more extensive range of stream definitions and handling activities. Dissimilar to OpenFlow version 1.0, which separates movement streams just in light of TCP (UDP)/IP header handle, this new interface should consider conventions run of the mill for WSN systems. Additionally, gaining information of intrigue (e.g. temperature > 40oC) in a few situations is more critical than knowing the node which sent the information, so characteristic based steering ought to be considered also.

## Benefits of SDN Approach

## 1. Energy Efficiency

One of the key prerequisites in WSNs is vitality productivity. Sensor nodes are typically battery-controlled, so vitality utilization straightforwardly impacts the system lifetime. This forces strict confinements on the outline and execution of steering calculations in the system. For instance, when the portal is excessively inaccessible from sensor nodes, coordinate transmission must be stayed away from in light of the fact that the vitality misfortune can be very broad. In any case, traditional multi-bounce correspondence, for example, Minimum Transmission Routing (MTE) regularly have similarly undesirable impact in light of the fact that the nodes nearest to the passage quickly deplete their batteries. By bringing together the system control plane, SDN permits execution of more complex directing calculations. The controller could be modified to occasionally gather data about current battery level of sensor nodes and also, utilize them to settle on vitality upgraded directing choices. Such directing choices should prompt expanded system lifetime through adjusted vitality utilization among the sensor nodes. Then again, since all control capacities are controlled by the controller, SDN sensor nodes don't expend vitality to run directing calculations and trade immense measures of control movement. Complex errands, for example, movement building, virtualization and QoS (Quality of Service) provisioning could be performed without effect on the system lifetime, since the control programming keeps running on machine having substantially more assets than customary system node (Zeng, Deze, et al., 2013).

## 2. Mobility Support

In a few situations sensor nodes are portrayed by abnormal state of versatility (e.g. VANET systems). Since that involves visit topology changes, merging time of conveyed steering convention might be critical and cause high bundle misfortune rate. On the opposite side, SDN gives better deceivability of the versatility occasions and permits dynamic changing of the stream table principles. For instance, the sensor node might be arranged to illuminate the controller about their versatility, or convention for portability administration could be actualized on the controller. Along these lines, the controller could track area of sensor nodes and auspicious refresh the stream table standards in the system (Orfanidis, C, 2016).

## 3. Network Management

In customary systems there is no interesting strategy for arranging the system gadgets. Indeed, arrangement components are merchant particular. Along these lines, the utilization of multi-seller organize parts essentially entangles the administration procedure. In WSNs administration multifaceted nature is much more articulated. Arrangement of another detecting application, or another system convention, requires re-programming of microcontrollers. Infrequently this requires physical access to the sensor node, which may not be doable. SDN guarantees to fundamentally rearrange organize arrangement and administration of system assets. Incorporated control plane modified works the sending equipment, along these lines dispensing with the requirement for independent adaptations of the control application for various sorts of sensor nodes. The significance of the system programmability will just increment with the developing enthusiasm for Internet of Things (IoT). Obviously it will be difficult to physically implement security and different arrangements to the bunch of gadgets with various capacities. The IoT organizations are relied upon to be in a general sense heterogeneous regarding utilized correspondence advancements

(ZigBee, Wi-Fi, NFC, and so forth.) and asset accessibility. While this makes open doors for an extensive variety of new applications, numerous new difficulties emerge, for example, sharing of system and sensor assets among applications, activity separation, QoS provisioning and network administration. In this specific circumstance, SDN capacities of system virtualization, concentrated asset allotment and dynamic load administration will be especially valuable (Zhang, B.; Li, G, 2009).

## WSN Management

Administration of WSN ought to consider definition of an arrangement of capacities that advance profitability and reconciliation in a sorted out way of the configuration, upkeep, operation and organization of the segments and administrations of the WSN. A few administration techniques have been proposed to oversee usefulness in the design of WSNs. These strategies consider WSN measurements, for example, vitality utilization, framework life expectancy, information inertness, framework resistance to flaws, exactness in information procurement or the Quality of Service and security.

WSN administration ought to be basic and hold fast to organize dynamic conduct, and additionally give efficiency being used of assets as proposed by Ruiz et al. In the MANNA (A management architecture for wireless sensor networks) design. The MANNA engineering considers administration arrangements for WSN administrations, capacities and models by taking a gander at administration of WSNs in three measurements that state usefulness deliberations (T. Luo, H.-P. Tan, and T. Quek, 2012):

- WSN functionalities which incorporate upkeep, configuration, sensor node actions (Sensing, preparing, correspondence)
- Management levels which incorporate application administrations and administration of system components (node groups, information total, and system availability).
- Management of useful territories, for example, security, blame checking, execution and configuration.

The structure of WSN administration plans exhibited depends on the above conventions and reflection elements anyway we re-arrange them as per utilitarian connections as takes after:

- **Network Configuration Administration:** All problems related with establishing configuration and operation are dealt with here. This incorporates convention usage, configuration of information procurement, arrangement of benefits, and organize the level programming issues.

- **Topology Administration:** This category of administration manages the concerns identified with the design of the WSN. Administration of sensor node area and appropriation, arrange action dispersion, node to node correspondence comprising entryway components fall under topology administration.

- **QoS Administration:** Data inactivity, framework execution, adaptation to internal failure, information securing precision are mostly the issues overseen under this classification to guarantee an ideal WSN nature of administration.

- **Energy Administration:** All parameters with respect to vitality utilization in the system are sorted here including vitality sources, vitality utilization minimization and framework life expectancy in connection to accessible vitality assets.

- **Security Administration:** In view of the prominence of WSNs, more delicate data is being communicated over such systems, in this way it is vital the system is shielded from noxious assaults. This would typically include the administration of system security functionalities, for example, encryption (key dispersion strategies), danger identification and recuperation which are arranged here.

- **Maintenance Administration:** Wireless sensor arrange perspectives identified with keeping up revise operation of the system are classified under this administration classification. Examination of system implementation, vitality levels and blames define some of these viewpoints.

As shall be discussed, depending on the availability of the management practices for the categories above, WSNs can be custom-made to meet at least one or more of the following design criteria:

- **Energy Efficiency:** This considers the capacity of a framework to monitor vitality or permit operation on constrained power for lengthy stretches bringing about enhanced system lifetime (Sherwood, Rob, et al., 2009).

- **Robustness:** This criteria guarantees that a framework executes not surprisingly paying little heed to changing natural conditions or plan necessities. A vigorous framework should create alluring execution in spite of system varieties, for example, node disappointment, control blackouts and dangers coming about because of node portability. A vital normal for a vigorous administration framework is organize reconfiguration.

- **Scalability:** WSN nodes are trusted upon to scale up vast numbers, in this manner a versatile administration framework should work efficiently at any system scale. Circulated administration assumes a critical part here while diminishing traffic overhead which may some way or another be altogether coordinated to a concentrated movement chief.

- **Adaptability:** These criteria refer to the ability of a system ability to meet the network disparities and task demands. The framework must have the capacity to work efficiently in fluctuating system conditions, for example, vitality fluctuations, topology variations and assignment diversity. The capacity to reconfigure and re-assignment additionally assumes a vital part in meeting these criteria.

## FUTURE RESEARCH DIRECTIONS

The arrangement of the broad writing in the spaces of SDN, MANET, and WSNs will give the potential chances to future research. Radio frequency identification (RFID) arrangements can be used to lessen the working expenses through diminishing work costs, upgrading computerization, enhancing the following strategy, and keeping the material misfortune. Semantic Web is the expansion of the World Wide Web that indexes data on a website page and reprocesses it so that different machines including PCs can comprehend the data. An examination of linkages among SDN, MANET, WSNs, RFID, and Semantic Web in worldwide operations would appear to be reasonable for future research endeavors.

## CONCLUSION

This part demonstrated the review of SDN; SDN controller and steering convention; OpenFlow-based SDN; the security worries for SDN; the outline of MANET; the security worries for MANET; the diagram of WSNs; WSNs and topology control; and the significance of WSNs. SDN includes a few categories of system novelty which are there for creating the system as flexible as the virtualized server and capacity framework of the present day server farm. SDN objective is to permit specialists and executives to quickly respond to the varying business necessities. In SDN, a system head can form the movement from a concentrated control reassure without touching the specific switches, and can convey directions to anywhere they are mandatory in the system.

MANET is an independent accretion of portable clients that impart over moderately data transfer capacity bound remote connections. Since the nodes are portable, the system topology may alter rapidly and unpredictably after some time. The system is decentralized, where all system activities (e.g., finding the topology and conveying the messages) must be implemented by the nodes themselves. MANETs require the productive circulated calculations to decide arrange association, connect booking, and directing. Nodes like to stem as meagre power importantly and communicate as infrequently as could be permitted, along these lines diminishing the probability of location or block attempt. A slip by in any of these prerequisites may debase the execution and reliability of the system.

WSNs comprise in an arrangement of spatially appropriated self-ruling gadgets, more often than not battery-fueled and intended to work for a drawn out stretch of time. Limiting the vitality utilization is a vital plan thought. Many steering, control administration, and information scattering conventions have been intended for WSNs where vitality mindfulness is a basic plan issue. Every sensor node involves the processes of identifying, making, transmission, mobilizer, position determining framework, and power units. Sensor nodes are sent in true conditions and decide some physical practices. Sensors are minor gadgets, low costing, and having low preparing capacities. Sensors take into account detecting over bigger land areas with more prominent precision. Expanding the processing abilities of present day sensors have empowered the current WSNs to execute many inquiries inside the system.

SDN, MANET, and WSNs turn into the developing parts of ICT applications and can be successfully used in worldwide operations. SDN, MANET, and WSNs can possibly build the productivity of operations in different enterprises, they can enrich the resource ability to perceive and their traceability, reduce the dependence on manual techniques, decrease the operational budgets, and provide valuable information to business exploration.

## REFERENCES

Costanzo, S. (2012). Software defined wireless networks: Unbridling sdns. *Software Defined Networking (EWSDN). European Workshop on. IEEE*, 1-6.

Costanzo, S., Galluccio, L., Morabito, G., & Palazzo, S. (2012). *Software defined wireless networks: Unbridling sdns*. EWSDN.

De Gante, A., Aslan, M., & Matrawy, A. (2014). Smart wireless sensor network management based on software-defined networking. *Communications (QBSC), 2014 27th Biennial Symposium on. IEEE*, 71-75. doi:10.1109/QBSC.2014.6841187

Lee, W. L., Datta, A., & Cardell-Oliver, R. (2006). Network management in wireless sensor networks. In *Handbook of Mobile Ad Hoc and Pervasive Communications*. Valencia, CA: American Scientific Publishers.

Luo, T., Tan, H.-P., & Quek, T. (2012). Sensor OpenFlow: Enabling Software-Defined Wireless Sensor Networks. *IEEE Communications Letters, 16*(11), 2012. doi:10.1109/LCOMM.2012.092812.121712

Luo, Tan, & Quek. (2012). Sensor OpenFlow: Enabling software-defined wireless sensor networks. *IEEE Communications Letters, 16*(11), 1896-1899.

McKeown, N., Anderson, T., Balakrishnan, H., & Rexford, J. (2008). OpenFlow: Enabling innovations in campus networks. *ACM SIGCOMM, 38*(2), 69–74. doi:10.1145/1355734.1355746

Muruganathan, S. D., Ma, D. C. F., Bhasin, R. I., & Fapojuwo, A. (2005). A centralized energy-efficient routing protocol for wireless sensor networks. *IEEE Communications Magazine, 43*(3), 8–13. doi:10.1109/MCOM.2005.1404592

Nunes, B. (2014). A survey of software-defined networking: Past, present, and future of programmable networks. *IEEE Communications Surveys & Tutorials, 16*(3), 1617-1634.

Olivier, Gonzalez, & Nolot. (2015). SDN Based Architecture for Clustered WSN. *Innovative Mobile and Internet Services in Ubiquitous Computing (IMIS), 9th International Conference on. IEEE*, 342 – 347.

Orfanidis, C. (2016). Increasing Robustness in WSN Using Software Defined Network Architecture. *Proceedings of the 2016 15th ACM/IEEE International Conference on Information Processing in Sensor Networks (IPSN)*, 1–2.

Ruiz, L. B., Nogueira, J. M., & Loureiro, A. A. (2003). Manna (2003): "A management architecture for wireless sensor networks. *IEEE Communications Magazine, 41*(2), 116–125. doi:10.1109/MCOM.2003.1179560

Sherwood, R. (2009). *Flow Visor: A network virtualization layer*. OpenFlow Switch Consortium, Tech. Rep: 1-13.

Tomovic, S., Pejanovic-Djurisic, M., & Radusinovic, I. (2014, October). SDN-based mobile networks: Concepts and benefits. *Wireless Personal Communications, 78*(3), 1629–1644. doi:10.1007/s11277-014-1909-6

Yang, F. (2014) OpenFlow-based load balancing for wireless mesh infrastructure. *Consumer Communications and Networking Conference (CCNC), IEEE 11th. IEEE*, 444-449.

Zeng, D. (2013). Evolution of software-defined sensor networks. *Mobile Ad-hoc and Sensor Networks (MSN), IEEE Ninth International Conference on. IEEE*, 410-413.

Zhang, B., & Li, G. (2009). Survey of Network Management Protocols in Wireless Sensor Network. *Proceedings of the 2009 International Conference on E-Business and Information System Security*, 1–5. doi:10.1109/EBISS.2009.5138098

## KEY TERMS AND DEFINITIONS

**Base Station (BS):** A fixed point of communication for customer cellular phones on a carrier network. The base station is connected to an antenna (or multiple antennae) that receives and transmits the signals in the cellular network to customer phones and cellular devices.

**Battery:** The gadget that creates power to give energy to gear.

**Cluster Head (CH):** A senor node. It is responsible for collecting data from member nodes inside the cluster.

**Hardware:** The physical gear that makes up a PC framework, for example, circuit sheets, console, mouse, screen, printer, control supply, and capacity gadgets.

**Internet of Things (IoT):** The interconnection via the Internet of computing devices embedded in everyday objects, enabling them to send and receive data.

**MANET:** Also known as wireless ad hoc network or ad hoc wireless network, is a continuously self-configuring, infrastructure-less network of mobile devices connected wirelessly.

**Minimum Transmission Routing (MTE):** An important design and performance characteristic of a computer network or there is a certain minimum level of delay that will be experienced due to the time it takes to transmit a packet serially through a link.

**Mobile Ad-Hoc Network:** The accumulation of remote versatile hosts shaping an impermanent system without the help of any brought together organization.

**Network:** The gathering of interconnected PCs and peripherals that is equipped for sharing programming and equipment assets among clients.

**QoS:** An advanced feature that prioritizes internet traffic for applications, online gaming, Ethernet LAN ports, or specified MAC addresses to minimize the impact of busy bandwidth.

**Radio Frequency Identification (RFID):** Uses electromagnetic fields to automatically identify and track tags attached to objects. The tags contain electronically stored information. Passive tags collect energy from a nearby RFID reader's interrogating radio waves.

**Sensing-as-a-Service (SaaS):** Providing sensing services using mobile phones via a cloud computing system.

**Sensor Nodes (SN):** Also known as a mote, is a node in a sensor network that is capable of performing some processing, gathering sensory information and communicating with other connected nodes in the network.

**Sensor OpenFlow (SOF):** Enabling software-defined wireless sensor networks.

**Sensor:** The gadget that identifies the adjustments in the encompassing conditions or in the condition of another gadget or a framework, and passes on this data in a specific way.

**Software-Defined Network:** The physical detachment of the system control plane from the sending plane, and where a control plane controls a few gadgets.

**Wireless Sensor Networks:** The remote systems comprising of spatially disseminated independent gadgets utilizing sensors to screen the physical or ecological conditions.

# Chapter 12
# Software–Defined Networking Paradigm in Wireless Sensor Networks

**Govind P. Gupta**
*National Institute of Technology Raipur, India*

## ABSTRACT

*Software-defined networking (SDN) is an emerging network design and management paradigm that offers a flexible way for reducing the complexity of the network management and configuration. SDN-based wireless sensor networks (SDWSNs) consist of a set of software-defined sensor nodes equipped with different types of sensors. In SDWSN, sensor node is able to conduct different sensing tasks according to the programs injected into it and functionalities of these nodes can also be dynamically configured by injecting different application-specific programs. SDWSNs adopt the characteristics of SDN and can provide energy efficient solutions for various problems such as topology management, sleep scheduling, routing, and localization, etc. This chapter discusses how to apply SDN model in the design of an energy-efficient protocol for wireless sensor networks and also presents an overview of SDN model proposed for wireless sensor networks and SDN-based resource management, routing, sleep scheduling algorithm, localization for SDWSNs. Finally, open research challenges are summarized.*

DOI: 10.4018/978-1-5225-3640-6.ch012

## INTRODUCTION

The advancement in the Micro Electrical Mechanical System (MEMS) and wireless communication technologies has enhanced the scope of wireless sensor networks (WSNs) in the different applications such as Smart Cities, Smart Grid, and Smart Environment etc (Akyildiz, 2002; Anastasi, 2009; Yick, 2008; Khan, 2016). A typical WSN consists of a set of sensor nodes and one or more sink nodes that are deployed over a monitoring area of interest in a structured or unstructured way (Khan, 2016). Wireless sensor nodes are generally operated by battery power thus requires an energy efficient operation to prolong the network lifetime.

In recent years, software defined networking (SDN) paradigm emerges as a new network design mechanism where control logic is decoupled from the network devices and leaving the network device with only data forwarding logic (Kreutz, 2015; Nunes, 2014; Jagadeesan, 2014; Bizanis, 2016; Jarraya, 2014; Olivier, 2015). This new paradigm offers various advantages over traditional paradigm such as energy efficient network operations, energy efficient resource allocations and flexible network management, multiple applications deployment and control over sensor nodes etc. (Haque, 2016; Gante, 2014; Luo, 2012; Zeng, 2013). The application of the SDN paradigm in the design of WSN emerges a new network called software defined Wireless Sensor Networks (SDWSNs). In SDWSN, most of the energy demanding operations such as routing decision, duty cycling, topology management, resource allocation, network coverage and connectivity planning etc. are migrated to the logically centralized SDN controllers, thus saves a lot of node energy (Kobo, 2017).

This book chapter first discuss generic model for SDWSN and presents different components of this model and its interactions in details. Next, it summarizes the various advantages offered by SDN paradigm to the WSN. SDN paradigm based Protocol design for Wireless Sensor Networks are discussed in Section 4. Finally some open research challenges are discussed in Section 5 and Section 6 concludes the book chapter.

## SOFTWARE DEFINED NETWORKING MODEL FOR WIRELESS SENSOR NETWORKS

Traditional architecture of a sensor node contains full fledge functionality with physical layer up to application layer. This traditional model of a sensor node makes it self-configurable and equipped with the ability to sense the physical phenomenon forwarding of the sensed data packet and interaction with its peer neighboring nodes. Although this model works well for fixed application-specific tasks, it does not provide flexibility and elasticity to change the application and control and very hard to manage due to its complexity and also does not provides energy efficient solutions.

In order to solve above said problems, recently SDN based WSN framework are proposed by various researcher in the (Jagadeesan, 2014; Bizanis, 2016; Jarraya, 2014; Olivier, 2015; Haque, 2016; Gante, 2014; Luo, 2012; Zeng, 2013). This section discussed a generic framework for SDWSN architecture and its functionality.

Figure 1 illustrates a generic architecture of software defined wireless sensor network which consists of three layers such as Application, Control and Data layer. Functionalities of these layers are discussed as follows:

1.  **Physical Infrastructure Layer:** In this layer, different kinds of the physical devices such as sensor nodes, gateway nodes, and sink nodes are included. These physical devices contains both hardware and software components. The hardware components of a typical sensor node consist of a sensing, radio and energy unit. A generic block diagram of SDN based wireless sensor node is illustrated in Figure 2. The software component of a sensor node consists of sensing module, data aggregation module, abstract layer and flow table. Sensing module performs the sampling of the sensor readings. The flow table of each node contains rules for forwarding the traffic which is provided by

*Figure 1. Generic architecture of software-defined wireless sensor networks*

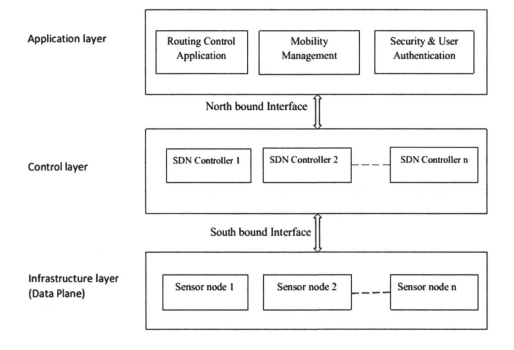

*Figure 2. A generic block diagram for SDN based wireless sensor node*

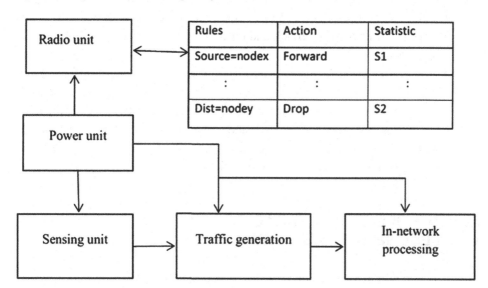

the control layer. Abstract layer provides an interface to interact with control layer via southbound interface. At this layer, each sensor nodes can have some important functionality and resources to sense the physical phenomenon, process the sensed data and forward it from one node to the another sensor node. However, these devices do not decide what to do. Decision making part of these devices is done at the control layer and passes it through southbound interface.

2.   **Control Layer:** This layer is a very significant layer in the SDWSN architecture as it performs all decision making functionalities. The main responsible of this layer is to formulate the flow rules, mapping and programming interface with both south bound and north bound interface. In the literature different approaches are proposed for the implementation of this layer. Generally these approaches are categorized as centralized, distributed and hybrid. In centralized controller approach, a single controller is used which controls the entire WSN network. This approach suffers from reliability and scalability issues. However, distributed controller approach overcome these issues and incorporated multiple controllers that are spatially distributed. In (Oliveira, 2014), distributed multiple controllers are used and these controllers are serially attached with sensor nodes and the sink node. Similarly, the authors in (Tsou, 2012) proposed a message exchange protocol called *SDNi* for message exchange between different interfaces in the multiple distributed controller environments. In the hybrid controller approach, controllers are implemented

such that it looks logically centralized but it is physically distributed apart. The main aim of this approach is to merge the good feature of centralized and distributed controller approach and ensure better scalability, availability and performance.

3.  **Application Layer:** At this layer, application developers develop different kinds of applications such as load balancing, sensor scheduling, sensor allocation, routing, security etc. SDWSN paradigm provides flexibility at the application layer to customize data aggregation and gathering without worrying about the required changes in the physical nodes. This feature simplifies the process of developing a new application at the application plane.

## ADVANTAGES OF SDN PARADIGM IN WIRELESS SENSOR NETWORK

The main aim of software defined wireless sensor network (SDWSN) is to provide flexibility by the virtue of decoupling of data and control plane. SDWSN provides following advantages in terms of energy saving, efficient network management and control, efficient and scalable localization, routing, mobility and security features.

-   **Energy Saving:** Sensor node is generally an energy constraint device that is operated by the limited energy source i.e. by using two AA batteries. Energy saving is a research challenge in the design and development of protocols for WSNs. Since in SDWSN, most of the energy consuming functionalities are performed in the SDN controllers at the control plane which has no scarcity of energy resources. Thus, SDWSN paradigm provides energy efficient operations and could enhance the network lifetime of WSNs. In (Wang, 2016), the authors have proposed a sleep scheduling protocols for SDWSN which provides energy efficient duly cycling for the nodes.
-   **Efficient Network Management and Control:** SDN paradigm provides an efficient and flexible approach for management and control of a large scale WSNs. This flexibility comes by the separation of control and forwarding elements. In SDWSN, forwarding elements are managed and controlled by the SDN controllers which provide flexible programmability to the infrastructure nodes. In (Oliveira, 2014), the authors have proposed TinySDN which used multiple controllers for efficient and flexible management and control of a SDN based network.
-   **Efficient and Scalable Localization and Routing:** Due to the features of multiple distributed controllers at the control plane, SDWSN provides a flexible paradigm for designing an efficient and scalable localization and

routing algorithms for the large scale WSN. Localization is a fundamental requirement for any WSN application. This is due to fact that sensor reading without location context is useless for many applications. In SDWSN, localization algorithm could be executed at the control plane or application layer which provides an efficient and scalable solution in terms of energy efficiency and localization error. Similarly, routing operations in the SDWSN can be decides at control plane which provides a fault tolerant and energy efficient routing operations.

- **Efficient Security Features:** It is supported and proved in the literature that centralized security management can simplify the realization and configuration of different security measures. This perspective could be easily implemented in the SDWSN and can provide a proactive monitoring and quick response to counter different kind of attacks.

## SDN PARADIGM BASED PROTOCOL DESIGN FOR WIRELESS SENSOR NETWORKS

In this section, state-of-art solutions are discussed that are designed for SDN paradigm based WSNs.

### SDN Paradigm Based Sleep Scheduling Algorithm

In WSN, Sleep scheduling mechanism is one of the popular mechanisms for saving and management of the scarce energy recourse of the sensor node. There are different types of sleep scheduling algorithms are proposed in literature (Wang, 2016; Yaxiong, 2010; Xiang, 2016) for the traditional WSN architecture. These algorithms are generally uses message exchange mechanism for establishing the sleep schedule among the neighboring sensor nodes. This result in high and unbalanced energy consumption during setup of sleep schedules. In order to overcome this problem, the authors in (Wang, 2016) have proposed a SDN based sleep scheduling approach, called SDN-ECCKN. In this approach, sleep scheduling process is executed at the controller rather than in the sensor nodes. For formulating the sleep scheduling, there is no message exchange between sensor nodes that is the main features of SDN-ECCKN. This causes energy efficient sleep schedule for SDWSN. The working of the SDN-ECCKN sleep scheduling protocol is described as follows:

- Lifetime of each sensor nodes is divided into multiple intervals and each interval has two sub-intervals, namely, beacon segment and executions segment.

- In the beacon segment, each sensor nodes keep itself awake and send beacon information to the SDN controller using multi-hop communication. During this segment, controller maintains full network topology at the controller. After this, controller employed the sleep scheduling algorithm proposed in (Yaxiong, 2010) for calculation of the sleep schedule of each node in the network and updates the topology information for the routing.
- In the executions segment, controller sends sleep schedule and updated routing information to the nodes and then each node executes these control information and updates its sleep schedule and routing topology.

## SDN Paradigm Based Routing Algorithm

In the traditional WSN architecture, routing operations are executed at each node that causes more energy consumption. However, in the SDN paradigm based WSN (SDWSN), routing operations are implemented at the control plane at various distributed SDN controllers. Since controller has enough energy resource, so there is saving the node energy at the infrastructure plane. The most related current work for routing the sensed data from sensor nodes to the sink is proposed in (Xiang, 2016). In (Shanmugapriya, 2015), PSO based clustering algorithm is proposed where this algorithm is executed at the SDN enabled sensor control server and generates an optimal set of Cluster Head. These CH nodes forms clusters and instruct its cluster members to complete the different tasks.

In (Han, 2014), a context aware and policy based routing method is proposed for SDWSN. In this method, routing process involves six phases such as Initialization, Topology discovery, Decision, Policy based routing and Enforcement Phase. In the initialization phase, sensor nodes send its energy and location information to the controller. In the enforcement phase, controller after the formation of routes enforces its knowledge to the flow table of each sensor node. In (Han, 2014), the authors have discussed a cluster based routing protocol for SDWSN, In this protocol, authors have assume three types of nodes such as normal node, master node, and centre node. The main job of normal node is to only receiving the data. However, master node is act as a controller and centre node is act as a relay node.

In (Yuan, 2014), the authors have described a novel idea for combining the AODV routing protocol with the OpenFlow. In the proposed scheme, an AODV daemon is used to implement the AODV routing algorithm and this scheme uses OpenvSwitch which acts as OpenFlow agent for facilitating the communication between the controller and the sensor nodes.

## SDN Paradigm Based WSN Management

Network management is a fundamental service which is provided by the network management applications in order to configure and run the various policies, controls and new patches. SDN based network management applications are generally implement through northbound interface of the SDN architecture. In (Yap, 2010), a northbound API is proposed, called OpenRoads, for facilitating the network management applications to define and control the policies on the SDN switches through the SDN controller. OpenRoads is a wireless OpenFlow API which uses FlowVisor to allow the management of the wireless networks using virtualization. Similarly, in (Huang, 2014), a SDN based network management framework is proposed for Internet of things. Since the framework proposed in (Huang, 2014) was for wireless networks, these model can also used in SDWSN architecture for the management of the various network related services and controls.

In (Bera, 2016), the authors have proposed a system; called Soft-WSN which is designed for the management of device as well as topology for software defined WSN. The sensor node specific task is managed by device management module. However, topology management module is responsible for control and management of topology in order to provide optimized network performance. In order to facilitate device and topology control and management from the software defined controller, different control rules and packet formats are defined in this research work.

## SDN Paradigm Based Localization

Localization is a fundament service in a typical application of WSN. This is due to fact that a sensor reading without its location is meaningless in most of the applications. In order to localize the sensor nodes, anchor nodes play a very important role. Anchor nodes know its location and with help of anchor nodes, localization scheme localize the normal sensor nodes that does not know its location. Different kinds of localization algorithms are proposed in literature for the traditional WSN architecture. These algorithms are generally distributed algorithm which exchanges number of messages for getting the location and distance information of the anchor nodes relative to the normal node for the estimation of its location. This process consumes high energy of the network. These distributed localization algorithms are generally suboptimal and less efficient in terms of accuracy and energy compared to centralized algorithm.

In order to solve these problems of localization, the authors in (Zhu, 2017) have proposed a SDN based anchor scheduling algorithm for the localization in the WSN. Main objective of the proposed algorithm to minimize number of active anchor nodes. Since SDN paradigm control the network activities through from the point of view of global network topology, it offers optimal solution for deciding the optimal number of active anchor nodes and how to estimates the location of normal sensor nodes at the SDN controllers with high accuracy. In the proposed algorithm, it is assume that an information table is maintained in the controller for each anchor node. This information is used to design the timer of the corresponding anchor node. In this scheme, controller determines a subset of active anchor nodes for each time slot and also ensures connectivity among the agents. The proposed scheme works in two phases: Initialization and anchor node scheduling. In the initialization phase, an agent node who does not know its location sends a hello packet to the anchor nodes in order to active them. After this, each active anchor node sends a packet which contains its location, residual energy and the hop counts with the agent $i$ to the SDN controller. In this phase, location of an agent I is estimated at the controller and also information table is constructed for each anchor node. In anchor scheduling phase, first information table is updated after expiration of time slot and after that controller decides the schedule of the anchor nodes based on the connectivity degree of the agents.

In (Zhu, 2016), a SDN based localization node selection algorithm is proposed for WSN. The proposed scheme works in two phases: Matrix Initialization and localization node selection. In the Matrix Initialization phase, SDN controller initializes the selection matrix such as if a node $x_i$ is within the communication range of agent node $x_j$, value of matrix entry $s_{ij}$ is *1* otherwite it is *0*. After initialization of selection matrix, SDN controller choose localization nodes that are used for the location estimation of the agent nodes which does not know its position.

## OPEN RESEARCH CHALLENGES

The research works in the area of software-defined wireless sensor networks are in a budding stage and generally requires major efforts in modeling and evaluation of systems and also a standard specification for sensor Openflow design model for wireless sensor nodes. In addition, there are many inherent research challenges that should be addresses for SND paradigm based WSNs such as operating system for sensor nodes, evaluation and quantification of processing at the node and at the SDN controller. In order to highlight the design challenges of SDWSN, this section discussed some of the important challenges as follows:

1. **Internal Processing vs. Logically Centralized Controller Processing:** For the SDN based WSN architecture; there is a trade-off between sensor node and logically centralized controllers in terms of processing load. Although, SDWSN pledges an enormous saving of node energy by transferring the

most of the decision logic to the controllers, the degree of this claim must be evaluated and verified by the application of the standard protocols. In addition, in-network processing i.e. data aggregation of the different sensors requires closer research attention.

2. **Duty Cycling:** In order to lessen the redundant transmission of sensor readings and to save the node energy, SDN paradigm based sensor node must support duty cycling. In duty cycling, each node turns off its radio and goes to the sleep state when it is not in use. Since duty cycling approach offers a huge amount of energy saving, there is a need to design an novel centralized algorithm for designing the optimal duty schedule for each node so that coverage and connectivity of the network is maintained.

3. **Flexible Rules and Policies for Sensor OpenFlow:** Since OpenFlow mechanism offers a novel approach to decouple the data and control plane in the SDN paradigm, SDWSN framework needs to focus on designing the simple and flexible rules for sensor Open flow and where to place these rules and policies is an emerging challenge in this area of research.

4. **Support of Node Mobility:** Since WSN is a application oriented network, node mobility as well as sink node mobility both offers various advantages in order to tackle various challenges such as energy balance problem, coverage and connectivity problem, energy hole problem etc. Since node mobility makes network topology dynamic, there is a design research challenge for SDWSN architecture which can support node mobility.

5. **Virtualization of the SDN Controller:** Since in cluster based SDWSN architecture, multiple controllers are deployed where each cluster has one controller, how to virtualized multi-controller sensor network and how to organize then is a research challenge.

6. **Reliability:** Since WSN uses wireless links for the communication and these links are generally unreliable and unstable. Sometimes dynamic network topology may cause unreliable network operations and management by the centralized controllers. The design of protocols for SDWSN should consider these issues also.

7. **Optimal Placement of Controllers:** In SDWSN architecture, SDN controller plays a major role in topology management, routing, duty cycling etc. However, optimal placement of these controllers and how to distribute loads to these controllers are an emerging research challenge in order to provide scalable solutions.

8. **Implementation and Evaluation Over a Sensor Platform:** In the literature, there are many research efforts in the design of protocols and frameworks for

SDWSN. These frameworks are generally only theoretical studies and simulated the proposed ideas. However, there is lacks of real time implementation of SDWSN framework in order to observe the actual benefits of SDN paradigm. So there is an open research challenge for implementation and evaluation of the proposed SDWSN framework over the SDN based sensor nodes.

9. **Standardization of North Bound and South Bound Interface:** The main aims of the north bound and south bound interface in SDWSN to facilitate different kinds of interactions with the SDN controllers. In order to provide interoperability, there is a need to standardize the interaction rules of both API.

10. **Security:** In the literature, most of the research works in the area of SDWSN focus on the architectural aspect of the network. In the reference to the SDWSN, there is a need to consider security issues such as threats to the compromise a SDN controller by the attackers, secure programmability of the SDN enabled sensor nodes etc.

## CONCLUSION

In this chapter, a generic framework for SDWSN and its different components are discussed. This chapter also discussed advantages of the SDN paradigm and flexibility and control offered by this paradigm in the protocol design for different operation in WSN. An overview of software defined networking model proposed for wireless sensor networks and SDN based resource management, routing, sleep scheduling algorithm, localization algorithms are discussed. In last, detailed discussions of open research challenges in the area of SDWSN are presented.

## REFERENCES

Akyildiz, I. F., Su, W., Sankarasubramaniam, Y., & Cayirci, E. (2002). Wireless sensor networks : A survey. *Computer Networks*, *38*(4), 393–422. doi:10.1016/S1389-1286(01)00302-4

Anastasi, G., Conti, M., Di Francesco, M., & Passarella, A. (2009). Energy conservation in wireless sensor networks: A survey. *Ad Hoc Networks*, *7*(3), 537–568. doi:10.1016/j.adhoc.2008.06.003

Bera, S., Misra, S., Roy, S. K., Obaidat, M. S. (2016). Soft-WSN: Software-Defined WSN Management System for IoT Applications. *IEEE Systems Journal*, 1-8.

Bizanis, N., & Kuipers, F. (2016). SDN and virtualization solutions for the Internet of Things: A survey. *IEEE Access: Practical Innovations, Open Solutions*, 1–1.

De Gante, A., Aslan, M., & Matrawy, A. (2014). Smart wireless sensor network management based on software-defined networking. *Proc. of 27th Bienn. Symp. Commun.*, 71–75. doi:10.1109/QBSC.2014.6841187

de Oliveira, B. T., Margi, C. B., & Gabriel, L. B. (2014). TinySDN: Enabling multiple controllers for software-defined wireless sensor networks. *Proc. IEEE Latin-Amer. Conf. Commun. (LATINCOM)*, 1–6.

Han, Z., & Ren, W. (2014). A Novel Wireless Sensor Networks Structure Based on the SDN. *International Journal of Distributed Sensor Networks*, *2014*(1), 1–8.

Haque, I. T., & Abu-Ghazaleh, N. (2016). *Wireless Software Defined Networking: a Survey and Taxonomy*. IEEE Communication Survey & Tutorials.

Huang, H., Zhu, J., & Zhang, L. (2014). An SDN-based Management Framework for IoT Devices. *Irish Signals System Conference-2014 China-irel. Int. Conf. Inf. Communication Technology (ISSC 2014/CIICT 2014), 25th IET*, 175–179.

Jagadeesan, N. A., & Krishnamachari, B. (2014). Software Defined Networking Paradigms in Wireless Networks: A Survey. *ACM Computer Survey, 47*(2), 27:1-27:11.

Jarraya, Y., Madi, T., & Debbabi, M. (2014). A Survey and a Layered Taxonomy of Software-Defined Networking. *IEEE Communications Surveys and Tutorials*, *16*(4), 1955–1980. doi:10.1109/COMST.2014.2320094

Khan, I., Belqasmi, F., Glitho, R., Crespi, N., Morrow, M., & Polakos, P. (2016). Wireless sensor network virtualization: A survey. *IEEE Communications Surveys and Tutorials*, *18*(1), 553–576. doi:10.1109/COMST.2015.2412971

Kobo, H. I., Abu-Mahfouz, A. M., & Hancke, G. P. (2017). A Survey on Software-Defined Wireless Sensor Networks: Challenges and Design Requirements. IEEE Access, 5, 1872-1899.

Kreutz, D., Ramos, F. M. V., Esteves Verissimo, P., Esteve Rothenberg, C., Azodolmolky, S., & Uhlig, S. (2015). Software Defined Networking: A Comprehensive Survey. *Proceedings of the IEEE*, *103*(1), 14–76. doi:10.1109/JPROC.2014.2371999

Luo, T., Tan, H.-P., & Quek, T. Q. S. (2012). Sensor OpenFlow: Enabling software-defined wireless sensor networks. *Commun. Lett. IEEE*, *16*(11), 1896–1899. doi:10.1109/LCOMM.2012.092812.121712

Nunes, B. A. A., Mendonca, M., Nguyen, X.-N., Obraczka, K., & Turletti, T. (2014). A Survey of Software-Defined Networking: Past, Present, and Future of Programmable Networks. *IEEE Communications Surveys and Tutorials, 16*(3), 1617–1634. doi:10.1109/SURV.2014.012214.00180

Olivier, F., Carlos, G., & Florent, N. (2015). SDN Based Architecture for Clustered WSN. *Proc. of 9th International Conference on Innovative Mobile and Internet Services in Ubiquitous Computing*, 342–347.

Shanmugapriya, S., & Shivakumar, M. (2015). Context Based Route Model for Policy Based routing in WSN using SDN approach. *BGSIT National Conference on Emerging Trends in Electronics and Communication*.

Tsou, T., Aranda, P., Xie, H., Sidi, R., Yin, H., & Lopez, D. (2012). SDNi: A message exchange protocol for software defined networks (SDNS) across multiple domains. Proc. Internet Eng. Task Force, 1–14.

Wang, Y., Chen, H., Wu, X., & Shu, L. (2016). An energy-efficient SDN based sleep scheduling algorithm for WSNs. *Journal of Network and Computer Applications, 59*, 39–45. doi:10.1016/j.jnca.2015.05.002

Xiang, W., Wang, N., & Zhou, Y. (2016, October 15). An Energy-Efficient Routing Algorithm for Software-Defined Wireless Sensor Networks. *IEEE Sensors Journal, 16*(20), 7393–7400. doi:10.1109/JSEN.2016.2585019

Yap, K., Kobayashi, M., Sherwood, R., Huang, T., Chan, M., Handigol, N., & Mckeown, N. (2010). OpenRoads : Empowering Research in Mobile Networks. *Computer Communication Review, 40*(1), 125–126. doi:10.1145/1672308.1672331

Yaxiong, Z., & Jie, W. (2010). Stochastic sleep scheduling for large scale wireless sensor networks. IEEE International Conference on Communications (ICC), 1–5.

Yick, J., Mukherjee, B., & Ghosal, D. (2008). Wireless sensor network survey. *Computer Networks, 52*(12), 2292–2330. doi:10.1016/j.comnet.2008.04.002

Yuan, A., Fang, H., & Wu, Q. (2014). OpenFlow based hybrid routing in Wireless Sensor Networks. *IEEE 9th International Conference on Intelligent Sensors, Sensor Networks and Information Processing (ISSNIP)*, 1-5.

Zeng, D., Miyazaki, T., Guo, S., Tsukahara, T., Kitamichi, J., & Hayashi, T. (2013). Evolution of Software-Defined Sensor Networks. *Proc. of IEEE 9th International Conference on Mobile Ad-hoc and Sensor Networks*, 410–413.

Zhu, Y., Yan, F., Zhang, Y., Zhang, R., & Shen, L. (2017, May). SDN-based Anchor Scheduling Scheme for Localization in Heterogeneous WSNs. *IEEE Communications Letters*, *21*(5), 1127–1130. doi:10.1109/LCOMM.2017.2657618

Zhu, Y., Zhang, Y., Xia, W., & Shen, L. (2016). A Software-Defined Network Based Node Selection Algorithm in WSN Localization. *IEEE 83rd Vehicular Technology Conference (VTC Spring)*, 1-5.

Zhuxiu, Y., Lei, W., Lei, S., Hara, T., & Zhenquan, Q. (2011). A balanced energy consumption sleep scheduling algorithm in wireless sensor networks. *Seventh international conference on wireless communications and mobile computing conference (IWCMC)*, 831–5.

# Chapter 13
# Software-Defined Storage

**Himanshu Sahu**
*University of Petroleum and Energy Studies, India*

**Ninni Singh**
*University of Petroleum and Energy Studies, India*

## ABSTRACT

*SDS along with SDN and software-defined compute (SDC; where in computing is virtualized and software defined) creates software-defined infrastructure (SDI). SDI is the set of three components—SDN, SDS, and SDC—making a new kind of software-defined IT infrastructure where centralization and virtualization are the main focus. SDI is proposed to have infrastructure developed over commodity hardware and software stack defined over it. SDS is exploiting the same concept of decoupling and centralization in reference to storage solutions as in SDN. The SDN works on decoupling the control plane with the data plane from a layer, three switches, or router, and makes a centralized decision point called the controller. The SDS works in a similar way by moving the decision making from the storage hardware to a centralized server. It helps in developing new and existing storage solutions over the commodity storage devices. The centralization helps to create a better dynamic solution for satisfying the customized user need. The solutions are expected to be cheaper due to the use of commodity hardware.*

## INTRODUCTION

Storage Network Industry Association (SNIA) defines SDS as

*SDS is Virtualized storage with a service management interface. SDS includes pools of storage with data service characteristics that may be applied to meet the requirements specified through the service management interface. (Carlson, 2014)*

DOI: 10.4018/978-1-5225-3640-6.ch013

The SDS is software stack that provides the centralized management interface over the commodity hardware. It can work as a part of cloud data centre or as standalone storage solution working as an end-product.

*From 2013 to 2020, the digital universe will grow by a factor of 10, from 4.4 ZB to 44ZB. It more than doubles every two years. (Turner, 2014)*

The large data required large amount of storage hardware and also there is requirement for fast and easy storage and retrieval of the data. Existing solution has improved to cope up this with innovations in the field of cloud storage (Azodolmolky, 2013). These may be considered as patch up solutions to the existing problems but they are not ready to for future. The Internet users are increasing day by day and also the data generated per users in increasing so in future the data size will become hard to manage. Not only that the information per bit is also decreasing due to rich media contents. After the emergence of IOT when each and everything will be connected to the internet the data generated will further increase (Gubbi, 2013).

## Traditional Storage System

The Traditional Storage system consists of consists of storage array, magnetic disks and tape libraries. The Tradition storage system has following features.

*Figure 1. Digital data growth*

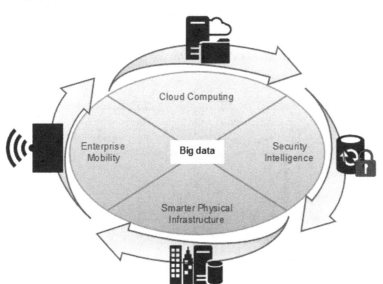

- **Application Dedicated:** In traditional storage system we use storage device dedicated to a particular application. Every application has its own storage associated with the application only.
- **Isolated Resources:** The Storage resources are isolated to one to one another. This leads to wastage of resources since the underutilized resource cannot be used by other application because storage is isolated and cannot be work as a pool.
- **Policies Unique to Vertical Solutions:** Since storage resources are dedicated and isolated the policy is limited to application dedicated storage.

Problems with traditional storage systems:

1. **Cost:** The traditional system is not capable of creating low cost solutions that will store the huge amount of data. The maintenance, operations and support is also needed which is also not efficient in traditional system.
2. **Choice:** The Traditional storage system is lacking the interoperability and flexibility due to dedicated resource to applications and unavailability of pooling of resources. The access to shared data is not possible.
3. **Cloud Deployment:** Cloud deployment is not possible by using traditional storage systems since pooling of resources in not available.

Unlike the traditional the SDS uses a software stack above the commodity hardware. The software defined stack in a centralized controlled and API is provided to develop applications over it. The isolated resources are converted into resource pools and the policies can be implemented globally (Carlson, 2014).

*Figure 2. Traditional storage system vs. SDS*

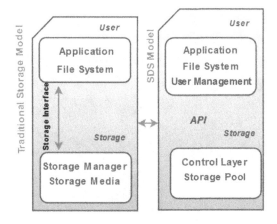

After considering all these factors it can be easily deduces Traditional storage management is too complex and inefficient for new data demands that storage technology not only need improvements but also a new innovation that is capable of handling the data. SDS may prove one such solution that is based on innovation and paradigm shift.

## BACKGROUND

Evolution of new technologies and trends in IT, such as mobile, cloud computing and Big Data has given the storage consumption and requirements new peak. Along with the exponential growth in the storage need, cheaper storage solutions have further created the abundance of digital data. It has created new opportunities with a need of cost effective control, management and access interface to efficiently process and store huge data. Current storage technologies need automation and management to successfully solve this extravagant data growth to provide efficient yet cost effective solutions.

## SDS Enablers

Now the question is what are the reasons that motivate SDS to become a strong contender for transforming storage market? The assemblage of technologies and events has motivated the venders to build modern storage architecture (Edition, I. P. C. (2014)). This new features incorporated modern storage architecture attracts many venders. In this section we elaborated the principles that make SDS different from others:

- **Virtual Controllers and VM-Aware Software:** VM-aware is a management service, which assembled in the data centre's software fabric to maintain I/O patterns and workloads of the virtual data centre. Software-defined storage (SDS) provides cost effective and promising efficiency only when storage services brought on each VM level. In addition to this SDS are capable enough to reproduce virtual software controllers, which scale, agile and easily provisioned the storage resources.
- **Flash Storage:** The emergence of flash facilitates in-system software control management which is not available on the hard drive as a sole module. Flash storage helps in transparently sharing server storage with other severs hosts.

- **Quick Failure Recovery:** SDS system is designed to deal with the failure. Because in SDS software layers have knowledge about all the status of software as well as hardware components, even if it is heavily scaled, extremely distributes system.

## Cloud Storage Data Centres and Software Defined Data Centres

Storage as a service (SAAS) is one of the major aspects of cloud computing. It relies on the data centre. Fast growing users and changing networking technologies also requires the change in the data centre technologies so that it can effectively serve the user requirements. Virtualization is one way to solve the large requirements of resource in a dynamic way.

Emergence of the new technologies such (VOIP, Multimedia Streaming Servers) has changed the data patterns i.e. (data generated from smart phones and IOT devices).This varied workload has been introduced into the existing environment.

Technology needs to change instead on upgradation of the old legacy software and propriety software environment which is not capable of full filing the changing need of storage devices.

*The way SDN has changed the current architecture of Data centre in the same way SDS will change the Storage architecture by providing the software infrastructure over existing storage hardware solutions.*

## SDN

The whole sole work is to design a centralized control APIs and algorithm. Software-defined networking (SDN) decouples the data primitives from control plane for devices (routers, switches, NICs). SDN programming that triggers the tasks are built upon data plane performs operations in networks like forwarding tables and traffic classification (based on addresses).

## FEATURES AND FUNCTIONALITIES OF SDS

Since SDS is a new technology the full features and functionalities are yet to be defined but provides possible features and functionalities (Carlson, 2014). The features can be summarized as below:

1.  **Scale-Out Architecture:** The SDS architecture is different from the existing scale up architecture. The storage can be upscale or downscale dynamically. It will easily adopt according to the user need.

2.  **Commodity Hardware:** The SDS is meant to support the commodity hardware so that the scale out process will be easier and the software storage solution is cheaper as compared to existing propriety solutions. Commodity hardware can be easily managed by the management interface due to availability of open interface. The SDS may also provide the feature that a user can also develop its own solution over commodity hardware. The SDS solutions are built in that way so that the user it can work with specialized hardware.

3.  **Resource Pooling:** The SDS is based on virtualization to support resource pooling. All the resources are virtualized and abstracted so that the resources are always available for pooling. The resources can be dynamically added or removed due to availability of centralized interface.

4.  **Abstraction:** In the SDS all the hardware are managed centrally. This provides a kind of abstraction so the system can be viewed managed and maintained as a whole not each storage devices. This provides easy debugging and maintenance of the storage devices.

5.  **Automation:** The SDS provides automation to the operations of configuration and monitoring. The automation helps to take necessary action by using polices defined in response to certain event.

6.  **Programmability:** The centralized management interface provides programmability to storage using API available. It helps in providing automation, monitoring and dynamic configuration of the storage system.

7.  **Policy Driven:** It allows the administrator to set the policy for data service and storage. The policies are implemented over the central management interface that governs the storage devices. SDS also has the capability that the end user can define the policy for the storage devices as per its convenience.

8.  **Data vs. Storage Services:** SDS provides the feature of separating the data services from the storages service. The Service may use the same path or different path depending on the application.

## Functionalities of SDS

The SDS system to provide all the expected features must provide the following functionalities. This functionality can be developed as an application over the provided or the system component. These functionalities help in fulfilling the business requirement and service level agreement (Coyne L. et. al (2017)).

1.  **Storage Virtualization:** Virtualization the most important concept used in cloud computing to support SaaS model. The SDS needs to provide the virtualization of storage resource so that the storage pools can be created and resource sharing can be done to maximize the resource utilization. The virtualization should support heterogeneous storage array and devices. Features like transparent data migration thin provisioning compression and de-duplication should be provided. These advanced features can be software defined or can be implemented using the vendor's native technology.

2.  **Policy Automation:** Automated provisioning is the functionality that improves the efficiency by removing the manual intervention from resource provisioning. Policy implementation based monitoring and analytics helps in better management of services. It also helps in the measurements and reports provided by the analytics tools. Policy automation also helps to deal with dynamic nature of request for provisioning of resources.

3.  **Analytics and Optimization:** Analytics helps in measuring the storage performances. The SDS analytics tools helps in measuring the tools to report them and compare them to required performance levels. These tools also help in optimization of the storage capacity usage. It collects the data and performance metrics to match with the automation workflows. It can also provide the chargeback model as required.

4.  **Availability, Backup, and Copy Management:** Availability is one of the most important features of any IT infrastructure. The SDS also needs to provide high availability of storage system. The availability is basically maintained with the help of fault tolerance and error recovery methods. The redundancy helps in making easy error recovery. The SDS need to provide backup and restore capability and local and remote copies for the purpose of disaster recovery.

5.  **Integration and API Services:** Integration of all functionalities is necessary since along with SDN and SDC the SDS provide the SDI. So all the feature must be integrated internally as well as externally to provide the SDI and with SDE enabled business application. Application programming interface is used to provide the specific interface that can help in integration with other application. The SDS provide northbound and south bound API for the integration.

6.  **Security:** Data security is the key factor of any storage system. SDS supports this feature to support authorized access of the data. Common features such as encryption, zoning, and Logical Unit number LUN masking are helpful in providing the security of data. Object based storage access can help to implement security at the object level security.

7.  **Massive Scale-Out Architecture:** Big data analytics is a growing field and it also a key driver for SDS. SDS provides rapid deployment of large storage capacity so it is really helpful in operating big data and analytics over there.

8.    **Cloud Accessibility:** Support of cloud implement is needed with the SDS so that is can provide the cloud services and also integrates with other cloud service provider. It needs to provide the storage as cloud storage to its user. Auto provisioning and chargeback models is helpful in that

## Role of Metadata in SDS

In traditional storage system the meta data generally contains information related data storage properties such as file index, file properties, file types and storage requirements but in the case of SDS meta data will serve other purposes such as to describe user requirements, define service level capabilities and control the data services.

## ARCHITECTURE OF SDS

## Data Access Protocols

Study of data access protocols are most needed since any storage architecture needs to know the data is accessed in a storage system. The SDS has introduced new way to access data called object based access along with traditional block and file based I/O (Coyne L. et. al (2017)).

*Figure 3. Data types in an SDS environment*

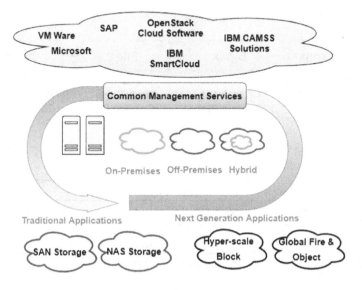

So there are 3 types of data access method available.

1. **Block I/O:** Block refers to block of common storage devices such as hard drive. Block I/O is also used in SAN architecture. Applications use the file I/O commands to manipulate bytes of data. The commands are passed to the operating system to operate on the storage. The operating system then translates those I/O requests into lower-level commands that use block I/O to manipulate the file system and the application data file.
2. **File I/O:** In file based I/O the application can directly access the file. The unit of data access is file not bits, bytes or blocks. In NAS environment the same is used for accessing the data.
3. **Object Based I/O:** This is the new way to access data in which data is seen as object described by a rich set of metadata. This type of file access is more beneficial when accessing large set of unstructured data.

Objects are stored in special repositories called Object Storage Devices (OSD)

## Software Defined Infrastructure (SDI)

- **Software Defined Infrastructure (SDI):** Software Defined Infrastructure (SDI) is the foundation for a fully integrated software defined environment, optimizing compute, storage and networking infrastructure so organizations can quickly adapt to changing business requirements. (Kandiraju, 2014)

*Figure 4. Data access method in SDS*

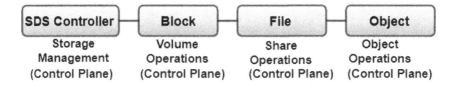

| | | | |
|---|---|---|---|
| **SDS Controller** | **Block** | **File** | **Object** |
| Storage Management (Control Plane) | Volume Operations (Control Plane) | Share Operations (Control Plane) | Object Operations (Control Plane) |

*Table 1.*

| | |
|---|---|
| **User Data** | Data coming from the user application |
| **Attributes** | The set of information about the data (richer when compared with traditional file systems) which improves data sharing among applications |
| **Metadata** | Set of information needed by the storage device to manage the object placement |
| **Object ID** | The unique identification code of the Object |

SDI consists of the software defined management interface for storage network and computing resources with the help of virtualization. The SDI consists of Software Defined Storage, Software defined networks and Software Defined Compute.

## SDI Features

SDI provides the following key features:

1. **Service Assurance:** It supports service assurance with the help of dynamic provisioning of resources. End to end policies management and monitoring helps better service and fault tolerance. The automation and programmability running on the top helps easier management of resource and dynamic provisioning.
2. **Provisioning Management:** SDI provides orchestration provisioning of resources which is not only dynamic but also optimized fulfilling requirement uniquely based on the applications requirement.
3. **Pooled Resources:** by using abstraction the network storage and computing resources are provided in the form of pooled resources. This provides optimal utilization of resources reduces resource wastage as well as provide global availability of resources.

*Figure 5. Software defined infrastructure*

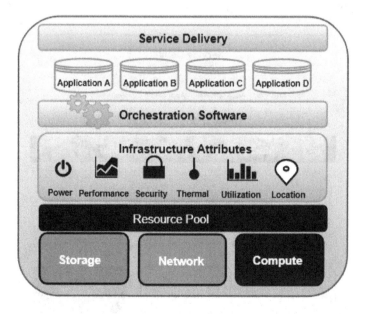

## SDS as a Key Component of SDI

SDS is software defined storage one of most important resource for an IT infrastructure. SDS framework delivers scalable, cost effective solutions to meet the need of current and future data storage requirements. The following are the supporting features provided by the SDS to support the SDI

1.  **Orchestrate:** Application access to diverse storage systems through SLAs, increasing flexibility and handling data complexity.
2.  **Provision:** Resources dynamically (pay-as-you grow), increasing efficiency.
3.  **Aggregate:** Diverse equipment, leverage legacy, increase flexibility, and drive down costs.
4.  **Abstract:** Software from hardware, providing flexibility and scalability.

## SDS Architecture

### SDS Reference Architecture

SDI architecture made up of three main components, SDS is one of them (Kandiraju, 2014). SDS reference architecture exhibit similar features of Storage defined networking (SDN) i.e. splitting of storage function into two separate layers:

*Figure 6. SDS as a key component of SDS*

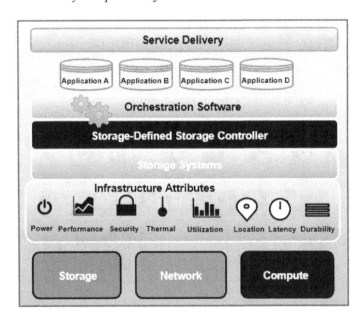

*Figure 7. SDS capabilities of the control plane and data plane*

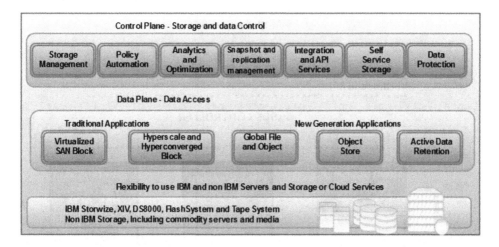

## SDS Data Plane

SDS data plane consists of storage related functions such as copy services, virtualization, tiering, RAID Protections, data deduplication and encryption. It acts as an interface to the hardware devices. It contains all possible access methods and a full range of access possibilities.

## SDS Control Plane

Control plane is a software layer that accomplishes virtualized storage assets. It consists of complex functions that are capable enough to run a business workload. It facilitates scalable, flexible, optimized and rapid storage capacity. SDS fulfils the present business requirements, i.e. control, agility, dynamic optimizing organization capabilities and efficiency

## SDS Controller

SDS controller is the heart of the SDS infrastructure which is the control and management plane proving resource provisioning, policy enforcement, coordination among the different components.

The SDS provides the following features

1.  **Centralized Management:** The SDS controller provides a centralized management point i.e. all the storage devices are visible and can be easily

*Figure 8. SDS controller*

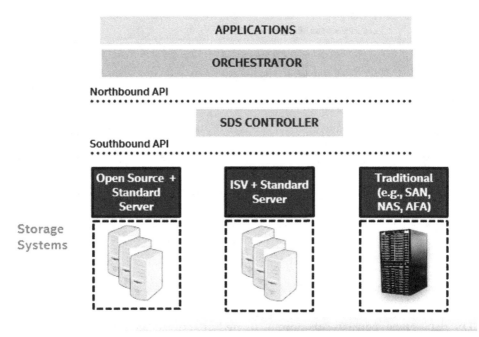

managed using the control plane. The SDS controller provides programmability such that the user specific control and provisioning application can be developed using this interface.

2. **Communication:** The SDS controller provides communication among applications, orchestrator and storage systems. It uses Northbound and southbound API.

3. **Resource Allocation:** The main benefit of SDS is the resource allocation that not only helps in optimizing resource utilization but also provides application specific storage. The resource allocation is done in that way so that it will meet the service level agreement.

## EXISTING SDS SOLUTION

After realizing the benefits of SDS many storage industry leaders came up with storage solutions based on SDS technology fully or partially. ViPR (DellEMC, (2017)), developed by emc2 and IBM storewize (IBM Storwize V7000 and Storwize V7000 Unified Disk Systems) are the solution based on SDS.

## ViPR

ViPR is basically an SDS controller developed by EMC. It is based on Storage as a Service (SaaS) model which reduces the complexity generated due to traditional storage system. It automates the storage provisioning reducing manual efforts and increasing efficiency. Viper is a commercial version of Open source project CorpHD (DellEMC, (2017)).

It centralizes and transforms storage into a simple and extensible platform by abstracting and pooling resources to deliver automated, policy-driven storage services on-demand via a self-service catalogue (DellEMC, (2017)).

Viper converts the storage array into in virtualized pool of storage array. The storage performance is limited due to heterogeneity of storage devices. Virtualized plays an important role address this problem.

Viper addresses these shortcomings and offers the similar kind of capabilities of virtualization by conceptualizing the storage services for the data path and embedding it in the storage control path. Viper provides support to object, block and file storage types. Viper is open and extensible solution such that, administrator has the ability of management and control over the whole storage devices using a centralized control i.e. a controller for storage networks (DellEMC, (2017)).

*Figure 9. Viper architecture*

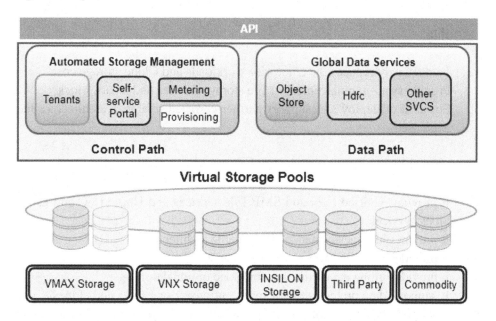

The features of ViPR can be summarized as below:

1.  **Automated Provisioning:** ViPR improves operational efficiency by automated provision and reclamation of storage resources.
2.  **Storage as a Service Model:** It is based on SaaS i.e. storage-as-a-service model and uses self-service catalogue to empower consumers.
3.  **Converged Infrastructure:** It supports converged infrastructure to speed-up deployment of cloud-based services on converged infrastructure
4.  **Multivendor Support:** It supports a variety of multivendor platforms (EMC & 3rd Party). ViPR manages block storage so it can work with OpenStack Cinder. Using the IaaS model it can integrate with VMware, OpenStack and Microsoft cloud stacks.
5.  **Open Community Based:** It is based on CorpHD so it will gain all the benefits of open source community-driven development.

## NexentaStor

NexentaStor offers unified block (iSCSI and FC) and file (SMB and NFS) storage service, that operates on standard industry hardware and supports hybrid, all-flash and disk scaling up to petabytes configurations (NexentaStor). It's very easier for IT administers to monitor, mange day to day tasks (creation of file systems, deploying pools etc.).

### Benefits

1.  It adequately reduces the enterprise workloads and Cloud storage cost.
2.  Provide swap-in replacement of file storage devices and legacy block.
3.  For ease of deploy and support partner certified reference architecture has been used.

### Functionality

1.  It provides Unified NFS and SMB File services and Unified FC and iSCSI block services
2.  It provides high performance and scalable architecture.
3.  It provides unlimited file system sizes
4.  It provides inline data reduction for space optimization.
5.  It supports data protection with space optimized snapshots and clones.
6.  It supports different replication for easy data back up

## IBM Storewize

Storwize provides a scalable, flexible and virtualized storage management solution for the cloud environments. It provides the functionality to support the virtualized data Storage. IBM Storwize provide the solution the management interface and analysis dashboard that in helpful for easier management (IBM Storwize V7000 and Storwize V7000 Unified Disk Systems).

Features of IBM storewize

1. Improve your business agility with flash storage and heterogeneous data services
2. Scale seamlessly, get higher flexibility and protect your investment with IBM Storwize system clustering
3. Transform the economics of data storage using IBM Real-time Compression
4. Optimize tiered storage—including flash storage—with IBM Easy Tier
5. Complement on-premises storage of all types with hybrid cloud capability
6. Address security needs by encrypting data on existing storage
7. Scale capacity quickly and easily into the petabyte range with high-density enclosures
8. Enable near-continuous availability of applications through dynamic migration

## CorpHD an SDN Controller

CorpHD is an Open source project of ViPR Controller of EMC. It is basically an SDS controller provide management and control services to various storage resources deployed by the cloud consumers (CorpHD Architecture). It provides an interface for the user and logical control by which user can work on legacy storage platform. It provides object, file and block access protocols.

### Key Highlights

1. Storage, manipulation, and analysis of unstructured data on arrays and commodity-based systems.
2. **Object:** Works across various commodity-based systems-EMC and other file-based arrays; compatible with Atmos, Amazon S3, Swift APIs.
3. **HDFS:** Builds a Big Data repository at scale and runs Hadoop analytic applications.

*Figure 10. Corp HD architecture*

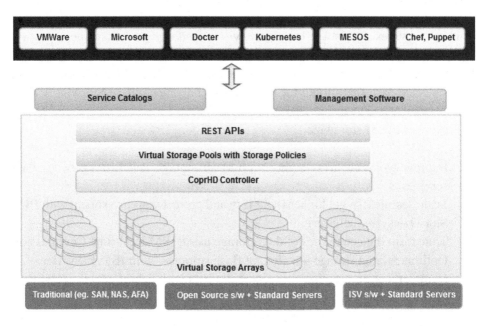

4. **Block:** Automates provisioning; adds block pools to CoprHD Service Catalog; powered by ScaleIO
5. **Storage Engine:** Writes object-related data (users, metadata and object location) to logical containers of contiguous disk space (128MB) called "chunks"
6. Information is indexed in append-only pattern.
7. Data protection on chunks that are snapped, journaled, and versioned; includes erasure coding; object recovery; HW monitoring; directs I/O to disks.
8. Does not overwrite data, requires locking or invalidates cache.
9. Write requests to same chunk happen simultaneously on different disk sets.
10. Throughput takes advantage of all spindles and NICs.
11. Small object payloads are aggregated in memory.
12. Provides geo protection against site failures; asynchronous replication.

A critical aspect of CoprHD's ability to adhere to application-based service requirements is timely awareness of the state of the physical infrastructure, including faults, performance challenges, and degradation, in addition to planned maintenance activities. Intel® Rack Scale Architecture management software provides this level of awareness, and through RESTful APIs makes this information available via push and pull queries.

## BENEFITS OF SDS IN BUSINESSES

Information technology (IT) revolutions are not only for IT benefits but also for socio-economic welfares. Advancement in technology delivers some concrete benefits before it becomes a trend.

With SDS, several business outcomes and drivers, both large and small, makes the technology, a majority success for several enterprises (DellEMC, 2017) (NexentaStor).

### Cloud-Scale Enterprise Architecture

Cloud and other service providers, generally, approach third party leaders, with various proposals, for the transformation of their workloads without any involvement of IT. It is the duty of Chief Information Officers (CIOs) to take necessary steps so that they can remain in control of their organizations' technology goals while still providing the kinds of services that the business demands. SDS systems provide easy and cheap way to transform workloads (NexentaStor).

### Support of IT Goals

While SDS systems are deployed as a part of a data centre i.e. software-defined data centre (SDDC) gives more flexibility to meet new workload needs as they arise. This is due to the elimination of storage as a discretely managed resource in the data-centre.

### Efficient Use of Existing Resources

In present environment, IT services runs both, on-premises and in a cloud provider's data-centre, whereas SDS schematics structure have power to provide services off-premises and cloud-based storage as a part of single-data fabric for the organization. Another feature of SDS is that, without sacrificing IT priorities, SDS is able to push archived data to less expensive offsite storage for the improvement of overall cost equations. SDS also helps IT to integrate, more deeply, into the infrastructure enabling new automation opportunities.

### Faster Payback From IT

New technologies like virtual desktop, data analytics and so on, requires more power, capacity and are dependent on well-designed storage systems. With the development of SDS techniques, technicians do not have to carefully design, and manage storage for business needs. The capability to scale in a linear fashion for both capacity and performance ensures that the storage system won't be a roadblock to new endeavours.

## CHALLENGES

It is a fact that every new technology, even with lot many benefits, also carry various challenges which cannot be ignored. Hence one cannot blindly favor software defined storage technology. There are various challenges to be resolved; some of them are listed below

### Legacy Data Storage

One of the biggest challenges of software defined storage is overcoming objections from data array customers who have invested time and money in their data storage systems. Existing storage arrays already have their own data and storage management software, and IT managers are already paying for some form of storage management-services.

### Cost

Another unknown factor is cost. Since SDS is largely cloud based some vendors are charging by the amount of data stored. However, customers really end up paying for the amount of data managed, since they have already paid for much of the storage devices already.

### Too Many Vendors

Since SDS is still a young technology there are at least 20 different SDS vendors eying for market share and each with a different approach. One of the challenges of software defined storage is a lack of common understanding; everyone is talking about SDS but it means something slightly different for each vendor or analyst.

### It's Not baked Yet

And as with any new technology, vendors are still working the bugs out of the deployments. SDS is a concept that is still evolving. It is surely coming, but it's not here just yet so vendors are still wooing early adopters willing to take the long view that the SDS-market-will-mature.

## A New Way of Thinking

For those who believe in SDN and IT as a service, SDS is a next logical step. For those used to running conventional data centers, the idea of using software defined networking, let alone storage as a service, is still very foreign and it will take some time for them to embrace it.

## CONCLUSION

After going through the challenges that are faced by the existing storage solutions and the promises SDS through SDI is providing and the solutions developed by the companies it seems quite feasible that the SDS in future will come up with solutions that are capable of solving current and future software problems.

The SDS is new technology and SDS solutions are also being provided by the storage giants. To increase the adaptability SDS need to more focused on the development of the solutions that incorporate and interoperate with the existing solutions. The SDS solution should contain the full spectrum of services that currently existing solutions are providing. The SDS solutions should not only be based on the commodity hardware but they should also be capable of running over the legacy storage solutions. The SDS solution should incorporate better solutions for data protection and data security. Finally SDS should grow gradually to achieve the acceptance and after standardization of all protocols it can fully replace the existing legacy solutions with a more open, cheaper, customizable, user oriented and reliable solutions that will be universally accepted and implemented.

## FUTURE DIRECTIONS

Software-defined storage (SDS) helps in fulfilling needs of information customers, who are concern with optimizing infrastructure at lower cost and must meet the necessity requirements. Software defined storage summaries software functionalities from hardware, as various applications require precise storage characteristics like performance, security, cost and so on. It also supports several physical or virtualized servers, additionally, virtualized all primary storage systems and networked systems to a common abstraction layer. SDS merges all types of storage systems into a single virtual scale-out storage offering unified automation, orchestration, provisioning, and management capabilities at the individual virtual machine (VM) level, while providing a central point of access to management functions.

As a replacement of dedicated storage arrays, software defined storage enables industry standard hardware which reduces initial entry and repeated costs. Thus provides better performance and more simplified storage management. Unifying major storage services into a single automated platform, averts the need for customers to purchase advanced storage features – snapshots, clones, DR, backup, thin provisioning, compression, de-duplication etc. – separately from multiple vendors.

- SDS provides an optimal storage platform for next generation infrastructure of on premise/private data centers that offers public cloud scale economics, universal access, and self-service automation to private clouds.
- SDS has potential to reduce operational and management expenses dramatically, using policy based automation, deployment simplicity, programmable flexibility, and centralized management while providing hardware independence and utilizing high-volume industry-standard components to lower storage system costs.
- SDS allows policy-driven data center automation that provides the facility to instantly provision storage resources based on workload demanded by each VM in virtualized data centers. These inherent capabilities of SDS will entice data-center managers to embrace and deploy SDS offerings and thereby improve their opex and capex, providing a quick return on investment (ROI).

## REFERENCES

Azodolmolky, S., Wieder, P., & Yahyapour, R. (2013). Cloud computing networking: challenges and opportunities for innovations. *IEEE Communications Magazine, 51*(7), 54-62.

Carlson, M., Yoder, A., Schoeb, L., Deel, D., Pratt, C., Lionetti, C., & Voigt, D. (2014). *Software defined storage*. Storage Networking Industry Assoc. working draft.

CoprHD Architecture. (n.d.). Retrieved from https://coprhd.atlassian.net/wiki/spaces/COP/pages/3211310/A+Short+Guide+to+the+CoprHD+Architecture /24

Coyne, L. (2017). *IBM Software-Defined Storage Guide*. Retrieved from http://ibm.com/redbooks //22

DellEMC. (n.d.). *Dell EMC Vipr Controller, Automate and Simplify Storage Management.* vailable: https://www.emc.com/collateral/data-sheet/h11750-emc-vipr-software-defined-storage-ds.pdf

Edition, I. P. C. (2014). Software Defined Storage For Dummies. Academic Press.

Foundation, O. N. (2012). Software-defined networking: The new norm for networks. *ONF White Paper, 2,* 2-6.

Gens, F. (2012). *IDC Predictions 2013: Competing on the 3rd Platform. Int.* Data Corporation.

Gubbi, J., Buyya, R., Marusic, S., & Palaniswami, M. (2013). Internet of Things (IoT): A vision, architectural elements, and future directions. *Future Generation Computer Systems, 29*(7), 1645–1660. doi:10.1016/j.future.2013.01.010

Hollis, C. (2013). *Introducing emc vipr: A breathtaking approach to software defined storage.* Academic Press.

IBM Storwize V7000 and Storwize V7000 Unified Disk Systems. (n.d.). IBM Corporation. Available:http://www-03.ibm.com/systems/storage/disk/storwize_v7000/

Kandiraju, G., Franke, H., Williams, M. D., Steinder, M., & Black, S. M. (2014). Software defined infrastructures. *IBM Journal of Research and Development, 58*(2/3), 2-1.

Monsanto, C., Reich, J., Foster, N., Rexford, J., & Walker, D. (2013, April). *Composing Software Defined Networks* (Vol. 13). NSDI.

NexentaStor. (n.d.). Retrieved from https://nexenta.com/products/nexentastor /25

Quintero, D., Genovese, W. M., Kim, K., Li, M. J. M., Martins, F., Nainwal, A., ... & Tiwary, A. (2015). *IBM Software Defined Environment.* IBM Redbooks.

Thereska, E., Ballani, H., O'Shea, G., Karagiannis, T., Rowstron, A., Talpey, T., & Zhu, T. et al. (2013). Ioflow: a software-defined storage architecture. In *Proceedings of the Twenty-Fourth ACM Symposium on Operating Systems Principles.* ACM. doi:10.1145/2517349.2522723

Turner, V., Gantz, J. F., Reinsel, D., & Minton, S. (2014). The digital universe of opportunities: Rich data and the increasing value of the internet of things. *IDC Analyze the Future, 16.*

## KEY TERMS AND DEFINITIONS

**Cloud Computing:** Cloud computing is a model for enabling convenient, on-demand network access to a shared pool of configurable computing resources (e.g., networks, servers, storage, applications, and services) that can be rapidly provisioned and released with minimal management effort or service provider interaction.

**Object Storage:** Object storage is a data storage architecture that treats data as objects.

**SDS Controller:** SDS controller is the heart of the SDS infrastructure which is the control and management plane proving resource provisioning, policy enforcement, coordination among the different components.

**Software-Defined Infrastructure:** Software-defined infrastructure (SDI) is the foundation for a fully integrated software defined environment, optimizing compute, storage and networking infrastructure so organizations can quickly adapt to changing business requirements.

**Software-Defined Network:** A networking paradigm based on decoupling the control plane from the data plane and putting the controller on a centralizes location (i.e., controller that provide a centralized management and control over the network).

**Software-Defined Storage:** Software-defined storage (SDS) is a methodology designed for data storage which decouples the programming that triggers the storage related job from physical storage hardware.

**Virtualization:** Virtualization is the technology to create virtual versions of computing resources such as storage, compute, or software.

# Chapter 14
# Learning With Software-Defined Area

**Anurag Tiwari**
*University of Petroleum and Energy Studies, India*

**Suneet Gupta**
*Bennett University, India*

## ABSTRACT

*The idea of software-defined networking (SDN) is a paradigm shift in computer networking. There are various advantages of SDN (e.g., network automation, fostering innovation in network using software, minimizing the CAPEX and OPEX cost with minimizing the power consumption in the network). SDN is one of the recently developed network-driven methodologies where the core of all lower-level services is operated by one centralized device. Developers tried to develop such approaches to make it easy for an administrator to control information flow from one node to another node. To obtain these services, lower-level static architecture is decoupled for the higher level. This chapter introduces a new approach that is based on complex network processing and forecasting for an event.*

## INTRODUCTION

Computer networking is one of the most emerging areas for researchers to introduce newly updated techniques for data communication. The process of data communication may be between various entities with help of communicating devices. As number of applications and entities increases inside a network, complexity of information flow increases. This information flow passes through numerous number of interconnecting

DOI: 10.4018/978-1-5225-3640-6.ch014

devices and networks. In networking, for information transfer mainly packet forwarding technique is used with applications of various numbers of complex protocols. This is the responsibility of the network administrator that modelling of infrastructure, processing of information and customizing all the processing must be tuned in a systematic manner. In most of cases, they have to deal such environment in a manual way but transferring such high level of networking policies into a lower level configuration commands are not an easy task. So there are lot of problems may rise with optimized results, network infrastructure management and performance retrieval index tuning.

To overcome such problems concept of "Programming in Networking" is developed. One of the main aims to introduce programmable "network concept" is that to facilitate multiple methodologies like management, functioning and controlling. Software Defined Networking (SDN) merges all those concepts, theories which are used to convert all described service manual to automation. This automation is achieved by decoupling networking hardware with control choices. It insures high index value corresponding to network performance evolution and management. Theoretically SDN is quite simple but at the time of implementation it creates lot of challenges. Networking technologies have evolved with a slower pace compared to other communication technologies for a long time and the hardware devices, i.e. switches, hub and routers have been developed by manufacturers traditionally. To communicate with the hardware devices, each vendor designed own firmware due to this the progress of innovations in the computer network area was not so speedy. In today's network architecture basically there are three logical planes defined as 1) Control plane 2) data plane 3) management plane. Generally, hardware related with network has been developed in tightly coupled control and data planes. Therefore, traditional networks are also known as "inside the box" paradigm. Such kinds of architecture considerably increase the cost of network administration and management with significant increments in the complexity. So, the market leaders and networking researchers joined the hands in order to rethink the design of traditional networks and proposals for a new networking paradigm, namely programmable networks (Campbell *et al.*, 1999), have emerged (e.g., active networks (Defense Advanced Research Projects Agency, 1997) and Open Signaling (*Campbell et al., 1999*). SDN is not a revolutionary proposal but it is a reshaping of earlier proposals investigated several years ago, mainly programmable networks and control–data plane separation projects (Yan *et al., 2007*). The objectives of SDN are to disconnect the control plane from the data plane. SDN is very often linked to the OpenFlow protocol (McKeown *et al. 2008*). After the advancement SDN also enables creating a global view of the network and offers a system-wide programming interface for controlling network devices.

Software defined networking comprises various types of networking related services and it makes networking environment agile and flexible by introducing virtualization inside it. To achieve such centralized control one industrial approach was initially used as a prime project by AT&T's and named as GeoPlex. In this project first time java was used to create multiple network API's and other function at the middle level of designing a network. This project focused its attention towards monitoring a network like collecting behavior of nodes present in channel and multiple activities happening inside network. This project started to use operations support system as a platform where various issues like network inventory, network configuration, management, service provisioning are handled by communication service providers. This project started to use operations support system as a platform where various issues like network inventory, network configuration, management, service provisioning are handled by communication service providers. After development of JAVA, SDN became a promoted technology by developers and it changed the fad of communication era.

In this chapter in the next section, we explain state of art and current running trends in software defined networking. In the section "Architecture of Software Defined Networking," we explain detailed architecture and scenarios related to its functionality. The section titled "Existing Platforms for Software Defined Working" covers existing platforms for SDN software testing with debugging and development with its simulation and emulation tools. The section titled "Machine Learning and SDN" presents relevant application areas for software development networking such as wireless networking and computer system houses. Finally, in the section titled "Future Scope of SDN in Virtualization and Wireless Networks" the future scope in SDN and possible optimization ways are defined.

## STATE OF ART

To promote processing, data flow, monitoring and controlling of data packets, developers created a map for automation in networking domain in decade of 90's. According to growth of the network the map is pictorially represented as shown in Figure 1.

To explain standards and working of SDN, Open Networking Foundation (ONF) developed a multivendor standard which is known as OPEN FLOW (N. McKeown *et al.*, 2008). Often term standard is replaced with protocol in networking. So OPEN FLOW defines an interface protocol which works between Open flow controller and Open flow switch. Open flow architecture. Open flow switch contains following functionalities:

*Figure 1. Open flow protocol with 1.3.0 switch specification*

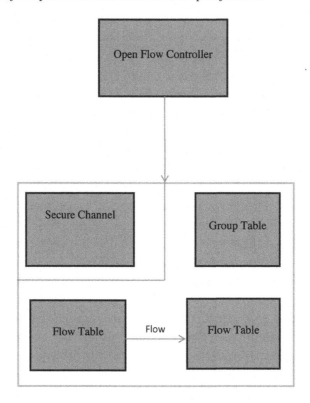

- Identification of data packets and categorizes them based on packet header information.
- Processing and modifications inside those packets.
- Option selections based on drop the packet or push the packet towards destination machine.

Like open flow protocols, there are many programmable effort are performed by developers. In this section we will represent some popular standards used in programmable network approach.

To implement programmable open flow switch IETF (Internet Engineering Task Force) implemented specific protocol called as General Switch Management Protocol (GSMP). This protocol is an asymmetric protocol and used for maintenance of states of labeled switches like frame relay, ATM etc.

Network configuration protocol is a network management based protocol which was developed by NETCONF working group. Functionality of network group is categorized into four layers (refer to Figure 2), which are as follows:

*Figure 2. Layer wise functionality distribution of network configuration protocol*

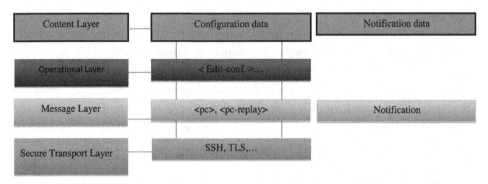

1. For configuration and notification of data content layer is responsible.
2. Operation, retrieval, editing of data is functionality of Operational layer.
3. Encoding of remote procedural calls and notification is provided by Message layer.
4. For security and reliability of data delivery Secure Transport Layer is responsible (Casado *et al., 2006*)

Some of the open sources to implement the SDN are described in the following table (refer Table 1).

*Table 1. Open sources for implementing SDN with description*

| S. No. | Tool Name | Description and Availability of Tool |
|---|---|---|
| 1 | Floodlight | • Apache licensed and java based application.<br>• Application of Open Flow protocol over virtual and physical switches.<br>• Controls to switch forwarding tables, traffic monitoring and controlling. |
| 2 | Indigo | • Work with physical and hypervisor switches both.<br>• Application of hardware abstraction layer(HAL) and set of network libraries for integration and management of network and controlling the network traffic. |
| 3 | Open Stack Networking Neutron | • Developed as cloud network controller (M. Casado *et al, 2007*)<br>• Focusing on network as a service (NaaS) |
| 4 | Open v Switch | • Multiple layer based switch used for network virtualization.<br>• Based on application of Netflow, sFlow etc.<br>• Includes services of Linux kernel 3.3 |
| 5 | OpenDaylight | • Based on Linux services but platform independent<br>• Support of OpenFlow protocol |

## ARCHITECTURE OF SOFTWARE DEFINED NETWORKING

Development of Software defined networking is started from development of java era. One main reason of this growth was compatible nature of Java, which shows that how effectively java well suited with distinct interfaces written in different platforms and languages. SDN working is based on two important platform components. These are network and topology virtualization. These both components develop customized collection of services with control plane. These collections of services can be divided into 3 components. Figure 3 represents these components

1.   Application Layer (Network Service Abstraction Layer)
2.   Control Layer
3.   Network Infrastructure

A clear explanation about above given component is described in Figure 3.
A clear explanation about the given component is described below.

- **Network Service Abstraction Layer:** In abstraction layer, different programs or applications communicate to SDN controller by North bound programming interfaces (NBI). In this layer application logic is interface drivers are coupled and offers multiple services with respective interface agents.

*Figure 3. Architectural components of software denied networking*

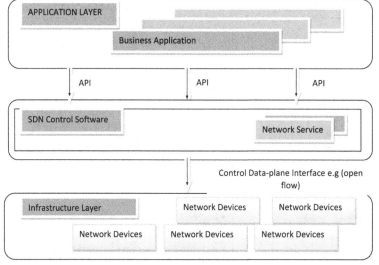

- **SDN Controller:** This state is core of complete logic. This centralized part of controller provides two important functions.
  - Conversion of all application layer oriented requirements into SDN data paths
  - Presenting applications into abstract view in the form of events and statics.

SDN controller consists of various types of NBI agents, control logic and CDPI (Control to data plain interfaces) drivers.

- **SDN Control to Data-Plane Interface (CDPI):** It is interface placed between SDN controller and SDN data path. Some of its main functions are:

  - Controlling over other operations
  - Reporting for statics presentation
  - Notification for events occurring
  - Capabilities notifications

Detailed description of Architectural model shown in Figure 1.

Figure 1 summarizes SDN into three layers. In this section, a detailed summary is given in terms of services, subcomponents and plains in Figure 4.

- **SDN Application:** SDN application term represents programs and services that are part of top layer services. These programs communicate with other entities based on network requirements and network controller automates these services based on network behavior. An SDN application represents application logic view of SDN modelling and applies NBI drivers and logic to connect with environment.
- **SDN Controller:** SDN controller works like a centralized entity inside SDN architecture and it controls following activities:
  - Translation of application layer services to SDN data paths.
  - Presenting an abstract view of application layer services.

Because of being a centralized SDN network entity it contains one or more than one NBI agents, control logic and CDPI drivers.

- **SDN Data Path:** SDN data path represents CDPI agent and one or more traffic routing servers corresponding routing function. These servers and

*Figure 4. SDN layer architecture*

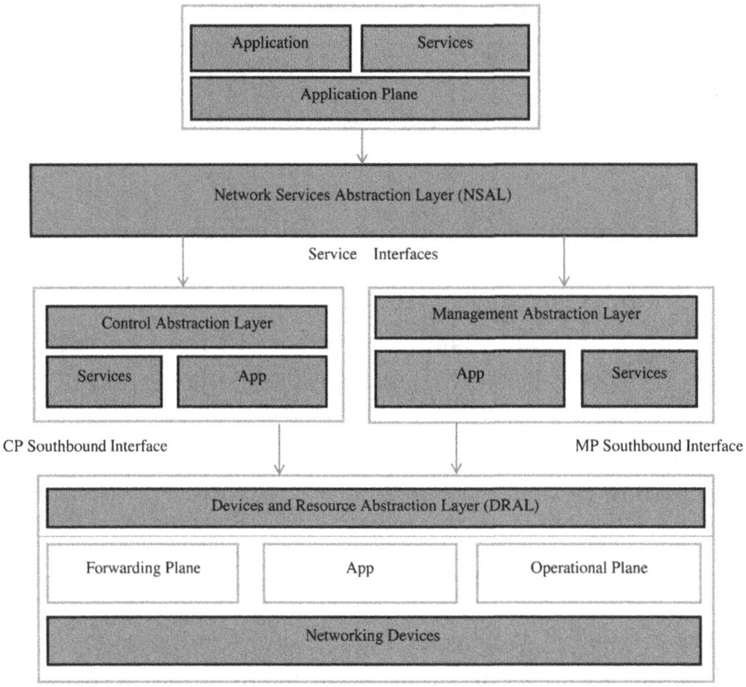

routing functions calculate optimize path of new upcoming packets. There is various algorithms work as routing logic for packets from one node to another node.

- **SDN Control to Data Plane Interface (CDPI):** SDN CDPI is an interface between control plane and data plane and functions like:
  ○ Programmable logic control for all routing operations
  ○ Event notification
  ○ Reporting for statistics of network

## EXISTING PLATFORMS FOR SOFTWARE DEFINED WORKING

CISCO XNC is software controller which consists of multiple modules as shown in fig.1 to provide solutions. Defined modules interact with each other by application of OSGI (Open Service Gateway Initiative) application framework. OSGI is a java based application framework which consists of multiple tightly coupled, dynamic loadable classes, configuration files that declares external dependencies.

## Classification of Services in CISCO XNC

Based on working, it is possible to classify inbuilt services of CISCO XNC into 4 categories.

1.  Southbound API modules enable services like interconnectivity and interoperability between network and controller. It controls over dynamic changes in network behavior with real time demands and responses.
2.  Advance infrastructure module is responsible for providing functional services. These services are controlling the degree of connectivity between various nodes and functioning among them, selection of optimal path for a data packet among various paths from source to destination. Metric standard for determining optimization level may be differing from level to level of network infrastructure.
3.  Network applications can be treated as various programs which work combined with network architecture and provide core group of services like network slicing.
4.  North-bound API's control interaction level between external services and controller.

## MACHINE LEARNING AND SDN

We are conducting research on methods to solve network management and operation problems using machine learning and data analytics. Machine learning can extract latent rules and generation models of network behavior through big data analytics, and those rules and models can be used for predicting and optimizing network management and operation, which improves network service and reduces costs. In this article, we introduce methods to predict and detect network failures using a social networking service (SNS) or network logs, extract workflows from operator logs, and predict mobile traffic from traffic generation factors.

To minimize the impact on services caused by a network failure, we must detect a failure or a fault that leads to a failure, before it occurs or as soon as possible after it occurs. Current failure detection methods are rule based, where rules between network logs and failure modes are set manually in advance. By trapping a log, we can detect a corresponding network failure. However, much progress has been made recently in software-based network function virtualization, which means that the network configuration is dynamically changing. Consequently, building those rules and updating them are difficult and time-consuming tasks. In addition, because of the increasing network complexity and the growing number of network roles, the monitoring information (network logs) obtained using existing methods is insufficient for monitoring the network status. To solve this problem, we are working on enhancing network monitoring and improving the accuracy of failure detection.

Current network monitoring techniques are based on the use of internal network data such as network logs and external network data such as service monitoring and user claims. To improve the coverage and agility of monitoring, we are implementing failure detection based on SNS data. However, because SNS data consist of free-format text messages and includes a huge number of messages other than those related to network outages; we explained a technique to accurately extract messages that correspond to network failures. In addition, by estimating the locations of such messages, we can estimate the location and the impact of the network failure.

Network logs that are used for network monitoring are divided into numerical logs such as CPU (central processing unit) and interface loads, and messages in text format such as syslog messages. Numerical logs are used for detecting network failures by applying predefined thresholds. However, defining thresholds for a huge number of logs is difficult. We apply statistical outlier detection based on a non-supervised machine learning method. In addition, we apply this method to obtain the time series of each log as well as the correlations among logs.

Text logs are used for failure detection by monitoring keywords. However, this involves looking at the relations between keywords. The network status is not directly monitored, and therefore, the accuracy needs to be improved. We adopt a machine learning technique such as clustering to monitor text logs that are not only keyword based but also message based and that generate patterns. We also try to merge both numerical logs and text logs to detect network failures that are not detected for them individually.

When network operators resolve network failures, if the resolution processes are not fixed and no manuals are available, operators must take action based on their knowledge, which of course depends on their experience. This increases the time needed to resolve the failure (the time-to-fix), especially for non-skilled operators. This in turn increases the need for Runbook automation (RBA), which enables auto-operation in the event of network failures. However, building a workflow (scenario) to be used for RBA is a time-consuming task.

To solve this problem, we take two approaches to extract and visualize workflows in resolving network failures. First, we develop a technique to extract workflows using a trouble ticket log where operators manually record the processes they carry out from the time a failure starts to when the problem has been resolved. However, these records consist of free-format text data, which means that the same process can be recorded using different words, and some processes may not be recorded. Therefore, we adopt a sequence alignment technique to adjust and complement these records.

However, some processes, specifically the initial processes implemented for critical failures, tend not to be recorded because the actions are taken prior to recording them. To extract workflows for such processes, we should not rely on trouble ticket logs, but rather use command logs. To extract command logs for graphical user interface (GUI) applications, we have developed a technique to independently build GUI command log sequences on applications

## TRAFFIC PREDICTION THROUGH ITS GENERATION PROCESS

Traffic prediction is based on using past values to extrapolate future values. However, the drawback of this method is that it cannot adapt to changes in the traffic generation mechanism such as application usage or popular content. Specifically, mobile traffic is critically affected by changes in human movement such as those occurring during sports or music events. We are developing a technique to predict future traffic based on not only past traffic values but also traffic generation mechanisms such as human movement patterns and application usages . We also adopt a method for long-term future traffic prediction by analyzing and feeding back prediction errors.

## FUTURE SCOPE OF SDN IN VIRTUALIZATION AND WIRELESS NETWORKS

In the recent years wireless communication based devices and their applications covered entire communication industry. Unfortunately huge demand of mobiles and other wireless network based entities have created a series of issues caused by inherent design of network. This section initially describes introduction of mobile wireless network with its functionality and then implementation of SDN with mobile network with virtualization specification.

Mobile wireless network (MWN) uses wireless data transfer among various communicating entities. Based on its structural and functional similarity, mobile wireless network is divided into multiple categories. Some important categories are:

- Wireless LAN
- wireless ad hoc network, also known as a wireless mesh network or mobile ad hoc network (MANET)
- Wireless metropolitan area networks
- Wireless wide area networks

Besides these network types there are so many other wireless network also exist. Although mobile networks provide various diversity level of communication to its users but it suffers from various challenging issues too. Some important issues related to wireless networks are:

- Tightly coupled modules and interfaces with various heterogeneous networks reduce flexibility and speed of data communication.
- Poor resource utilization and high contradiction level among various uncommon spectrums generate worst situations for data communication among entities.
- Existence of various heterogeneous wireless network create problem for connection establishment among various unlike communicating infrastructures.
- Mobile networks always known for their diminished quality of services (QOS) and quality of experience (QOE) because of uncertainty of heterogeneous environment and protocol stacks.

To overcome such type of issues till a certain level, software defined networking is introduced in wireless communication domain. One basic issue present in wireless network is defined as tight coupling between several modules is advocated by decoupling control and data planes. The decoupling process makes network more flexible by introducing SDN controller as intermediate. In recent years academia as well industry both are focused to extend SDN applications in mobile wireless networks. Such type of extended network is called as software defined wireless network (SDWN). SDWN benefits in several ways as per structural a functional point of view. Some important benefits are:

- Optimization in wireless resource management, convergence of heterogeneous network into a homogeneous network environment.
- A programmable environment for customization of client server based services option
- Least coupling among various components present in architecture

To expand various levels of services and inbuilt applications inside SDWN, industry added network virtualization theory in it. Network virtualization enables to various concurrent virtual network to run on similar kind of shared resources. Researchers named this theory as network wireless virtualization (NWV). Although NWV and SDWN both are different technologies but researchers are trying to merge both these technologies to face new challenges. These challenges are:

## Challenge 1: Diverse Heterogeneous Networks vs. Vertical Constructing and Operating

Solution: There are various heterogeneous networks like LTE, Wimax, UMTS, WLAN exists in mobile communication technology and all these are quite unlike in architecture and functionality point of view. It is very hard to interconnect these entire networks over a common platform. To overcome this challenge SDWN keeps status of current running heterogeneous networks. Based on status of a network SDN controller creates view and schedules view for forwarding data packets rules and data processing. For resource sharing, SDWN enables control plane based on real time network environment.

## Challenge 2: Capability Crisis vs. Low Resource Utilization

Solution: Industrial survey argues that in next 20 years there will be a huge crisis for mobile spectrum for communication. Developers and scientists proved that the main reason for this crisis is improper utilization of network resources. To overcome this issue WNV proposed concept of unique physical network which makes heterogeneous environment interoperable for functionality point of view.

Some other challenges are:

- Innovation expectations v.s. network ossification
- Service and application proliferating v.s. poor QoS and QoE
- Rapid growth of traffic and subscribers v.s. increasing cost and stagnant revenues

## CURRENT ONGOING RESEARCH IN SDWN

Wireless network is one of the favorite areas of research for developers and scholars. Mainly they are focusing their work for optimization of resource distribution policy, energy conservation and service customization. To gain such types of optimization developers are working over architecture modifications. OpenRoad project was an initial work where physical infrastructure independency was achieved. Physical infrastructure independency term is mainly used for such scenario where a user can move among various networks. In this project all network devices are managed under NOX (first OpenFlow controller). Developers included network virtualization by introducing FlowVisor (A network virtualization layer). FlowVisor enables to work

*Table 2. Summary of current research work in SDN*

| Project Name | Year | Network | Network Position | Summary |
|---|---|---|---|---|
| OpenRoad | 2009 | Wi-Fi | OpenFlow switch | Wireless infrastructure independency |
| Odin | 2012 | Wlan | OpenFlow switch | New prototypes were included programmability |
| OpenRF | 2013 | Wlan | Access network | Programmable data plane was included for wireless network. |
| SoftRAN | 2013 | LTE | Access network | Implementation of radio access network |
| OpenRAN | 2013 | Heterogeneous | Access network | Application of Cloud- computing network for heterogeneous wireless network |
| CellSDN | 2012 | LTE | Access + core | |
| SoftCell | 2013 | LTE | Core network | Traffic control functionality |
| MobileFlow | 2013 | LTE | Carrier network | |
| SoftCOM | 2013 | Heterogeneous | Access + core | Cloud based infrastructure |
| OpenRadio | 2012 | General | Access network | Programmable wireless data plane |

from a common platform containing various logical networks based infrastructure. It also controls bandwidth distribution, topological architecture of network, traffic control etc. Recently OpenRadio is developed for introducing more programming in data plane to gain customization. In Table 2 a summary of recent work is given.

# REFERENCES

Caesar, M., Caldwell, D., Feamster, N., Rexford, J., Shaikh, A., & van der Merwe, J. (2005). Design and implementation of a routing control platform. *Proc. ACM/ USENIX NSDI*, 15–28.

Casado, M., Freedman, M. J., Pettit, J., Luo, J., McKeown, N., & Shenker, S. (2007). Ethane: Taking control of the enterprise. *Proceedings SIGCOMM Conference on Applications, Technology, Architecture, Protocols Computer Communication*, 1–12.

Casado, M., Garfinkel, T., Akella, A., Freedman, M. J., Boneh, D., McKeown, N., & Shenker, S. (2006). SANE: A protection architecture for enterprise networks. *Proceedings USENIX Security Symposium*, 1–15.

Feamster, N., Rexford, J., & Zegura. (2013). *The Road to SDN: An Intellectual History of Programmable Networks*. ACM Queue, Tech. Rep.

Greenberg, A., Hjalmtysson, G., Maltz, D. A., Myers, A., Rexford, J., Xie, G., & Zhang, H. et al. (2005). A clean slate 4D approach to network control and management. *Computer Communication Review*, *35*(5), 41–54. doi:10.1145/1096536.1096541

McKeown, N., Anderson, T., Balakrishnan, H., Parulkar, G., Peterson, L., Rexford, J., & Turner, J. et al. (2008). OpenFlow: Enabling Innovation in Campus Networks. *Computer Communication Review*, *38*(2), 69–74. doi:10.1145/1355734.1355746

Yan, H., Maltz, D. A., Ng, T. S. E., Gogineni, H., Zhang, H., & Cai, Z. (2007). Tesseract: A 4D network control plane. *Proceedings Symposium on Networked Systems Design & Implementation*, 369–382.

## KEY TERMS AND DEFINITIONS

**Flood Light:** Flood light is an open flow controller that is used to control network remotely by specific protocol.

**GeoPlex:** GeoPlex is a middleware code word that is frequently used to explain integrated global connectivity.

**Indigo:** Indigo is an open source project developed for controlling hypervisor switch in network.

**OpenDaylight:** Linux-based networking project for automation of network by application of SDN.

**SDN:** Software-defined networking is a technology that enables the network administrator to automate network infrastructure in terms of initialize, control, change, and management.

# Related References

To continue our tradition of advancing information science and technology research, we have compiled a list of recommended IGI Global readings. These references will provide additional information and guidance to further enrich your knowledge and assist you with your own research and future publications.

Abramowicz, W., Stolarski, P., & Tomaszewski, T. (2013). Legal ontologies in ICT and law. In *Digital rights management: Concepts, methodologies, tools, and applications* (pp. 34–49). Hershey, PA: IGI Global. doi:10.4018/978-1-4666-2136-7.ch003

Adamich, T. (2012). Materials-to-standards alignment: How to "chunk" a whole cake and even use the "crumbs": State standards alignment models, learning objects, and formative assessment – methodologies and metadata for education. In L. Tomei (Ed.), *Advancing education with information communication technologies: Facilitating new trends* (pp. 165–178). Hershey, PA: IGI Global. doi:10.4018/978-1-61350-468-0.ch014

Adomi, E. E. (2011). Regulation of internet content. In E. Adomi (Ed.), *Frameworks for ICT policy: Government, social and legal issues* (pp. 233–246). Hershey, PA: IGI Global. doi:10.4018/978-1-61692-012-8.ch015

Aggestam, L. (2011). Guidelines for preparing organizations in developing countries for standards-based B2B. In *Global business: Concepts, methodologies, tools and applications* (pp. 206–228). Hershey, PA: IGI Global. doi:10.4018/978-1-60960-587-2.ch114

Akowuah, F., Yuan, X., Xu, J., & Wang, H. (2012). A survey of U.S. laws for health information security & privacy. *International Journal of Information Security and Privacy*, 6(4), 40–54. doi:10.4018/jisp.2012100102

Akowuah, F., Yuan, X., Xu, J., & Wang, H. (2013). A survey of security standards applicable to health information systems. *International Journal of Information Security and Privacy, 7*(4), 22–36. doi:10.4018/ijisp.2013100103

Al Hadid, I. (2012). Applying the certification's standards to the simulation study steps. In E. Abu-Taieh, A. El Sheikh, & M. Jafari (Eds.), *Technology engineering and management in aviation: Advancements and discoveries* (pp. 294–307). Hershey, PA: IGI Global. doi:10.4018/978-1-60960-887-3.ch017

Al Mohannadi, F., Arif, M., Aziz, Z., & Richardson, P. A. (2013). Adopting BIM standards for managing vision 2030 infrastructure development in Qatar. *International Journal of 3-D Information Modeling, 2*(3), 64-73. doi:10.4018/ij3dim.2013070105

Al-Nu'aimi, A. A. (2011). Using watermarking techniques to prove rightful ownership of web images. *International Journal of Information Technology and Web Engineering, 6*(2), 29–39. doi:10.4018/jitwe.2011040103

Alejandre, G. M. (2013). IT security governance legal issues. In D. Mellado, L. Enrique Sánchez, E. Fernández-Medina, & M. Piattini (Eds.), *IT security governance innovations: Theory and research* (pp. 47–73). Hershey, PA: IGI Global. doi:10.4018/978-1-4666-2083-4.ch003

Alexandropoulou-Egyptiadou, E. (2013). The Hellenic framework for computer program copyright protection following the implementation of the relative european union directives. In *Digital rights management: Concepts, methodologies, tools, and applications* (pp. 738–745). Hershey, PA: IGI Global. doi:10.4018/978-1-4666-2136-7.ch033

Ali, S. (2012). Practical web application security audit following industry standards and compliance. In J. Zubairi & A. Mahboob (Eds.), *Cyber security standards, practices and industrial applications: Systems and methodologies* (pp. 259–279). Hershey, PA: IGI Global. doi:10.4018/978-1-60960-851-4.ch013

Alirezaee, M., & Afsharian, M. (2011). Measuring the effect of the rules and regulations on global malmquist index. *International Journal of Operations Research and Information Systems, 2*(3), 64–78. doi:10.4018/joris.2011070105

Alirezaee, M., & Afsharian, M. (2013). Measuring the effect of the rules and regulations on global malmquist index. In J. Wang (Ed.), *Optimizing, innovating, and capitalizing on information systems for operations* (pp. 215–229). Hershey, PA: IGI Global. doi:10.4018/978-1-4666-2925-7.ch011

Alves de Lima, A., Carvalho dos Reis, P., Branco, J. C., Danieli, R., Osawa, C. C., Winter, E., & Santos, D. A. (2013). Scenario-patent protection compared to climate change: The case of green patents. *International Journal of Social Ecology and Sustainable Development, 4*(3), 61–70. doi:10.4018/jsesd.2013070105

Amirante, A., Castaldi, T., Miniero, L., & Romano, S. P. (2013). Protocol interactions among user agents, application servers, and media servers: Standardization efforts and open issues. In D. Kanellopoulos (Ed.), *Intelligent multimedia technologies for networking applications: Techniques and tools* (pp. 48–63). Hershey, PA: IGI Global. doi:10.4018/978-1-4666-2833-5.ch003

Anker, P. (2013). The impact of regulations on the business case for cognitive radio. In T. Lagkas, P. Sarigiannidis, M. Louta, & P. Chatzimisios (Eds.), *Evolution of cognitive networks and self-adaptive communication systems* (pp. 142–170). Hershey, PA: IGI Global. doi:10.4018/978-1-4666-4189-1.ch006

Antunes, A. M., Mendes, F. M., Schumacher, S. D., Quoniam, L., & Lima de Magalhães, J. (2014). The contribution of information science through intellectual property to innovation in the Brazilian health sector. In G. Jamil, A. Malheiro, & F. Ribeiro (Eds.), *Rethinking the conceptual base for new practical applications in information value and quality* (pp. 83–115). Hershey, PA: IGI Global. doi:10.4018/978-1-4666-4562-2.ch005

Atiskov, A. Y., Novikov, F. A., Fedorchenko, L. N., Vorobiev, V. I., & Moldovyan, N. A. (2013). Ontology-based analysis of cryptography standards and possibilities of their harmonization. In A. Elçi, J. Pieprzyk, A. Chefranov, M. Orgun, H. Wang, & R. Shankaran (Eds.), *Theory and practice of cryptography solutions for secure information systems* (pp. 1–33). Hershey, PA: IGI Global. doi:10.4018/978-1-4666-4030-6.ch001

Ayanso, A., & Herath, T. (2012). Law and technology at crossroads in cyberspace: Where do we go from here? In A. Dudley, J. Braman, & G. Vincenti (Eds.), *Investigating cyber law and cyber ethics: Issues, impacts and practices* (pp. 57–77). Hershey, PA: IGI Global. doi:10.4018/978-1-61350-132-0.ch004

Ayanso, A., & Herath, T. (2014). Law and technology at crossroads in cyberspace: Where do we go from here? In *Cyber behavior: Concepts, methodologies, tools, and applications* (pp. 1990–2010). Hershey, PA: IGI Global. doi:10.4018/978-1-4666-5942-1.ch105

Aydogan-Duda, N. (2012). Branding innovation: The case study of Turkey. In N. Ekekwe & N. Islam (Eds.), *Disruptive technologies, innovation and global redesign: Emerging implications* (pp. 238–248). Hershey, PA: IGI Global. doi:10.4018/978-1-4666-0134-5.ch012

Bagby, J. W. (2011). Environmental standardization for sustainability. In Z. Luo (Ed.), *Green finance and sustainability: Environmentally-aware business models and technologies* (pp. 31–55). Hershey, PA: IGI Global. doi:10.4018/978-1-60960-531-5.ch002

Bagby, J. W. (2013). Insights from U.S. experience to guide international reliance on standardization: Achieving supply chain sustainability. *International Journal of Applied Logistics*, *4*(3), 25–46. doi:10.4018/jal.2013070103

Baggio, B., & Beldarrain, Y. (2011). Intellectual property in an age of open source and anonymity. In *Anonymity and learning in digitally mediated communications: Authenticity and trust in cyber education* (pp. 39–57). Hershey, PA: IGI Global. doi:10.4018/978-1-60960-543-8.ch003

Balzli, C. E., & Fragnière, E. (2012). How ERP systems are centralizing and standardizing the accounting function in public organizations for better and worse. In S. Chhabra & M. Kumar (Eds.), *Strategic enterprise resource planning models for e-government: Applications and methodologies* (pp. 55–72). Hershey, PA: IGI Global. doi:10.4018/978-1-60960-863-7.ch004

Banas, J. R. (2011). Standardized, flexible design of electronic learning environments to enhance learning efficiency and effectiveness. In A. Kitchenham (Ed.), *Models for interdisciplinary mobile learning: Delivering information to students* (pp. 66–86). Hershey, PA: IGI Global. doi:10.4018/978-1-60960-511-7.ch004

Bao, C., & Castresana, J. M. (2011). Interoperability approach in e-learning standardization processes. In F. Lazarinis, S. Green, & E. Pearson (Eds.), *Handbook of research on e-learning standards and interoperability: Frameworks and issues* (pp. 399–418). Hershey, PA: IGI Global. doi:10.4018/978-1-61692-789-9.ch020

Bao, C., & Castresana, J. M. (2012). Interoperability approach in e-learning standardization processes. In *Virtual learning environments: Concepts, methodologies, tools and applications* (pp. 542–560). Hershey, PA: IGI Global. doi:10.4018/978-1-4666-0011-9.ch307

Barrett, B. (2011). Evaluating and implementing teaching standards: Providing quality online teaching strategies and techniques standards. In F. Lazarinis, S. Green, & E. Pearson (Eds.), *Developing and utilizing e-learning applications* (pp. 66–83). Hershey, PA: IGI Global. doi:10.4018/978-1-61692-791-2.ch004

Berleur, J. (2011). Ethical and social issues of the internet governance regulations. In D. Haftor & A. Mirijamdotter (Eds.), *Information and communication technologies, society and human beings: Theory and framework (festschrift in honor of Gunilla Bradley)* (pp. 466–476). Hershey, PA: IGI Global. doi:10.4018/978-1-60960-057-0.ch038

Bhattathiripad, V. P. (2014). Software copyright infringement and litigation. In *Judiciary-friendly forensics of software copyright infringement* (pp. 35–55). Hershey, PA: IGI Global. doi:10.4018/978-1-4666-5804-2.ch002

Bin, X., & Chuan, T. K. (2011). The effect of business characteristics on the methods of knowledge protections. *International Journal of Social Ecology and Sustainable Development*, *2*(3), 34–60. doi:10.4018/jsesd.2011070103

Bin, X., & Chuan, T. K. (2013). The effect of business characteristics on the methods of knowledge protections. In E. Carayannis (Ed.), *Creating a sustainable ecology using technology-driven solutions* (pp. 172–200). Hershey, PA: IGI Global. doi:10.4018/978-1-4666-3613-2.ch013

Bin, X., & Chuan, T. K. (2013). The effect of business characteristics on the methods of knowledge protections. In *Digital rights management: Concepts, methodologies, tools, and applications* (pp. 1283–1311). Hershey, PA: IGI Global. doi:10.4018/978-1-4666-2136-7.ch063

Bogers, M., Bekkers, R., & Granstrand, O. (2012). Intellectual property and licensing strategies in open collaborative innovation. In C. de Pablos Heredero & D. López (Eds.), *Open innovation in firms and public administrations: Technologies for value creation* (pp. 37–58). Hershey, PA: IGI Global. doi:10.4018/978-1-61350-341-6.ch003

Bogers, M., Bekkers, R., & Granstrand, O. (2013). Intellectual property and licensing strategies in open collaborative innovation. In *Digital rights management: Concepts, methodologies, tools, and applications* (pp. 1204–1224). Hershey, PA: IGI Global. doi:10.4018/978-1-4666-2136-7.ch059

Bourcier, D. (2013). Law and governance: The genesis of the commons. In F. Doridot, P. Duquenoy, P. Goujon, A. Kurt, S. Lavelle, N. Patrignani, & A. Santuccio et al. (Eds.), *Ethical governance of emerging technologies development* (pp. 166–183). Hershey, PA: IGI Global. doi:10.4018/978-1-4666-3670-5.ch011

Bousquet, F., Fomin, V. V., & Drillon, D. (2011). Anticipatory standards development and competitive intelligence. *International Journal of Business Intelligence Research*, *2*(1), 16–30. doi:10.4018/jbir.2011010102

Bousquet, F., Fomin, V. V., & Drillon, D. (2013). Anticipatory standards development and competitive intelligence. In R. Herschel (Ed.), *Principles and applications of business intelligence research* (pp. 17–30). Hershey, PA: IGI Global. doi:10.4018/978-1-4666-2650-8.ch002

Brabazon, A. (2013). Optimal patent design: An agent-based modeling approach. In B. Alexandrova-Kabadjova, S. Martinez-Jaramillo, A. Garcia-Almanza, & E. Tsang (Eds.), *Simulation in computational finance and economics: Tools and emerging applications* (pp. 280–302). Hershey, PA: IGI Global. doi:10.4018/978-1-4666-2011-7.ch014

Bracci, F., Corradi, A., & Foschini, L. (2014). Cloud standards: Security and interoperability issues. In H. Mouftah & B. Kantarci (Eds.), *Communication infrastructures for cloud computing* (pp. 465–495). Hershey, PA: IGI Global. doi:10.4018/978-1-4666-4522-6.ch020

Briscoe, D. R. (2012). Globalization and international labor standards, codes of conduct, and ethics: An International HRM perspective. In C. Wankel & S. Malleck (Eds.), *Ethical models and applications of globalization: Cultural, socio-political and economic perspectives* (pp. 1–22). Hershey, PA: IGI Global. doi:10.4018/978-1-61350-332-4.ch001

Briscoe, D. R. (2014). Globalization and international labor standards, codes of conduct, and ethics: An International HRM perspective. In *Cross-cultural interaction: Concepts, methodologies, tools and applications* (pp. 40–62). Hershey, PA: IGI Global. doi:10.4018/978-1-4666-4979-8.ch004

Brooks, R. G., & Geradin, D. (2011). Interpreting and enforcing the voluntary FRAND commitment. *International Journal of IT Standards and Standardization Research*, *9*(1), 1–23. doi:10.4018/jitsr.2011010101

Brown, C. A. (2013). Common core state standards: The promise for college and career ready students in the U.S. In V. Wang (Ed.), *Handbook of research on teaching and learning in K-20 education* (pp. 50–82). Hershey, PA: IGI Global. doi:10.4018/978-1-4666-4249-2.ch004

Buyurgan, N., Rardin, R. L., Jayaraman, R., Varghese, V. M., & Burbano, A. (2011). A novel GS1 data standard adoption roadmap for healthcare providers. *International Journal of Healthcare Information Systems and Informatics*, *6*(4), 42–59. doi:10.4018/jhisi.2011100103

Buyurgan, N., Rardin, R. L., Jayaraman, R., Varghese, V. M., & Burbano, A. (2013). A novel GS1 data standard adoption roadmap for healthcare providers. In J. Tan (Ed.), *Healthcare information technology innovation and sustainability: Frontiers and adoption* (pp. 41–57). Hershey, PA: IGI Global. doi:10.4018/978-1-4666-2797-0.ch003

Campolo, C., Cozzetti, H. A., Molinaro, A., & Scopigno, R. M. (2012). PHY/MAC layer design in vehicular ad hoc networks: Challenges, standard approaches, and alternative solutions. In R. Aquino-Santos, A. Edwards, & V. Rangel-Licea (Eds.), *Wireless technologies in vehicular ad hoc networks: Present and future challenges* (pp. 70–100). Hershey, PA: IGI Global. doi:10.4018/978-1-4666-0209-0.ch004

Cantatore, F. (2014). Copyright support structures. In *Authors, copyright, and publishing in the digital era* (pp. 81–93). Hershey, PA: IGI Global. doi:10.4018/978-1-4666-5214-9.ch005

Cantatore, F. (2014). History and development of copyright. In *Authors, copyright, and publishing in the digital era* (pp. 10–32). Hershey, PA: IGI Global. doi:10.4018/978-1-4666-5214-9.ch002

Cantatore, F. (2014). Research findings: Authors' perceptions and the copyright framework. In Authors, copyright, and publishing in the digital era (pp. 147-189). Hershey, PA: IGI Global. doi:10.4018/978-1-4666-5214-9.ch008

Cassini, J., Medlin, B. D., & Romaniello, A. (2011). Forty years of federal legislation in the area of data protection and information security. In H. Nemati (Ed.), *Pervasive information security and privacy developments: Trends and advancements* (pp. 14–23). Hershey, PA: IGI Global. doi:10.4018/978-1-61692-000-5.ch002

Charlesworth, A. (2012). Addressing legal issues in online research, publication and archiving: A UK perspective. In C. Silva (Ed.), *Online research methods in urban and planning studies: Design and outcomes* (pp. 368–393). Hershey, PA: IGI Global. doi:10.4018/978-1-4666-0074-4.ch022

Chaudhary, C., & Kang, I. S. (2011). Pirates of the copyright and cyberspace: Issues involved. In R. Santanam, M. Sethumadhavan, & M. Virendra (Eds.), *Cyber security, cyber crime and cyber forensics: Applications and perspectives* (pp. 59–68). Hershey, PA: IGI Global. doi:10.4018/978-1-60960-123-2.ch005

Chen, L., Hu, W., Yang, M., & Zhang, L. (2011). Security and privacy issues in secure e-mail standards and services. In H. Nemati (Ed.), *Security and privacy assurance in advancing technologies: New developments* (pp. 174–185). Hershey, PA: IGI Global. doi:10.4018/978-1-60960-200-0.ch013

Ciaghi, A., & Villafiorita, A. (2012). Law modeling and BPR for public administration improvement. In K. Bwalya & S. Zulu (Eds.), *Handbook of research on e-government in emerging economies: Adoption, E-participation, and legal frameworks* (pp. 391–410). Hershey, PA: IGI Global. doi:10.4018/978-1-4666-0324-0.ch019

Ciptasari, R. W., & Sakurai, K. (2013). Multimedia copyright protection scheme based on the direct feature-based method. In K. Kondo (Ed.), *Multimedia information hiding technologies and methodologies for controlling data* (pp. 412–439). Hershey, PA: IGI Global. doi:10.4018/978-1-4666-2217-3.ch019

Clark, L. A., Jones, D. L., & Clark, W. J. (2012). Technology innovation and the policy vacuum: A call for ethics, norms, and laws to fill the void. *International Journal of Technoethics*, *3*(1), 1–13. doi:10.4018/jte.2012010101

Cooklev, T. (2013). The role of standards in engineering education. In K. Jakobs (Ed.), *Innovations in organizational IT specification and standards development* (pp. 129–137). Hershey, PA: IGI Global. doi:10.4018/978-1-4666-2160-2.ch007

Cooper, A. R. (2013). Key challenges in the design of learning technology standards: Observations and proposals. In K. Jakobs (Ed.), *Innovations in organizational IT specification and standards development* (pp. 241–249). Hershey, PA: IGI Global. doi:10.4018/978-1-4666-2160-2.ch014

Cordella, A. (2011). Emerging standardization. *International Journal of Actor-Network Theory and Technological Innovation*, *3*(3), 49–64. doi:10.4018/jantti.2011070104

Cordella, A. (2013). Emerging standardization. In A. Tatnall (Ed.), *Social and professional applications of actor-network theory for technology development* (pp. 221–237). Hershey, PA: IGI Global. doi:10.4018/978-1-4666-2166-4.ch017

Curran, K., & Lautman, R. (2011). The problems of jurisdiction on the internet. *International Journal of Ambient Computing and Intelligence*, *3*(3), 36–42. doi:10.4018/jaci.2011070105

Dani, D. E., Salloum, S., Khishfe, R., & BouJaoude, S. (2013). A tool for analyzing science standards and curricula for 21st century science education. In M. Khine & I. Saleh (Eds.), *Approaches and strategies in next generation science learning* (pp. 265–289). Hershey, PA: IGI Global. doi:10.4018/978-1-4666-2809-0.ch014

De Silva, S. (2012). Legal issues with FOS-ERP: A UK law perspective. In R. Atem de Carvalho & B. Johansson (Eds.), *Free and open source enterprise resource planning: Systems and strategies* (pp. 102–115). Hershey, PA: IGI Global. doi:10.4018/978-1-61350-486-4.ch007 de Vries, H. J. (2011). Implementing standardization education at the national level. *International Journal of IT Standards and Standardization Research*, 9(2), 72–83. doi:10.4018/jitsr.2011070104

de Vries, H. J. (2013). Implementing standardization education at the national level. In K. Jakobs (Ed.), *Innovations in organizational IT specification and standards development* (pp. 116–128). Hershey, PA: IGI Global. doi:10.4018/978-1-4666-2160-2.ch006

de Vuyst, B., & Fairchild, A. (2012). Legal and economic justification for software protection. *International Journal of Open Source Software and Processes*, 4(3), 1–12. doi:10.4018/ijossp.2012070101

Dedeke, A. (2012). Politics hinders open standards in the public sector: The Massachusetts open document format decision. In C. Reddick (Ed.), *Cases on public information management and e-government adoption* (pp. 1–23). Hershey, PA: IGI Global. doi:10.4018/978-1-4666-0981-5.ch001

Delfmann, P., Herwig, S., Lis, L., & Becker, J. (2012). Supporting conceptual model analysis using semantic standardization and structural pattern matching. In S. Smolnik, F. Teuteberg, & O. Thomas (Eds.), *Semantic technologies for business and information systems engineering: Concepts and applications* (pp. 125–149). Hershey, PA: IGI Global. doi:10.4018/978-1-60960-126-3.ch007

den Uijl, S., de Vries, H. J., & Bayramoglu, D. (2013). The rise of MP3 as the market standard: How compressed audio files became the dominant music format. *International Journal of IT Standards and Standardization Research*, 11(1), 1–26. doi:10.4018/jitsr.2013010101

Dickerson, J., & Coleman, H. V. (2012). Technology, e-leadership and educational administration in schools: Integrating standards with context and guiding questions. In V. Wang (Ed.), *Encyclopedia of e-leadership, counseling and training* (pp. 408–422). Hershey, PA: IGI Global. doi:10.4018/978-1-61350-068-2.ch030

Dindaroglu, B. (2013). R&D productivity and firm size in semiconductors and pharmaceuticals: Evidence from citation yields. In I. Yetkiner, M. Pamukcu, & E. Erdil (Eds.), *Industrial dynamics, innovation policy, and economic growth through technological advancements* (pp. 92–113). Hershey, PA: IGI Global. doi:10.4018/978-1-4666-1978-4.ch006

Ding, W. (2011). Development of intellectual property of communications enterprise and analysis of current situation of patents in emerging technology field. *International Journal of Advanced Pervasive and Ubiquitous Computing*, 3(2), 21–28. doi:10.4018/japuc.2011040103

Ding, W. (2013). Development of intellectual property of communications enterprise and analysis of current situation of patents in emerging technology field. In T. Gao (Ed.), *Global applications of pervasive and ubiquitous computing* (pp. 89–96). Hershey, PA: IGI Global. doi:10.4018/978-1-4666-2645-4.ch010

Dorloff, F., & Kajan, E. (2012). Balancing of heterogeneity and interoperability in e-business networks: The role of standards and protocols. *International Journal of E-Business Research*, 8(4), 15–33. doi:10.4018/jebr.2012100102

Dorloff, F., & Kajan, E. (2012). Efficient and interoperable e-business –Based on frameworks, standards and protocols: An introduction. In E. Kajan, F. Dorloff, & I. Bedini (Eds.), *Handbook of research on e-business standards and protocols: Documents, data and advanced web technologies* (pp. 1–20). Hershey, PA: IGI Global. doi:10.4018/978-1-4666-0146-8.ch001

Driouchi, A., & Kadiri, M. (2013). Challenges to intellectual property rights from information and communication technologies, nanotechnologies and microelectronics. In *Digital rights management: Concepts, methodologies, tools, and applications* (pp. 1474–1492). Hershey, PA: IGI Global. doi:10.4018/978-1-4666-2136-7.ch075

Dubey, M., & Hirwade, M. (2013). Copyright relevancy at stake in libraries of the digital era. In T. Ashraf & P. Gulati (Eds.), *Design, development, and management of resources for digital library services* (pp. 379–384). Hershey, PA: IGI Global. doi:10.4018/978-1-4666-2500-6.ch030

Egyedi, T. M. (2011). Between supply and demand: Coping with the impact of standards change. In *Global business: Concepts, methodologies, tools and applications* (pp. 105–120). Hershey, PA: IGI Global. doi:10.4018/978-1-60960-587-2.ch108

Egyedi, T. M., & Koppenhol, A. (2013). The standards war between ODF and OOXML: Does competition between overlapping ISO standards lead to innovation? In K. Jakobs (Ed.), *Innovations in organizational IT specification and standards development* (pp. 79–90). Hershey, PA: IGI Global. doi:10.4018/978-1-4666-2160-2.ch004

Egyedi, T. M., & Muto, S. (2012). Standards for ICT: A green strategy in a grey sector. *International Journal of IT Standards and Standardization Research*, 10(1), 34–47. doi:10.4018/jitsr.2012010103

El Kharbili, M., & Pulvermueller, E. (2012). Semantic policies for modeling regulatory process compliance. In S. Smolnik, F. Teuteberg, & O. Thomas (Eds.), *Semantic technologies for business and information systems engineering: Concepts and applications* (pp. 311–336). Hershey, PA: IGI Global. doi:10.4018/978-1-60960-126-3.ch016

El Kharbili, M., & Pulvermueller, E. (2013). Semantic policies for modeling regulatory process compliance. In *IT policy and ethics: Concepts, methodologies, tools, and applications* (pp. 218–243). Hershey, PA: IGI Global. doi:10.4018/978-1-4666-2919-6.ch011

Ervin, K. (2014). Legal and ethical considerations in the implementation of electronic health records. In J. Krueger (Ed.), *Cases on electronic records and resource management implementation in diverse environments* (pp. 193–210). Hershey, PA: IGI Global. doi:10.4018/978-1-4666-4466-3.ch012

Escayola, J., Trigo, J., Martínez, I., Martínez-Espronceda, M., Aragüés, A., Sancho, D., & García, J. et al. (2012). Overview of the ISO/ieee11073 family of standards and their applications to health monitoring. In W. Chen, S. Oetomo, & L. Feijs (Eds.), *Neonatal monitoring technologies: Design for integrated solutions* (pp. 148–173). Hershey, PA: IGI Global. doi:10.4018/978-1-4666-0975-4.ch007

Escayola, J., Trigo, J., Martínez, I., Martínez-Espronceda, M., Aragüés, A., Sancho, D., . . . García, J. (2013). Overview of the ISO/IEEE11073 family of standards and their applications to health monitoring. In User-driven healthcare: Concepts, methodologies, tools, and applications (pp. 357-381). Hershey, PA: IGI Global. doi:10.4018/978-1-4666-2770-3.ch018

Espada, J. P., Martínez, O. S., García-Bustelo, B. C., Lovelle, J. M., & Ordóñez de Pablos, P. (2011). Standardization of virtual objects. In M. Lytras, P. Ordóñez de Pablos, & E. Damiani (Eds.), *Semantic web personalization and context awareness: Management of personal identities and social networking* (pp. 7–21). Hershey, PA: IGI Global. doi:10.4018/978-1-61520-921-7.ch002

Falkner, N. J. (2011). Security technologies and policies in organisations. In M. Quigley (Ed.), *ICT ethics and security in the 21st century: New developments and applications* (pp. 196–213). Hershey, PA: IGI Global. doi:10.4018/978-1-60960-573-5.ch010

Ferrer-Roca, O. (2011). Standards in telemedicine. In A. Moumtzoglou & A. Kastania (Eds.), *E-health systems quality and reliability: Models and standards* (pp. 220–243). Hershey, PA: IGI Global. doi:10.4018/978-1-61692-843-8.ch017

Ferullo, D. L., & Soules, A. (2012). Managing copyright in a digital world. *International Journal of Digital Library Systems*, *3*(4), 1–25. doi:10.4018/ijdls.2012100101

Fichtner, J. R., & Simpson, L. A. (2011). Legal issues facing companies with products in a digital format. In T. Strader (Ed.), *Digital product management, technology and practice: Interdisciplinary perspectives* (pp. 32–52). Hershey, PA: IGI Global. doi:10.4018/978-1-61692-877-3.ch003

Fichtner, J. R., & Simpson, L. A. (2013). Legal issues facing companies with products in a digital format. In *Digital rights management: Concepts, methodologies, tools, and applications* (pp. 1334–1354). Hershey, PA: IGI Global. doi:10.4018/978-1-4666-2136-7.ch066

Folmer, E. (2012). BOMOS: Management and development model for open standards. In E. Kajan, F. Dorloff, & I. Bedini (Eds.), *Handbook of research on e-business standards and protocols: Documents, data and advanced web technologies* (pp. 102–128). Hershey, PA: IGI Global. doi:10.4018/978-1-4666-0146-8.ch006

Fomin, V. V. (2012). Standards as hybrids: An essay on tensions and juxtapositions in contemporary standardization. *International Journal of IT Standards and Standardization Research*, *10*(2), 59–68. doi:10.4018/jitsr.2012070105

Fomin, V. V., & Matinmikko, M. (2014). The role of standards in the development of new informational infrastructure. In M. Khosrow-Pour (Ed.), *Systems and software development, modeling, and analysis: New perspectives and methodologies* (pp. 149–160). Hershey, PA: IGI Global. doi:10.4018/978-1-4666-6098-4.ch006

Fomin, V. V., Medeisis, A., & Vitkute-Adžgauskiene, D. (2012). Pre-standardization of cognitive radio systems. *International Journal of IT Standards and Standardization Research*, *10*(1), 1–16. doi:10.4018/jitsr.2012010101

Francia, G., & Hutchinson, F. S. (2012). Regulatory and policy compliance with regard to identity theft prevention, detection, and response. In T. Chou (Ed.), *Information assurance and security technologies for risk assessment and threat management: Advances* (pp. 292–322). Hershey, PA: IGI Global. doi:10.4018/978-1-61350-507-6.ch012

Francia, G. A., & Hutchinson, F. S. (2014). Regulatory and policy compliance with regard to identity theft prevention, detection, and response. In *Crisis management: Concepts, methodologies, tools and applications* (pp. 280–310). Hershey, PA: IGI Global. doi:10.4018/978-1-4666-4707-7.ch012

Fulkerson, D. M. (2012). Copyright. In D. Fulkerson (Ed.), *Remote access technologies for library collections: Tools for library users and managers* (pp. 33–48). Hershey, PA: IGI Global. doi:10.4018/978-1-4666-0234-2.ch003

Galinski, C., & Beckmann, H. (2014). Concepts for enhancing content quality and eaccessibility: In general and in the field of eprocurement. In *Assistive technologies: Concepts, methodologies, tools, and applications* (pp. 180–197). Hershey, PA: IGI Global. doi:10.4018/978-1-4666-4422-9.ch010

Gaur, R. (2013). Facilitating access to Indian cultural heritage: Copyright, permission rights and ownership issues vis-à-vis IGNCA collections. In *Digital rights management: Concepts, methodologies, tools, and applications* (pp. 817–833). Hershey, PA: IGI Global. doi:10.4018/978-1-4666-2136-7.ch038

Geiger, C. (2011). Copyright and digital libraries: Securing access to information in the digital age. In I. Iglezakis, T. Synodinou, & S. Kapidakis (Eds.), *E-publishing and digital libraries: Legal and organizational issues* (pp. 257–272). Hershey, PA: IGI Global. doi:10.4018/978-1-60960-031-0.ch013

Geiger, C. (2013). Copyright and digital libraries: Securing access to information in the digital age. In *Digital rights management: Concepts, methodologies, tools, and applications* (pp. 99–114). Hershey, PA: IGI Global. doi:10.4018/978-1-4666-2136-7.ch007

Gencer, M. (2012). The evolution of IETF standards and their production. *International Journal of IT Standards and Standardization Research*, *10*(1), 17–33. doi:10.4018/jitsr.2012010102

Gillam, L., & Vartapetiance, A. (2014). Gambling with laws and ethics in cyberspace. In R. Luppicini (Ed.), *Evolving issues surrounding technoethics and society in the digital age* (pp. 149–170). Hershey, PA: IGI Global. doi:10.4018/978-1-4666-6122-6.ch010

Grandinetti, L., Pisacane, O., & Sheikhalishahi, M. (2014). Standardization. In *Pervasive cloud computing technologies: Future outlooks and interdisciplinary perspectives* (pp. 75–96). Hershey, PA: IGI Global. doi:10.4018/978-1-4666-4683-4.ch004

Grant, S., & Young, R. (2013). Concepts and standardization in areas relating to competence. In K. Jakobs (Ed.), *Innovations in organizational IT specification and standards development* (pp. 264–280). Hershey, PA: IGI Global. doi:10.4018/978-1-4666-2160-2.ch016

Grassetti, M., & Brookby, S. (2013). Using the iPad to develop preservice teachers' understanding of the common core state standards for mathematical practice. In D. Polly (Ed.), *Common core mathematics standards and implementing digital technologies* (pp. 370–386). Hershey, PA: IGI Global. doi:10.4018/978-1-4666-4086-3.ch025

Gray, P. J. (2012). CDIO Standards and quality assurance: From application to accreditation. *International Journal of Quality Assurance in Engineering and Technology Education*, *2*(2), 1–8. doi:10.4018/ijqaete.2012040101

Graz, J., & Hauert, C. (2011). The INTERNORM project: Bridging two worlds of expert- and lay-knowledge in standardization. *International Journal of IT Standards and Standardization Research, 9*(1), 52–62. doi:10.4018/jitsr.2011010103

Graz, J., & Hauert, C. (2013). The INTERNORM project: Bridging two worlds of expert- and lay-knowledge in standardization. In K. Jakobs (Ed.), *Innovations in organizational IT specification and standards development* (pp. 154–164). Hershey, PA: IGI Global. doi:10.4018/978-1-4666-2160-2.ch009

Grobler, M. (2012). The need for digital evidence standardisation. *International Journal of Digital Crime and Forensics, 4*(2), 1–12. doi:10.4018/jdcf.2012040101

Grobler, M. (2013). The need for digital evidence standardisation. In C. Li (Ed.), *Emerging digital forensics applications for crime detection, prevention, and security* (pp. 234–245). Hershey, PA: IGI Global. doi:10.4018/978-1-4666-4006-1.ch016

Guest, C. L., & Guest, J. M. (2011). Legal issues in the use of technology in higher education: Copyright and privacy in the academy. In D. Surry, R. Gray Jr, & J. Stefurak (Eds.), *Technology integration in higher education: Social and organizational aspects* (pp. 72–85). Hershey, PA: IGI Global. doi:10.4018/978-1-60960-147-8.ch006

Gupta, A., Gantz, D. A., Sreecharana, D., & Kreyling, J. (2012). The interplay of offshoring of professional services, law, intellectual property, and international organizations. *International Journal of Strategic Information Technology and Applications, 3*(2), 47–71. doi:10.4018/jsita.2012040104

Hai-Jew, S. (2011). Staying legal and ethical in global e-learning course and training developments: An exploration. In V. Wang (Ed.), *Encyclopedia of information communication technologies and adult education integration* (pp. 958–970). Hershey, PA: IGI Global. doi:10.4018/978-1-61692-906-0.ch058

Halder, D., & Jaishankar, K. (2012). Cyber space regulations for protecting women in UK. In *Cyber crime and the victimization of women: Laws, rights and regulations* (pp. 95–104). Hershey, PA: IGI Global. doi:10.4018/978-1-60960-830-9.ch007

Han, M., & Cho, C. (2013). XML in library cataloging workflows: Working with diverse sources and metadata standards. In J. Tramullas & P. Garrido (Eds.), *Library automation and OPAC 2.0: Information access and services in the 2.0 landscape* (pp. 59–72). Hershey, PA: IGI Global. doi:10.4018/978-1-4666-1912-8.ch003

Hanseth, O., & Nielsen, P. (2013). Infrastructural innovation: Flexibility, generativity and the mobile internet. *International Journal of IT Standards and Standardization Research, 11*(1), 27–45. doi:10.4018/jitsr.2013010102

Hartong, M., & Wijesekera, D. (2012). U.S. regulatory requirements for positive train control systems. In F. Flammini (Ed.), *Railway safety, reliability, and security: Technologies and systems engineering* (pp. 1–21). Hershey, PA: IGI Global. doi:10.4018/978-1-4666-1643-1.ch001

Hasan, H. (2011). Formal and emergent standards in KM. In D. Schwartz & D. Te'eni (Eds.), *Encyclopedia of knowledge management* (2nd ed.; pp. 331–342). Hershey, PA: IGI Global. doi:10.4018/978-1-59904-931-1.ch032

Hatzimihail, N. (2011). Copyright infringement of digital libraries and private international law: Jurisdiction issues. In I. Iglezakis, T. Synodinou, & S. Kapidakis (Eds.), *E-publishing and digital libraries: Legal and organizational issues* (pp. 447–460). Hershey, PA: IGI Global. doi:10.4018/978-1-60960-031-0.ch021

Hauert, C. (2013). Where are you? Consumers' associations in standardization: A case study on Switzerland. In K. Jakobs (Ed.), *Innovations in organizational IT specification and standards development* (pp. 139–153). Hershey, PA: IGI Global. doi:10.4018/978-1-4666-2160-2.ch008

Hawks, V. D., & Ekstrom, J. J. (2011). Balancing policies, principles, and philosophy in information assurance. In M. Dark (Ed.), *Information assurance and security ethics in complex systems: Interdisciplinary perspectives* (pp. 32–54). Hershey, PA: IGI Global. doi:10.4018/978-1-61692-245-0.ch003

Henningsson, S. (2012). International e-customs standardization from the perspective of a global company. *International Journal of IT Standards and Standardization Research*, *10*(2), 45–58. doi:10.4018/jitsr.2012070104

Hensberry, K. K., Paul, A. J., Moore, E. B., Podolefsky, N. S., & Perkins, K. K. (2013). PhET interactive simulations: New tools to achieve common core mathematics standards. In D. Polly (Ed.), *Common core mathematics standards and implementing digital technologies* (pp. 147–167). Hershey, PA: IGI Global. doi:10.4018/978-1-4666-4086-3.ch010

Heravi, B. R., & Lycett, M. (2012). Semantically enriched e-business standards development: The case of ebXML business process specification schema. In E. Kajan, F. Dorloff, & I. Bedini (Eds.), *Handbook of research on e-business standards and protocols: Documents, data and advanced web technologies* (pp. 655–675). Hershey, PA: IGI Global. doi:10.4018/978-1-4666-0146-8.ch030

Higuera, J., & Polo, J. (2012). Interoperability in wireless sensor networks based on IEEE 1451 standard. In N. Zaman, K. Ragab, & A. Abdullah (Eds.), *Wireless sensor networks and energy efficiency: Protocols, routing and management* (pp. 47–69). Hershey, PA: IGI Global. doi:10.4018/978-1-4666-0101-7.ch004

Hill, D. S. (2012). An examination of standardized product identification and business benefit. In E. Kajan, F. Dorloff, & I. Bedini (Eds.), *Handbook of research on e-business standards and protocols: Documents, data and advanced web technologies* (pp. 387–411). Hershey, PA: IGI Global. doi:10.4018/978-1-4666-0146-8.ch018

Hill, D. S. (2013). An examination of standardized product identification and business benefit. In *Supply chain management: Concepts, methodologies, tools, and applications* (pp. 171–195). Hershey, PA: IGI Global. doi:10.4018/978-1-4666-2625-6.ch011

Holloway, K. (2012). Fair use, copyright, and academic integrity in an online academic environment. In V. Wang (Ed.), *Encyclopedia of e-leadership, counseling and training* (pp. 298–309). Hershey, PA: IGI Global. doi:10.4018/978-1-61350-068-2.ch022

Hoops, D. S. (2011). Legal issues in the virtual world and e-commerce. In B. Ciaramitaro (Ed.), *Virtual worlds and e-commerce: Technologies and applications for building customer relationships* (pp. 186–204). Hershey, PA: IGI Global. doi:10.4018/978-1-61692-808-7.ch010

Hoops, D. S. (2012). Lost in cyberspace: Navigating the legal issues of e-commerce. *Journal of Electronic Commerce in Organizations*, *10*(1), 33–51. doi:10.4018/jeco.2012010103

Hopkinson, A. (2012). Establishing the digital library: Don't ignore the library standards and don't forget the training needed. In A. Tella & A. Issa (Eds.), *Library and information science in developing countries: Contemporary issues* (pp. 195–204). Hershey, PA: IGI Global. doi:10.4018/978-1-61350-335-5.ch014

Hua, G. B. (2013). The construction industry and standardization of information. In *Implementing IT business strategy in the construction industry* (pp. 47–66). Hershey, PA: IGI Global. doi:10.4018/978-1-4666-4185-3.ch003

Huang, C., & Lin, H. (2011). Patent infringement risk analysis using rough set theory. In Q. Zhang, R. Segall, & M. Cao (Eds.), *Visual analytics and interactive technologies: Data, text and web mining applications* (pp. 123–150). Hershey, PA: IGI Global. doi:10.4018/978-1-60960-102-7.ch008

Huang, C., Tseng, T. B., & Lin, H. (2013). Patent infringement risk analysis using rough set theory. In *Digital rights management: Concepts, methodologies, tools, and applications* (pp. 1225–1251). Hershey, PA: IGI Global. doi:10.4018/978-1-4666-2136-7.ch060

Iyamu, T. (2013). The impact of organisational politics on the implementation of IT strategy: South African case in context. In J. Abdelnour-Nocera (Ed.), *Knowledge and technological development effects on organizational and social structures* (pp. 167–193). Hershey, PA: IGI Global. doi:10.4018/978-1-4666-2151-0.ch011

Jacinto, K., Neto, F. M., Leite, C. R., & Jacinto, K. (2014). Accessibility in u-learning: Standards, legislation, and future visions. In F. Neto (Ed.), *Technology platform innovations and forthcoming trends in ubiquitous learning* (pp. 215–236). Hershey, PA: IGI Global. doi:10.4018/978-1-4666-4542-4.ch012

Jakobs, K., Wagner, T., & Reimers, K. (2011). Standardising the internet of things: What the experts think. *International Journal of IT Standards and Standardization Research*, 9(1), 63–67. doi:10.4018/jitsr.2011010104

Juzoji, H. (2012). Legal bases for medical supervision via mobile telecommunications in Japan. *International Journal of E-Health and Medical Communications*, 3(1), 33–45. doi:10.4018/jehmc.2012010103

Kallinikou, D., Papadopoulos, M., Kaponi, A., & Strakantouna, V. (2011). Intellectual property issues for digital libraries at the intersection of law, technology, and the public interest. In I. Iglezakis, T. Synodinou, & S. Kapidakis (Eds.), *E-publishing and digital libraries: Legal and organizational issues* (pp. 294–341). Hershey, PA: IGI Global. doi:10.4018/978-1-60960-031-0.ch015

Kallinikou, D., Papadopoulos, M., Kaponi, A., & Strakantouna, V. (2013). Intellectual property issues for digital libraries at the intersection of law, technology, and the public interest. In *Digital rights management: Concepts, methodologies, tools, and applications* (pp. 1043–1090). Hershey, PA: IGI Global. doi:10.4018/978-1-4666-2136-7.ch052

Kaupins, G. (2012). Laws associated with mobile computing in the cloud. *International Journal of Wireless Networks and Broadband Technologies*, 2(3), 1–9. doi:10.4018/ijwnbt.2012070101

Kaur, P., & Singh, H. (2013). Component certification process and standards. In H. Singh & K. Kaur (Eds.), *Designing, engineering, and analyzing reliable and efficient software* (pp. 22–39). Hershey, PA: IGI Global. doi:10.4018/978-1-4666-2958-5.ch002

Kayem, A. V. (2013). Security in service oriented architectures: Standards and challenges. In *Digital rights management: Concepts, methodologies, tools, and applications* (pp. 50–73). Hershey, PA: IGI Global. doi:10.4018/978-1-4666-2136-7.ch004

Kemp, M. L., Robb, S., & Deans, P. C. (2013). The legal implications of cloud computing. In A. Bento & A. Aggarwal (Eds.), *Cloud computing service and deployment models: Layers and management* (pp. 257–272). Hershey, PA: IGI Global. doi:10.4018/978-1-4666-2187-9.ch014

Khansa, L., & Liginlal, D. (2012). Regulatory influence and the imperative of innovation in identity and access management. *Information Resources Management Journal, 25*(3), 78–97. doi:10.4018/irmj.2012070104

Kim, E. (2012). Government policies to promote production and consumption of renewable electricity in the US. In M. Tortora (Ed.), *Sustainable systems and energy management at the regional level: Comparative approaches* (pp. 1–18). Hershey, PA: IGI Global. doi:10.4018/978-1-61350-344-7.ch001

Kinsell, C. (2014). Technology and disability laws, regulations, and rights. In B. DaCosta & S. Seok (Eds.), *Assistive technology research, practice, and theory* (pp. 75–87). Hershey, PA: IGI Global. doi:10.4018/978-1-4666-5015-2.ch006

Kitsiou, S. (2010). Overview and analysis of electronic health record standards. In J. Rodrigues (Ed.), *Health information systems: Concepts, methodologies, tools, and applications* (pp. 374–392). Hershey, PA: IGI Global. doi:10.4018/978-1-60566-988-5.ch025

Kloss, J. H., & Schickel, P. (2011). X3D: A secure ISO standard for virtual worlds. In A. Rea (Ed.), *Security in virtual worlds, 3D webs, and immersive environments: Models for development, interaction, and management* (pp. 208–220). Hershey, PA: IGI Global. doi:10.4018/978-1-61520-891-3.ch010

Kotsonis, E., & Eliakis, S. (2011). Information security standards for health information systems: The implementer's approach. In A. Chryssanthou, I. Apostolakis, & I. Varlamis (Eds.), *Certification and security in health-related web applications: Concepts and solutions* (pp. 113–145). Hershey, PA: IGI Global. doi:10.4018/978-1-61692-895-7.ch006

Kotsonis, E., & Eliakis, S. (2013). Information security standards for health information systems: The implementer's approach. In *User-driven healthcare: Concepts, methodologies, tools, and applications* (pp. 225–257). Hershey, PA: IGI Global. doi:10.4018/978-1-4666-2770-3.ch013

Koumaras, H., & Kourtis, M. (2013). A survey on video coding principles and standards. In R. Farrugia & C. Debono (Eds.), *Multimedia networking and coding* (pp. 1–27). Hershey, PA: IGI Global. doi:10.4018/978-1-4666-2660-7.ch001

Krupinski, E. A., Antoniotti, N., & Burdick, A. (2011). Standards and guidelines development in the american telemedicine association. In A. Moumtzoglou & A. Kastania (Eds.), *E-health systems quality and reliability: Models and standards* (pp. 244–252). Hershey, PA: IGI Global. doi:10.4018/978-1-61692-843-8.ch018

Kuanpoth, J. (2011). Biotechnological patents and morality: A critical view from a developing country. In S. Hongladarom (Ed.), *Genomics and bioethics: Interdisciplinary perspectives, technologies and advancements* (pp. 141–151). Hershey, PA: IGI Global. doi:10.4018/978-1-61692-883-4.ch010

Kuanpoth, J. (2013). Biotechnological patents and morality: A critical view from a developing country. In *Digital rights management: Concepts, methodologies, tools, and applications* (pp. 1417–1427). Hershey, PA: IGI Global. doi:10.4018/978-1-4666-2136-7.ch071

Kulmala, R., & Kettunen, J. (2012). Intellectual property protection and process modeling in small knowledge intensive enterprises. In *Organizational learning and knowledge: Concepts, methodologies, tools and applications* (pp. 2963–2980). Hershey, PA: IGI Global. doi:10.4018/978-1-60960-783-8.ch809

Kulmala, R., & Kettunen, J. (2013). Intellectual property protection in small knowledge intensive enterprises. *International Journal of Cyber Warfare & Terrorism*, *3*(1), 29–45. doi:10.4018/ijcwt.2013010103

Küster, M. W. (2012). Standards for achieving interoperability of egovernment in Europe. In E. Kajan, F. Dorloff, & I. Bedini (Eds.), *Handbook of research on e-business standards and protocols: Documents, data and advanced web technologies* (pp. 249–268). Hershey, PA: IGI Global. doi:10.4018/978-1-4666-0146-8.ch012

Kyobe, M. (2011). Factors influencing SME compliance with government regulation on use of IT: The case of South Africa. In F. Tan (Ed.), *International enterprises and global information technologies: Advancing management practices* (pp. 85–116). Hershey, PA: IGI Global. doi:10.4018/978-1-60960-605-3.ch005

Lam, J. C., & Hills, P. (2011). Promoting technological environmental innovations: What is the role of environmental regulation? In Z. Luo (Ed.), *Green finance and sustainability: Environmentally-aware business models and technologies* (pp. 56–73). Hershey, PA: IGI Global. doi:10.4018/978-1-60960-531-5.ch003

Lam, J. C., & Hills, P. (2013). Promoting technological environmental innovations: The role of environmental regulation. In Z. Luo (Ed.), *Technological solutions for modern logistics and supply chain management* (pp. 230–247). Hershey, PA: IGI Global. doi:10.4018/978-1-4666-2773-4.ch015

Laporte, C., & Vargas, E. P. (2012). The development of international standards to facilitate process improvements for very small entities. In S. Fauzi, M. Nasir, N. Ramli, & S. Sahibuddin (Eds.), *Software process improvement and management: Approaches and tools for practical development* (pp. 34–61). Hershey, PA: IGI Global. doi:10.4018/978-1-61350-141-2.ch003

Laporte, C., & Vargas, E. P. (2014). The development of international standards to facilitate process improvements for very small entities. In *Software design and development: Concepts, methodologies, tools, and applications* (pp. 1335–1361). Hershey, PA: IGI Global. doi:10.4018/978-1-4666-4301-7.ch065

Lautman, R., & Curran, K. (2013). The problems of jurisdiction on the internet. In K. Curran (Ed.), *Pervasive and ubiquitous technology innovations for ambient intelligence environments* (pp. 164–170). Hershey, PA: IGI Global. doi:10.4018/978-1-4666-2041-4.ch016

Layne-Farrar, A. (2011). Innovative or indefensible? An empirical assessment of patenting within standard setting. *International Journal of IT Standards and Standardization Research*, 9(2), 1–18. doi:10.4018/jitsr.2011070101

Layne-Farrar, A. (2013). Innovative or indefensible? An empirical assessment of patenting within standard setting. In K. Jakobs (Ed.), *Innovations in organizational IT specification and standards development* (pp. 1–18). Hershey, PA: IGI Global. doi:10.4018/978-1-4666-2160-2.ch001

Layne-Farrar, A., & Padilla, A. J. (2011). Assessing the link between standards and patents. *International Journal of IT Standards and Standardization Research*, 9(2), 19–49. doi:10.4018/jitsr.2011070102

Layne-Farrar, A., & Padilla, A. J. (2013). Assessing the link between standards and patents. In K. Jakobs (Ed.), *Innovations in organizational IT specification and standards development* (pp. 19–51). Hershey, PA: IGI Global. doi:10.4018/978-1-4666-2160-2.ch002

Lee, H., & Huh, J. C. (2012). Korea's strategies for ICT standards internationalisation: A comparison with China's. *International Journal of IT Standards and Standardization Research*, 10(2), 1–13. doi:10.4018/jitsr.2012070101

Li, Y., & Wei, C. (2011). Digital image authentication: A review. *International Journal of Digital Library Systems*, 2(2), 55–78. doi:10.4018/jdls.2011040104

Li, Y., Xiao, X., Feng, X., & Yan, H. (2012). Adaptation and localization: Metadata research and development for Chinese digital resources. *International Journal of Digital Library Systems*, 3(1), 1–21. doi:10.4018/jdls.2012010101

Lim, W., & Kim, D. (2013). Do technologies support the implementation of the common core state standards in mathematics of high school probability and statistics? In D. Polly (Ed.), *Common core mathematics standards and implementing digital technologies* (pp. 168–183). Hershey, PA: IGI Global. doi:10.4018/978-1-4666-4086-3.ch011

Linton, J., & Stegall, D. (2013). Common core standards for mathematical practice and TPACK: An integrated approach to instruction. In D. Polly (Ed.), *Common core mathematics standards and implementing digital technologies* (pp. 234–249). Hershey, PA: IGI Global. doi:10.4018/978-1-4666-4086-3.ch016

Liotta, A., & Liotta, A. (2011). Privacy in pervasive systems: Legal framework and regulatory challenges. In A. Malatras (Ed.), *Pervasive computing and communications design and deployment: Technologies, trends and applications* (pp. 263–277). Hershey, PA: IGI Global. doi:10.4018/978-1-60960-611-4.ch012

Lissoni, F. (2013). Academic patenting in Europe: Recent research and new perspectives. In I. Yetkiner, M. Pamukcu, & E. Erdil (Eds.), *Industrial dynamics, innovation policy, and economic growth through technological advancements* (pp. 75–91). Hershey, PA: IGI Global. doi:10.4018/978-1-4666-1978-4.ch005

Litaay, T., Prananingrum, D. H., & Krisanto, Y. A. (2011). Indonesian legal perspectives on biotechnology and intellectual property rights. In S. Hongladarom (Ed.), *Genomics and bioethics: Interdisciplinary perspectives, technologies and advancements* (pp. 171–183). Hershey, PA: IGI Global. doi:10.4018/978-1-61692-883-4.ch012

Litaay, T., Prananingrum, D. H., & Krisanto, Y. A. (2013). Indonesian legal perspectives on biotechnology and intellectual property rights. In *Digital rights management: Concepts, methodologies, tools, and applications* (pp. 834–845). Hershey, PA: IGI Global. doi:10.4018/978-1-4666-2136-7.ch039

Losavio, M., Pastukhov, P., & Polyakova, S. (2014). Regulatory aspects of cloud computing in business environments. In S. Srinivasan (Ed.), *Security, trust, and regulatory aspects of cloud computing in business environments* (pp. 156–169). Hershey, PA: IGI Global. doi:10.4018/978-1-4666-5788-5.ch009

Lu, B., Tsou, B. K., Jiang, T., Zhu, J., & Kwong, O. Y. (2011). Mining parallel knowledge from comparable patents. In W. Wong, W. Liu, & M. Bennamoun (Eds.), *Ontology learning and knowledge discovery using the web: Challenges and recent advances* (pp. 247–271). Hershey, PA: IGI Global. doi:10.4018/978-1-60960-625-1.ch013

Lucas-Schloetter, A. (2011). Digital libraries and copyright issues: Digitization of contents and the economic rights of the authors. In I. Iglezakis, T. Synodinou, & S. Kapidakis (Eds.), *E-publishing and digital libraries: Legal and organizational issues* (pp. 159–179). Hershey, PA: IGI Global. doi:10.4018/978-1-60960-031-0.ch009

Lyytinen, K., Keil, T., & Fomin, V. (2010). A framework to build process theories of anticipatory information and communication technology (ICT) standardizing. In K. Jakobs (Ed.), *New applications in IT standards: Developments and progress* (pp. 147–186). Hershey, PA: IGI Global. doi:10.4018/978-1-60566-946-5.ch008

Macedo, M., & Isaías, P. (2013). Standards related to interoperability in EHR & HS. In M. Sicilia & P. Balazote (Eds.), *Interoperability in healthcare information systems: Standards, management, and technology* (pp. 19–44). Hershey, PA: IGI Global. doi:10.4018/978-1-4666-3000-0.ch002

Madden, P. (2011). Greater accountability, less red tape: The Australian standard business reporting experience. *International Journal of E-Business Research*, 7(2), 1–10. doi:10.4018/jebr.2011040101

Maravilhas, S. (2014). Quality improves the value of patent information to promote innovation. In G. Jamil, A. Malheiro, & F. Ribeiro (Eds.), *Rethinking the conceptual base for new practical applications in information value and quality* (pp. 61–82). Hershey, PA: IGI Global. doi:10.4018/978-1-4666-4562-2.ch004

Marshall, S. (2011). E-learning standards: Beyond technical standards to guides for professional practice. In F. Lazarinis, S. Green, & E. Pearson (Eds.), *Handbook of research on e-learning standards and interoperability: Frameworks and issues* (pp. 170–192). Hershey, PA: IGI Global. doi:10.4018/978-1-61692-789-9.ch008

Martino, L., & Bertino, E. (2012). Security for web services: Standards and research issues. In L. Jie-Zhang (Ed.), *Innovations, standards and practices of web services: Emerging research topics* (pp. 336–362). Hershey, PA: IGI Global. doi:10.4018/978-1-61350-104-7.ch015

McCarthy, V., & Hulsart, R. (2012). Management education for integrity: Raising ethical standards in online management classes. In C. Wankel & A. Stachowicz-Stanusch (Eds.), *Handbook of research on teaching ethics in business and management education* (pp. 413–425). Hershey, PA: IGI Global. doi:10.4018/978-1-61350-510-6.ch024

McGrath, T. (2012). The reality of using standards for electronic business document formats. In E. Kajan, F. Dorloff, & I. Bedini (Eds.), *Handbook of research on e-business standards and protocols: Documents, data and advanced web technologies* (pp. 21–32). Hershey, PA: IGI Global. doi:10.4018/978-1-4666-0146-8.ch002

Medlin, B. D., & Chen, C. C. (2012). A global perspective of laws and regulations dealing with information security and privacy. In *Cyber crime: Concepts, methodologies, tools and applications* (pp. 1349–1363). Hershey, PA: IGI Global. doi:10.4018/978-1-61350-323-2.ch609

Mehrfard, H., & Hamou-Lhadj, A. (2011). The impact of regulatory compliance on agile software processes with a focus on the FDA guidelines for medical device software. *International Journal of Information System Modeling and Design*, 2(2), 67–81. doi:10.4018/jismd.2011040104

Mehrfard, H., & Hamou-Lhadj, A. (2013). The impact of regulatory compliance on agile software processes with a focus on the FDA guidelines for medical device software. In J. Krogstie (Ed.), *Frameworks for developing efficient information systems: Models, theory, and practice* (pp. 298–314). Hershey, PA: IGI Global. doi:10.4018/978-1-4666-4161-7.ch013

Mendoza, R. A., & Ravichandran, T. (2011). An exploratory analysis of the relationship between organizational and institutional factors shaping the assimilation of vertical standards. *International Journal of IT Standards and Standardization Research*, 9(1), 24–51. doi:10.4018/jitsr.2011010102

Mendoza, R. A., & Ravichandran, T. (2012). An empirical evaluation of the assimilation of industry-specific data standards using firm-level and community-level constructs. In M. Tavana (Ed.), *Enterprise information systems and advancing business solutions: Emerging models* (pp. 287–312). Hershey, PA: IGI Global. doi:10.4018/978-1-4666-1761-2.ch017

Mendoza, R. A., & Ravichandran, T. (2012). Drivers of organizational participation in XML-based industry standardization efforts. In M. Tavana (Ed.), *Enterprise information systems and advancing business solutions: Emerging models* (pp. 268–286). Hershey, PA: IGI Global. doi:10.4018/978-1-4666-1761-2.ch016

Mendoza, R. A., & Ravichandran, T. (2013). An exploratory analysis of the relationship between organizational and institutional factors shaping the assimilation of vertical standards. In K. Jakobs (Ed.), *Innovations in organizational IT specification and standards development* (pp. 193–221). Hershey, PA: IGI Global. doi:10.4018/978-1-4666-2160-2.ch012

Mense, E. G., Fulwiler, J. H., Richardson, M. D., & Lane, K. E. (2011). Standardization, hybridization, or individualization: Marketing IT to a diverse clientele. In U. Demiray & S. Sever (Eds.), *Marketing online education programs: Frameworks for promotion and communication* (pp. 291–299). Hershey, PA: IGI Global. doi:10.4018/978-1-60960-074-7.ch019

Metaxa, E., Sarigiannidis, M., & Folinas, D. (2012). Legal issues of the French law on creation and internet (Hadopi 1 and 2). *International Journal of Technoethics*, *3*(3), 21–36. doi:10.4018/jte.2012070102

Meyer, N. (2012). Standardization as governance without government: A critical reassessment of the digital video broadcasting project's success story. *International Journal of IT Standards and Standardization Research*, *10*(2), 14–28. doi:10.4018/jitsr.2012070102

Miguel da Silva, F., Neto, F. M., Burlamaqui, A. M., Pinto, J. P., Fernandes, C. E., & Castro de Souza, R. (2014). T-SCORM: An extension of the SCORM standard to support the project of educational contents for t-learning. In F. Neto (Ed.), *Technology platform innovations and forthcoming trends in ubiquitous learning* (pp. 94–119). Hershey, PA: IGI Global. doi:10.4018/978-1-4666-4542-4.ch006

Moon, A. (2014). Copyright and licensing essentials for librarians and copyright owners in the digital age. In N. Patra, B. Kumar, & A. Pani (Eds.), *Progressive trends in electronic resource management in libraries* (pp. 106–117). Hershey, PA: IGI Global. doi:10.4018/978-1-4666-4761-9.ch006

Moralis, A., Pouli, V., Grammatikou, M., Kalogeras, D., & Maglaris, V. (2012). Security standards and issues for grid computing. In *Grid and cloud computing: Concepts, methodologies, tools and applications* (pp. 1656–1671). Hershey, PA: IGI Global. doi:10.4018/978-1-4666-0879-5.ch708

Moreno, L., Iglesias, A., Calvo, R., Delgado, S., & Zaragoza, L. (2012). Disability standards and guidelines for learning management systems: Evaluating accessibility. In R. Babo & A. Azevedo (Eds.), *Higher education institutions and learning management systems: Adoption and standardization* (pp. 199–218). Hershey, PA: IGI Global. doi:10.4018/978-1-60960-884-2.ch010

Moro, N. (2013). Digital rights management and corporate hegemony: Avenues for reform. In H. Rahman & I. Ramos (Eds.), *Ethical data mining applications for socio-economic development* (pp. 281–299). Hershey, PA: IGI Global. doi:10.4018/978-1-4666-4078-8.ch013

Mula, D., & Lobina, M. L. (2012). Legal protection of the web page. In H. Sasaki (Ed.), *Information technology for intellectual property protection: Interdisciplinary advancements* (pp. 213–236). Hershey, PA: IGI Global. doi:10.4018/978-1-61350-135-1.ch008

Mula, D., & Lobina, M. L. (2013). Legal protection of the web page. In *Digital rights management: Concepts, methodologies, tools, and applications* (pp. 1–18). Hershey, PA: IGI Global. doi:10.4018/978-1-4666-2136-7.ch001

Mulcahy, D. (2011). Performativity in practice: An actor-network account of professional teaching standards. *International Journal of Actor-Network Theory and Technological Innovation, 3*(2), 1–16. doi:10.4018/jantti.2011040101

Mulcahy, D. (2013). Performativity in practice: An actor-network account of professional teaching standards. In A. Tatnall (Ed.), *Social and professional applications of actor-network theory for technology development* (pp. 1–16). Hershey, PA: IGI Global. doi:10.4018/978-1-4666-2166-4.ch001

Mustaffa, M. T. (2012). Multi-standard multi-band reconfigurable LNA. In A. Marzuki, A. Rahim, & M. Loulou (Eds.), *Advances in monolithic microwave integrated circuits for wireless systems: Modeling and design technologies* (pp. 1–23). Hershey, PA: IGI Global. doi:10.4018/978-1-60566-886-4.ch001

Nabi, S. I., Al-Ghmlas, G. S., & Alghathbar, K. (2012). Enterprise information security policies, standards, and procedures: A survey of available standards and guidelines. In M. Gupta, J. Walp, & R. Sharman (Eds.), *Strategic and practical approaches for information security governance: Technologies and applied solutions* (pp. 67–89). Hershey, PA: IGI Global. doi:10.4018/978-1-4666-0197-0.ch005

Nabi, S. I., Al-Ghmlas, G. S., & Alghathbar, K. (2014). Enterprise information security policies, standards, and procedures: A survey of available standards and guidelines. In *Crisis management: Concepts, methodologies, tools and applications* (pp. 750–773). Hershey, PA: IGI Global. doi:10.4018/978-1-4666-4707-7.ch036

Naixiao, Z., & Chunhua, H. (2012). Research on open innovation in China: Focus on intellectual property rights and their operation in Chinese enterprises. *International Journal of Asian Business and Information Management, 3*(1), 65–71. doi:10.4018/jabim.2012010106

Naixiao, Z., & Chunhua, H. (2013). Research on open innovation in China: Focus on intellectual property rights and their operation in Chinese enterprises. In *Digital rights management: Concepts, methodologies, tools, and applications* (pp. 714–720). Hershey, PA: IGI Global. doi:10.4018/978-1-4666-2136-7.ch031

Ndjetcheu, L. (2013). Social responsibility and legal financial communication in African companies in the south of the Sahara: Glance from the OHADA accounting law viewpoint. *International Journal of Innovation in the Digital Economy, 4*(4), 1–17. doi:10.4018/ijide.2013100101

Ng, W. L. (2013). Improving long-term financial risk forecasts using high-frequency data and scaling laws. In B. Alexandrova-Kabadjova, S. Martinez-Jaramillo, A. Garcia-Almanza, & E. Tsang (Eds.), *Simulation in computational finance and economics: Tools and emerging applications* (pp. 255–278). Hershey, PA: IGI Global. doi:10.4018/978-1-4666-2011-7.ch013

Noury, N., Bourquard, K., Bergognon, D., & Schroeder, J. (2013). Regulations initiatives in France for the interoperability of communicating medical devices. *International Journal of E-Health and Medical Communications*, *4*(2), 50–64. doi:10.4018/jehmc.2013040104

Null, E. (2013). Legal and political barriers to municipal networks in the United States. In A. Abdelaal (Ed.), *Social and economic effects of community wireless networks and infrastructures* (pp. 27–56). Hershey, PA: IGI Global. doi:10.4018/978-1-4666-2997-4.ch003

O'Connor, R. V., & Laporte, C. Y. (2014). An innovative approach to the development of an international software process lifecycle standard for very small entities. *International Journal of Information Technologies and Systems Approach*, *7*(1), 1–22. doi:10.4018/ijitsa.2014010101

Onat, I., & Miri, A. (2013). RFID standards. In A. Miri (Ed.), *Advanced security and privacy for RFID technologies* (pp. 14–22). Hershey, PA: IGI Global. doi:10.4018/978-1-4666-3685-9.ch002

Orton, I., Alva, A., & Endicott-Popovsky, B. (2013). Legal process and requirements for cloud forensic investigations. In K. Ruan (Ed.), *Cybercrime and cloud forensics: Applications for investigation processes* (pp. 186–229). Hershey, PA: IGI Global. doi:10.4018/978-1-4666-2662-1.ch008

Ortt, J. R., & Egyedi, T. M. (2014). The effect of pre-existing standards and regulations on the development and diffusion of radically new innovations. *International Journal of IT Standards and Standardization Research*, *12*(1), 17–37. doi:10.4018/ijitsr.2014010102

Ozturk, Y., & Sharma, J. (2011). mVITAL: A standards compliant vital sign monitor. In C. Röcker, & M. Ziefle (Eds.), Smart healthcare applications and services: Developments and practices (pp. 174-196). Hershey, PA: IGI Global. doi:10.4018/978-1-60960-180-5.ch008

Ozturk, Y., & Sharma, J. (2013). mVITAL: A standards compliant vital sign monitor. In IT policy and ethics: Concepts, methodologies, tools, and applications (pp. 515-538). Hershey, PA: IGI Global. doi:10.4018/978-1-4666-2919-6.ch024

Parsons, T. D. (2011). Affect-sensitive virtual standardized patient interface system. In D. Surry, R. Gray Jr, & J. Stefurak (Eds.), *Technology integration in higher education: Social and organizational aspects* (pp. 201–221). Hershey, PA: IGI Global. doi:10.4018/978-1-60960-147-8.ch015

Parveen, S., & Pater, C. (2012). Utilizing innovative video chat technology to meet national standards: A Case study on a STARTALK Hindi language program. *International Journal of Virtual and Personal Learning Environments, 3*(3), 1–20. doi:10.4018/jvple.2012070101

Pawlowski, J. M., & Kozlov, D. (2013). Analysis and validation of learning technology models, standards and specifications: The reference model analysis grid (RMAG). In K. Jakobs (Ed.), *Innovations in organizational IT specification and standards development* (pp. 223–240). Hershey, PA: IGI Global. doi:10.4018/978-1-4666-2160-2.ch013

Pina, P. (2011). The private copy issue: Piracy, copyright and consumers' rights. In T. Strader (Ed.), *Digital product management, technology and practice: Interdisciplinary perspectives* (pp. 193–205). Hershey, PA: IGI Global. doi:10.4018/978-1-61692-877-3.ch011

Pina, P. (2013). Between Scylla and Charybdis: The balance between copyright, digital rights management and freedom of expression. In Digital rights management: Concepts, methodologies, tools, and applications (pp. 1355-1367). Hershey, PA: IGI Global. doi:10.4018/978-1-4666-2136-7.ch067

Pina, P. (2013). Computer games and intellectual property law: Derivative works, copyright and copyleft. In *Digital rights management: Concepts, methodologies, tools, and applications* (pp. 777–788). Hershey, PA: IGI Global. doi:10.4018/978-1-4666-2136-7.ch035

Pina, P. (2013). The private copy issue: Piracy, copyright and consumers' rights. In *Digital rights management: Concepts, methodologies, tools, and applications* (pp. 1546–1558). Hershey, PA: IGI Global. doi:10.4018/978-1-4666-2136-7.ch078

Piotrowski, M. (2011). QTI: A failed e-learning standard? In F. Lazarinis, S. Green, & E. Pearson (Eds.), *Handbook of research on e-learning standards and interoperability: Frameworks and issues* (pp. 59–82). Hershey, PA: IGI Global. doi:10.4018/978-1-61692-789-9.ch004

Ponte, D., & Camussone, P. F. (2013). Neither heroes nor chaos: The victory of VHS against Betamax. *International Journal of Actor-Network Theory and Technological Innovation, 5*(1), 40–54. doi:10.4018/jantti.2013010103

Pradhan, A. (2011). Pivotal role of the ISO 14001 standard in the carbon economy. *International Journal of Green Computing*, *2*(1), 38–46. doi:10.4018/jgc.2011010104

Pradhan, A. (2011). Standards and legislation for the carbon economy. In B. Unhelkar (Ed.), *Handbook of research on green ICT: Technology, business and social perspectives* (pp. 592–606). Hershey, PA: IGI Global. doi:10.4018/978-1-61692-834-6.ch043

Pradhan, A. (2013). Pivotal role of the ISO 14001 standard in the carbon economy. In K. Ganesh & S. Anbuudayasankar (Eds.), *International and interdisciplinary studies in green computing* (pp. 38–46). Hershey, PA: IGI Global. doi:10.4018/978-1-4666-2646-1.ch004

Prentzas, J., & Hatzilygeroudis, I. (2011). Techniques, technologies and patents related to intelligent educational systems. In G. Magoulas (Ed.), *E-infrastructures and technologies for lifelong learning: Next generation environments* (pp. 1–28). Hershey, PA: IGI Global. doi:10.4018/978-1-61520-983-5.ch001

Ramos, I., & Fernandes, J. (2011). Web-based intellectual property marketplace: A survey of current practices. *International Journal of Information Communication Technologies and Human Development*, *3*(3), 58–68. doi:10.4018/jicthd.2011070105

Ramos, I., & Fernandes, J. (2013). Web-based intellectual property marketplace: A survey of current practices. In S. Chhabra (Ed.), *ICT influences on human development, interaction, and collaboration* (pp. 203–213). Hershey, PA: IGI Global. doi:10.4018/978-1-4666-1957-9.ch012

Rashmi, R. (2011). Biopharma drugs innovation in India and foreign investment and technology transfer in the changed patent regime. In P. Ordóñez de Pablos, W. Lee, & J. Zhao (Eds.), *Regional innovation systems and sustainable development: Emerging technologies* (pp. 210–225). Hershey, PA: IGI Global. doi:10.4018/978-1-61692-846-9.ch016

Rashmi, R. (2011). Optimal policy for biopharmaceutical drugs innovation and access in India. In P. Ordóñez de Pablos, W. Lee, & J. Zhao (Eds.), *Regional innovation systems and sustainable development: Emerging technologies* (pp. 74–114). Hershey, PA: IGI Global. doi:10.4018/978-1-61692-846-9.ch007

Rashmi, R. (2013). Biopharma drugs innovation in India and foreign investment and technology transfer in the changed patent regime. In *Digital rights management: Concepts, methodologies, tools, and applications* (pp. 846–859). Hershey, PA: IGI Global. doi:10.4018/978-1-4666-2136-7.ch040

Reed, C. N. (2011). The open geospatial consortium and web services standards. In P. Zhao & L. Di (Eds.), *Geospatial web services: Advances in information interoperability* (pp. 1–16). Hershey, PA: IGI Global. doi:10.4018/978-1-60960-192-8.ch001

Rejas-Muslera, R., Davara, E., Abran, A., & Buglione, L. (2013). Intellectual property systems in software. *International Journal of Cyber Warfare & Terrorism*, *3*(1), 1–14. doi:10.4018/ijcwt.2013010101

Rejas-Muslera, R. J., García-Tejedor, A. J., & Rodriguez, O. P. (2011). Open educational resources in e-learning: standards and environment. In F. Lazarinis, S. Green, & E. Pearson (Eds.), *Handbook of research on e-learning standards and interoperability: Frameworks and issues* (pp. 346–359). Hershey, PA: IGI Global. doi:10.4018/978-1-61692-789-9.ch017

Ries, N. M. (2011). Legal issues in health information and electronic health records. In *Clinical technologies: Concepts, methodologies, tools and applications* (pp. 1948–1961). Hershey, PA: IGI Global. doi:10.4018/978-1-60960-561-2.ch708

Riillo, C. A. (2013). Profiles and motivations of standardization players. *International Journal of IT Standards and Standardization Research*, *11*(2), 17–33. doi:10.4018/jitsr.2013070102

Rodriguez, E., & Lolas, F. (2011). Social issues related to gene patenting in Latin America: A bioethical reflection. In S. Hongladarom (Ed.), *Genomics and bioethics: Interdisciplinary perspectives, technologies and advancements* (pp. 152–170). Hershey, PA: IGI Global. doi:10.4018/978-1-61692-883-4.ch011

Rutherford, M. (2013). Implementing common core state standards using digital curriculum. In D. Polly (Ed.), *Common core mathematics standards and implementing digital technologies* (pp. 38–44). Hershey, PA: IGI Global. doi:10.4018/978-1-4666-4086-3.ch003

Rutherford, M. (2014). Implementing common core state standards using digital curriculum. In *K-12 education: Concepts, methodologies, tools, and applications* (pp. 383–389). Hershey, PA: IGI Global. doi:10.4018/978-1-4666-4502-8.ch022

Ryan, G., & Shinnick, E. (2011). Knowledge and intellectual property rights: An economics perspective. In D. Schwartz & D. Te'eni (Eds.), *Encyclopedia of knowledge management* (2nd ed.; pp. 489–496). Hershey, PA: IGI Global. doi:10.4018/978-1-59904-931-1.ch047

Ryoo, J., & Choi, Y. (2011). A taxonomy of green information and communication protocols and standards. In B. Unhelkar (Ed.), *Handbook of research on green ICT: Technology, business and social perspectives* (pp. 364–376). Hershey, PA: IGI Global. doi:10.4018/978-1-61692-834-6.ch026

Saeed, K., Ziegler, G., & Yaqoob, M. K. (2013). Management practices in exploration and production industry. In S. Saeed, M. Khan, & R. Ahmad (Eds.), *Business strategies and approaches for effective engineering management* (pp. 151–187). Hershey, PA: IGI Global. doi:10.4018/978-1-4666-3658-3.ch010

Saiki, T. (2014). Intellectual property in mergers & acquisitions. In J. Wang (Ed.), *Encyclopedia of business analytics and optimization* (pp. 1275–1283). Hershey, PA: IGI Global. doi:10.4018/978-1-4666-5202-6.ch117

Santos, O., & Boticario, J. (2011). A general framework for inclusive lifelong learning in higher education institutions with adaptive web-based services that support standards. In G. Magoulas (Ed.), *E-infrastructures and technologies for lifelong learning: Next generation environments* (pp. 29–58). Hershey, PA: IGI Global. doi:10.4018/978-1-61520-983-5.ch002

Santos, O., Boticario, J., Raffenne, E., Granado, J., Rodriguez-Ascaso, A., & Gutierrez y Restrepo, E. (2011). A standard-based framework to support personalisation, adaptation, and interoperability in inclusive learning scenarios. In F. Lazarinis, S. Green, & E. Pearson (Eds.), *Handbook of research on e-learning standards and interoperability: Frameworks and issues* (pp. 126–169). Hershey, PA: IGI Global. doi:10.4018/978-1-61692-789-9.ch007

Sarabdeen, J. (2012). Legal issues in e-healthcare systems. In M. Watfa (Ed.), *E-healthcare systems and wireless communications: Current and future challenges* (pp. 23–48). Hershey, PA: IGI Global. doi:10.4018/978-1-61350-123-8.ch002

Scheg, A. G. (2014). Common standards for online education found in accrediting organizations. In *Reforming teacher education for online pedagogy development* (pp. 50–76). Hershey, PA: IGI Global. doi:10.4018/978-1-4666-5055-8.ch003

Sclater, N. (2012). Legal and contractual issues of cloud computing for educational institutions. In L. Chao (Ed.), *Cloud computing for teaching and learning: Strategies for design and implementation* (pp. 186–199). Hershey, PA: IGI Global. doi:10.4018/978-1-4666-0957-0.ch013

Selwyn, L., & Eldridge, V. (2013). Governance and organizational structures. In *Public law librarianship: Objectives, challenges, and solutions* (pp. 41–71). Hershey, PA: IGI Global. doi:10.4018/978-1-4666-2184-8.ch003

Seo, D. (2012). The significance of government's role in technology standardization: Two cases in the wireless communications industry. In C. Reddick (Ed.), *Cases on public information management and e-government adoption* (pp. 219–231). Hershey, PA: IGI Global. doi:10.4018/978-1-4666-0981-5.ch009

Seo, D. (2013). Analysis of various structures of standards setting organizations (SSOs) that impact tension among members. *International Journal of IT Standards and Standardization Research, 11*(2), 46–60. doi:10.4018/jitsr.2013070104

Seo, D. (2013). Background of standards strategy. In *Evolution and standardization of mobile communications technology* (pp. 1–17). Hershey, PA: IGI Global. doi:10.4018/978-1-4666-4074-0.ch001

Seo, D. (2013). Developing a theoretical model. In *Evolution and standardization of mobile communications technology* (pp. 18–42). Hershey, PA: IGI Global. doi:10.4018/978-1-4666-4074-0.ch002

Seo, D. (2013). The 1G (first generation) mobile communications technology standards. In *Evolution and standardization of mobile communications technology* (pp. 54–75). Hershey, PA: IGI Global. doi:10.4018/978-1-4666-4074-0.ch005

Seo, D. (2013). The 2G (second generation) mobile communications technology standards. In *Evolution and standardization of mobile communications technology* (pp. 76–114). Hershey, PA: IGI Global. doi:10.4018/978-1-4666-4074-0.ch006

Seo, D. (2013). The 3G (third generation) of mobile communications technology standards. In *Evolution and standardization of mobile communications technology* (pp. 115–161). Hershey, PA: IGI Global. doi:10.4018/978-1-4666-4074-0.ch007

Seo, D. (2013). The significance of government's role in technology standardization: Two cases in the wireless communications industry. In K. Jakobs (Ed.), *Innovations in organizational IT specification and standards development* (pp. 183–192). Hershey, PA: IGI Global. doi:10.4018/978-1-4666-2160-2.ch011

Seo, D., & Koek, J. W. (2012). Are Asian countries ready to lead a global ICT standardization? *International Journal of IT Standards and Standardization Research, 10*(2), 29–44. doi:10.4018/jitsr.2012070103

Sharp, R. J., Ewald, J. A., & Kenward, R. (2013). Central information flows and decision-making requirements. In J. Papathanasiou, B. Manos, S. Arampatzis, & R. Kenward (Eds.), *Transactional environmental support system design: Global solutions* (pp. 7–32). Hershey, PA: IGI Global. doi:10.4018/978-1-4666-2824-3.ch002

Shen, X., Graham, I., Stewart, J., & Williams, R. (2013). Standards development as hybridization. *International Journal of IT Standards and Standardization Research, 11*(2), 34–45. doi:10.4018/jitsr.2013070103

Sherman, M. (2013). Using technology to engage students with the standards for mathematical practice: The case of DGS. In D. Polly (Ed.), *Common core mathematics standards and implementing digital technologies* (pp. 78–101). Hershey, PA: IGI Global. doi:10.4018/978-1-4666-4086-3.ch006

Singh, J., & Kumar, V. (2013). Compliance and regulatory standards for cloud computing. In R. Khurana & R. Aggarwal (Eds.), *Interdisciplinary perspectives on business convergence, computing, and legality* (pp. 54–64). Hershey, PA: IGI Global. doi:10.4018/978-1-4666-4209-6.ch006

Singh, S., & Paliwal, M. (2014). Exploring a sense of intellectual property valuation for Indian SMEs. *International Journal of Asian Business and Information Management, 5*(1), 15–36. doi:10.4018/ijabim.2014010102

Singh, S., & Siddiqui, T. J. (2013). Robust image data hiding technique for copyright protection. *International Journal of Information Security and Privacy, 7*(2), 44–56. doi:10.4018/jisp.2013040103

Spies, M., & Tabet, S. (2012). Emerging standards and protocols for governance, risk, and compliance management. In E. Kajan, F. Dorloff, & I. Bedini (Eds.), *Handbook of research on e-business standards and protocols: Documents, data and advanced web technologies* (pp. 768–790). Hershey, PA: IGI Global. doi:10.4018/978-1-4666-0146-8.ch035

Spinello, R. A., & Tavani, H. T. (2008). Intellectual property rights: From theory to practical implementation. In H. Sasaki (Ed.), *Intellectual property protection for multimedia information technology* (pp. 25–69). Hershey, PA: IGI Global. doi:10.4018/978-1-59904-762-1.ch002

Spyrou, S., Bamidis, P., & Maglaveras, N. (2010). Health information standards: Towards integrated health information networks. In J. Rodrigues (Ed.), *Health information systems: Concepts, methodologies, tools, and applications* (pp. 2145–2159). Hershey, PA: IGI Global. doi:10.4018/978-1-60566-988-5.ch136

Stanfill, D. (2012). Standards-based educational technology professional development. In V. Wang (Ed.), *Encyclopedia of e-leadership, counseling and training* (pp. 819–834). Hershey, PA: IGI Global. doi:10.4018/978-1-61350-068-2.ch060

Steen, H. U. (2011). The battle within: An analysis of internal fragmentation in networked technologies based on a comparison of the DVB-H and T-DMB mobile digital multimedia broadcasting standards. *International Journal of IT Standards and Standardization Research, 9*(2), 50–71. doi:10.4018/jitsr.2011070103

Steen, H. U. (2013). The battle within: An analysis of internal fragmentation in networked technologies based on a comparison of the DVB-H and T-DMB mobile digital multimedia broadcasting standards. In K. Jakobs (Ed.), *Innovations in organizational IT specification and standards development* (pp. 91–114). Hershey, PA: IGI Global. doi:10.4018/978-1-4666-2160-2.ch005

Stoll, M., & Breu, R. (2012). Information security governance and standard based management systems. In M. Gupta, J. Walp, & R. Sharman (Eds.), *Strategic and practical approaches for information security governance: Technologies and applied solutions* (pp. 261–282). Hershey, PA: IGI Global. doi:10.4018/978-1-4666-0197-0. ch015

Suzuki, O. (2013). Search efforts, selective appropriation, and the usefulness of new knowledge: Evidence from a comparison across U.S. and non-U.S. patent applicants. *International Journal of Knowledge Management, 9*(1), 42-59. doi:10.4018/jkm.2013010103

Tajima, M. (2012). The role of technology standardization in RFID adoption: The pharmaceutical context. *International Journal of IT Standards and Standardization Research, 10*(1), 48–67. doi:10.4018/jitsr.2012010104

Talevi, A., Castro, E. A., & Bruno-Blanch, L. E. (2012). Virtual screening: An emergent, key methodology for drug development in an emergent continent: A bridge towards patentability. In E. Castro & A. Haghi (Eds.), *Advanced methods and applications in chemoinformatics: Research progress and new applications* (pp. 229–245). Hershey, PA: IGI Global. doi:10.4018/978-1-60960-860-6.ch011

Tauber, A. (2012). Requirements and properties of qualified electronic delivery systems in egovernment: An Austrian experience. In S. Sharma (Ed.), *E-adoption and technologies for empowering developing countries: Global advances* (pp. 115–128). Hershey, PA: IGI Global. doi:10.4018/978-1-4666-0041-6.ch009

Telesko, R., & Nikles, S. (2012). Semantic-enabled compliance management. In S. Smolnik, F. Teuteberg, & O. Thomas (Eds.), *Semantic technologies for business and information systems engineering: Concepts and applications* (pp. 292–310). Hershey, PA: IGI Global. doi:10.4018/978-1-60960-126-3.ch015

Tella, A., & Afolabi, A. K. (2013). Internet policy issues and digital libraries' management of intellectual property. In S. Thanuskodi (Ed.), *Challenges of academic library management in developing countries* (pp. 272–284). Hershey, PA: IGI Global. doi:10.4018/978-1-4666-4070-2.ch019

Tiwari, S. C., Gupta, M., Khan, M. A., & Ansari, A. Q. (2013). Intellectual property rights in semi-conductor industries: An Indian perspective. In S. Saeed, M. Khan, & R. Ahmad (Eds.), *Business strategies and approaches for effective engineering management* (pp. 97–110). Hershey, PA: IGI Global. doi:10.4018/978-1-4666-3658-3.ch006

Truyen, F., & Buekens, F. (2013). Professional ICT knowledge, epistemic standards, and social epistemology. In T. Takševa (Ed.), *Social software and the evolution of user expertise: Future trends in knowledge creation and dissemination* (pp. 274–294). Hershey, PA: IGI Global. doi:10.4018/978-1-4666-2178-7.ch016

Tummons, J. (2011). Deconstructing professionalism: An actor-network critique of professional standards for teachers in the UK lifelong learning sector. *International Journal of Actor-Network Theory and Technological Innovation, 3*(4), 22–31. doi:10.4018/jantti.2011100103

Tummons, J. (2013). Deconstructing professionalism: An actor-network critique of professional standards for teachers in the UK lifelong learning sector. In A. Tatnall (Ed.), *Social and professional applications of actor-network theory for technology development* (pp. 78–87). Hershey, PA: IGI Global. doi:10.4018/978-1-4666-2166-4.ch007

Tuohey, W. G. (2014). Lessons from practices and standards in safety-critical and regulated sectors. In I. Ghani, W. Kadir, & M. Ahmad (Eds.), *Handbook of research on emerging advancements and technologies in software engineering* (pp. 369–391). Hershey, PA: IGI Global. doi:10.4018/978-1-4666-6026-7.ch016

Tzoulia, E. (2013). Legal issues to be considered before setting in force consumer-centric marketing strategies within the European Union. In H. Kaufmann & M. Panni (Eds.), *Customer-centric marketing strategies: Tools for building organizational performance* (pp. 36–56). Hershey, PA: IGI Global. doi:10.4018/978-1-4666-2524-2.ch003

Unland, R. (2012). Interoperability support for e-business applications through standards, services, and multi-agent systems. In E. Kajan, F. Dorloff, & I. Bedini (Eds.), *Handbook of research on e-business standards and protocols: Documents, data and advanced web technologies* (pp. 129–153). Hershey, PA: IGI Global. doi:10.4018/978-1-4666-0146-8.ch007

Uslar, M., Grüning, F., & Rohjans, S. (2013). A use case for ontology evolution and interoperability: The IEC utility standards reference framework 62357. In M. Khosrow-Pour (Ed.), *Cases on performance measurement and productivity improvement: Technology integration and maturity* (pp. 387–415). Hershey, PA: IGI Global. doi:10.4018/978-1-4666-2618-8.ch018

van de Kaa, G. (2013). Responsible innovation and standardization: A new research approach? *International Journal of IT Standards and Standardization Research*, *11*(2), 61–65. doi:10.4018/jitsr.2013070105

van de Kaa, G., Blind, K., & de Vries, H. J. (2013). The challenge of establishing a recognized interdisciplinary journal: A citation analysis of the international journal of IT standards and standardization research. *International Journal of IT Standards and Standardization Research*, *11*(2), 1–16. doi:10.4018/jitsr.2013070101

Venkataraman, H., Ciubotaru, B., & Muntean, G. (2012). System design perspective: WiMAX standards and IEEE 802.16j based multihop WiMAX. In G. Cornetta, D. Santos, & J. Vazquez (Eds.), *Wireless radio-frequency standards and system design: Advanced techniques* (pp. 287–309). Hershey, PA: IGI Global. doi:10.4018/978-1-4666-0083-6.ch012

Vishwakarma, P., & Mukherjee, B. (2014). Knowing protection of intellectual contents in digital era. In N. Patra, B. Kumar, & A. Pani (Eds.), *Progressive trends in electronic resource management in libraries* (pp. 147–165). Hershey, PA: IGI Global. doi:10.4018/978-1-4666-4761-9.ch008

Wasilko, P. J. (2011). Law, architecture, gameplay, and marketing. In M. Cruz-Cunha, V. Varvalho, & P. Tavares (Eds.), *Business, technological, and social dimensions of computer games: Multidisciplinary developments* (pp. 476–493). Hershey, PA: IGI Global. doi:10.4018/978-1-60960-567-4.ch029

Wasilko, P. J. (2012). Law, architecture, gameplay, and marketing. In *Computer engineering: concepts, methodologies, tools and applications* (pp. 1660–1677). Hershey, PA: IGI Global. doi:10.4018/978-1-61350-456-7.ch703

Wasilko, P. J. (2014). Beyond compliance: Understanding the legal aspects of information system administration. In I. Portela & F. Almeida (Eds.), *Organizational, legal, and technological dimensions of information system administration* (pp. 57–75). Hershey, PA: IGI Global. doi:10.4018/978-1-4666-4526-4.ch004

White, G. L., Mediavilla, F. A., & Shah, J. R. (2011). Information privacy: Implementation and perception of laws and corporate policies by CEOs and managers. *International Journal of Information Security and Privacy*, *5*(1), 50–66. doi:10.4018/jisp.2011010104

White, G. L., Mediavilla, F. A., & Shah, J. R. (2013). Information privacy: Implementation and perception of laws and corporate policies by CEOs and managers. In H. Nemati (Ed.), *Privacy solutions and security frameworks in information protection* (pp. 52–69). Hershey, PA: IGI Global. doi:10.4018/978-1-4666-2050-6. ch004

Whyte, K. P., List, M., Stone, J. V., Grooms, D., Gasteyer, S., Thompson, P. B., & Bouri, H. et al. (2014). Uberveillance, standards, and anticipation: A case study on nanobiosensors in U.S. cattle. In M. Michael & K. Michael (Eds.), *Uberveillance and the social implications of microchip implants: Emerging technologies* (pp. 260–279). Hershey, PA: IGI Global. doi:10.4018/978-1-4666-4582-0.ch012

Wilkes, W., Reusch, P. J., & Moreno, L. E. (2012). Flexible classification standards for product data exchange. In E. Kajan, F. Dorloff, & I. Bedini (Eds.), *Handbook of research on e-business standards and protocols: Documents, data and advanced web technologies* (pp. 448–466). Hershey, PA: IGI Global. doi:10.4018/978-1-4666-0146-8.ch021

Wittkower, D. E. (2011). Against strong copyright in e-business. In *Global business: Concepts, methodologies, tools and applications* (pp. 2157–2176). Hershey, PA: IGI Global. doi:10.4018/978-1-60960-587-2.ch720

Wright, D. (2012). Evolution of standards for smart grid communications. *International Journal of Interdisciplinary Telecommunications and Networking*, *4*(1), 47–55. doi:10.4018/jitn.2012010103

Wurster, S. (2013). Development of a specification for data interchange between information systems in public hazard prevention: Dimensions of success and related activities identified by case study research. *International Journal of IT Standards and Standardization Research*, *11*(1), 46–66. doi:10.4018/jitsr.2013010103

Wyburn, M. (2011). Copyright and ethical issues in emerging models for the digital media reporting of sports news in Australia. In M. Quigley (Ed.), *ICT ethics and security in the 21st century: New developments and applications* (pp. 66–85). Hershey, PA: IGI Global. doi:10.4018/978-1-60960-573-5.ch004

Wyburn, M. (2013). Copyright and ethical issues in emerging models for the digital media reporting of sports news in Australia. In *Digital rights management: Concepts, methodologies, tools, and applications* (pp. 290–309). Hershey, PA: IGI Global. doi:10.4018/978-1-4666-2136-7.ch014

Xiaohui, T., Yaohui, Z., & Yi, Z. (2012). The management system of enterprises' intellectual property rights: A case study from China. *International Journal of Asian Business and Information Management*, *3*(1), 50–64. doi:10.4018/jabim.2012010105

Xiaohui, T., Yaohui, Z., & Yi, Z. (2013). The management system of enterprises' intellectual property rights: A case study from China. In *Digital rights management: Concepts, methodologies, tools, and applications* (pp. 1092–1106). Hershey, PA: IGI Global. doi:10.4018/978-1-4666-2136-7.ch053

Xuan, X., & Xiaowei, Z. (2012). The dilemma and resolution: The patentability of traditional Chinese medicine. *International Journal of Asian Business and Information Management*, *3*(3), 1–8. doi:10.4018/jabim.2012070101

Yang, C., & Lu, Z. (2011). A blind image watermarking scheme utilizing BTC bitplanes. *International Journal of Digital Crime and Forensics*, *3*(4), 42–53. doi:10.4018/jdcf.2011100104

Yastrebenetsky, M., & Gromov, G. (2014). International standard bases and safety classification. In M. Yastrebenetsky & V. Kharchenko (Eds.), *Nuclear power plant instrumentation and control systems for safety and security* (pp. 31–60). Hershey, PA: IGI Global. doi:10.4018/978-1-4666-5133-3.ch002

Zouag, N., & Kadiri, M. (2014). Intellectual property rights, innovation, and knowledge economy in Arab countries. In A. Driouchi (Ed.), *Knowledge-based economic policy development in the Arab world* (pp. 245–272). Hershey, PA: IGI Global. doi:10.4018/978-1-4666-5210-1.ch010

# Compilation of References

A & M. (2012, April). *Ten Things to look for in an SDN Controller*. Retrieved April, 2017, from http://www.webtorials.com/content/2012/08/2012-application-service-delivery-han

Aditess. (2016). *Tailoring the needs for NFV-to-SDN convergence: An opportunity for the ARCADIA framework*. Retrieved from http://www.arcadia-framework.eu/tailoring-needs-nfv-sdn-convergence-opportunity-arcadia-framework/

Advantages of Software Defined Networking. (2014). Retrieved from http://www.ingrammicroadvisor.com/data-center/7-advantages-of-software-defined-networking

Akyildiz, I. F., Su, W., Sankarasubramaniam, Y., & Cayirci, E. (2002). Wireless sensor networks : A survey. *Computer Networks*, *38*(4), 393–422. doi:10.1016/S1389-1286(01)00302-4

Aleplidis, E., Pentikousis, K., Denazis, S., Salim, J. H., Meyer, D., & Koufopavlou, O. (2015). *Software-defined networking (SDN): Layers and Eugen Borcoci*. InfoSystems Conference, Rome, Italy.

Algarni. (2013). Software-Defined Networking Overview and Implementation. Academic Press.

Alsulaiman, M., Alyahya, A., Alkharboush, R., & Alghafis, N. (2009). Intrusion Detection System Using Self-Organizing Maps. *2009 Third International Conference on Network and System Security*, 397-402. doi:10.1109/NSS.2009.62

Anastasi, G., Conti, M., Di Francesco, M., & Passarella, A. (2009). Energy conservation in wireless sensor networks: A survey. *Ad Hoc Networks*, *7*(3), 537–568. doi:10.1016/j.adhoc.2008.06.003

Azodolmolky, S., Wieder, P., & Yahyapour, R. (2013). Cloud computing networking: challenges and opportunities for innovations. *IEEE Communications Magazine, 51*(7), 54-62.

Bahnasse, A., & El Kamoun, N. (2014). Policy-based Management of a Secure Dynamic and Multipoint Virtual Private Network. *Global Journal of Computer Science and Technology, 14*(8).

Bahnasse, A., & Elkamoun, N. (2015). Study and evaluation of the high availability of a Dynamic Multipoint Virtual Private Network. *Revue MéDiterranéEnne Des TéLéCommunications, 5*(2).

Barona López, L. I., Valdivieso Caraguay, A. L., Monge, M. A. S., & García Villalba, L. J. (2017). *Key Technologies in the Context of Future Networks: Operational and Management Requirements*. Retrieved from http://www.mdpi.com/1999-5903/9/1/1

Bera, S., Misra, S., Roy, S. K., Obaidat, M. S. (2016). Soft-WSN: Software-Defined WSN Management System for IoT Applications. *IEEE Systems Journal*, 1-8.

Bizanis, N., & Kuipers, F. (2016). SDN and virtualization solutions for the Internet of Things: A survey. *IEEE Access: Practical Innovations, Open Solutions*, 1–1.

Bogineni, K., Davidson, D., Slauson, A., Molocznik, L., Martin, C., McBean, K., & Smith, K. (2016). SDN-NFV reference architecture. Verizon.

Bogineni, K., Davidson, D., Slauson, A., Molocznik, L., Martin, C., McBean, K., . . . Smith, K. (2016). SDN-NFV reference architecture. New York: Verizon.

Build SDN Agilely. (2017). Retrieved from https://osrg.github.io/ryu/

Caesar, M., Caldwell, D., Feamster, N., Rexford, J., Shaikh, A., & van der Merwe, J. (2005). Design and implementation of a routing control platform. *Proc. ACM/USENIX NSDI*, 15–28.

Campbell, A. T., Katzela, I., Miki, K., & Vicente, J. (1999). Open signaling for ATM, internet and mobile networks (OPENSIG'98). *Computer Communication Review*, *29*(1), 97–108. doi:10.1145/505754.505762

Cao, Zhang, Huang, Zhang, & Gu. (2009). The design, Implementation and performance analysis of transport-MPLS network. *IEEE Journal*, 46-49.

Carlson, M., Yoder, A., Schoeb, L., Deel, D., Pratt, C., Lionetti, C., & Voigt, D. (2014). *Software defined storage*. Storage Networking Industry Assoc. working draft.

Casado, M., Freedman, M. J., Pettit, J., Luo, J., McKeown, N., & Shenker, S. (2007). Ethane: Taking control of the enterprise. *Proceedings SIGCOMM Conference on Applications, Technology, Architecture, Protocols Computer Communication*, 1–12.

Casado, M., Freedman, M. J., Pettit, J., Luo, J., McKeown, N., & Shenker, S. (2007, August). Ethane: Taking control of the enterprise. *Computer Communication Review*, *37*(4), 1–12. doi:10.1145/1282427.1282382

Casado, M., Garfinkel, T., Akella, A., Freedman, M. J., Boneh, D., McKeown, N., & Shenker, S. (2006). SANE: A protection architecture for enterprise networks. *Proceedings USENIX Security Symposium*, 1–15.

Casado, M., Koponen, T., Shenker, S., & Tootoonchian, A. (2012, August). Fabric: a retrospective on evolving SDN. In *Proceedings of the first workshop on Hot topics in software defined networks* (pp. 85-90). ACM. doi:10.1145/2342441.2342459

Chiosi, M., Clarke, D., Willis, P., Reid, A., Feger, J., Bugenhagen, M., & Benitez, J. (2012). Network functions virtualization: An introduction, benefits, challenges and call for action. In *SDN and OpenFlow World Congress* (pp. 22-24). Academic Press.

Chiosi, M., Clarke, D., Willis, P., Reid, A., Feger, J., Bugenhagen, M., & Benitez, J. (2012, October). Network functions virtualization: An introduction, benefits, challenges and call for action. In *SDN and OpenFlow World Congress* (pp. 22-24). Academic Press.

Chowdhury, N. M. K., & Boutaba, R. (2009). Network virtualization: State of the art and research challenges. *IEEE Communications Magazine, 47*(7), 20–26. doi:10.1109/MCOM.2009.5183468

Chowdhury, N. M. K., & Boutaba, R. (2010). A survey of network virtualization. *Computer Networks, 54*(5), 862–876. doi:10.1016/j.comnet.2009.10.017

Chua, R. (2017). *2017 NFV Report Series Part I: Foundations of NFV: NFV Infrastructure and VIM Report Available Now.* Retrieved from https://www.sdxcentral.com/articles/announcements/nfv-infrastructure-vim-report-avialable/2017/04/

Chui, B., Yang, Z., & Ding, W. (2004). A load balancing algorithm supporting QoS for traffic engineering in MPLS networks. *4th international conference on computer & Information technology*, 436-441.

Cisco, V. N. I. (2016). *Cisco visual networking index: Global mobile data traffic forecast update, 2016–2021.* Retrieved from https://www.cisco.com/c/en/us/solutions/collateral/service-provider/visual-networking-index-vni/complete-white-paper-c11-481360.html

Cisco. (2005). *DiffServ --The Scalable End-to-End QoS Model.* Retrieved March 30, 2017, from https://www.cisco.com/en/US/technologies/tk543/tk766/technologies_white_paper09186a00800a3e2f.html

Cisco. (2010). *Cisco visual networking index: Global mobile data traffic forecast update, 2009–2014.* Author.

Civanlar, S., Parlakisik, M., Tekalp, A. M., Gorkemli, B., Kaytaz, B., & Onem, E. (2010). *A qos-enabled openflow environment for scalable video streaming.* IEEE Globecom Workshops. doi:10.1109/GLOCOMW.2010.5700340

Controller Benchmarker. (2008). Retrieved from https://www. openflow.org/wk/index.php/Oflops

CoprHD Architecture. (n.d.). Retrieved from https://coprhd.atlassian.net/wiki/spaces/COP/pages/3211310/A+Short+Guide+to+the+CoprHD+Architecture /24

Costanzo, S. (2012). Software defined wireless networks: Unbridling sdns. *Software Defined Networking (EWSDN). European Workshop on*, 1-6.

Costanzo, S. (2012). Software defined wireless networks: Unbridling sdns. *Software Defined Networking (EWSDN). European Workshop on. IEEE*, 1-6.

Costanzo, S., Galluccio, L., Morabito, G., & Palazzo, S. (2012). *Software defined wireless networks: Unbridling sdns.* EWSDN.

Coyne, L. (2017). *IBM Software-Defined Storage Guide.* Retrieved from http://ibm.com/redbooks //22

CPqD. (n.d.). *What is it?* Retrieved from http://cpqd.github.io/RouteFlow/

D'souza, Sundharan, Lokanath, & Mittal. (2016). Improving QoS in a Software-Defined Network. *Capstone Research Paper*, 1-9.

Darabinejad, B., Rasoul, S., & Fayyeh, M. (2014). An introduction to software defined networking. *International Journal of Intelligent Information Systems*, *3*(6), 71-74.

Darabinejad, B., Rasoul, S., & Fayyeh. (2014). An introduction to software defined networking. *International Journal of Intelligent Information Systems, 3*(6), 71-74.

De Gante, A., Aslan, M., & Matrawy, A. (2014). Smart wireless sensor network management based on software-defined networking. *Communications (QBSC), 2014 27th Biennial Symposium on*, 71-75.

De Gante, A., Aslan, M., & Matrawy, A. (2014). Smart wireless sensor network management based on software-defined networking. *Communications (QBSC), 2014 27th Biennial Symposium on. IEEE*, 71-75. doi:10.1109/QBSC.2014.6841187

de Oliveira, B. T., Margi, C. B., & Gabriel, L. B. (2014). TinySDN: Enabling multiple controllers for software-defined wireless sensor networks. *Proc. IEEE Latin-Amer. Conf. Commun. (LATINCOM)*, 1–6.

DellEMC. (n.d.). *Dell EMC Vipr Controller, Automate and Simplify Storage Management.* vailable: https://www.emc.com/collateral/data-sheet/h11750-emc-vipr-software-defined-storage-ds.pdf

Doria, A. (2002). General Switch Management Protocol V3. *RFC 3292*.

Doria, A., Hellstrand, F., Sundell, K., & Worster, T. (2002). General Switch Management Protocol V3. *RFC 3292*. Retrieved from https://tools.ietf.org/html/rfc3292

Doria, A., Salim, J.H., Haas, R., Khosravi, H., Wang, W., Dong, L., … Halpern, J. (2010). *Forwarding and control element separation (forces) protocol specification.* Academic Press.

Dumka, A., Mandoria, H. L., Fore, V., & Dumka, K. (2015). *Implementation of QoS Algorithm in the Integrated Services (IntServ) MPLS Network.* Paper published in 2nd International Conference on Computing for Sustainable Global Development (INDIAcom), New Delhi, India.

Edition, I. P. C. (2014). Software Defined Storage For Dummies. Academic Press.

Egilmez, A. T. H. E., & Civanlar, S. (2012). A distributed qos routing architecture for scalable video streaming over multidomain openflow networks. *Proc. IEEE International Conference on Image Processing (ICIP 2012)*. doi:10.1109/ICIP.2012.6467340

Egilmez, H. E., Dane, S. T., Gorkemli, B., & Tekalp, A. M. (2012). *Openqos: Openflow controller design and test network for multimedia delivery with quality of service.* NEM Summit.

Enns, R. (2006). *NETCONF Configuration Protocol.* Retrieved from https://tools.ietf.org/pdf/rfc4741.pdf

Erickson, D. (2013). *What is Beacon?* Retrieved from https://openflow.stanford.edu/display/Beacon/Home

Erickson, D. (2011). *Open Networking Foundation Formed to Speed Network Innovation.* Portland, OR: Open Networking Foundation.

ETSI. (2012). *Network Functions Virtualisation: An Introduction, Benefits, Enablers, Challenges & Call for Action.* Retrieved from https://portal.etsi.org/nfv/nfv_white_paper.pdf

ETSI. (2013a). *Network Functions Virtualisation: Network Operator Perspectives on Industry Progress.* Retrieved from https://portal.etsi.org/nfv/nfv_white_paper2.pdf

ETSI. (2013b). *ETSI NFV 001 V1.1.1, 2013-10, NFV Use Cases.* Retrieved from http://www.etsi.org/deliver/etsi_gs/NFV/001_099/001/01.01.01_60/gs_NFV001v010101p.pdf

ETSI. (2013c). *ETSI GS NFV 004 v1.1.1 2013-10, NFV Virtualization Requirements.* Retrieved from http://www.etsi.org/deliver/etsi_gs/NFV/001_099/004/01.01.01_60/gs_NFV004v010101p.pdf

ETSI. (2014a). *Network Functions Virtualisation (NFV): Network Operator Perspectives on Industry Progress.* Retrieved from https://portal.etsi.org/Portals/0/TBpages/NFV/Docs/NFV_White_Paper3.pdf

ETSI. (2014b). *Network Functions Virtualization (NFV); Terminology for Main Concepts in NFV.* Retrieved from http://www.etsi.org/deliver/etsi_gs/NFV/001_099/003/01.02.01_60/gs_NFV003v010201p.pdf

ETSI. (2014c). *ETSI GS NFV 002 v1.2.1 2014-12, NFV Architectural Framework.* Retrieved from http://www.etsi.org/deliver/etsi_gs/NFV/001_099/002/01.02.01_60/gs_NFV002v010201p.pdf

Feamster, N., Rexford, J., & Zegura. (2013). *The Road to SDN: An Intellectual History of Programmable Networks.* ACM Queue, Tech. Rep.

Feamster, N., Rexford, J., & Zegura, E. (2014). The road to SDN: An intellectual history of programmable networks. *Computer Communication Review*, *44*(2), 87–98. doi:10.1145/2602204.2602219

Foundation, O. N. (2012). Software-defined networking: The new norm for networks. *ONF White Paper, 2,* 2-6.

Franciscus, W. X., Gregory, M. A., Khandakar, A., & Gomez, K. M. (2017). Multi-domain Software Defined Networking: Research status and challenges. *Journal of Network and Computer Applications.* doi:10.1016/j.jnca.2017.03.004

Fundation, O. N. (2012). Software-defined networking: The new norm for networks. *ONF White Paper, 2*, 2-6.

Gens, F. (2012). *IDC Predictions 2013: Competing on the 3rd Platform. Int.* Data Corporation.

Goransson, P., Black, C., & Culver, T. (2016). *Software Defined Networks: A Comprehensive Approach.* Burlington: Morgan Kaufmann.

Govindarajan, K., Meng, K. C., & Ong, H. (2014). Realizing the Quality of Service (QoS) in Software-Defined Networking (SDN) based Cloud infrastructure. *2nd International Conference on Information and Communication Technology (ICoICT)*, 505 – 510.

Govindarajan, K., Meng, K. C., & Ong, H. (2013). A literature review on Software-Defined Networking (SDN) research topics, challenges and solutions. *Fifth International Conference on Advanced Computing (ICoAC)*, 293-299. doi:10.1109/ICoAC.2013.6921966

Greenberg, A., Hjalmtysson, G., Maltz, D. A., Myers, A., Rexford, J., Xie, G., & Zhang, H. (2005, October). A clean slate 4D approach to network control and management. *Computer Communication Review, 35*(5), 41–54. doi:10.1145/1096536.1096541

Gubbi, J., Buyya, R., Marusic, S., & Palaniswami, M. (2013). Internet of Things (IoT): A vision, architectural elements, and future directions. *Future Generation Computer Systems, 29*(7), 1645–1660. doi:10.1016/j.future.2013.01.010

Gude, N., Koponen, T., Pettit, J., Pfaff, B., Casado, M., McKeown, N., & Shenker, S. (2008). NOX: Towards an operating system for networks. *Computer Communication Review, 38*(3), 105–110. doi:10.1145/1384609.1384625

H. (2012). Software Defined Networking (SDN): A Revolution in Computer Network. *IOSR Journal of Computer Engineering, 15*(5), 103-106. Retrieved from http://ict.unimap.edu.my/images/doc/ SDN%20IBM%20WhitePaper.pdf

Hakiria, A., Gokhalec, A., Berthoua, P., & Schmidt, D. C. (2014). Gayraud Thierry, "Software-defined Networking: Challenges and Research Opportunities for Future Internet. *International Council for Computer Communication, Elsevier, 2014*, 1–26.

Haleplidis, E., Pentikousis, K., Denazis, S., Salim, J. H., Meyer, D., & Koufopavlou, O. (2015). *Software-defined networking (SDN): Layers and architecture terminology* (No. RFC 7426).

Haleplidis. (2015). *Software-Defined Networking (SDN): Layers and Architecture Terminology* (RFC 7426). Retrieved from http://tools.ietf.org/search/rfc7426

Han, B., Gopalakrishnan, V., Ji, L., & Lee, S. (2015). Network function virtualization: Challenges and opportunities for innovations. *IEEE Communications Magazine, 53*(2), 90–97. doi:10.1109/MCOM.2015.7045396

Han, Z., & Ren, W. (2014). A Novel Wireless Sensor Networks Structure Based on the SDN. *International Journal of Distributed Sensor Networks, 2014*(1), 1–8.

Haque, I. T., & Abu-Ghazaleh, N. (2016). *Wireless Software Defined Networking: a Survey and Taxonomy*. IEEE Communication Survey & Tutorials.

Heller, B., Sherwood, R., & McKeown, N. (2012). The controller placement problem. *HotSDN*, *12*, 1–6.

Hernandez-Valencia, E., Izzo, S., & Polonsky, B. (2015). How will NFV/SDN transform service provider opex? *IEEE Network*, *29*(3), 60–67. doi:10.1109/MNET.2015.7113227

Hollis, C. (2013). *Introducing emc vipr: A breathtaking approach to software defined storage*. Academic Press.

HowSDN Works. (n.d.). Retrieved from http://cdn.ttgtmedia.com/rms/editorial/HowSDNWorks-SoftwareDefinedNetworks-Ch4.pdf

Huang, H., Zhu, J., & Zhang, L. (2014). An SDN-based Management Framework for IoT Devices. *Irish Signals System Conference-2014 China-irel. Int. Conf. Inf. Communication Technology (ISSC 2014/CIICT 2014), 25th IET*, 175–179.

IBM Storwize V7000 and Storwize V7000 Unified Disk Systems. (n.d.). IBM Corporation. Available:http://www-03.ibm.com/systems/storage/disk/storwize_v7000/

Ingram Micro Advisor. (n.d.). *7 Advantages of Software Defined Networking*. Retrieved from http://www.ingrammicroadvisor.com/data-center/7-advantages-of-software-defined-networking

Jagadeesan, N. A., & Krishnamachari, B. (2014). Software Defined Networking Paradigms in Wireless Networks: A Survey. *ACM Computer Survey, 47*(2), 27:1-27:11.

Jain, R. (2014). *OpenFlow, Software Defined OpenFlow, Software Defined Networking (SDN) and Network Networking (SDN) and Network Function Virtualization (NFV)*. Tutorial at 2014 IEEE 15th International Conference on High Performance Switching and Routing, Vancouver, Canada.

Jain, R., & Paul, S. (2013). Network virtualization and software defined networking for cloud computing: A survey. *IEEE Communications Magazine*, *51*(11), 24–31. doi:10.1109/MCOM.2013.6658648

Jarraya, Y., Madi, T., & Debbabi, M. (2014). A Survey and a Layered Taxonomy of Software-Defined Networking. *IEEE Communications Surveys and Tutorials*, *16*(4), 1955–1980. doi:10.1109/COMST.2014.2320094

Jarschel, M., Lehrieder, F., Magyari, Z., & Pries, R. (2012). A flexible OpenFlow-controller benchmark. *Software Defined Networking*, 48-53. doi:10.1109/EWSDN.2012.15

Kanaumi, Y., Saito, S., Kawai, E., Ishii, S., Kobayashi, K., & Shimojo, S. (2013). Rise: A wide-area hybrid openflow network testbed. *IEICE Transactions*, *96-B*(1), 108–118. doi:10.1587/transcom.E96.B.108

Kandiraju, G., Franke, H., Williams, M. D., Steinder, M., & Black, S. M. (2014). Software defined infrastructures. *IBM Journal of Research and Development, 58*(2/3), 2-1.

Khan, I., Belqasmi, F., Glitho, R., Crespi, N., Morrow, M., & Polakos, P. (2016). Wireless sensor network virtualization: A survey. *IEEE Communications Surveys and Tutorials, 18*(1), 553–576. doi:10.1109/COMST.2015.2412971

Kim, H., & Feamster, N. (2013). Improving network management with software defined networking. *Communications Magazine, IEEE, 51*(2), 114–119. doi:10.1109/MCOM.2013.6461195

Kind, M., Westphal, F., Gladisch, A., & Topp, S. (2012). Split architecture: Applying the software defined networking concept to carrier networks. In *World Telecommunications Congress* (pp. 1–6). WTC. Retrieved from http://www.fp7-sparc.eu/

Kobo, H. I., Abu-Mahfouz, A. M., & Hancke, G. P. (2017). A Survey on Software-Defined Wireless Sensor Networks: Challenges and Design Requirements. IEEE Access, 5, 1872-1899.

Kolias, C. (2014). Bundling NFV and SDN for Open Networking. Proceedings of NetSeminar at Stanford.

Kolias, C. (2014). *Bundling NFV and SDN for Open Networking.* Retrieved from http://netseminar. stanford.edu/seminars/05_22_14.pdf

Kolias. (2014). *Bundling NFV and SDN for Open Networking.* NetSeminar @ Stanford.

Kotani, D., Suzuki, K., & Shimonishi, H. (2012). A Design and Implementation of OpenFlow Controller Handling IP Multicast with Fast Tree Switching. *Applications and the Internet (SAINT), 2012 IEEE/IPSJ 12th International Symposium,* 60-67. doi:10.1109/SAINT.2012.17

Kreutz, D., Ramos, F. M. V., Esteves Verissimo, P., Esteve Rothenberg, C., Azodolmolky, S., & Uhlig, S. (2015). Software Defined Networking: A Comprehensive Survey. *Proceedings of the IEEE, 103*(1), 14–76. doi:10.1109/JPROC.2014.2371999

Lee, W. L., Datta, A., & Cardell-Oliver, R. (2006). Network management in wireless sensor networks. In *Handbook of Mobile Ad Hoc and Pervasive Communications*. Valencia, CA: American Scientific Publishers.

Luo, Tan, & Quek. (2012). Sensor OpenFlow: Enabling software-defined wireless sensor networks. *IEEE Communications Letters, 16*(11), 1896-1899.

Luo, T., Tan, H.-P., & Quek, T. (2012). Sensor OpenFlow: Enabling Software-Defined Wireless Sensor Networks. *IEEE Communications Letters, 16*(11), 2012. doi:10.1109/LCOMM.2012.092812.121712

Marcondes, C. (2013). *A Survey of Software-Defined Networking: Past, Present and Future of Programmable for Wireless Mobile & Adhoc Networks.* Retrieved from https://www.google. ro/?gws_rd=ssl#q=ETSI+NFV+USe+cases++tutorial

Martini, B., Baroncelli, F, Martini, V., & Castoldi, P. (2009). ITU-T RACF implementation for application-driven QoS control in MPLS networks. *IEEE Journal,* 422-429.

Matias, J., Garay, J., Toledo, N., Unzilla, J., & Jacob, E. (2015). Toward an SDN-enabled NFV architecture. *IEEE Communications Magazine, 53*(4), 187–193. doi:10.1109/MCOM.2015.7081093

McKeown, N., & Anderson, T. (2005). *OpenFlow: Enabling Innovation in Campus Networks.* Retrieved from http://www.openflow.org/documents/openflow-wp-latest.pdf

McKeown, N., Anderson, T., Balakrishnan, H., Parulkar, G., Peterson, L., & Rexford, J. (2008). OpenFlow: Enabling Innovation in Campus Networks. *ACM Communications Review.* Retrieved 2017-01-11 from https://dl.acm.org/citation.cfm?id=1355734.1355746

McKeown, N., Anderson, T., Balakrishnan, H., Parulkar, G., Peterson, L., Rexford, J., & Turner, J. (2008). OpenFlow: Enabling innovation in campus networks. *ACM SIGCOMM Computer Communication Review, 38*(2), 69-74.

McKeown, N., Anderson, T., Balakrishnan, H., Parulkar, G., Peterson, L., Rexford, J., & Turner, J. et al. (2008). OpenFlow: Enabling innovation in campus networks. *Computer Communication Review, 38*(2), 69–74. doi:10.1145/1355734.1355746

Melno Park. (2017). *Open Networking Foundation Unveils New Open Innovation Pipeline to Transform Open Networking.* Open Networking Foundation.

Mendonca, M. (2005). *A Survey of Software-Defined Networking: Past, Present and Future of Programmable Networks.* Retrieved from http://hal.inria.fr/hal-00825087/

Metzler, J., & Metzler, A. (2015). *The 2015 Guide to SDN and NFV.* Retrieved from https://www.a10networks.com/sites/default/files/resource-files/2015Ebook-A10-all.pdf

MetzlerJ. (2015). Retrieved from http://www.webtorials.com/content/2014/11/the-2015-guide-to-sdn-nfv.html

Mijumbi, R., Serrat, J., Gorricho, J. L., Bouten, N., De Turck, F., & Boutaba, R. (2016). Network function virtualization: State-of-the-art and research challenges. *IEEE Communications Surveys and Tutorials, 18*(1), 236–262. doi:10.1109/COMST.2015.2477041

Mirkovic, J., & Reiher, P. (2004). A Taxonomy of DDoS Attack and DDoS defense Mechanisms. *ACM SIGCOMM Computer Communications Review, 34*(2), 39–53. doi:10.1145/997150.997156

Mohammad, M. S., & Marc, S. (2015). *Early Detection of DDoS Attacks against SDN Controllers.* Department of Systems and Computer Engineering, Carleton University.

Monge, A. S., & Szarkowicz, K. G. (2015). *MPLS in the SDN Era: Interoperable Scenarios to Make Networks Scale to New Services.* O'Reilly Media, Inc.

Monsanto, C., Reich, J., Foster, N., Rexford, J., & Walker, D. (2013, April). *Composing Software Defined Networks* (Vol. 13). NSDI.

Muruganathan, S. D., Ma, D. C. F., Bhasin, R. I., & Fapojuwo, A. (2005). A centralized energy-efficient routing protocol for wireless sensor networks. *IEEE Communications Magazine, 43*(3), 8–13. doi:10.1109/MCOM.2005.1404592

Nakashima, T., Sueyoshi, T., & Oshima, S. (2010). Early DoS/DDoS Detection Method using Short-term Statistics. *International Conference on Complex, Intelligent and Software Intensive Systems*, 168-173.

Needham, R. M. (1994). Denial of service: An example. *Communications of the ACM, 37*(11), 42–46. doi:10.1145/188280.188294

NexentaStor. (n.d.). Retrieved from https://nexenta.com/products/nexentastor /25

NFV and SDN. What's the Difference? (2013). Retrieved from https://www.sdxcentral.com/articles/contributed/nfv-and-sdn-whats-the-difference/2013/03/

NFV-ISG. (2015). *White paper on Network Functions Virtualization, whitepaper3*. Retrieved from https://portal.etsi.org/Portals/0/TBpages/NFV/Docs/NFV_White_Paper3.pdf

NFV-ISG. (2015). *White paper on Network Functions Virtualization, whitepaper3*. Retrieved September 2017, from https://portal.etsi.org/Portals/0/TBpages/NFV/Docs/NFV_White_Paper3.pdf

Noble, S., (2017). *Building Modern Networks*. Birmingham: Packt Publishing.

Noyes, K. (2009). *Google and other titans form Open Networking Foundation*. Retrieved January 15, 2017, from https://www.computerworld.com.au/article/380663/google_other_titans_form_open_networking_foundation/?fp=4&fpid=78268965

Nunes, B. (2014). A survey of software-defined networking: Past, present, and future of programmable networks. *IEEE Communications Surveys & Tutorials, 16*(3), 1617-1634.

Nunes, B. A. A., Mendonca, M., Nguyen, X. N., Obraczka, K., & Turletti, T. (2014). A survey of software-defined networking: Past, present, and future of programmable networks. *IEEE Communications Surveys and Tutorials, 16*(3), 1617–1634. doi:10.1109/SURV.2014.012214.00180

Olivier, F., Gonzalez, C., & Nolot, F. (2015). SDN Based Architecture for Clustered WSN. *Innovative Mobile and Internet Services in Ubiquitous Computing (IMIS), 9th International Conference on*, 342 – 347.

Olivier, Gonzalez, & Nolot. (2015). SDN Based Architecture for Clustered WSN. *Innovative Mobile and Internet Services in Ubiquitous Computing (IMIS), 9th International Conference on. IEEE*, 342 – 347.

Olivier, F., Carlos, G., & Florent, N. (2015). SDN Based Architecture for Clustered WSN. *Proc. of 9th International Conference on Innovative Mobile and Internet Services in Ubiquitous Computing*, 342–347.

ONF SDN. (n.d.). *Open networking foundation*. Retrieved from https://www.opennetworking.org/

ONF White Paper. (2012). *Software-defined networking: The new norm for networks*. Retrieved from http://www.bigswitch.com/sites/default/files/sdn_resources/onf-whitepaper.pdf

Open Networking Foundation. (2011). *Open Networking Foundation Formed to Speed Network Innovation*. Retrieved January 18, 2017 from https://www.opennetworking.org/news-and-events/press-releases/onf-formed-to-speed-network-innovation/

Open Networking Foundation. (n.d.). *OpenFlow-Enabled SDN and Network Functions Virtualization*. Retrieved from https://www.opennetworking.org/images/stories/downloads/sdn-resources/solutionbriefs/sb-sdn-nvf-solution.pdf

Open Networking Foundation. (n.d.). *Software-Defined Networking (SDN) Definition*. Retrieved from https://www.opennetworking.org/sdn-resources/sdn-definition

Open Networking. (2017). *OpenFlow Table Type Patterns*. Retrieved April 20, 2017 from https://www.opennetworking.org

OpenFlow Controllers. (n.d.). Retrieved from https://www.packtpub.com/books/content/openflow-controllers

OpenFlow Switch Consortium. (2017). Retrieved August 3, 2017, from http://www. openflow.org/

OpenFlow. (n.d.). Retrieved March 27, 2017, from https://www.opennetworking.org/sdn-resources/

Orfanidis, C. (2016). Increasing Robustness in WSN Using Software Defined Network Architecture. *Proceedings of the 2016 15th ACM/IEEE International Conference on Information Processing in Sensor Networks (IPSN),* 1–2.

Oulai, D., Chamberland, S., & Pierre, S. (2009). End-to-end Quality of Service constrained routing and admission control for MPLS network. *Journal of Communications and Networks (Seoul), 2*(3).

Pate, P. (2013). *NFV and SDN: What's the Difference?* Retrieved from https://www.sdxcentral.com/articles/contributed/nfv-and-sdn-whats-the-difference/2013/03/

PC Mag. (n.d.). *Definition of: Wire Protocol*. Retrieved March 29, 2017, from https://www.pcmag.com/encyclopedia/term/54750/wire-protocol

Quintero, D., Genovese, W. M., Kim, K., Li, M. J. M., Martins, F., Nainwal, A., ... & Tiwary, A. (2015). *IBM Software Defined Environment*. IBM Redbooks.

Rao, S. (2014, March). *SDN Series Part Four: Ryu, a Rich-Featured Open Source SDN Controller Supported by NTT Labs*. Retrieved May, 2017, from https://thenewstack.io/tag/sdn-series/

Reid, A. (2013). *Network Functions Virtualization and ETSI NFV ISG*. Retrieved from http://www.commnet.ac.uk/documents/commnet workshop networks/CommNets EPSRC workshop Reid.pdf

Reid, A. (n.d.). *Network Functions Virtualization and ETSI NFV ISG*. Retrieved from http://www.commnet.ac.uk/documents/commnet workshop networks/CommNets EPSRC workshop Reid.pdf

Riera, J. F., Escalona, E., Batalle, J., Grasa, E., & Garcia-Espin, J. A. (2014, June). Virtual network function scheduling: Concept and challenges. In *Smart Communications in Network Technologies (SaCoNeT), 2014 International Conference on* (pp. 1-5). IEEE.

Road to SDN. (2013). Retrieved from http://queue.acm.org/detail.cfm?id=2560327

Rouse, M. (2013). *What is FlowVisor?* Retrieved from http://searchsdn.techtarget.com/definition/FlowVisor

RouteFlow. (2015). Retrieved from https://sites.google.com/site/routeflow/home

Ruiz, L. B., Nogueira, J. M., & Loureiro, A. A. (2003). Manna (2003): "A management architecture for wireless sensor networks. *IEEE Communications Magazine, 41*(2), 116–125. doi:10.1109/MCOM.2003.1179560

SDN Controller. (n.d.). Retrieved from http://searchsdn.techtarget.com/definition/SDN-controller-software-defined-networking-controller

SDX Central. (n.d.). *What Is Ryu Controller?* Retrieved from https://www.sdxcentral.com/sdn/definitions/sdn-controllers/open-source-sdn controllers/what-is-ryu-controller/

Shanmugapriya, S., & Shivakumar, M. (2015). Context Based Route Model for Policy Based routing in WSN using SDN approach. *BGSIT National Conference on Emerging Trends in Electronics and Communication.*

Sherwood, R. (2009). *Flow Visor: A network virtualization layer.* OpenFlow Switch Consortium, Tech. Rep: 1-13.

Stanford. (2014). *Flowvisor.* Retrieved from https://openflow.stanford.edu/display/DOCS/Flowvisor

Su, W. L., Huang, W. Y. S., & Hu, K. Y. (2013). Design of Event-Based Intrusion Detection System on OpenFlow Network. *IEEE International Conference on Dependable Systems and Networks (SDN) 2013*, 1-2.

Tewari, Dumka, & Khan. (2012). Sync Preempted Probability Algorithm in the Integrated Services (IntServ) MPLS Network. *International Journal of Science and Research, 3*(6), 696-698.

Thereska, E., Ballani, H., O'Shea, G., Karagiannis, T., Rowstron, A., Talpey, T., & Zhu, T. et al. (2013). Ioflow: a software-defined storage architecture. In *Proceedings of the Twenty-Fourth ACM Symposium on Operating Systems Principles.* ACM. doi:10.1145/2517349.2522723

Tomar, R., Kumar, H., Dumka, A., & Anand, A. (2015). Traffic management in MPLS network using GNS simulator using class for different services. *2015 2nd International Conference on Computing for Sustainable Global Development (INDIACom).*

Tomovic, S., Pejanovic-Djurisic, M., & Radusinovic, I. (2014, October). SDN-based mobile networks: Concepts and benefits. *Wireless Personal Communications, 78*(3), 1629–1644. doi:10.1007/s11277-014-1909-6

Tootoonchian & Ganjali, Y. (2010). HyperFlow: A Distributed Control Plane for OpenFlow. *Proceedings of 2010 Internet Network Management Conference on Research on Enterprise Networking (INM/WREN).*

Tsou, T., Aranda, P., Xie, H., Sidi, R., Yin, H., & Lopez, D. (2012). SDNi:A message exchange protocol for software defined networks (SDNS) across multiple domains. Proc. Internet Eng. Task Force, 1–14.

Turner, V., Gantz, J. F., Reinsel, D., & Minton, S. (2014). The digital universe of opportunities: Rich data and the increasing value of the internet of things. *IDC Analyze the Future, 16*.

Voellmy, A., & Wang, J. (2012). Scalable Software Defined Network Controllers. *SIGCOMM, 12*, 1–2.

Wang, B., Zheng, Y., & Lou, W. (2014). DDoS Attack Protection in the Era of Cloud Computing and Software-Defined Networking. *2014 IEEE 22nd International Conference on Network Protocols (ICNP)*, 624-629. doi:10.1109/ICNP.2014.99

Wang, A., Guo, Y., & Hao, F. (2013). Scotch: Elastically Scaling up SDN Control-Plane using vSwitch based Overlay. In *Proceedings of the 10th ACM International on Conference on emerging Networking Experiments and Technologies*. ACM.

Wang, Y., Chen, H., Wu, X., & Shu, L. (2016). An energy-efficient SDN based sleep scheduling algorithm for WSNs. *Journal of Network and Computer Applications, 59*, 39–45. doi:10.1016/j.jnca.2015.05.002

What Are SDN Controllers (or SDN Controllers Platforms)? (n.d.). Retrieved from https://www.sdxcentral.com/sdn/definitions/sdn-controllers/

What Is Ryu Controller? (n.d.). Retrieved from https://www.sdxcentral.com/sdn/definitions/sdn-controllers/open-source-sdn-controllers/what-is-ryu-controller/

Wilkins, S. (2014, November 25). *A Guide To Software Defined Networking (SDN) Solutions - Software Defined Networking: What It Is And Isn't*. Retrieved from http://www.tomsitpro.com/articles/software-defined-networking-solutions,2-835.html

Xiang, W., Wang, N., & Zhou, Y. (2016, October 15). An Energy-Efficient Routing Algorithm for Software-Defined Wireless Sensor Networks. *IEEE Sensors Journal, 16*(20), 7393–7400. doi:10.1109/JSEN.2016.2585019

Xia, W., Wen, Y., Foh, C. H., Niyato, D., & Xie, H. (2015). A survey on software-defined networking. *IEEE Communications Surveys and Tutorials, 17*(1), 27–51. doi:10.1109/COMST.2014.2330903

Yang, F. (2014) OpenFlow-based load balancing for wireless mesh infrastructure. *Consumer Communications and Networking Conference (CCNC), IEEE 11th. IEEE*, 444-449.

Yang, F. (2014). OpenFlow-based load balancing for wireless mesh infrastructure. *Consumer Communications and Networking Conference (CCNC), IEEE 11th*, 444-449.

Yang, H.H., & Quek, T.Q.S. (2016). *Massive MIMO Meets Small Cell: Backhaul and Cooperation*. New York: Springer.

Yan, H., Maltz, D. A., Ng, T. S. E., Gogineni, H., Zhang, H., & Cai, Z. (2007). Tesseract: A 4D network control plane. *Proceedings Symposium on Networked Systems Design & Implementation*, 369–382.

Yap, K., Kobayashi, M., Sherwood, R., Huang, T., Chan, M., Handigol, N., & Mckeown, N. (2010). OpenRoads : Empowering Research in Mobile Networks. *Computer Communication Review, 40*(1), 125–126. doi:10.1145/1672308.1672331

Yaxiong, Z., & Jie, W. (2010). Stochastic sleep scheduling for large scale wireless sensor networks. IEEE International Conference on Communications (ICC), 1–5.

Yick, J., Mukherjee, B., & Ghosal, D. (2008). Wireless sensor network survey. *Computer Networks, 52*(12), 2292–2330. doi:10.1016/j.comnet.2008.04.002

Yuan, A., Fang, H., & Wu, Q. (2014). OpenFlow based hybrid routing in Wireless Sensor Networks. *IEEE 9th International Conference on Intelligent Sensors, Sensor Networks and Information Processing (ISSNIP)*, 1-5.

Zeng, D. (2013). Evolution of software-defined sensor networks. *Mobile Ad-hoc and Sensor Networks (MSN), IEEE Ninth International Conference on,* 410-413.

Zeng, D. (2013). Evolution of software-defined sensor networks. *Mobile Ad-hoc and Sensor Networks (MSN), IEEE Ninth International Conference on. IEEE,* 410-413.

Zeng, D., Miyazaki, T., Guo, S., Tsukahara, T., Kitamichi, J., & Hayashi, T. (2013). Evolution of Software-Defined Sensor Networks. *Proc. of IEEE 9th International Conference on Mobile Ad-hoc and Sensor Networks*, 410–413.

Zhang, B., & Li, G. (2009). Survey of Network Management Protocols in Wireless Sensor Network. *Proceedings of the 2009 International Conference on E-Business and Information System Security*, 1–5. doi:10.1109/EBISS.2009.5138098

Zhang, D., & Ionescu, D. (2007). QoS performance Analysis in Deployment of DiffServ-aware MPLS Traffic Engineering. *8th ACIS International Conference on Software Engineering, Artificial Intelligence, Networking and Parallel/Distributed Computing, IEEE 2007*, 963-967. doi:10.1109/SNPD.2007.541

Zhijing, Q., Denker, G., Giannelli, C., Bellavista, P., & Venkatasubramanian, N. (2014). A software defined network for Internet of Things. *IEEE Network Operation and Management Symposium (NOMS)*.

Zhu, Y., Zhang, Y., Xia, W., & Shen, L. (2016). A Software-Defined Network Based Node Selection Algorithm in WSN Localization. *IEEE 83rd Vehicular Technology Conference (VTC Spring)*, 1-5.

Zhuxiu, Y., Lei, W., Lei, S., Hara, T., & Zhenquan, Q. (2011). A balanced energy consumption sleep scheduling algorithm in wireless sensor networks. *Seventh international conference on wireless communications and mobile computing conference (IWCMC)*, 831–5.

Zhu, Y., Yan, F., Zhang, Y., Zhang, R., & Shen, L. (2017, May). SDN-based Anchor Scheduling Scheme for Localization in Heterogeneous WSNs. *IEEE Communications Letters*, *21*(5), 1127–1130. doi:10.1109/LCOMM.2017.2657618

Zimmerman, M., Allan, D., Cohn, M., Damouny, N., Kolias, C., Maguire, J., . . . Shirazipour, M. (2014). *ONF SOLUTION BRIEF - OpenFlow-enabled SDN and Network Functions Virtualization.* Retrieved from https://www.opennetworking.org/

# About the Contributors

**Ankur Dumka** is working as Assistant Professor-Senior Scale in University of Petroleum & Energy Studies, Dehradun. He is having a long experience of 8+ years in the field of industry and academics. He is associated with smart city Dehradun as academic expert committee member and coordinator in terms of projects related to IT. He is having 25 + international papers in reputed conference and journals. He is also authored a book on MPLS with German Publisher. He had also contributed 6 chapters for reputed publishers. He is also editorial board members of many reputed conference and journals including scopus and IEEE. He is also guest editor of IJNCDS (Scopus Indexed Inderscience Journal), guest editor for IJNCR (ACM digital library -IGI Global journal) and many more. He is associated with many societies and organization for welfare of educationalist societies.

\* \* \*

**Govind P. Gupta** received his PhD degree from Indian Institute of Technology, Roorkee, India, in 2014. He is currently an Assistant Professor in the Department of Information Technology at National Institute of Technology, Raipur, India. His current research interests include Integration of Internet of Things (IoT) with Cloud Computing, Security issues with IoT, Software-defined Networking, Wireless Sensor Networks, and Big Data Processing. He is a professional member of the ACM, IEEE and CSI.

**Suneet K. Gupta** received PhD degree from Indian Institute of Technology, Dhanbad in year 2016. Currently he is working with Bennett University, Gr. Noida India in Computer Science Engineering department. Dr. Gupta is the member of IEEE and ACM. He has contributed 13 research papers and authored two books. He acted as referees in many reputed international journals i.e Computer Network, Computer Communication. His Ph.D. work is in the field of wireless sensor networks. His main interest of research is on developing energy efficient routing and clustering algorithms with fault tolerant wireless sensor networks and Biomedical engineering.

**Misha Hungyo** is currently working in Nokia Networks as R&D Software Engineer. She completed her M.Tech from Motilal Nehru National Institute of Technology, Allahabad, and B.Tech from National Institute of Technology, Durgapur. Her current research interests include Cloud Computing, Software-defined Networking(SDN) with Internet of Things(IOT) and 5th Generation(5G) Technology.

**Ravi Prakash**, alumni of IET Lucknow and Jamia Millia Islamia has demonstrated his intellectual, interpersonal and managerial skills with vast industry and teaching experience. He has an extensive experience of more than 20 years in Institutional Building, Teaching, Consultancy and Research & Industry. He is internationally recognized as a known Professor in the area of IT & Management and is known in the field of academics as an institution builder, a writer, professor, distinguished academician, a top class trainer. His areas of interests include Software Engineering, Data Mining, Computer Networks and Database Systems. He has published various research papers in SCOPUS Impact Factor Journals. Mr. Prakash is a Life Member of ISTE and IETE. He is also the member of Indian Science Congress. Mr. Prakash has delivered a number of invited talks on Research Methodology, Statistical Computing, Embedded Systems and Software Engineering issues at various institutions. Presently he is working as a Senior Faculty in the School of Computer Science and Engineering, UPES Dehradun. Before joining UPES, he was an academician in BIT Mesra Ranchi and Amity University Noida. Specialties: Researcher in the field of Data Networks & Software Engineering. A very good command on Oracle. Have taught more than 100 batches on Oracle (SQL, PL/SQL) and DBA in the last 15 years.

**Anushree Sah** is highly experienced IT professional having an experience of more than 11 years in the field of IT industry and education. The author has worked with the renowned companies like Oracle Financial Services & Software Ltd., Western Union, Dencare Ltd., DIT University, UPES etc. The author has completed her bachelor's in Computer Science and Engineering and has Master's degree from University of Greenwich, London, U.K. She holds various academic and administrative responsibilities in her current working place. The author specializes in Programming Languages, Web Technologies, Building Enterprise Application, Service Oriented Computing and Cloud Computing. She has several research papers, conference proceedings, Book Chapters and Project.

**Himanshu Sahu** received his Master's degree from Motilal National Institute of Technology, Allahabad, India, in 2015. He has got his bachelor's degree from University of Allahabad, India in 2012. He is currently working as an Assistant Professor in the Department of Informatics, School of Computer Science and Engineering, UPES Dehradun, India. His current research interests include Computer Networks, Network Security, Software-defined Networking, Cyber Forensics, Wireless Sensor Networks, Machine Learning and Recommender Systems.

**Ajay Sharma** completed his PhD Degree from Singhania University Pacheri Beri, (Rajasthan), in 2013. Prior to this, He completed his M.Tech (2004) in Computer Science & Engg. from 'A' Grade NAAC Accredited state technical University of Haryana Guru Jambheshwar University of Science & Technology. He is currently guiding five Ph.D scholars. He has also guided four M.Tech Students. His current research area is cryptographic protocol, symmetric encryption, asymmetric encryption and biometric template security. He has more than eleven years teaching as well as administrative experience. He is the author/co-author of more than 30 publications in National/International journals and conferences with impact factor up to 5.49. He is in editorial/reviewer board of Science Alert, New York, USA. He is a life member of CSTA, IAENG, IAOE, and WASE. He had conducted workshops on various area of computer science to enhance the skill set of faculties as well as students.

**Ninni Singh** is pursuing Ph.D. from University of Petroleum and Energy Studies, Dehradun in the dept. of Computer Science and Engineering. She is graduated from HItkarini College of Engineering and Technology, Jabalpur Madhya Pradesh, India and post graduated from Jaypee University of Information and Technology, Solan Himachal Pradesh, India. She joined the academic teaching profession in January 2015. She served as a Teaching Associate in Jaypee University of Information and Technology, Solan Himachal Pradesh, India for a total period of about 2 years. After having served as a Teaching Associate for about 2 years, she switched over to the Research Scholar in the dept. of CSE in August, 2015 and held the SRF (Senior Research Fellow) position on DST sponsored project funded by Govt. of India. Her areas of Interest are artificial intelligence, expert System, cryptography and network security, distributed system, wireless sensor and mesh network.

**Subodh Srivastava** is currently working as Assistant Professor in VNRVJIET (JNTU), Hyderabad, India. Before to join current institution, he had been visiting faculty at IIT (BHU), Varanasi, U.P for two years. He has seven years of teaching and Industry experiences. He earned his Ph.D from IIT (BHU), Varanasi. His researches areas are Image Processing, Pattern Classification and their Medical Applications.

**Anurag Tiwari** received his Master's degree from Indian Institute of Information Technology, Allahabad in year 2016. Currently he is working with University of Petroleum and Energy studies (Dehradun) as an assistant professor, India in Computer Science Engineering department. His post-graduation work was in the field of Data Science. His main interest of research is on Cognitive science, Artificial Intelligence, NLP, Machine learning, wireless sensor networks and Biomedical engineering.

**Ravi Tomar** is currently working in the capacity of Assistant Professor (Senior Scale) in School of Computer Science & Engineering at University of Petroleum & Energy Studies, Dehradun, India. His current research interests include Information Dissemination on Vehicular Ad-hoc Networks; he has authored many papers on Image Processing. He has guided and presented IoT based projects on National Level. On the research side, Prof. Tomar has contributed over 30 research articles in various reputed National/International conference/journals.

# Index

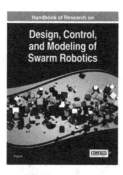

Stay Current on the Latest Emerging Research Developments

# Become an IGI Global Reviewer for Authored Book Projects

## The overall success of an authored book project is dependent on quality and timely reviews.

In this competitive age of scholarly publishing, constructive and timely feedback significantly decreases the turnaround time of manuscripts from submission to acceptance, allowing the publication and discovery of progressive research at a much more expeditious rate. Several IGI Global authored book projects are currently seeking highly qualified experts in the field to fill vacancies on their respective editorial review boards:

### Applications may be sent to:
### development@igi-global.com

Applicants must have a doctorate (or an equivalent degree) as well as publishing and reviewing experience. Reviewers are asked to write reviews in a timely, collegial, and constructive manner. All reviewers will begin their role on an ad-hoc basis for a period of one year, and upon successful completion of this term can be considered for full editorial review board status, with the potential for a subsequent promotion to Associate Editor.

If you have a colleague that may be interested in this opportunity, we encourage you to share this information with them.

# Information Resources Management Association

Advancing the Concepts & Practices of Information Resources Management in Modern Organizations

# Become an IRMA Member

Members of the **Information Resources Management Association (IRMA)** understand the importance of community within their field of study. The Information Resources Management Association is an ideal venue through which professionals, students, and academicians can convene and share the latest industry innovations and scholarly research that is changing the field of information science and technology. Become a member today and enjoy the benefits of membership as well as the opportunity to collaborate and network with fellow experts in the field.

## IRMA Membership Benefits:

- **One FREE Journal Subscription**
- **30% Off Additional Journal Subscriptions**
- **20% Off Book Purchases**
- Updates on the latest events and research on Information Resources Management through the IRMA-L listserv.
- Updates on new open access and downloadable content added to Research IRM.
- A copy of the Information Technology Management Newsletter twice a year.
- A certificate of membership.

## IRMA Membership $195

Scan code or visit **irma-international.org** and begin by selecting your free journal subscription.

Membership is good for one full year.

Printed in the United States
By Bookmasters